I0752774

Easel to Edifice

Intersections in the Principles and Practice of C.R. Mackintosh and Henry van de Velde

---

Judith E. Stone

EASEL TO EDIFICE

Intersections in the Principles and Practice of C.R. Mackintosh and Henry van de Velde

---

Judith E. Stone

COMMON GROUND RESEARCH NETWORKS 2019

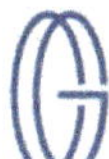

First published in 2018
as part of the Arts in Society Book Imprint
doi: 10.18848/978-1-86335-024-2/CGP (Full Book)

BISAC Codes: DES008000, ARC005070, ARC006000

Common Ground Research Networks
2001 South First Street, Suite 202
University of Illinois Research Park
Champaign, IL USA
61821

Library of Congress Cataloging-in-Publication Data

Names: Stone, Judith E., author.
Title: Easel to edifice : intersections in the principles and practice of C.R. Mackintosh and Henry van de Velde / Judith E. Stone.
Description: Champaign, IL : Common Ground Research Networks, 2018. | Includes bibliographical references.
Identifiers: LCCN 2018031752 (print) | LCCN 2018040594 (ebook) | ISBN 9781863350242 (pdf) | ISBN 9781863350228 (hardback : alk. paper) | ISBN 9781863350235 (pbk. : alk. paper)
Subjects: LCSH: Mackintosh, Charles Rennie, 1868-1928--Criticism and interpretation. | Velde, Henry van de, 1863-1957--Criticism and interpretation. | Art nouveau. | Four (Group of artists) | XX (Group of artists)
Classification: LCC N6797.M23 (ebook) | LCC N6797.M23 S76 2018 (print) | DDC 709.03/49--dc23
LC record available at https: //lccn.loc.gov/2018031752

Cover Photo Credit: Wikimedia Commons

Table of Contents

ACKNOWLEDGEMENTS

For the completion of “Easel to Edifice,” I am first of all indebted to three Common Ground Research Networks editors. The first is Stephanie Turza, for several years Journals Editor for Common Ground, now Book Production Manager at Elsevier Press. Ms. Turza's informed enthusiasm for the book's focal subject, an in-depth comparison of two Art Nouveau masters, added to her vigorous encouragement when I suggested proposing “Easel to Edifice” to Common Ground, set me on a seven-year journey to its eventual publication I've never for a moment regretted, demanding as the journey proved to be.

I am indebted as well to Jeremy Boehme, now Common Ground Production Manager, and Phillip Kisubika, currently Managing Books Editor, for their prompt and thorough responses to technical questions I raised regarding such issues as selecting appropriate illustrations for each chapter topic and preparing the verbal material necessary for presenting “Easel to Edifice” effectively to potential readers..

Further, I am grateful to Peter Trowles, Mackintosh Curator at the Glasgow School of Art's Archives and Collection Centre, and Pamela Robertson, Senior Curator of Mackintosh Studies at the Hunterian Museum, for their efforts in replying to my queries concerning the influence of ukiyo-e prints on Mackintosh’s flower studies, the impact of Japanese architectural traditions on Mackintosh's own building projects, and the interaction between visiting Japanese engineers and their Scottish counterparts in late 19th Century Glaswegian shipyards.

To Jon Long, skilled custom framer and computer wizard, I owe a debt of gratitude for the many hours we spent together locating and sending via his office computer illustrations for each of the book's twelve chapters. I hasten to add that Mr. Long's patience in fielding my comments on each image's link to corresponding points in the text was in itself invaluable.

To my daughter Sylvia Orli, naturalist and Supervisor in the Smithsonian's Botany Department, and to my son David Stone, Information Director for the organization Amazon Conservation Team, I give deep thanks for both their thoughtful, insightful feedback and unstinting support as I wended my way through a wealth of information outlining the achievements of the books central figures, Charles Rennie Mackintosh and Henry van de Velde.

Lastly, but most importantly, I have no words to fully express my gratitude to my late husband, Donald Promish, who passed away midway through the writing of “Easel to Edifice.” A world class physicist and mathematician, Don spent 35 years as a highly regarded Decision Analyst with the United States Navy in Warminster, Pennsylvania. His expertise in matters of engineering, and the field’s application to shipbuilding, contributed massively to chapters dealing with both architecture per se, and the construction of seaworthy vessels. Yet more critical to the book’s development and completion was Don’s faith in my ability to carry out my intentions for “Easel to Edifice” successfully. Without his steadfast devotion, “Easel to Edifice” would have remained merely an intriguing idea.

CHAPTER 1

Charles Rennie Mackintosh: Sketches, Competition Drawings, and Perspectives

"Drawing is the philosophy of art."
—Anonymous

"An architect's sketchbook will probably give the historian a far greater insight into his design processes than many of his finished drawings for specific buildings. The sketchbook enables one to experiment, to play around with composition, plan, elevation, or section, to concentrate on specific features or ornament, even to doodle; it will remain a record of, hopefully, private thoughts, and need have none of the deliberation or precision of measured drawing. Such sketchbooks will probably have a dual purpose that of 'thinking aloud' while developing some new project, along with that of recording things seen, some striking detail drawn both for its own sake and its possible future usefulness. Perhaps the camera has replaced this latter function, perhaps architecture today does not draw as heavily on details of earlier buildings whatever the reason, few architects' sketchbooks of today will be so revealing to the historian of tomorrow as those of Charles Rennie Mackintosh." (Billcliffe: 9)

So, Roger Billcliffe introduces his monograph, Architectural Sketches and Flower Drawings by Charles Rennie Mackintosh, an illustrated, profoundly appreciative study published in 1977. In the decades since Billciffe's enlightening tribute appeared, the camera has indeed largely supplanted the traditional sketchbook, as portable record keeper of intriguing and potentially useful architectural forms and features on the built landscape, ancient and modern, urban, suburban, and rural. Billcliffe's reflective, faintly melancholy "perhaps" would no longer find a place in a discussion of the 21st Century architect's technical strategy for developing ideas.

The shift from the sketchbook to the camera is a *fait accompli*, a done deal. Nonetheless, the camera's advantages its increasingly lighter weight and compactness, its speed and flexibility in capturing both overall structure and functional or decorative detail might be a mixed blessing: what the photographer-architect gains in sheer quantity and variety of views in a relatively short time period, he loses in the draughtsman architect's experience of lingering over the singular qualities of, say, a cornice, a door handle, a street light, an indistinct form in the distant cityscape or countryside, as his pencil attempts to define its shape and recreate its surface. Sketching, then, does go hand in hand with a more gradual, meditative, and thorough process of observation. And since the sketchbook page allows for juxtaposition of one detail with another, or progressively closer, tighter observation of a single detail on the same sheet, the architect who sketches, rather than shoots, images can be considering 3-D structural, material, and stylistic relationships in full scale future projects, even as he adjusts sketched studies or study fragments to each other on the small scale 2-D surface.

Moreover, it's likely that the current, pervasive use of computer-aided design (CAD) both in professional architecture and design offices and in academic programs throughout the globe would have stunned, baffled, or, just as likely, aroused the skeptic in Billcliffe, whose sensitive analysis of his subject's skill in drawing and painting suggests a cautious purist, or a technological Luddite. With regard to the minimum required elements in contemporary CAD processing, the facts are irrefutable. While the camera, at least, still necessitates physical travel, from city to city, region to region, country to country, thus ensuring direct exposure to buildings and the environment in which they function, CAD use demands only two essential components in one enclosed space: state-of-the art computer apparatus and an accomplished operator-designer with an informed, nimble imagination. Certainly, the CAD-reliant designer or architect must mobilize both exceptional technological sophistication and mental agility in his *modus operandi*. Nevertheless, to initiate and then shepherd a project to completion, he needn't, in strict terms, stir from his seat, even should his curiosity compel him to "search" architectural and design precedent elsewhere on the planet.

As a result, in CAD use, as in the photographic warehousing of images, while something is gained speed and flexibility in creative genesis, development, and final realization something equally, if not more critical to functional, stylistic, and aesthetic success is lost: the immense profit gleaned from immediate, multi-sensory encounter with the place itself, with, for example, the modest local church with its idiosyncratic tower, the hidden pocket of vernacular dwellings, the town green ringed with intriguing municipal and commercial buildings, the Scottish baronial manor.

Worth emphasis as well, in weighing the relative merits of the sketchbook, the camera, and CAD use, is the power of memory, that is, the emotion-infused, and for that reason all the more potent memory of that first-hand encounter. How much more invigorating and durable is the recollection of the Duomo approached on foot in Florence, than a few miniaturized glimpses of the High Renaissance cathedral on an illuminated screen? As Steele notes, "Mackintosh had an assimilative heuristic ability based on keen observation and memory. This ability allowed him to transform various divergent references into a cohesive statement in which each was distilled and strengthened." (Steele 49) His prodigious memory, in turn, was nourished by the extensive travel, the voracious habits of observation, and the constant sketching he engaged in throughout his life.

An analogy in the realm of hypothesis emerges here: perhaps, since Mackintosh was eventually able to coordinate his devotion to hand craftsmanship with the advantages of innovative industrial fabrication, so he might also have seen fit to capitalize on the quick, if occasionally deceptive camera eye, or the malleability of the computer-aided design process, had these been options at the turn into the 20th

Century. Possibly, given his wide ranging curiosity, he would have had a go at each option However, conjecture aside, the concrete legacy we do have from the Scottish master is a treasure trove of sketchbooks, elegant, meticulous project perspectives, and carefully crafted, compositionally flawless watermedia paintings, dating from his involvement with The Four in the 1890s to the end of his prolific career in Port-Vendres in 1928. All this two-dimensional wealth, always achieved on paper with pencil, pen, and translucent watercolor, would assure Mackintosh a secure niche in Western art history, had he never designed a piece of furniture or fabric, or draughted formal elevations, sections or floor plans for a building and followed them through to completion.

As a young man with architectural ambitions, Mackintosh took his sketchbooks everywhere, setting down not only schematic studies of entire buildings, but the particularities of hinges, shutters, railings, roof tiles, lamp posts, and interior light fixtures and furnishings; a notorious perfectionist when it counted, he attended as well to the surface qualities of the stone, brick, wood, or harling with which walls were constructed or cladded. These were working sketchbooks, repositories of visual data chosen not randomly, but with the conscious (or subconscious) intention of feeding their specifics into future projects. The degree of polish in the sketchbook images increased with the years: the later sketches done in Sussex and Kent can more accurately be described as finished drawings than loose, informal studies, their pictorial elements often harmonized with an overlay of transparent watercolor wash. Tellingly, the increased polish does coincide, in a kind of inverse ratio, with the decline in commissions Mackintosh saw beginning ca. 1910.

Important to note, in sketchbook entries made in the countryside around Glasgow and in southern England, is his habitual focus on workaday, unpretentious vernacular structures: inns, barns and other utilitarian farm buildings, humble homes for farmworkers and tradesmen; local parish churches. As to the latter, full scale cathedrals rarely drew his interest before his sketching tour of Italy in 1892, although he did attempt to capture the grandeur of Glasgow Cathedral. In addition, buildings modern for their time, that is, the late 19th and early 20th Centuries, almost never figure in his studies.

More curious, and what will eventually prove ironic, is the limited number of rapid sketches and finished drawings of Scottish subjects beyond Glasgow's immediate environs, in marked contrast to the range and variety of sketches done in England, where Mackintosh often spent his holidays. In fact, he made an impressive number of sketching tours of southern England from 1894 onwards, "where he would have seen the kind of vernacular architecture that provided inspiration for many Arts and Crafts architects," including William Morris, mentor to Mackintosh himself and to Francis Newberry, Glasgow School of Art Director. (Escritt"177) According to Billcliffe, a tome entitled The Castellated and Domesticated Architecture of Scotland (1887-1892) was "all the source material he needed," or thought he needed, for his native country. (Billcliffe: 10)

As for observational precision, in both loose sketches and drawings taken to a higher level of finish,"punctiliousness and absolute accuracy in the use of historical detail was not his way; he can be said to be striving toward a free style of architecture having affinities with the past but not dependent on it." (Billcliffe: 10) His focus was selective, not comprehensive, in the recording of each structure. This subtle, but important distinction squares with what we know of Mackintosh's rejection of then-rampant historicism, a distaste he shared with his Art Nouveau peers on the European continent. Intuitively targeting architectural features that synchronized with his increasingly well defined personal objectives, he dismissed those that were irrelevant to his vision.

This filtering process, through which he separated the architecturally essential from the superfluous, intrusive, or distracting, conventionally began at the sketchbook stage and continued through the sequence of perspectives Mackintosh developed for each commission. This point is most easily illustrated in the series of perspectives developed for the two stages of construction of the Glasgow School of Art, (1897-99;1906-09), in which we can see the progressive elimination of residual classical allusions cornices, pillars and plinths that served, in Mackintosh's mind, no pragmatic or stylistic purpose for what architectural scholars now term "the first modern building."

The complement to the progressive removal of the extraneous or anachronistic was Mackintosh's surprising willingness to scuttle decisions represented graphically in each successive perspective drawing as the developing project required it. "His practice of making design alterations while construction proceeded was consistent with his view that drawings indicated an intentional design framework, and were not final or immutable." (Bernard: 20) A paradox for Mackintosh admirers, then, is the high degree of linear and tonal refinement, attention to specifics, and sheer drama in all the perspectives, set against their provisional nature as predictors of the built structures themselves.

The refusal to reflexively reproduce *in toto* all that lay before his eyes, in sketches, in perspective drawings, and ultimately in his commissioned built structures, lines up with Mackintosh's selective appropriation, rather than full bore mimicry, of certain salient features of the Scottish, as opposed to Palladian or Italian Renaissance, manor house. He was drawn to the manor's trademark characteristics: its broad, unembellished exterior walls; its round tower with internal spiral staircase; its additive, and therefore asymmetrical layout; its seemingly random placement of windows, corresponding primarily, if not only to the need for light in each room.

However, in perspectives done for his most significant commissions, Mackintosh assimilated relevant baronial manor features with others absorbed from Classicism, Gothic Revival norms, and even from the rough, utilitarian factory structures ringing Glasgow. His personal brand of eclecticism had its source in tandem demands of utility and stylistic coherence, while by no means resembling the superficial flamboyance of pastiche architecture.

In a lifetime of sketchbook activity, Mackintosh never produced a drawing, rudimentary or polished, that appeared merely dry or mechanical. Even the least consequential in subject or degree of finish stand up as works of art in themselves. Like all great draughtsmen, he used the shape of the page and the versatility of the pencil or pen to their utmost. He drew quickly, incorporating mistakes into the overall image, rather than rubbing them out. Some of the more captivating drawings involve superimposition of a sketch taken from one source onto another, with the added dimension of scale change, as if in unconscious anticipation of Surrealist strategies of the 1920s. The build-up or layering of images stretched out over significant time periods as well. As a rule, Mackintosh returned to and expanded on material stored in earlier sketchbooks, a habit we can verify in noting as much as a ten-year spread between drawings on adjacent pages. (Billcliffe: 11) Conveniently for scholars and historians, the architect signed and dated all his sketches.

Evidence points to a far more methodical creative figure in Mackintosh than is commonly supposed, given his legendary moody, volatile personality. Almost never guided by "Idle fancy" or "speculation" in his choice of subjects for the sketchbooks of the mid to late 1890s, when his career was at its peak, he chose buildings "whose features would be incorporated in his own work, without prejudicing or dominating the style he wished to create." (Billcliffe: 10) Most commonly, these choices rested on qualities of dependable functionality, ratified by time-honored use, rather than the enticements of current, perhaps ephemeral fashion. One can easily perceive, for example, the resemblance between the bay windows in the main entrance of the Glasgow School of Art and sketches done of similarly placed bay windows in traditional homes at Lyme. Regis (Billcliffe: 14)

Indeed, the sheer quantity "of specific references to the sketchbooks in his designs are more numerous for them to be dismissed as coincidence." (Billcliffe: 10) Further proof of a systematic, rather than erratic, disorderly practitioner is supplied by Mackintosh's packrat habits: he saved and organized in his office not only sketchbooks, but several hundred drawings, diaries, account books, letters, journals, and photographs, the latter mainly cut from periodicals, long after the immediate application of these items had passed, and right up to his death. A strong sense of "parts to whole" generally drives such systematic preservation of what might seem, at first glance, useless clutter. Mackintosh clearly had an ingrained sense that even the most trivial element in his working environment might someday come in handy.

In examining the entire corpus of an architect's drawings, it's tempting to train the light exclusively on studies and completed renderings of large architectural forms and smaller particulars. However, doing so in considering Mackintosh would be a grave error. Far more than most of his Art Nouveau peers, he sustained a passionate involvement with the world of organic growth throughout his productive life, an involvement that sustained him in his period of professional decline and the disheartenment that followed There is, as the phrase goes, "history" in this intense involvement with the natural world.

While there is no precedent for his architectural bent in Mackintosh's family history, what does strike us as prophetic is that, from age 10, the nascent artist-designer accompanied his father in the latter's love of gardening. Promotion to the rank of superintendant had allowed Mackintosh senior, a policeman, to move his wife and 11 children from a Glasgow tenement rooms to Dennistoun, a quiet suburb on the city's outskirts. The Mackintosh "Garden of Eden," so named with tender irony, was actually a modest patch of ground adjoining a nearby vacant home. Tending the garden in his father's company instilled in the young Charles "a love of nature that remained with him thoughout his life." (Steele 7) The exquisitely minimal watercolor paintings of flowers that streamed steadily from the Mackintosh studio at every point in his career provide evidence for this simple observation. Moreover, his practice of extracting curvilinear shapes from his already spare plant and flower studies, then translating them into wrought iron functional or decorative elements for his commissioned projects, confirms further the compelling force exerted by the natural world, always in flux, never static, on his growth as designer and architect.

As to exterior design, his "decorative motifs, confined to doorways, windows, railings, and so on, are always simple, reduced to their essence, often stylized abstractions of those natural forms which Mackintosh spent so long studying and drawing." (Steele 49) The wrought iron fence and stanchions guarding the broad north wall and entrance to the Glasgow School of Art combine to form a case in point. "Masterpieces of the blacksmith's craft, they represent the same combination of human judgment and machine-milled precision as the steel hulls then being carefully shaped and riveted together along Clydeside. White hot iron bars straight from the fire, intuitively hammered into tapering sections were transformed into tendrils and stylised roses." (Steele 49)

A similar transformation can be seen in the design for the *interior* walls of Hill House, in Helensburgh, the home commissioned by the publisher Walter Blackie for his family in 1902. A stenciled, stylized organic repeat, abstracted from flower sketches and painted in soft pastels, runs along the top edges of the walls of such white-painted spaces as the bedroom and dining room. While the medium, water-based tempera, differs radically from the tough, industrially-produced wrought iron, the design springs are the same: lovingly crafted, intimate studies of plants and flowers. (Steele 122)

Important to note as well is the inevitable inclusion of trees and shrubbery, rendered in ink, in formal perspective drawings for projects planned for open tracts of land outside Glasgow proper. In most instances, these renderings were anything but what we would now dismiss as "window dressing." The varieties of plantings and their location in the perspectives were as integral to Mackintosh's concept as the shape and placement of entryways and the pitch of the roof. Mackintosh hardly matched Frank Lloyd Wright in the American architect's near-dictatorial control of every aspect of his *Gesamtkunstwerk*. Nevertheless, no account of the Scotchman's collaboration with Walter Blackie in the planning of Hill House omits his insistence that the landscape features depicted in the perspectives govern, without deviation, the actual planting and maintenance of the home's grounds. (Bernard 40) The architect's unyielding stance is legend here the trees, bushes, and hedges were to be selected, planted, and clipped exactly as the perspectives indicated.

Ironically, Mackintosh was far more pliable and sympathetic to the Blackies' wishes where the interior of Hill House was concerned, altering plans, sections, elevations, and perspectives in response to the family's evolving needs. The progressive nature of Mackintosh's project perspectives noted earlier comes into play here. For example, the architect readily reconfigured the plans for one wing of the home to accommodate a nursery for a daughter born even as Hill House was under construction. *Á propos* is Barbara Bernard's comment regarding Mackintosh's flexible, incremental approach to solving spatial problems for important commissions: "Mackintosh saw building, not as a single creative act, but as a social process in which the adaptation of the original design to suit the needs of the client was vital." (Bernard 10) (It is interesting to note that compromise did not extend to the lawn and gardens framing the Blackie home, an area of inflexibility that bespeaks the architect's deepest attachment, that is, to the natural world., He could bend to practical necessity, even to his patron's taste, as he did to Blackie's own stubborn attachment to his own heavy, ungainly oak furniture. But in issues of landscaping, Mackintosh stood his ground.)

The heightened response to the natural world described above was intensified during Mackintosh's youth by "long rambles into the surrounding countryside," walks originally intended as physical therapy for a contracted sinew. "Charles used this time alone to observe and sketch nature and architecture," (Bernard 8) a second deceptively simple, declarative statement that goes far in suggesting the origin of the dynamic duality in Mackintosh's professional activity: an enduring need to express his responses to the natural and manmade environment in freehand art-making for its own sake, accompanied by the accelerating desire, as he matured, to bring his sketched observations to bear on his professional architectural practice. Drawings of vernacular buildings on Glasgow's outskirts, completed from the late 1870s to the early to mid-1880s "laid the foundation of an architectural vocabulary he was to use throughout his career." (Bernard 8)

On separate pages in these formative sketchbooks, were early flower studies, coupled with deft, schematic sketches of country gardens or stretches of uncultivated countryside, both giving context to studies of rural structures. The striking contrast between drawings of controlled, domesticated nature, of gardens and cultivated fields, and studies of the natural world left untouched, generated another Mackintosh preoccupation: the relationship, fluent or disjunctive, between the manmade and the naturally occurring landscapes. In fact, as an easel artist and as *de facto* leader of The Four, whose members drew inspiration from continental Symbolism, Mackintosh tended to see beyond the hard biological, facts of organic growth. In his encounters with a landscape both tamed and tranquil and wild and unruly, Mackintosh saw metaphorically: "This dichotomy of symbolism: nature as a beneficent provider and a potential threat to be mastered is a theme that recurs throughout his work." (Steele 41)

In sum, the whole of Mackintosh's childhood and pre-adolescent drawing experience contributed significantly to the formation of his distinctive mature style. The singular impact of this style lies in the contrapuntal "contrast between strong right angles and floral-inspired motifs with subtle curves." (www.charles renniemackintosh.com) We are most likely to associate the sinuous curves and arabesques typical of Art Nouveau with the craft of Henry van de Velde, the second focal figure in this study, and with the Brussels interiors of van de Velde's compatriot, Victor HortaMoreover, we link geometric Art Nouveau with the *Wiener Werkstätte* founder, Josef Hoffmann, with whom Mackintosh is most frequently associated. But clearly, only the Scotchman brought both fundamental linear elements, the curve and the straight line, to bear in a single built structure, inside and out.

Further, unlike both van de Velde and Horta, for whom the curve served as defining edge, or strategy in surface ornament, Mackintosh did not perceive its sinuousity as an abstraction, several degrees removed from its organic source. He'd sketched those plants and flowers, held them in his hands and smelled their odor, in a Scottish countryside still not nearly as populated and pocked with manufacturing sites as that of Belgium. The flourishing, productive, but toxic necklace of factories surrounding Glasgow had not yet infiltrated the bucolic quiet of rural areas further beyond the city's precincts.

In 1884, at age 16, Mackintosh was apprenticed to the architect John Hutchison, an appointment that suggests both trust in his charge on the part of the veteran practitioner and a high degree of certainty regarding his future calling in Charles. On the flip side of an otherwise profitable arrangement, Mackintosh received no pay during the first year of the apprenticeship, although he did have the expectation of ten shillings per week, if he stayed on for five years! In the same year, Mackintosh enrolled in evening classes at the Glasgow School of Art, an academy dedicated primarily, until the mid-1880s, to what we now term "fine" or "easel art." An overview of the School's evening curriculum for hopeful architects shows us an adequate, if not extensive and thorough, course of study. Classes were offered in architectural graphics, building construction, geometry, and freehand and perspective drawing in a program that paired essential architectural instruction with the opportunity for more independent, less restrictive personal expression.

A closer look at Mackintosh's situation as a whole, however, in Glasgow of the early 1880s, reveals few other options for a more sophisticated architectural education, and an antiquated training program "rooted in the stylistic wrangles of the preceding generation." By all accounts, the common lot of Glaswegian novices was little more than the adornment of the master architect's structure. (Bernard 8) Very likely, then, we can attribute the high velocity of Mackintosh's eventual rise in Glasgow's architectural ranks to several interrelated factors: (1) his prodigious talent, skill, and diligence as a draughtsman; (2) his readiness to assume responsibility for complex building projects at an age - late teens and early twenties - considered unusually young by any standard; (3) the assumption of the School's directorship, in 1884, by the Francis (Fra) Newberry, who reformed the curriculum so as to substantially expand the GSA's offerings in the applied arts.

In the mid-1880s, Mackintosh entered a field of enterprise that continued through the period of his greatest professional success: the winning of prizes for excellence in drawings created expressly for architectural competitions. After his marriage to Margaret Macdonald, in 1901, the competition drawings often reflected their collaborative efforts, such as those for The House for an Art Lover, completed in 1902. Derived primarily from Mackintosh's growing backlog of sketches and finished work on paper, these renderings manifested his gift for expressive line, his idiosyncratic, but always satisfying compositional sense, and theatrical qualities rare in formal competition pieces. The drawings, guided and restricted by technical protocols and practical considerations of budget, location, and use, also displayed Mackintosh's facility with architectural graphic techniques learned at the Glasgow School of Art.

Most importantly, the drawings that won prizes convincingly delineated concepts for 3-D structures on 2-D surfaces. Spatial relationships and construction materials were easily read; structural proportions appeared organically adjusted to each other and to the whole; the overall structure, as rendered, suggested a full scale, built result that would be elegant, imposing and fully functional.

Of great value was the prize money Mackintosh received in 1891, for the design of a public hall, an award that funded what became for Mackintosh a landmark sketching tour of Italy. The motive for the award, rather long-windedly titled The Alexander Thomson Travelling Studentship, merits emphasis: the competition and the prize were created "for furtherance of the study of ancient classic architecture, with special reference to the principles illustrated in Mr. Thomson's work." (Bernard 90) Mackintosh presented to the jurors a sober, symmetrical, no-frills municipal structure. The drawing's unmistakable debt to classical proportional harmony and monumentality predicts the allegiance to classicism that would inform so many of his projects in the brief period, ca. 1896-1909, of his greatest productivity. No historicist steal or fussy pastiche, the rendering of the proposed hall distilled and melded together seamlessly the components of the Greek temple that both moved Mackintosh aesthetically and seemed appropriate for an urban administrative structure. In the jurors' eyes, he had brought the classical architectural spirit, as well as its specifics, its symmetry, its pillars, its architrave into the modern age.

The sketching tour of Italy is a staple in the biographies of 19th Century British and European creative figures. The painted, carved, and constructed wealth at every turn on the "Boot" had no match elsewhere for novice painters, sculptors, and architects bent on absorbing classical, that is, Greek, Roman, and Renaissance tradition, stylistic and technical, in the formative stages of their careers. It is common knowledge that, in the pre-modern period, this tradition dominated and directed academic instruction, setting the criteria for critical approbation, along with steady commissions and income, throughout Europe and Great Britain. As a result, seizing the opportunity to sketch one's way through Italy, was simply *de rigeur*. (Needless to say, the vast majority of ardent careerists in art and architecture on tour in Italy, sketchbooks and drawing tools in hand, were male.)

No exception, Mackintosh drew prolifically throughout his months-long Italian trip, which also took him through areas of Belgium and France. He added marginal comments as he progressed: "strange projections!," or "striking irregularities!," he noted, as he sketched, for example, the Ducal Palace in Venice. (Bernard 9) Working independently, far removed from mentors, colleagues, and friends in Glasgow, he drew mainly in pencil, in a style increasingly less hesitant than in sketches of the 1880s. He combined long-view accounts of arches, campaniles, loggias, churches and cathedrals, with tightly observed, detailed examinations of structural and ornamental particularities. His subjects varied widely, ranging from Orvieto's cathedral, to the Forum's Arch of Titus, to more secluded, less frequently visited and documented rural villas, mentally calculating the possible application of each study to his own future projects.

What survives the journey is a 76-page sketchbook and 30 watercolor and pencil drawings, certainly an impressive corpus, but only a portion of the total actually accomplished. While direct integration of sketched material in future projects proved, in the end, short term, the Italian journey itself, which opened the door to an utterly new architectural, cultural, and natural landscape, contributed substantially to Mackintosh's confidence, not to mention his stylistic, aesthetic, and technical maturation.

The solid impact the Italian tour had on Mackintosh's developing architectural vision can be seen in his design for an extension to the Glasgow Herald building, an assignment he carried out in 1893. The extension was one of Mackintosh's first responsibilities for Honeyman and Keppie, the architectural firm he joined in 1889 as a junior draughtsman. Ironically, the extension was deemed a project "not warranting the attentions of a senior member of the firm." (Steele 25) Planned to provide more space for the Herald's newspaper production and warehousing, the extension, as conceived by Mackintosh, boasted an impressive tower, clearly Italianate in its origins, with its source in the young architect's sketches of *campanili*. No architectural self-indulgence, the unignorably Italianate swelling capping the tower served a down-to-earth function: it housed an 8,000 gallon, water tank, intended as a reserve for firefighting. (Steele 25) The tower itself incorporated two additional technological innovations: diatomic concrete flooring, for insulation and soundproofing, and a large capacity hydropneumatic lift.

A marvel of compression, the Herald Tower, now known as the Lighthouse, succeeded in quoting an Italian Renaissance architectural norm, while simultaneously exploiting Glaswegian industrial sophistication in its infrastructure. The completed extension itself attracted critical praise in the Glasgow press, slightly undercut by a subtle gibe for "modernity verging on eccentricity." However, in 1895, the final perspective drawing for the tower drew praise in the journal British Architect, praise hardly effusive, but all the more telling for its restraint: "This admirable drawing sets forth one of the most noticeable modern buildings in Glasgow, a building which may fairly claim to be a genuinely modern development. not innocent of a quality of proportion and emphasis such as make architecture a thing independent of mere style." (Bernard 8)

Divided critical response aside, hindsight demands that attention be paid to Mackintosh's *modus operandi* in the processing of his concept for the Glasgow Herald tower extension. Here, as elsewhere, he clarified his vision for the extension through a series of ever more resolved perspective drawings. Oddly, given their popularity with patrons, these drawings were carried out in a style that was generally "considered too fanciful and romantic for the professional norms of the time," given his tendency to "romanticize the context." (Steele 31) Such was the case for the Herald Tower perspectives, each a work of art in its own right, so that in this case, as in preparatory work for other commissions, we can only conclude that Mackintosh was driven as much by his *painterly* impulses as by the practical exigencies of his profession.

A frequently reproduced perspective for a building housing the offices of the Herald's competition, the Glasgow Record, also assigned to Mackintosh in this period, reinforces this observation. The dramatic force of the drawing is intensified by the almost impossibly steep technical perspective with which the building's facade, seen at an angle, is depicted; the drawing's appeal is further heightened by a soft, strategic watercolor overlay, unique for the period in professional draughting. In the 1890s, at least in Glasgow, architectural perspectives were only completed in black and white. Nevertheless, while both formal project drawings and completed commissions by the emerging architect seemed questionable, even outrageous to the reactionary wing of the Glasgow press, Honeyman and Keppie apparently respected him enough to entrust him with increasingly more demanding commissions. This, despite Mackintosh's clear commitment to The Four, the avant garde group whose members were together responsible for "the vision that became world famous as the Glasgow style" (www.The Four.com).

CHAPTER 2

Avant Garde Art Groups in 1890s Glasgow: The Glasgow Boys and the Four

"Not a line was drawn without purpose and rarely was a single motif employed that had not some allegorical meaning."
—Herbert MacNair

Without deeper investigation, it's tempting to lump together, and see as one, the quite distinct art groups, all cutting edge for their time, that formed in Glasgow in the late 19th Century. Indeed, one prominent feature does unite them: a shared determination to reject the conservative stylistic guidelines for successful painting, as well as the prescribed options for image content, that governed studio activity in nearby, far more cosmopolitan Edinburgh. In addition, the members of all the movements defined themselves primarily as individuals participating in "loose collectives," in which rigid organizational structure was absent and the emergence of dominant leaders discouraged. Moreover, the painting of all the Glaswegian artists reflected to some degree their exposure to the norms of composition the asymmetry, the severe cropping, the diagonal movement as well as the rich, saturated color and stylized organic forms that characterized the Japanese woodblock or *ukiyo-é* prints flooding European urban centers from the late 1860s on.

Nevertheless, these renegade Glaswegian art groups did differ significantly in a number of ways: in stylistic direction, in choice of subject, and in degree of involvement in the applied, as well as the "fine" arts. The Glasgow Boys rarely, if ever, engaged in the design and crafting of functional objects, while the Four, and even more so the Glasgow Girls, did so increasingly as they mobilized their collective energies. Just as importantly, those affiliated with one or another group took their creative cues from contrasting foreign influences: the Glasgow Boys found stimulus in the mid-19th Century French Realists and Impressionists, while the sympathies of the Four were with the French and Belgian Symbolists, and, with the exception of C.R.Mackintosh, the English Pre-Raphaelite Brotherhood.

The Glasgow Boys constituted a movement virtually off the art historical map now, but, in their own time, these artists were enthusiastically embraced by vanguard cultural circles in their vibrant home city. While the Glasgow Boys' 21 individualistic members hardly formed a homogeneous group, the overall thrust of their efforts can be described as the interpretation and expansion, in Scottish terms, of breakthroughs made by mid-19th Century French Realists, and by their inheritors, French Impressionists who cut their ties with the Salon and the conservative Parisian art establishment from the early 1870s on. Working primarily in oil, the greater number of Glasgow Boys focused their energies on prosaic scenes in the rural areas on the outskirts of their home city or along the coastline. They dwelt lovingly on what they perceived as the singularly Scottish features of the landscape, pastoral or rugged, cultivated or forested, and everywhere marked by serene lochs.

The undated "Sands of Morar," by William York Macgregor, embodies well the style and substance most characteristic of the Glasgow Boys' concerns: the visible, "painterly" brushstrokes are quick and decisive; the dominant shadowed areas on the hills in the background, barely relieved by flecks of light, suggest the transient quality of cloud cover in a northern sky; the deep greens and crimsons of grasses, bushes, and low-slung trees that line the wide swathe of sand leading to the lake suggest an unyielding, as opposed to a lush, fertile countryside. This is a landscape typical of Scotland, rather than France, Holland, or Italy, where Western landscape painting had its birth in the 17th Century. Important to note, in "Sands of Morar," is the sheer quantity of pictorial space occupied by the sand, which becomes a kind of pale yellow void or negative space, as well as the work's pronounced compositional asymmetry, and the freewheeling cropping of image content, especially at the bottom of the piece. These are trademark Japanese compositional strategies that the Glasgow Boys, Macgregor included, borrowed freely from the Japanese ukiyo-é prints available to them in increasingly cosmopolitan Glasgow.

Like their French Impressionist counterparts, Monet, Pissarro, *et al*, they worked most commonly *en plein air*, concerning themselves with the effects of light on the human eye's understanding of surface and edge. Needless to say, in doing so, they were forced to work quickly, in order to capture the shifting, fugitive qualities of sunlight, shadow, shade and atmosphere, moist or dry, at different times of day and in different weather and seasons. It is telling that, in contriving their pastoral Scottish scenes, the Glasgow Boys elected to sidestep the otherwise unignorable presence of Glasgow's booming, late 19th Century industrial behemoth, which encircled the city "in a belt of coal mines, blast furnaces, factories. shipyards, docks and railways." (Steele 19) They filtered out the intricate tangle of railyards and rumbling locomotives, the spewing smokestacks and blazing furnaces, together with the downside of industrial growth soot, grime, polluted air, ramshackle housing, and rampant disease, that combined to form both the source and the collatoral damage of Glasgow's economic primacy. The visual signs of vigorous industrial productivity, at once thrilling and destructive, hardly lent themselves to a Scotch version of French Impressionism

In the group's deletion of the pervasive signs of industrial presence in Glasgow, there is some paradox. Like Manet, Monet, Pissarro, and Degas, with full acknowledgement of the stylistic and substantive distinctions *within* the Impressionist movement, the Glasgow Boys were also inheritors of the changes introduced in the mid-19th Century by the French Realists, Courbet, Millet, and Daumier. Indeed, these earlier artists had paved the way for the upheaval in painting that shocked the Parisian critics and public attending the Impressionist *Salon des Indépendents* in 1873.

In more specific terms, the paintings of the Glasgow Boys often recall the quasi-spiritual homage to farmers and field workers, and to the rhythms and rigors of farm life, "the epic hymn to labor" (Rosenblum 90), we see in the oils and pastels of the Barbizon painter, Jean François Millet. However, in the Glasgow Boys' work, the allusions to Millet seem more commonly drawn from the Frenchman's early paintings, which idealize the daily ritual of agricultural labor, than to mature paintings such as "The Gleaners" (1857), whose warm palette, volumetric shapes, and asymmetrical, but harmonious composition ironically reveal, rather than disguise, the socioeconomic inequities in rural life, the unbridgeable divide between farm worker and farm owner. Unignorable as well, in some Glasgow Boys' paintings, are echoes of the more sentimental, even hackneyed motifs of Millet's contemporary, Jules Bastien-Lepage, as in Thomas Millie Dow's allegorical "Spring." (1886)

Some Glasgow Boys seem to have been on the fence in their representation of the Scotch human condition. For example, Sir James Guthrie's "To Pastures New" (1883), appears, at first glance, another excessively sweet *genre* piece. However, on closer examination, the painting does manifest the artist's absorption of Realist principles, particularly those of Courbet and Daumier, in his scrutiny of the nitty gritty realities of lower class life, such as worn out clothing and heavy workshoes. Is this a peaceful scene of a contented little girl carrying out her daily chores, or is she an impoverished, exploited child doing a job fit for an older, stronger adult?

However, unavailable altogether in Glasgow Boy paintings is the uncompromising, brutal naturalism of Courbet's depictions of rural experience at its grimmest and most soul-deadening, such as "The Stonebreakers" (1849) or "The Burial at Ornans" (1849-50). Nor were the artists moved to action in their studios by Daumier's compassionate, shoot-from-the-hip portrayals, in dulled, broken color, of punishing lower class life in mid-19th Century Paris. Monet, in his paintings of crowds engulfed in smoke in the Gare St. Lazare train shed, and Degas, in his pastels of milliners and laundresses, had come within shouting distance of gritty, contemporary urban realism, but the Glasgow Boys, for the most part, kept their distance from Glasgow's seamier realities.

Finally, unmistakable in the group's landscape work in particular, is the merging of French Impressionist delight in the effects of lambent light on contour and surface with the spirit, if not the actual cultural artifacts, of the Celtic Revival. The Revival was a movement championed in Scotland by the proto-environmentalist and urban planner Patrick Geddes, who urged artists in all media to draw creatively from regional *Scottish*, rather than English or continental cultural experience. In many cases, very well travelled, some even venturing as far as North Africa to paint, the Glasgow Boys exhibited solo and as a group not only in their own country, but in England and in major European capitals. That said, their unprecedented celebration of their native landscape surely reflects Geddes' impact, as does the rapidity with which the term "Celtic Twilight" comes to mind when one contemplates the more haunting of these artists' scenes of fields, hills, forests, and lakes in late afternoon or evening.

The Celtic Revival had a similar influence on the painting and applied art of the Four, a group too small and perhaps too interconnected personally, to qualify as a "movement." However, the Celtic impact manifests itself in their work in more concrete ways: in the group's appropriation of decorative floral and figurative motifs found in ancient, pre-Roman Celtic jewelry and weaponry, in embroidered fabric contrived in later centuries corresponding to the Medieval and Renaissance periods in Europe; in the entwined serpentine forms of ornamental carving and joinery in the ruins of early Christian sacred spaces. The very lettering with which the four artist-designers signed their work finds its source in the memorials incised on 17th Century Scottish tombstones (www.glasgowschool.com). The intricate curvilinear patterning of Celtic design, and the intrinsic bond between ornamental form and utilitarian function in all aspects of Celtic craft, rang true for the Four. As a result, the Celtic model served as compelling motivator in both fine and applied art, rather than one of many fads or fashions to adopt, and possibly discard, as their careers progressed.

The Four painted exclusively in watercolor, an exigent medium demanding a deft, self-assured stroke of the brush, similar to that of the oriental calligrapher. In this, they followed the precedent set by the English watermedia masters of the 19th Century, the seascape artist J.M.W.Turner and the illustrator Arthur Rackham among them. Like Rackham, and unlike Turner, they drew their images more commonly from the mental terrain of the imagination than from the physical, here-and-now, peopled or unpeopled, countryside surrounding Glasgow. Their continental mentors were the European Symbolists: Rédon, Moreau, and the Nabis, of the latter, particularly Maurice Denis, whose gentle, patterned allusions to Catholic ritual, conveying a trance-like mood, often resemble the work of the Four, in style, content, and atmosphere.

In terms of content, no visual element woven into The Four's painted compositions lacked metaphoric value. As Herbert MacNair pointed out, even the smallest notation in paintings and drawings completed by the group during their most productive period, the mid-1890s, carried symbolic import: "'not a line was drawn without purpose, and rarely was a single motif employed that had not some allegorical weight." (Escritt: 178) Of course, symbolic pictorial art, such as medieval altarpiece diptychs and triptychs, demands a community of viewers who understand the allegorical content exactly as the artist intends it. For this reason, it will be useful to discuss, later in this chapter, the impact of both Theosophy and Rosicrucianism on the work of The Four, Charles Rennie Mackintosh, Margaret and Frances Macdonald, and Herbert MacNair, since these esoteric movements, so popular in Glasgow in the late 1800s, communicate spiritual concepts exclusively through parable and visual symbol.

Lastly, as one might expect, in the imaginative cosmos bodied forth in painting by the Four, precision in anatomy and perspective were irrelevant. For that matter, attempts at accurate representation of concrete phenomena and day-to-day events played no role in their pictures: compositions involving figures, more often clothed than nude, in natural settings were organized, or better put, orchestrated in symbolic rather than logical or realistic terms, while pictorial space remained flat, as in a panoramic, densely detailed 12th Century tapestry.

In the early 1890s, while still students at the Glasgow School of Art, Charles Rennie Mackintosh, the Macdonald sisters, and Herbert MacNair were brought together and encouraged to exhibit as a group by Francis (Fra) Newberry, the School's innovative director. An ambitious, hands-on leader, Newberry noted affinities between the four students in work required for courses and in their independently produced painting and craft. (Steele 11) Relatively young himself, having taken over the leadership of GSA in 1884, at age 30, Newberry had arrived in Glasgow fresh from exposure to modernist developments in London and fired up with plans for updating and expanding the School's conservative curriculum. In light of the changes wrought by the new regime, it seems imperative, at this juncture, to comment on the school as Newberry found it, and then on GSA's expanded program as engineered by its progressive new executive leader.

Conservative though its course offerings were in 1884, the Glasgow School of Art had long boasted one forward-looking feature that distinguished it from most art schools elsewhere on the British Isles and, for that matter, throughout the European continent: its student body was co-ed.

Even before the advent of Newberry, young Scotch women had been as welcome in the School's program as their male counterparts. A caveat: the women were required to enter the school building through a separate door and, as one might expect, weren't permitted to attend life drawing classes in which the models posed nude. Those restrictions stated, nevertheless the young women's vital contribution to the academy's quality work in the fine arts, and ultimately even more so in the applied arts, was unparalleled elsewhere in England and in Europe.

While the School of Art did offer a limited set of evening classes for aspiring architects before Newberry's arrival, what he found in Glasgow in 1884 was an art college dedicated primarily to educating easel painters. In London, Newberry had had the benefit of immersion in the wave of enthusiasm for the Arts and Crafts Movement that had swept the city and reached its peak in the early 1880s. His respect for William Morris, who had set up shop in London 30 years earlier, was enormous; his favorable response to Morris's passionate advocacy of traditional hand craftsmanship was equaled by his admiration for the designer's now legendary utopian idealism.

Morris believed, somewhat naïvely, in an ideal socioeconomic setting in which skilled craftsmen, using techniques pre-dating the Industrial Revolution, would produce well-designed functional ware for a stratum of society hitherto deprived of "good taste" in their homes. He had faith that this model would inevitably result in a more stable, harmonious, and productive workmen's community than had emerged in the period following what we now term the Machine Age. Sadly, the pesky issue of cost for one-of-a-kind goods made by hand was disregarded in his calculations.

Once installed as Director at GSA, Newberry converted his enthusiasm for Morris's ideals into a concrete overhaul of the school's curriculum. He introduced courses in an impressive range of applied arts, in pottery, embroidery, metalwork, stained glass, and wood carving, and carried his innovative zeal further in promoting student work through exhibitions open to the Glaswegian public. Clearly, the presence of young women in the applied arts studios allowed for an exceptional level of excellence in craft areas previously reserved for the domestic realm. There, mothers passed on techniques to daughters whose efforts as embroiderers, weavers, seamstresses and painters of ceramics were mainly used, displayed, or both, in the privacy of the family home. It is interesting, however, that stereotypes regarding gender preferences in the applied arts were often turned on their heads in Newberry's creative cauldron. The Macdonald sisters, for example, became accomplished metalworkers, as well as painters, textile designers, book designers and illustrators, and, in the case of Frances, embroiderer.

Like so many facilitators in the late 19th Century, a period that witnessed a societal groundswell of dissatisfaction with cheap, shoddy, factory-made goods, Newberry fostered an educational environment in which "high" art for its own sake and the applied arts occupied the same rung on the ladder of cultural esteem. He was guided in his aesthetic preferences, in part, by the Arts and Crafts principle of "honesty," which insisted that construction materials and processes should "show," undisguised, in the final product, and, in part, by a fervent allegiance to the organic world as ultimate design source and reference point for both easel and applied artists. In these, as in other creative biases, he found a kindred spirit in his young student-turned-colleague, Charles Rennie Mackintosh.

Nourishing Newberry's relatively Spartan aesthetic program were the streamlined forms of Japanese functional objects that flowed into European urban centers shortly after Commodore Matthew Perry sailed into Tokyo Harbor in 1854 and the Japanese lifted their centuries' long ban on trade with the West. In London, Newbury's exposure to Japanese metal and enamelware, kimonos, fans, and screens, ceramic serving ware, and finely crafted, inlaid carpentry goods for which stylized surface patterns and elegant contours were "ornament" enough had reinforced his instinctive distaste for surface frills lacking utilitarian purpose or aesthetic appeal. So, as a natural consequence, tacked-on floral bulges, disguised joints, and paper-thin veneers were discouraged at the Glasgow School of Art.

The expansion of curriculum into the applied arts at GSA served the booming shipbuilding industry in Glasgow well, especially given the potential for adapting skills acquired at GSA in wood and metal construction to shipboard needs. Moreover, the shipbuilding industry "employed countless draughtsmen" (Escritt: 175) whose inventiveness was put to work for purposes as varied as the design of hulls for cargo ships and the contriving of light fittings for luxury liners. The Glasgow School of Art, as it developed under Newberry's guidance, represented "the marriage of the city's strong industrial and municipal traditions." In fact, "it was partly as a response to the needs of local industry that the governors of the existing art school were able to relocate to a new site and commission a purpose-designed building to replace their cramped accommodation on Sauchiehall Street." (Escritt: 175)

Mackintosh was still an employee, rather than a partner, at Honeyman and Keppie when the Board of Governors at GSA established a competition for the design of the new Glasgow School of Art building. His official status in the firm was still fairly low. Nevertheless, his stark, strictly utilitarian draughted solutions submitted to the jurors won him the commission for a structure that was ultimately built in two stages: the first, 1896 to1899 and the second, 1906 to1909. The drawings, winners in a field of 11 competitors, reflect the combined impact of three architectural models in which ornament is kept to a minimum: the Greek classical tradition; the Scottish baronial manor; and the rough brick, all-business factory buildings on the fringes of Glasgow.

So, given the severe quality of the overall plan for the School, based on a functionally-directed "E" shape, it is striking that Mackintosh's parallel involvement with the Four eventually guided his design of the few curvilinear decorative elements on GSA's facades. For example, the rose-like ironwork along the windows of the north front, built during the first stage of construction, "bears more than a passing resemblance to the floral elements in Mackintosh's Symbolist-influenced watercolours of the mid-1890s, such as *Part-Seen, Part-Imagined* of 1896, in which a floating female figure surrounded by a halo is entwined by plant stems, some headed with stylized rose flowers in varying stages of bloom." (Billcliffe 11)

By 1896, the Four had collectively produced enough stylistically coherent furniture, posters, glass and metalwork, and painted narrative panels to mount an exhibit for the Arts and Crafts Society in London in the same year. Their combined efforts were not well received by the English public and some mainstream journalists, who shared the general Glaswegian distaste for what was perceived as ghoulish imagery depicting, according to one pundit, "hobgoblins by misty moonlight." Hence, the derisive alternative name "Spook School." Luckily, however, one perceptive British critic was able to buck the negative critical tide. Gleeson White, Editor of the influential periodical The Studio, was intrigued, rather than repulsed by The Four's distinctive art and craft. His journey to Glasgow to meet The Four was followed by the publication of two congratulatory articles in The Studio in the following year. White's prescient "Part Seen, Part Imagined," 1896.recognition of The Four's advances in the applied arts in particular accounted for the spread of the group's reputation throughout Britain and the coining of the term "The Glasgow Style."

Of still greater importance, his insightful observations stimulated interest in the work of the Scotch foursome on the continent, primarily in German-speaking centers like Berlin and Vienna. (Important to emphasize is the potency of the illustrated periodical, in alternatively generating or derailing reputations in the late 19th Century, a potency analogous to that of the Internet in our own time.)

Members of the Four functioned as professional partners, with Charles *de facto* leader, but their bonds were also romantic and lasting. Frances and Herbert married in 1899; Charles and Margaret in 1901. Not surprisingly, considerable attention has recently been directed at the invisibility of both sisters in the traditional record of the Four's achievements. Margaret, in particular, attracts substantial scholarly study, given her much-debated, but undeniable participation in the completion of Charles' commissions. One commentator writes, in the now-familiar language of Feminist criticism: "Macdonald, along with her sister, is one of the many 'marginalized wives' who suffered from patriarchal art historical discourse. She was celebrated in her time by many of her peers, including her husband, who once wrote in a letter to Margaret: "Remember, you are half if not three-quarters of all my architectural achievements" (www.margaretmacdonald.com). Elsewhere, Mackintosh is quoted as saying, in a similar, humble vein, "Margaret has genius, I have only talent."

Margaret's accomplishments, both as autonomous artist and designer and as Charles' collaborator, have indeed received their rightful due in recent decades. That she had a hand, quite literally, in the draughting of numerous Mackintosh perspectives and competition drawings is proven by the presence of both partners' signatures on many pieces. Still more intriguing is current scholarship pointing to her influence on Gustav Klimt, Vienna Secession leader, most strikingly on Klimt's monumental, floor-to-ceiling Beethoven Frieze created for the Secession Exhibition of 1902. However, the informed audience for modern design has little awareness *of* and, consequently, still less appreciation *for* the painting and craft of Frances Macdonald, not to mention the contributions of Herbert MacNair, during The Four's short-lived, but fertile association.

Initially, Frances' career kept pace with that of her sister, at least throughout the 1890s. They enrolled at the Glasgow School of Art in the same year, 1891, and left the school together, in the mid-1890s, to set up a shared studio. The overlapping design efforts of the two women were both extensive and consuming: in addition to working in textile design, embroidery, and metalwork, they devoted their energies to graphic design, book illustration, and decorative, allegorical painting in the context of the Four.

In painting, Frances, like Margaret, worked in watercolor on narrow, rectangular panels; she most commonly depicted elongated, apparently boneless and melancholic female figures that reflect the influence of both the Medievalist Pre-Raphaelites and the Aesthete Aubrey Beardsley. John Everett Millais' sweet-visaged, but virtually dematerialized, "Ophelia" (1852), dead by her own hand and floating in a stream surrounded by lush growth, is clearly the ancestor of the fantasy realm depicted by Frances and Margaret, and by Herbert MacNair, in the early stages of their creative alliance. Figures, usually female, merge with fecund nature in a state that is neither fully alive and vigorous nor, unlike Ophelia, moribund, or stone cold.

However, be it noted that, despite Beardsley's clear influence, in neither Frances's nor Margaret's depictions of ethereal young women do we sense the undercurrent of sinister eroticism that runs through the illustrator's's Japanese-influenced ink drawings, such as those that illustrate Oscar Wilde's "Salomé." The paintings of all the members of the Spook School may have been symbol-laden, often nocturnal dreamscapes, but rarely did Charles, Margaret, Frances, or Herbert venture into the terrain of real menace or danger.

As a duo, the Macdonald sisters mounted joint exhibitions in London and in Liverpool, where Frances eventually lived with Herbert during his stint as design instructor at the Liverpool School of Architecture and Applied Art. At the same time, The Four continued to present themselves as a cohesive group, exhibiting together well into the first decade of the 20th Century, long after Charles had established a major career as an architect and distanced himself artistically from the Four's trademark "fairy pictures" of the 1890s.

Oddly,however, while we can easily locate critical appraisal of the Rose Boudoir, Charles' and Margaret's jointly contrived installation for the Turin International Design Exhibition (1902), we must dig harder in order to unearth critical response to the Writing Room, the prototypically Scottish Art Nouveau environment for quiet study created for the same event by Frances and Herbert. Both interiors, each stylistically integrated and reflective of Celtic and Japanese influence, were developed under the auspices of the entrepreneurial Fra Newberry. However, only the Mackintosh-Macdonald *Gesamtkunswerk* appears to have drawn critical attention.

More provocative still, as one of many fraught curiosities in the annals of art and design history, is the rumor of a series of watercolors painted by Frances later in life, when The Four had effectively disbanded. These paintings reputedly addressed the conflicting choices facing gifted, ambitious women of her time, chiefly the choice between professional advancement and marriage, or, more pointedly, marriage and motherhood. (www.francesmaçdonald.com)

The lingering, nagging conundrum of fame who attains and keeps it, and who passes into obscurity without it is far too complex a sociological problem to tackle here, in an overview of the interwoven lives of the Four. Nevertheless, some conjecture, grounded in the evidence so far available, seems in order. Herbert MacNair is arguably the least well recognized of the Four, so it is ironic that he actually outlived the others by decades, dying in 1955. Taking into account MacNir's involvement in the vanguard Four, his training in Newberry's progressive curriculum at GSA, and his own career as design instructor at the School of Architecture and Applied Arts in Liverpool (1898 to 1905), one can infer that his impact on the direction of British design practice in the early 20th Century, while as yet undefined, was substantial. MacNair is, in fact, the only member of the Four to have divided his professional time between personal studio work and the preparation of students for careers in the applied arts.

His role as mentor apparently extended to his relationship with his far more ambitious, charismatic brother-in-law. MacNair, for example, is credited with convincing Mackintosh that semi-abstract symbolic elements should find a place in the architect's plans for Queens Cross Church (1897-99) built to serve a poor neighborhood, "slotted into a cramped corner lot amid tenements and warehouses." (www.charlesrenniemackintoshand margaretmacdonald.com) The vaulted wooden ceiling of the Queens Cross nave, banded with undisguised steel beams, is clearly referential to an inverted ship's hull, or, just as likely, an inverted Noah's arc, and reflects MacNair's influence. Both architect and designer were concerned that the church interior communicate in recognizable ways to a congregation comprising, in large part, craftsmen and tradesmen in the shipbuilding industry. MacNair's input can also be detected in the carving on the sides of the pulpit, where abstracted bird wings seem to embrace and protect stylized young plant shoots, a symbolic motif drawn from St. Matthew, to whom the church was originally dedicated.

In the end, however, it's hard to claim that Herbert MacNair was as fully dedicated to making decorative or expressive images, or functional objects, as was Mackintosh, or that his motives and goals for design education were as intensely felt as those of Newberry or Henry van de Velde. MacNair had never designed an innovative curriculum for teaching the applied arts, as had both those committed educators, nor, of course, had he generated a program for bringing architects, designers, and industrialists together, as had van de Velde for the *Deutsche Werkbund.*

Such a claim is further undercut by his destruction not only of Frances', but his own body of work, at her death, and his subsequent disheartenment and distancing from all productive activity in the decades that followed. Some would argue that the committed artist, architect, or designer, no matter how grief stricken, would find it impossible to destroy what he, or she, had produced and that the dedicated teacher would eventually find his, or her, way back into the educational realm (The career of Henry van de Velde provides the case in point.) MacNair left behind neither a substantial corpus of fine and/or applied art nor a structured, cogent program for design education, although his long-range influence on students in Liverpool was undoubtedly significant. Therefore, while it is unreasonable and unfair to deny him some responsibility for the development of the Glasgow Style, there is a persuasive explanation for his secondary position in the reputation shared by The Four.

Despite the spirit world invoked by the “Spook School” in their painting, there is no solid proof that any of the four artists had direct affiliation with the two esoteric societies, the Theosophists and the Rosicrucians, whose related brands of mysticism lured so many adherents in Glasgow in the late 19th Century. Mackintosh had been raised Catholic and accepted commissions for churches of all denominations. Of those commissions, only one, Queens Cross Church, was carried beyond plans and perspectives to completion. However, he had little truck with theological abstractions, or with theories of any kind, especially those imposed from the outside, as they applied to his painting. “I care not the least for theories or for this or that dogma as far as the practice of art is concerned but take my stand on what I consider my personal ideal.” (Senior, quoting Mackintosh)

Nevertheless, in view of the pervasive symbolic elements in the paintings of the Four, Charles’ included, as well as the popularity of the Theosophists and Rosicrucians among Glaswegian artists and intellectuals of the period, it makes sense to search out areas of possible consonance between the belief systems of these societies and the thought and practice of The Four.

Theosophical thinking rests on several assumptions that might have resonated with Mackintosh’s private search for “the soul that lies beneath appearances” In a set of interlocked attitudes similar to, but not identical with those of Christianity, the Theosophists assert the irrefutable reality of God’s essence, from which they deduce the fundamentally spiritual, rather than material, nature of the universe. As in many channels of mainstream Christianity, God, for the theosophist, is the transcendent source of all being, and all good; evil in the world, on the other hand, derives directly from man’s desire for finite goods and can be overcome by complete absorption in the infinite. Needless to say, this degree of “absorption” would have been a formidable challenge in Glasgow, a city whose trademarks in the 1880s and 1890s were round-the-clock industrial production and rampant commercialism.

The Rosicrucians, for their part, claim that their order has been in existence since the days of ancient Egypt and has, over the course of time, included many of the world’s sages. Less structured in terms of theological or ethical principles than the Theosophists, the Rosicrucians deal heavily in occult symbols notably the rose, the cross, the swastika, and the pyramid and with hard-to-parse mystical writings that borrow from other mystical sources, such as the Jewish Kabbalah. Importantly for students of the Celtic Revival, Rosicrucian symbolism figures centrally in the writings of the Irish poet William Butler Yeats and is particularly evident in the collection called “The Rose.”

Significantly, in their exposure to Theosophical and Rosicrucian attitudes, The Four would have been exposed to both societies’ emphasis on the interpretation of sacred writing through allegory or visual symbol, an interpretive strategy reminiscent of the means by which Roman Catholicism speaks to its adherents: parable and visual iconography. Since Celtic tradition communicates through visual symbols as well, there would have been a good fit between the expressive technique used by the Four, all of whom incorporated in their work symbols borrowed from both their Christian and Celtic heritages, and Theosophist and Rosicrucian reliance on visual emblems that stand for elusive spiritual abstractions. The cross-cultural emblem of growth and fecundity, the "Tree of Life," comes to mind here. By extension, an audience of Glaswegians familiar with the combined specifics of Theosophical, Rosicrucian, Catholic, and Celtic visual metaphor would have recognized and understood the import of those symbols in the paintings of the Four.

Modern Theosophy is articulated largely through vocabulary drawn from Indian, rather than Western philosophic discourse. Not surprisingly, then, Patrick Geddes, Celtic Revival leader in Scotland, was also a Theosophist. Geddes, a dedicated ecologist and urban planner before the terms were invented, had spent years in India supervising renovation and expansion projects for Bombay. (www.patrick geddes.com) His concern for preserving, rather than remodeling or leveling, traditional Hindu temples and shrines in an otherwise "rehabilitated" Indian city was no doubt informed by his revelatory encounter with the liturgical and iconographical wealth he found inside.

The eclectic admixture of Hindu, Theosophical, and Celtic mysticism informing Geddes' otherwise pragmatic mindset goes some distance in explaining his rejection, like Mackintosh, of random-sort historicism in late 19th CenturyWestern architecture, as well as what he correctly perceived and deplored as the flattening of regional differences in sterile, efficiency-obsessed Modernism. In India, Geddes attended to practical issues of trade and commerce, acquisition of suitable land for construction, and provision for futher urban growth. Nonetheless, underpinning his clear-sighted hold on the practical demands of city planning was a bedrock interest in social harmony and individual peace of mind, conditions he believed would be nourished by preservation of old fashioned traditions, whenever possible, as the urban modernization process took place. Indeed, Geddes' concern for the preservation of regional "facts on the ground," physical and social, guided the renewal program he directed in Edinburgh, one that drew inspiration from its specifically Celtic past.

At no point, did Charles Rennie Mackintosh incorporate the so-called "fairy world" in his paintings with The Four to quite the degree that did his three colleagues. His affection for the sensuous realities of the organic world, combined with his ever-greater immersion in the practical exigencies of architecture, rendered such misty, ethereal image-making increasingly difficult. By the end of the 1890s, Mackintosh was investing his skills in drawing and watercolor painting either into the progressive perspectives for projects discussed earlier, or into the flower paintings that both stimulated his design vision, and stayed the turbulence in his psyche. However, a few paintings from the early 1890s, when the Four first merged their efforts, give persuasive evidence that Charles was probably, at least at the start, as touched as the others by the currents of mysticism that flowed through Glaswegian cultural life in that period.

With "Harvest Moon" (1892-93), Mackintosh began a series of symbolic watercolors almost certainly influenced by Theosophical or Rosicrucian thought. The rose itself, as pervasive in ancient Rosicrucian symbology as in well-tended Scottish gardens, appears through the tangle of organic growth on the lower half of the picture plane. A murky layering of clouds in the night sky, thought in Gnostic circles to suggest levels of spiritual being, hovers above the organic tangle on the upper half of the image. Straddling the two halves, which clearly represent the earthly and celestial realms, is a "moon maiden," strangely octopus-like in shape, silhouetted against the golden "harvest moon," and its aura. Bisecting the painting, and the moon maiden, is a branch, and beneath the undulating maiden a naked, prone, more recognizably human woman, who, according to one latter day Gnostic analyst, exists in a lower, more physical zone than the moon maiden above her.

Charles was in his mid-20s when he painted this striking image, which seems not so much to separate as to wed the fantastical cosmos of symbolic fairies and ghosts with the earthly realm of plants, flowers, and thicket-like undergrowth. From a technical standpoint, the intricate web of stems, branches, flowers and fruits below seem to engage Mackintosh's attention far more than the moon maiden and her earthly counterpart, and the indeterminate cloud cover above. The tightly rendered stems and branches, forming a highly controlled, geometric lattice-work screen, suggests a creative bias that will eventually emerge full blown in the architect's mature designs for furniture, textiles, and wrought iron ornamental and practical elements on the exterior of his built structures. In "Harvest Moon," the still impressionable, idealistic young Mackintosh obviously attempts to convey the superiority of the dematerialized sphere of the spirit. It is, however, a quixotic attempt, as it is equally obvious that the mundane truths of the natural world, visible, tangible, but hardly crass or base, lure and rivet his imaginative faculties far more.

CHAPTER 3

Les Vingt: The Avant Garde Artist in the Belgian Metropolis

On October 28, 1883, *Les Vingt*, *Les XX*, or The Twenty, Belgium's singular late 19th Century avant garde art group, was founded in Brussels. Actually, on that particular autumn day, only 13 artists "signed their names to a folio marked with a double X, declaring the formation of *Le Cercle des Vingt* or *Les XX*, "but seven more soon added their names to the initial signatories." (Canning, "Soyons nous "28) The membership comprised painters, sculptors, graphic artists, and, in the final three of the group's ten-year lifespan, designers in the decorative arts: promotional posters for theatrical events; book cover design and illustration; embroidery and tapestry; ceramics; glasswork. While primarily Belgian and, with one notable exception, the painter Anna Boch, male, the organization's unusual inclusiveness, in terms of both permanent members and invited exhibitors, reflected both its determination to reach beyond Belgium's borders and the increasingly international demographic of its home city.

The immediate catalyst for the group's formation was the rejection of James Ensor's provocative "Woman Eating Oysters" (1882), by the official Antwerp and Brussels salons, *and* by the more liberal, artist-run society *L'Essor* (Flight). Viewed as "daring for its examination of the intersection of feminine space, pleasure and social propriety," the piece, with its loose rendering and painterly surface, depicts a woman seated alone at her dining room table, clearly savoring a meal of oysters. Although the scene seems innocuous enough in our own time, Susan Canning accurately notes that "In Ensor's time, such a bold representation of female appetite and self-indulgence was rarely seen." (Canning, "In the Realm of the Social" 79)

Obviously, however, a single source of dissatisfaction doesn't adequately explain the founding of an art organization radical for its period. The initial group of Les Vingt artists comprised in large part dissenting members of *L'Essor*, whose hopes for that progressive society had been thwarted by its conservative exhibition policies, its increasingly top-down governance, and its dependence on the royal patronage of King Leopold II. As a result, Ensor and his colleagues left *L'Essor*, moving on to generate "a new exhibition society devoted to showing a broad range of modern art by Belgian artists and those invited from other countries."

The operant phrase here is "broad range." Accounts differ as to the number of nations represented in the annual exhibitions held from 1884 to 1893. However, even a cursory scan of the painting and sculpture on show each year reveals initially a preponderance of Realist and Impressionist painting, later a larger body of Neo-Impressionist and Symbolist work accomplished by artists not only from Belgium, but from Holland, France, Germany, England, and even geographically remote Greece.

While substantial numbers of foreign artists participated in one or several *salons*, with a select few given solo exhibits, a smaller, but still significant number were invited into the fold as permanent members. Among the latter were the Symbolists Jan Toorop from Holland and Odilon Redon from France, the prodigiously gifted, but defiantly scrappy, expatriate American painter and printmaker James McNeill Whistler, and the most influential, albeit critically divisive sculptor of the late19th and early 20th Centuries, Auguste Rodin

Emblematic of the group's often shape-shifting approach to the choice of permanent non-Belgian members is the invitation extended to the French *Pointilliste* Paul Signac. Signac's well-known anarchist affiliation, in combination with his experimental divisioniste approach to the canvas, appears to have synchronized well with the alliance between *Les Vingt* and the reformist *Parti Oeuvrier Belge* (Belgian Workers Party), at least on a superficial level. In general terms, Signac certainly subscribed to the egalitarian platform outlined in 1885 by P.O.B. leaders.

However, some scrutiny of the French painter's personal bead on anarchism seems *à propos* here, early in the discussion of *Les Vingt*, given that, in the late 19th Century, anarchism was "then associated with ideas of replacing the existing order with loosely federated, mutually supporting groups.' (Escritt: 68) Signac defined the anarchist position in strictly artistic terms, an interpretation that deviated from that of the politically-oriented anarchist mainstream: An anarchist painter is not one who creates anarchist paintings, but one who, without care for money, without desire for recompense fights with all his individuality against bourgeois conventions and officials." (Levine 59) Here, admittedly, Signac does declare his distaste for bourgeois convention and, by implication, an immutable *status quo* imposed from on high by an entrenched establishment. In this sense, in his emphatic individualism, he is a classic anarchist.

Nevertheless, his narrow, somewhat skewed definition also suggests either a cavalier attitude toward the concrete concerns of the rural and industrial workers who were, in principle, in league with the artist members of *Les Vingt*, or simple tunnel vision. Anarchism at its core emphasizes self-determination, the right of the individual to plot the direction of his life, liberated from the restraints of an authoritarian officialdom. Moreover, in contrast with socialism, the anarchist puts little stock in collective action, action in which the individual's interests have been so fully merged with those of the group that he has sacrificed the pivotal right to independent decision-making.

So far, so good, as to *avant garde* artists and lower class laborers sharing common cause through the anarchist lens. Nevertheless, it's unlikely that the workers represented by the *P.O.B.* would have subscribed to an agenda like that of Signac, one "without care for money, without desire for recompense" and apparently indifferent to their demand for a living wage. In the end, however, *Les Vingt* was not only a highly politicized, but a strikingly flexible organization as to its membership. So, an artist member like Signac, who espoused a personal, non-purist anarchism, was better than an artist with no altruistic, anti-establishment, anti-authoritarian leanings at all.

In light, then, of *Les Vingt's* strikingly eclectic international membership, one can conclude that close bonds and mutual support between the group's artists rested more heavily on stylistic similarities and loosely defined attitudinal sympathies than on national origin or strict political agenda. Indeed, Canning points out that the group explicitly proposed to hold an exhibit in Brussels each February, in which each member could show his artwork "alongside the work of select invited artists, both Belgian and foreign, who shared the same aesthetic concerns." (Canning, *"Soyons nous"* 28) The group's goal was twofold: to revive the local art scene and bring contemporary developments in the visual arts to the Belgian public; once achieved, these goals would ultimately make Brussels the 'center of a magnificent *avant garde* art movement,' (Canning, *"Soyons nous"* 28) not only in the visual arts, but in all the creative fields. And in fact, by the mid-1880s, the exhibits sponsored and organized by *Les Vingt* had become more popular than those of the official Salon, the latter cossetted by artistic convention.

By the early 1890s, *Les Vingt* salons had ventured further into modern terrain, integrating painting and sculpture with the decorative craft of emerging Art Nouveau designers. Moreover, "*Les XX* interjected their salons into the public discourse of official culture, further encouraging the Brussels populace to view their salons as the *avant garde* equivalent of the *Triennial*," (Canning, "Soyons nous 33), a yearly exhibition event which toook place in Brussels, Antwerp, and Ghent, providing a dependable venue for artists trained in Belgium's traditional academies Given theprogressive leanings of Octave Maus, principal *Les Vingt* founder, and most of the group's members, the popularity of *Les Vingt* opening receptions, or *vernissages,* among conservative government officials may seem odd, in defiance of social logic However, the *vernissages* had in fact become fashionable, must-attend events as early as 1885, when state ministers, Senate members, and Belgian aristocrats could be seen rubbing shoulders with and lavishing kudoes on exhibiting artists and their supportive middle class patrons.

Especially telling was the sheer number of attendees, an astounding1500 at the 1887 reception, by all accounts making it next to impossible for visitors to see, much less quietly contemplate the serene, patterned expanse of that exhibit's groundbreaking *pièce de resistance*, Georges Seurat's *"L'Aprés Midi sur La Grande Jatte."* No matter, since the source of *Les Vingt's* prestige among the conservative elite lay not so much in that group's genuine appreciation for the often mystifying art work on display as in the work's very innovative nature. If the art was in the cultural vanguard, it followed that so would be Belgium itself.

In addition to governmental concern for demonstrating Belgium's leadership in European culture, the source of *Les Vingt's* fashionability, and related profitability, lay in a mix of factors: sophisticated advertising in widely displayed posters; meticulously designed catalogues, which attendees could take home and peruse for future purchases; innovative, easy-on-the-eye installations From 1884 to 1886, *Les Vingt's* annual exhibitions were installed in the stately, monumental, but decidely stodgy *Palais des Beaux Arts* (1884-1886). However, starting in 1887 and continuing into1893, the exhibits were mounted in the newly established *Musée d'Art moderne*, together with the lectures and concerts that played a critical role in the group's activities. Given the innovative quality of the installations themselves, as organized by a committee of artist-members, the modern museum lent itself far better to the cutting edge look of the exhibitions as a whole. Naturally, the newer building and its galleries were far better suited to the experimental work on display.

From the outset, *Les Vingt* policy ensured that each artist's set of pieces be hung separately, so as to give both the work and its creator their visual due. While the installations grew increasingly complex by the year, the show's organizers were still adamant in rejecting the cluttered, floor-to-ceiling arrangement favored by establishment *salons* in Brussels and their more celebrated counterparts in Paris. Paintings were hung from a railing at eye level, with pieces by different artists but similar style exhibited together from 1886 on. (Canning, "*Soyons nous*" 34) Especially noteworthy was the refusal to separate fine from applied art, even in the early salons, when craft entries were rare: decorative art, like medallions and hand-bound books with tooled leather covers, were shown in the same rooms with paintings and sculpture, suggesting that, in terms of absolute value, the applied arts were on a par with painting and sculpture.

As a result of this visual democracy, in terms of the artists and their work, the notion of *individualism*, a concept that recurs with stunning frequency in virtually every study of *Les Vingt*, held sway within a larger context of a unified, harmonious artistic whole. This was a concept vigorously promoted by Maus, by Edmond Picard, fellow lawyer and editor of the group's journal, *L'Art moderne,* and by *Les Vingt* members. The group's unified stance was reinforced by the prominent placement of its double "X" emblem, designed by Fernand Khnopff, on the wall of each exhibition chamber.

While not commercially motivated to a fault, as had been its timidly experimental predecessor *L'Essor* (Flight), *Les Vingt* was definitely interested in making a profit, its members realizing that self-sufficiency and longevity were "dependent upon their ability to attract a paying public and to promote and sell the work on view." (Canning, "*Soyons nous*" 34) To this end, the editors of *L'Art moderne* launched publicity campaigns worthy of any aggressive public relations assault in our own time. The journal published a list of exhibiting artists before each salon, and a second list of works sold after the salon's closing. Also published were reviews of each show by favorable critics, together, surprisingly, with "extracts of negative reviews by hostile critics." (Canning, "*Soyons nous*" 34) Further heating up the pages of *L'Art moderne* were articles on the nature and importance of socially-directed art, as well as extracts from published socialist and anarchist writing, such as Prince Kropotkin's tellingly titled "Words of a Revolutionary." (Canning, "In the Realm of the Social" 80)

This effective editorial strategy clearly capitalized on the time-honored universal taste for contrroversy Together with the innovative art itself, innovatively installed in *Les Vingt* salons, the strategy assisted in the furtherance of the "group's radical avant garde image in the public eye" (Canning, "*Soyons nous*" 34) that is to say, the viewing public raced to the *salon vernissages* as if to a fire. Added to this cumulus of tactics designed to seduce the potential customer, including the occasional resort to shock value, were the posters and catalogues designed by the artist members. Repeating and further illuminating the information in *L'Art moderne*, the catalogues for every salon featured comprehensive, handwritten accounts of all the artists and sometimes complemented by drawings. Each artist was given a separate page, thereby heightening the reader's awareness of important stylistic distinctions between artist members. In addition, rather than masking *Les Vingt's* anarcho-socialist underpinnings, the catalogues promulgated the group's left wing bias through red catalogue covers, with the Les XX emblem embossed in black (Canning, "*Soyons nous*" 35).

Later catalogues reflected greater attention to paper choice and quality, layout, and type, carried out in tandem with the expanded presence of decorative craft in the Les Vingt exhibits of 1891-1893. Covers designed by Symbolist artist George Lemmen functioned symbolically to convey the group's dual role as exponent of avant garde art-making and as champion of socioeconomic reform. The 1891 catalogue cover depicts a red sun labelled "*Les XX*" above a turbulent sea; the 1892 cover features a banner with *Les XX*'s emblem partially obscuring a fruit-laden tree, the abundance of fruit signifying the creative fecundity of *Les Vingt's* artists. (Canning, "*Soyons nous*" 35) In 1896, Octave Maus sent copies of these elegant catalogues to Siegfried Bing's *Galérie Art Nouveau*, for inclusion in an exhibit on the modern book.

There is an unmistakable link between the favorable impression made on Bing by the catalogues and Lemmen's eventual collaboration with Henry van de Velde in contriving showrooms for Bing's gallery in 1896. *Les Vingt's* three-pronged effort at wooing the public, striking departures in installation, informative, provocative editorial tactics in "*L'Art moderne*," catalogues showcasing each artist separately, very shortly paid off. As the salons became more and more popular, work by *Vingtistes* and their invited guests sold, and well. As Canning notes, "By establishing a reputation for selling work, many more artists were willing to exhibit in *Les Vingt*, and, in turn, the participation of the 'invités' insured Les XX's fame and fortune." (Canning, "*Soyons nous*" 34)

The openness of *Les Vingt* to foreign participation in the exhibitions also extended to artists cutting ties with the past in other areas: in literature, for example the French Symbolist poet Stéphane Mallarmé was asked to read his evocative Symbolist poetry to a rapt Belgian audience as well as lecture on the equally elusive verse of the Belgian poet Auguste Villiers de l'Isle-Adam, for the 1890 Salon. In music, concerts presented in 1891 and 1892 exposed Brussels' Western European listeners to the Eastern European minor key melodies and unfamiliar, "exotic" rhythms, chords, and harmonies informing the surging compositions of Russian composers Alexander Borodin and Nikolai Rimsky-Korsakov. Indeed, the Russians' populist musical agenda, manifest in their borrowings from Russian folk music, resonated with the intimate bond between *Les Vingt* and *Le Parti Oeuvrier Belge*. The *P.O.B.* agenda responded not only to the pragmatic dissatisfactions and needs, but also to the tastes and tangible folk arts of a lower class barely represented in canonic European classical music, theater, dance, or the visual arts until the mid-19th century.

To both enrichen and complicate an already diverse creative mix, two distinct linguistic entities within Les Vingt's Belgian majority strove to maintain a productive, albeit strained, solidarity: the Flemish artists from the agricultural north, its time-honored trade and cultural centers Antwerp, Bruges, Ghent, and Louvain tracing theirroots to the Medieval period, and the French-speaking Wallons from Belgium's industrialized southern region. Efforts at maintaining administrative equality, or even social calm and equilibrium, within this bi-lingual and bi-cultural organization were obviously not so easy. In strict factual terms, a majority of French-speaking artists and writers controlled the affairs of *Les Vingt* in its early years, reflecting the traditionally dominant position of French speakers in Belgium's political, professional, and commercial circles.

This dominance would affect the layout and content of *Les Vingt's* critical journalistic voice itself, *L' Art moderne,* founded by Octave Maus and Edmond Picard in1881. Its first issue published on March 6, 1881, the periodical reflected the anarcho-socialist perspective of its lawyer-editors and promoted a social role for art, albeit one that did include material gain in its objectives: " 'We wish to smooth the way, to facilitate the rapport between the artists and the public, so that each day Art can gain the beneficial social influence that it should obtain, so that artists also will be able to possess the important material and moral position which they are owed.'" "(Canning, *"Soyons nous"* 30-31)

According to Maus and Picard, the artists, in particular the artists rejecting the outdated creative norms of the academies, and the working class public, were social and economic brethren. Both had long been owed greater recognition; both had long been economically shortchanged. Long overdue were both the appropriate respect and commensurate income their efforts deserved. In addition to attacking the tradition-bound Brussels Academy of Fine Arts and its annual showcase, the official *Salon, L'Art moderne* agitated for the introduction of art, chiefly the decorative applied arts, into the everyday life of all Belgian citizens, a goal it shared with the Arts and Crafts Movement gaining momentum across the English Channel.

Be it said, however, that, at first, the journal's impassioned polemic succeeded in driving away as much of the literate public as it attracted, at least until its emotionally charged voice became a more familiar journalistic presence. Indeed, *L'Art moderne's* editorial stridency even intimidated a small number of the very artists whose careers the journal hoped to promote. "Unnerved by the hostile reaction of the rhetoric of *L'Art moderne*, a few of the more conservative members left the group." Fortunately for the group as a whole, their places were quickly filled by the Belgians Anna Boch Felicien Rops and Henry van de Velde, all "modern" artists of greater moral fiber, and by the eminent foreign artists noted earlier.

While *L'Art moderne* was an indisputably francophone journal, its stated goals, like those of socialism itself, disavowed national and class boundaries. There is paradox here: while the historic Belgian centers for education and the arts lay in its Flemish cities, the dominance, across the board, of its French-speaking populace owed its authority not to the productivity of its thriving industrial south, but to the nation's border with its *soi-disant* culturally superior neighbor, France. All of Belgium, for that matter, had been virtually owned and controlled by Spanish, Austrian, French, and finally Dutch Hapsburg rulers for hundreds of years before unification and independence in 1830. (Murphy and Strikwerda 19)

Indeed, these were centuries when French was the lingua franca of governmental affairs, as well as cultural and commercial interchange, throughout the entire European continent. This linguistic hegemony was perpetuated in Brussels long after Belgium had freed itself from Hapsburg control. Ambitious newcomers to the city from elsewhere in Belgium those seeking influential positions in the courts, the military, or on the higher rungs of government administration; those seeking education in law or medicine; those bent on success in commerce were either native French speakers, or Flemings with fluency in that language. (Murphy and Strikwerda 20)

A leap ahead into Henry van de Velde's career post -*Les Vingt* seems appropriate here. Given *Les Vingt's* "French connection," and the international make-up of the group's exhibition calendar, lectures, and musical performances, it is not in the least remarkable that van de Velde travelled comfortably southward to Paris in 1895, two years after the group disbanded. There, at Siegfried Bing's invitation, he masterminded and installed three showrooms in the Art Nouveau impresario's *Galérie Art Nouveau* Not so remarkable either, when viewed in historic context, is van de Velde's 1899 move eastward to Germany, where he built and sustained a dual career, at the outset in interior design and architecture, later in the overhaul of applied arts education, through his curriculum development for Weimar's *Kunstgewerbeschule.* The Belgian master had been conditioned, throughout his four-year affiliation with *Les Vingt*, to the assumption that national borders were porous and would remain so indefinitely.

Van de Velde's internationalist outlook had been nourished by his fidelity to both the objectives of the *Parti Oeuvrier Belge* and to William Morris's moralizing views on the necessary link between well-designed functional goods and social reform. This outlook apparently served him well through a 16-year immersion in German commercial, cultural and educational life. However, as our jump ahead makes clear, rising 20th Century nationalistic sentiment trumped an earlier surge of cultural reciprocity, so that van de Velde's native idealism, nurtured by the years with *Les Vingt*, proved an unfortunate blind spot.

The uniqueness of *Les Vingt*, among European avant garde groups of the same period, is thus already evident in the symbiotic mix of artists, writers, and composers working together in a creative crucible. Also unprecedented is the welcome extended to artists with similar sensibilities from other European cultural centers, as well as the four distinct stylistic directions, Naturalism, Symbolism, Impressionism, Post-Impressionism, often on display simultaneously in the ten successive exhibitions. Few, if any art movements of the same or later periods could claim such expansive inclusiveness.

That said, perhaps what most sets *Les Vingt* apart from other art societies is the identity of its founder, Octave Maus. With no artistic training or achievement to his credit, Maus operated effectively on three parallel, but non-creative professional tracks: as lawyer, as publisher and journalist, as cultural entrepreneur. Indeed, one might say that, were it not for the atypical bond between *Les Vingt* and the *P.O.B.*, the motives of this lawyer-publisher-impresario in organizing and leading an eclectic group of artists would remain opaque. However, that bond was the propulsive force driving Maus's organizational activities. As noted earlier, he operated on a central guiding assumption, one which viewed art-making as a potent form of political speech.

Les Vingt, like all avant garde movements in rebellion against the status quo, was formed as a concerted reaction to staid academic guidelines for art-making long in place throughout the continent and the British Isles. Ironically, as we know, the academic tradition under siege had itself begun, in the late 13th Century, as a reaction against the strictures of Medieval art, whose artifacts can be found pervasively in Gothic cathedrals and museum collections throughout the Western world. However, by the late 19th Century, the technical and stylistic advances of the 15th and 16th Century Italian Renaissance, the tremendous technical strides in depicting anatomy and perspective, had hardened and ossified into a rigid set of formulae for portraiture, landscape, still life, and genre painting, as well as figurative sculpture. The results were predictable, repetitive, and, as often as not, insipid.

No *Les Vingt* member opposed the traditional Brussels Academy straitjacket with more wit and vitriol than James Ensor, painter of "Woman Eating Oysters" and probably the most dynamic figure in the 19th Century Brussels avant garde. Having migrated from rural Flemish Ostend to cosmopolitan Brussels while still in his teens, Ensor had dropped out of the academy after a mere three years of study. Not content to simply leave the school, he'd published a diaristic account of his studies, "Three weeks at the Academy," which constituted "a witty upending of his professors and the tired traditions of the official art school." (Canning, "In the Realm of the Social" 76)

Ensor deployed visually devastating tactics masks, skeletons, scatological imagery in his unsparing caracatures of establishment villains in Belgian society, what he perceived as the corrupt, venal institution of the Catholic Church; the military; indolent, entitled aristocrats; smug Brussels burghers; Leopold II himself. (Canning, "In the Realm of the Social" 76) While "*L'Art moderne*" served up provocative diatribes and catalyzed critical debate, Ensor bodied forth the very essence of the phrase *"épater la bourgeoisie"* in his scathingly critical work, its stylistic strategies so much at odds with those of the academies.

Nevertheless, some credit is due the much-maligned traditional course of study, in Brussels, Antwerp, and elsewhere, given the technical skills it allowed the architect-to-be, Henry van de Velde and others like him, in the preparation of perspectives for future projects. The established academies *did* offer methodical instruction in the manipulation of the tools of the studio trade, they *did* insist on accuracy in the depiction of the human face and figure, albeit *via* casts of classical sculpture, and they *did* instruct students in the tenets of point perspective, developed five centuries earlier in Renaissance Florence. Of the twenty original *Les Vingt* members, fifteen had attended art academies in Brussels or Antwerp;.Of the Belgian artists who later joined the group, seven, including van de Velde, had been steeped in the now superannuated academic training (Canning, *"Soyons nous"* 32) For that matter, given the relative restraint and artistic conservatism of many original group members, their participation in both the official and *Les Vingt* Salons in the mid-1880s should be no surprise.

The innovations in technique, style, and subject matter deployed by Les Vingt artists were matched in house-cleaning spirit by the group's impressively egalitarian administrative structure, initiated and sustained by Maus. This structure was adopted and implemented by *Les Vingt* members as an artist-friendly antidote to the hierarchical framework favored by the official Brussels Salon and even by *L'Essor*, spiritual forerunner to *Les Vingt*. In fact, many of the original *Les Vingt* artist members had left *L'Essor*, in part in reaction to the society's "strong bureaucratic element," a hierarchical system in which twenty Essorians legislated exhibition policy for a much larger community of member artists.

According to the new régime, *Les Vingt* had *no* president and *no* long term governing committees. The administrative process, focussed on selecting and inviting artists for exhibitions, was carried out by a short-term rotating committee of three members, who together orchestrated the installations. (Canning, *"Soyons nous"* 35) The membership, feeding ideas to the troika of exhibition planners, also determined and scheduled the literary readings, lectures, and discussions, as well as the increasingly important musical performances that complemented the visual art experience. Indeed, in considering the "multi-media" nature of the annual exhibitions contrived for *Les Vingt* by its membership, one might define them as the artistic equivalent of a composer's, or an architect's, *Gesamtkunstwerk*. If so, then *Les Vingt's* coordination of three media for its annual salons anticipates the "total work[s] of art" of Mackintosh, Hoffmann, Horta, and van de Velde to come.

The active personal investment of all its members in *Les Vingt* activities extended to the scouting of new talent, particularly beyond Belgium's borders. Naturally, ties between Belgian and French artists were the strongest, since so many permanent members had visited or studied in Paris in the 1870s and '80s. The reciprocity between the two artistic communities, strengthened by the participation of French artists in *Les Vingt* salons from 1885 on, was further buttressed in 1887 by the involvement of several *Vingtistes* in the first exhibit of *Galérie Georges Petit in Paris* Of the initial members, Théo van Rysselberghe, an avid francophile, played the most prominent role in bringing French modernism to Brussels. (Canning, *"Soyons nous"* 35)

Responsible for inviting Caillebotte, Gauguin, Signac, and van Gogh to exhibit, van Rysselberghe also discovered the work of Henri de Toulouse Lautrec, whose work was first shown not in Paris, but in the 1888 *Les Vingt* salon.(Canning, *"Soyons nous"* 36) Lautrec provides a crucial 19th Century bridge between the worlds of easel and decorative art for two reasons: his mastery of lithographic techniques in designing posters for *Le Moulin Rouge* and other Parisian performance halls, and the absorption of Japanese compositional and stylistic norms into all his graphic work. Doubtless, the sinuous contour, asymmetry, and decidedly non-Western cropping energizing the posters Lautrec exhibited in *Les Vingt* salons of the 1890s, were surely not lost on Henry van de Velde. Nor, for that matter, would have been the subjects of Lautrec' acerbic, but compassionate portrayals: the *demi-mondaines* of Parisian nightlife, whose glamor and celebrity were ephemeral, but whose marginal position in staid, middle class French society was permanent.

Paul Signac brought more than *pointilliste* technique and a personal take on anarchist principles to *Les Vingt*, both before and after his election to full membership in 1891. He accompanied Seurat to the 1887 Salon, in which *"L'Après-Midi sur la Grande Jatte"* held pride of place; he acted as intermediary between the group and French avant garde luminaries, providing Maus with the addresses of Camille

Pissarro and Paul Gauguin; he arranged for the 1892 Seurat retrospective in Brussels, after his colleague's premature death of tuberculosis. (Canning, *"Soyons nous"* 37)

Only slightly less important for *Les Vingt's* expansion beyond Belgium's borders were its contacts with London. Founding member Alfred William (Willy) Finch, half-English himself, requested Whistler's invitation to first *Les Vingt* salon, and nominated the outspoken, truculent American for permanent membership in 1886. Whistler was also championed by standing *Les Vingt* members Fernand Khnopff and Georges Lemmen, both involved as well in bringing the Pre-Raphaelites and the British Arts and Crafts Movement to the attention and the galleries of *Les Vingt* salons. In the course of their travels to London, all three artists developed interest in the writings of William Morris and John Ruskin, while Lemmen urged the exhibit of Walter Crane's illustrated books in the 1891 Salon (Canning, *"Soyons nous"* 37) As a result, Henry van de Velde, like so many other Belgian artists, was drawn into the Arts and Crafts orbit without actually travelling to London.

Maus himself acted, or claimed he acted, merely as secretary, ceding artistic authority to the member artists of the selection committee whose tenure was long enough to be effective, but not so long as to become rigid or autocratic. Nevertheless, it would be an error to minimize Maus's duties and effectiveness as what we now term art "facilitator." He secured the artists' participation in each salon in written contracts signed by all parties involved, arranging for the shipment of work from both Belgian and foreign studios. His close ties with Belgium's conservative government smoothed the way for *Les Vingt*'s initial exhibits in the traditional Palace of Fine Arts, a prestigious, if not cutting edge, venue, and later in the *Musée d'Art moderne.* Again, with Picard, and later with the Symbolist poet Verhaeren, a more moderate editorial voice, he developed *Les Vingt*'s polemic through the incisive editorials and reviews published in *L'Art moderne.* And as a lawyer specializing in issues of copyright, he was in a prime position to inform the artists of their rights in issues regarding resale of purchased work or graphic reproduction in journals and periodicals. (Canning, *"Soyons nous"* 38)

Of even greater importance, Maus also shares credit with Picard for the expanding presence of decorative art and craft in *Les Vingt*'s salons, from 1889 on. Examples of such work had been confined mainly to book design and illustration in the first five salons. The 1889 Salon brought ceramics and glasswork into the fine art mix of mainly Neo-Impressionist and Symbolist painting and sculpture. *Les Vingt* salons from 1891 to 1893 saw the full integration of decorative with easel art, with the ornamental objects often placed on stands as though literally on equal standing with the other artwork (Canning *"Soyons nous"* 44)

The 1891 Salon, for instance, combined work by Seurat, Pissarro, and Sisley with a retrospective for the now-deceased van Gogh. Extending the scope of an already eclectic installation were posters and book illustrations by the Arts and Crafts master, Walter Crane, several early attempts at ceramics by Willy Finch," and three ceramic vases, accompanied by a rough, totemic wooden sculpture, by Gauguin. In 1892, a retrospective of Seurat's paintings, including "*La Cirque*" and "*La Parade*," shared exhibit space with an array of objects that included sketches for embroidery pieces by van de Velde, these last his earliest ventures into the applied arts. By 1893, and its final exhibition, *Les Vingt* had moved more assertively into the realms of both decorative and functional design, with the display of a table by Finch, as well as a more substantial entry by van de Velde: a sweeping, stylized tapestry, reflecting both the Japanese influence and the consolidation of his trademark whiplash curve. The tapestry represented a momentous and definitive shift in creative direction for the Belgian Art Nouveau master.

The involvement of Maus, Picard, and *Les Vingt* membership as a whole in decorative art did not spring exclusively from simple delight in beautiful crafted objects for their own sake. The motives, like so many in the group's agenda, lay in its socialist underpinnings and its avowed dedication to improving the living conditions for the underclass. In their shared editorial stance, Maus and Picard lay emphasis on the artificiality and arranged nature of all art-making, "the underlying decorative nature of all art." As Picard observed or, more accurately put, pontificated in *L'Art moderne,* "decorative art played an essential role in society as it instructed the masses in the universal principles of beauty, thereby raising their living standards and the aesthetic values of the whole community." (Canning, *"Soyons nous"* 43)

Of course, one is bound to look askance at the condescension, the implicit *noblesse oblige,* qualifying the idealism that brought Art Nouveau design to the Brussels public, *via* Les Vingt's final three salons. Nevertheless, praise is due the editors of *L'Art moderne* for their efforts in bridging the traditional gap in status between the fine and the applied arts, as had their counterparts in England's Arts and Crafts Movement, and for bringing innovative craft, indeed the first Art Nouveau decorative objects, into the public arena.

On balance, Maus's determination and organizational gifts, as well as the contacts he didn't hesitate to use, were in large part responsible for the successes of *Les Vingt's* salons, and for its relative longevity. Essential to state, however, is the ambiguous nature of its leader's long term impact on the group. As *Les Vingt's* centrality in Brussels' art scene grew more secure, Maus became more cautious in planning *Les Vingt* exhibits, constrained by those otherwise profitable ties with a Parliament dominated by the Catholic Party and headed not by an elected President, but by a hereditary monarch. Indicative of Maus's growing caution was his attempt, in 1891, to block the exhibition of James Ensor's "satirical indictment of the Belgian legal system," *"Les Bons Juges"* an attempt generated by his fear that public outrage and a governmental edict would close the salon altogether. Note that his erstwhile ally, Picard, disagreed, and engineered the showing of the painting in the *Les Vingt* salon of 1892. (Canning, *"Soyons nous"* 38)

Important to emphasize is that paintings by the dauntless, iconoclastic Ensor served both as immediate triggers for the founding of *Les Vingt*0 in 1884 and the final rift between Maus and Picard, in 1892. Moreover, Maus's pro-French orientation led to increasing friction within the group as his grip on the reins grew tighter.

While francophone *Vingtistes* like van Rysselberghe found favor with their founder, supporters of a more universally Belgian focus viewed Maus's pro-French bias and increasing aversion to risk a poor fit with their intentions for an avant garde group of artists comprising two distinct cultural strains. (Canning, *"Soyons nous"* 38-39) In the end, Maus's growing dissatisfaction with the group's democratic orientation, which ironically he himself had fostered, together with his drive for more control over the content of exhibitions, drove a wedge into *Les Vingt'*s 10-year solidarity. The group dissolved in 1893.

On the heels of the *Les Vingt's* demise was the formation of *La Libre aesthéthique*, Maus's creature and a society over which he exerted far greater administrative and artistic control.(Canning, *"Soyons nous"* 39) Surely Henry van de Velde, having witnessed the rising tensions and clash of egos and interests dividing a group of creative figures originally brought together by shared motives, would balk at the prospect of total authority wielded by another increasingly doctrinaire leader, Hermann Muthesius, founder of the *Deutscher Werkbund* and its dominant, energizing force

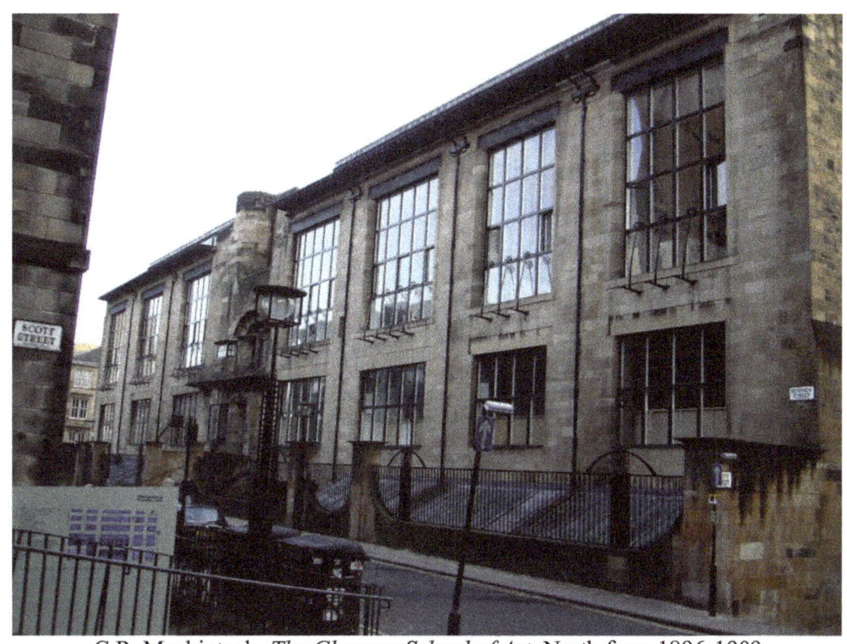

C.R. Mackintosh, *The Glasgow School of Art*, North face, 1896-1909

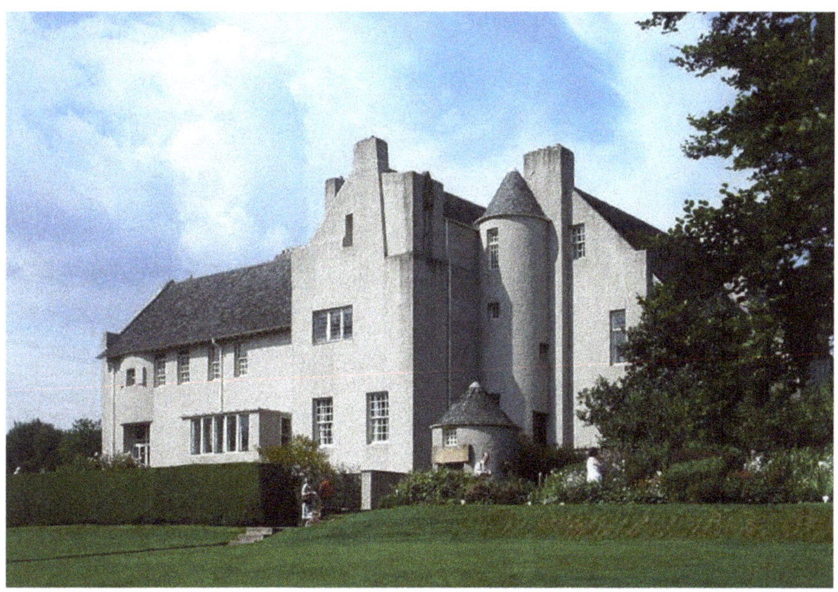
C.R.Mackintosh, *Hill House, Helensburgh*: exterior view with landscaping, 1902-04

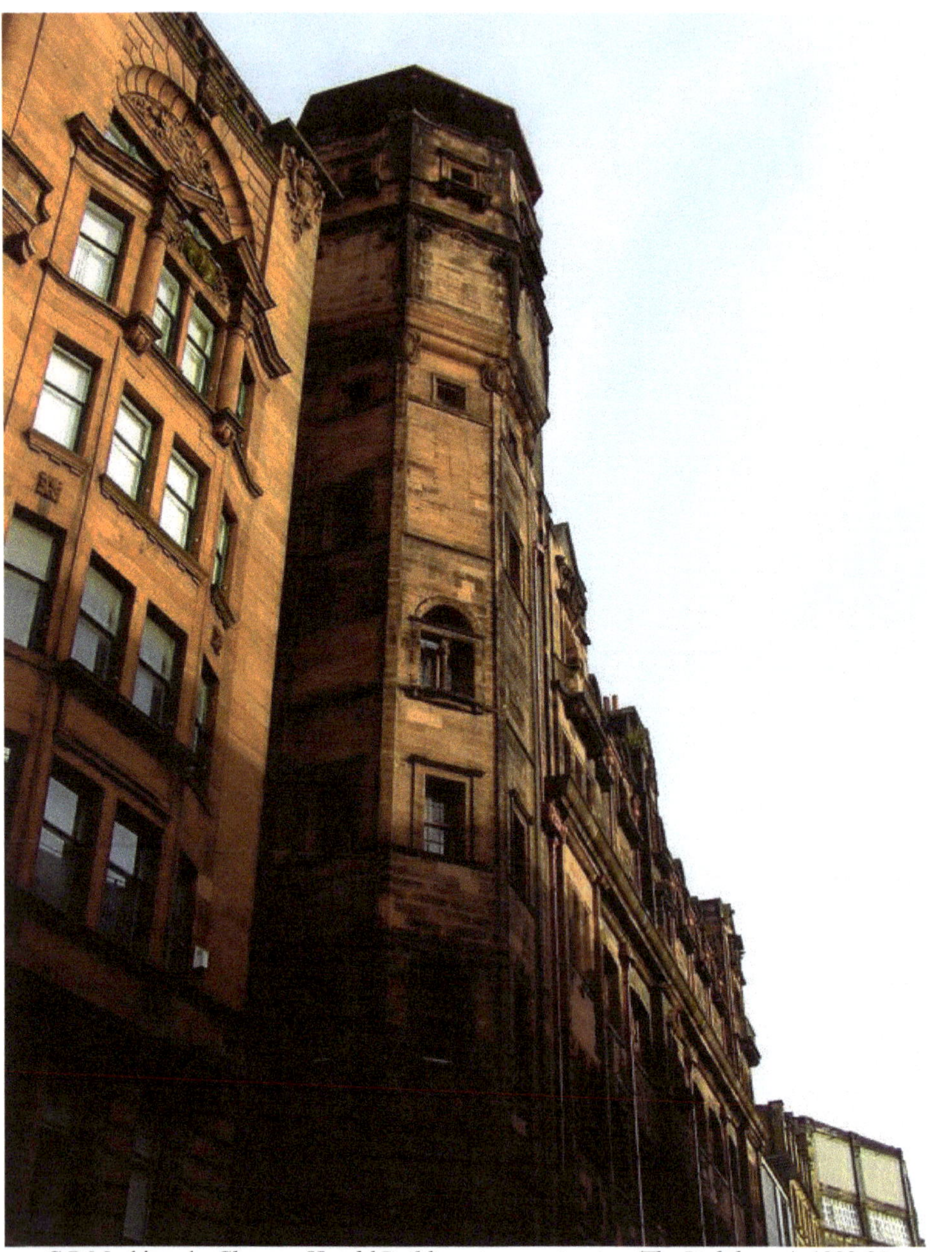

C.R.Mackintosh, *Glasgow Herald Building, tower extension (The Lighthouse)*, 1893-95

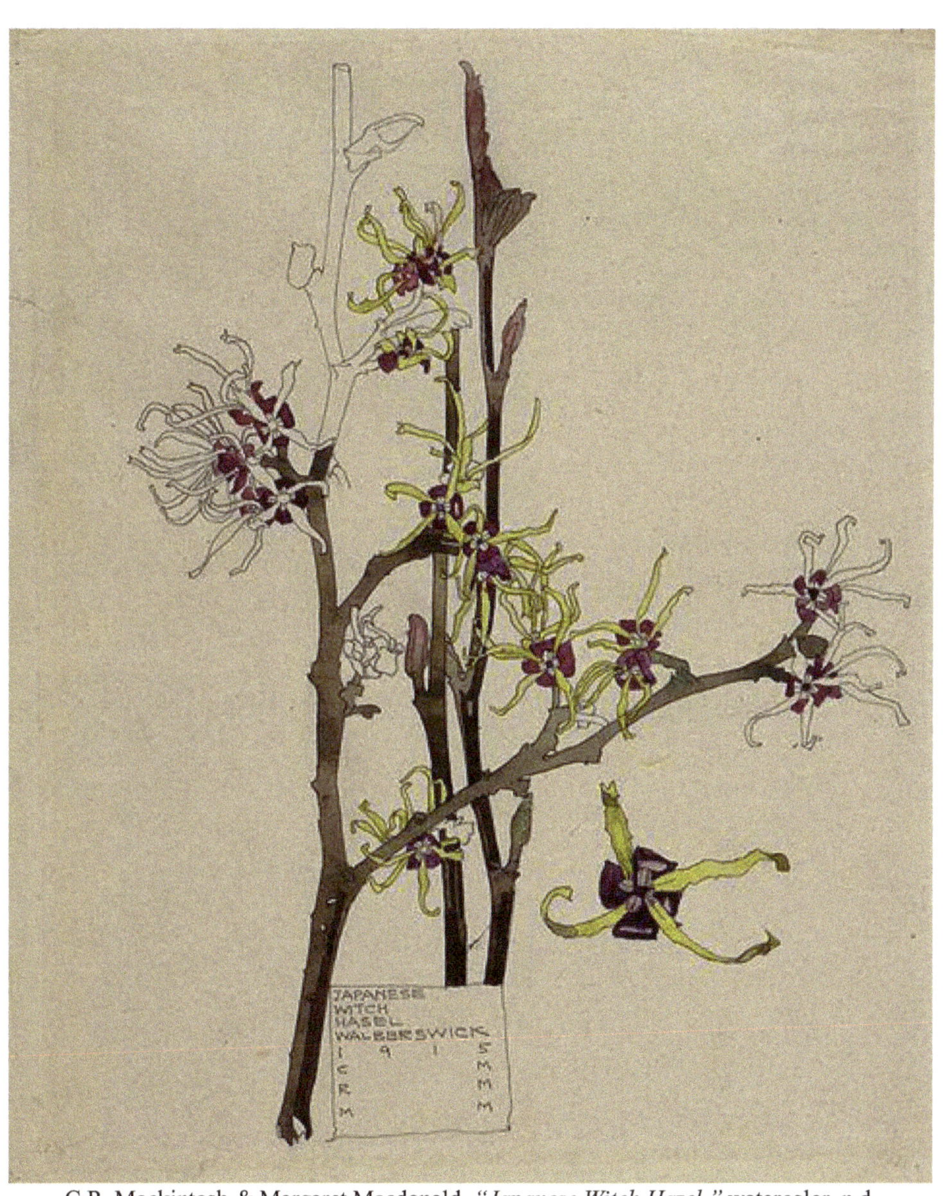

C.R. Mackintosh & Margaret Macdonald, *"Japanese Witch Hazel,"* watercolor, n.d.

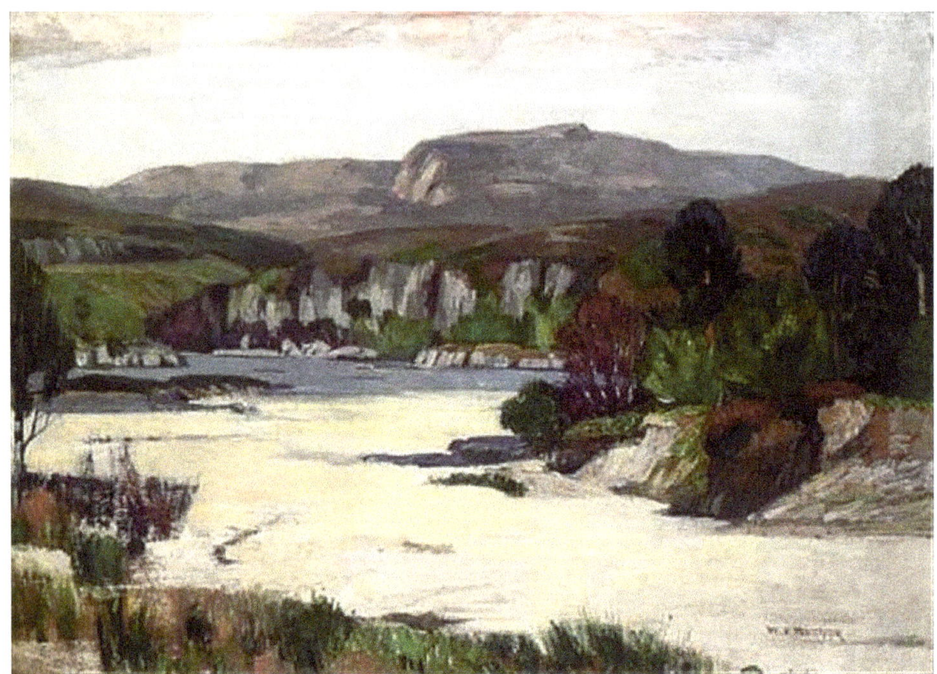

William York MacGregor, *"Sands of Morar,"* oil, n.d.

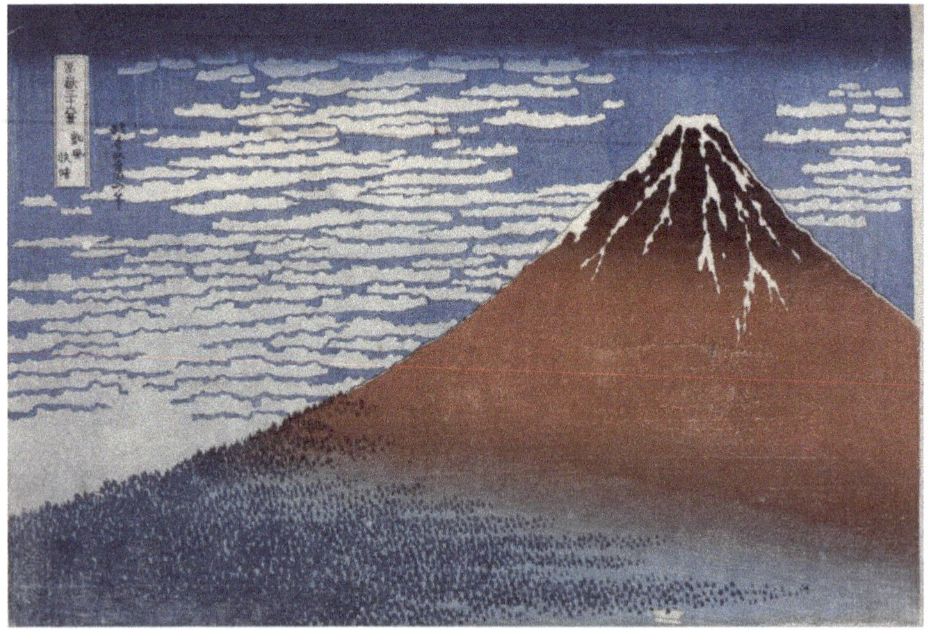

Hokusai, *"Fine Wind, Clear Morning,"* Japanese woodblock print, n.d.

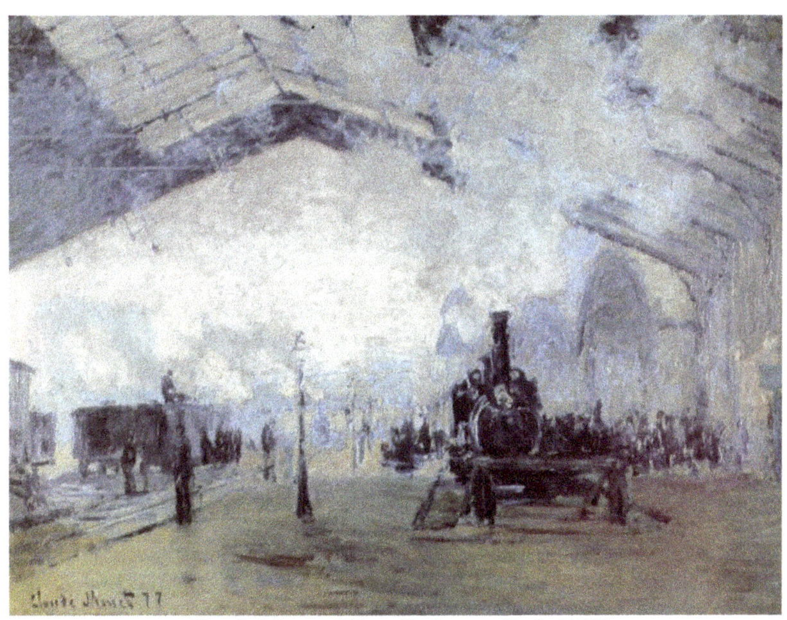

Claude Monet, "Gare St. Lazare," oil, 1877

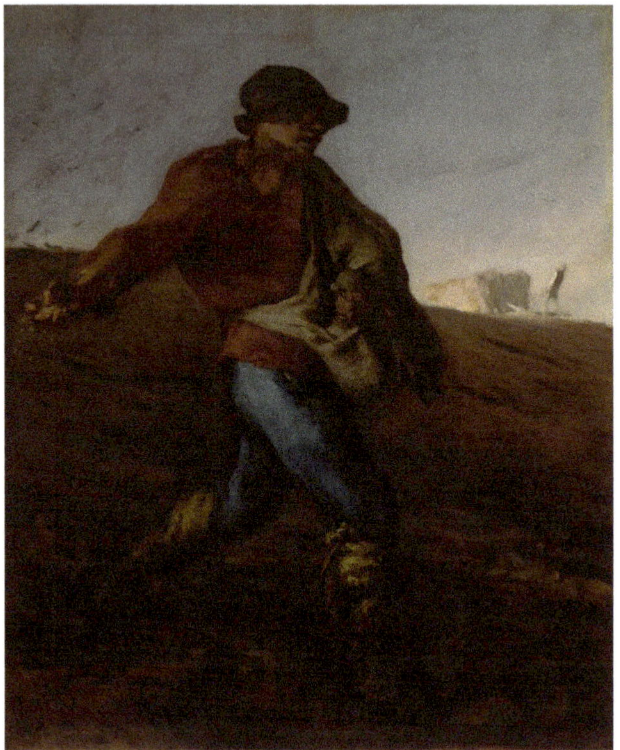

Jean François Millet, *"The Sower,"* oil, 1850

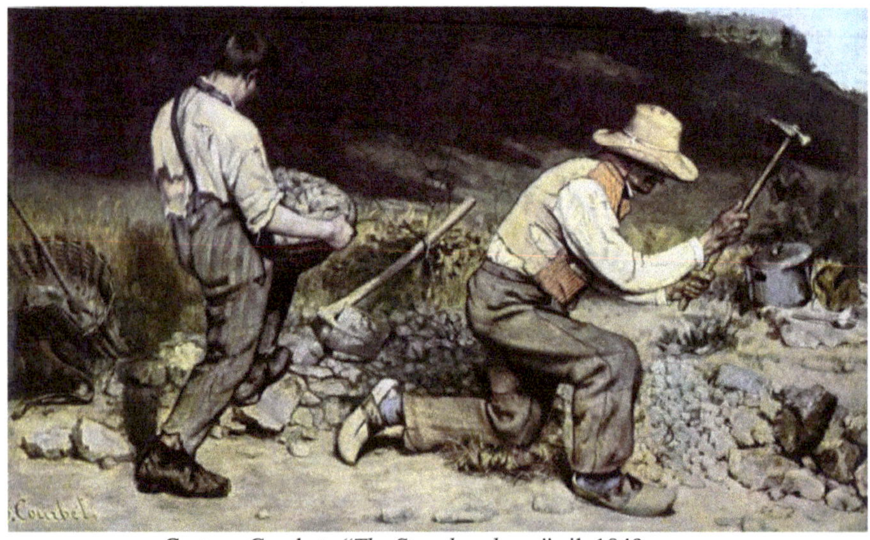

Gustave Courbet, *"The Stonebreakers,"* oil, 1849

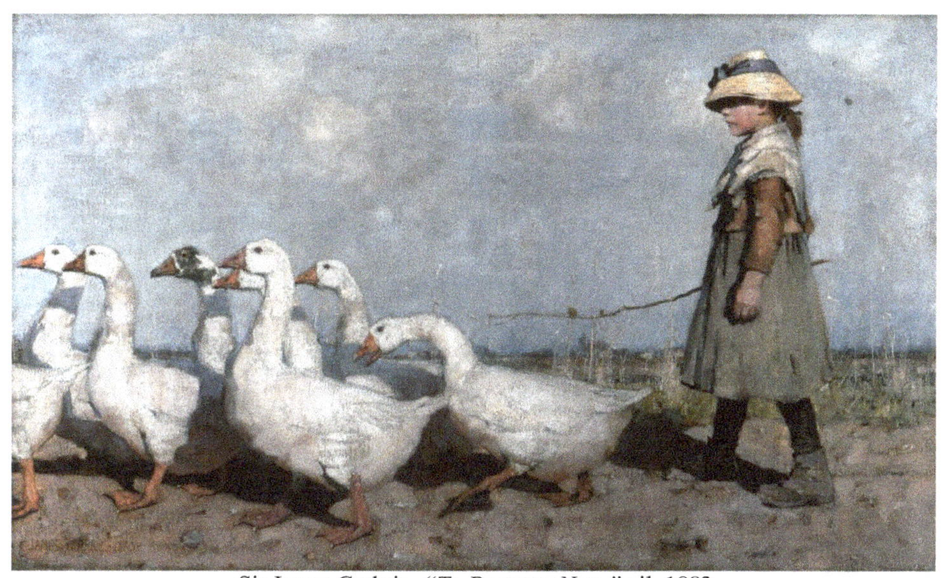

Sir James Guthrie, *"To Pastures New,"* oil, 1883

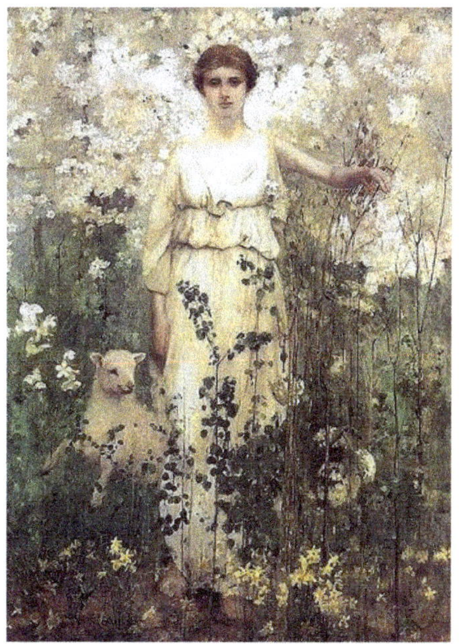

Thomas Millie Dow, *"Spring,"* watercolor, 1886

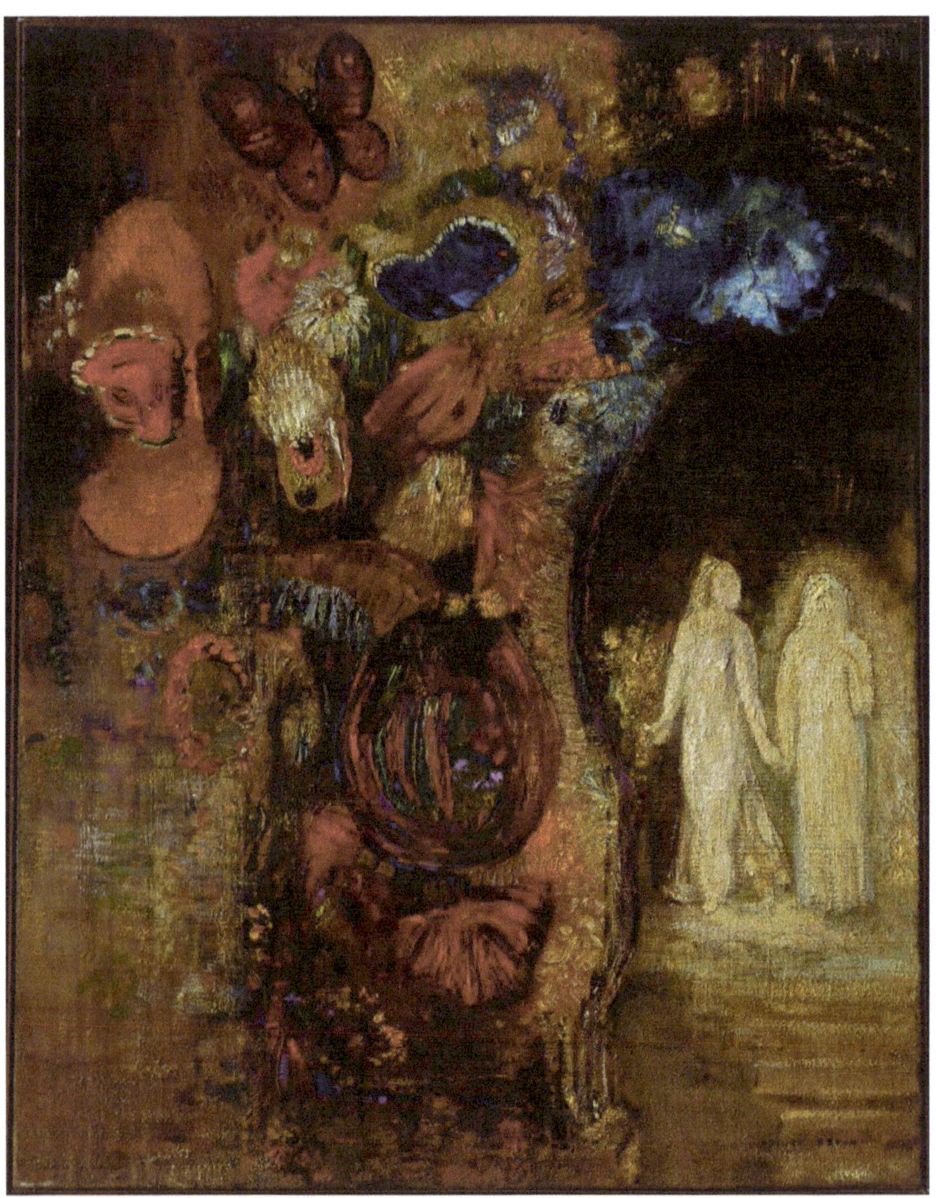

Odilon Redon, *"Apparition,"* mixed media, n.d.

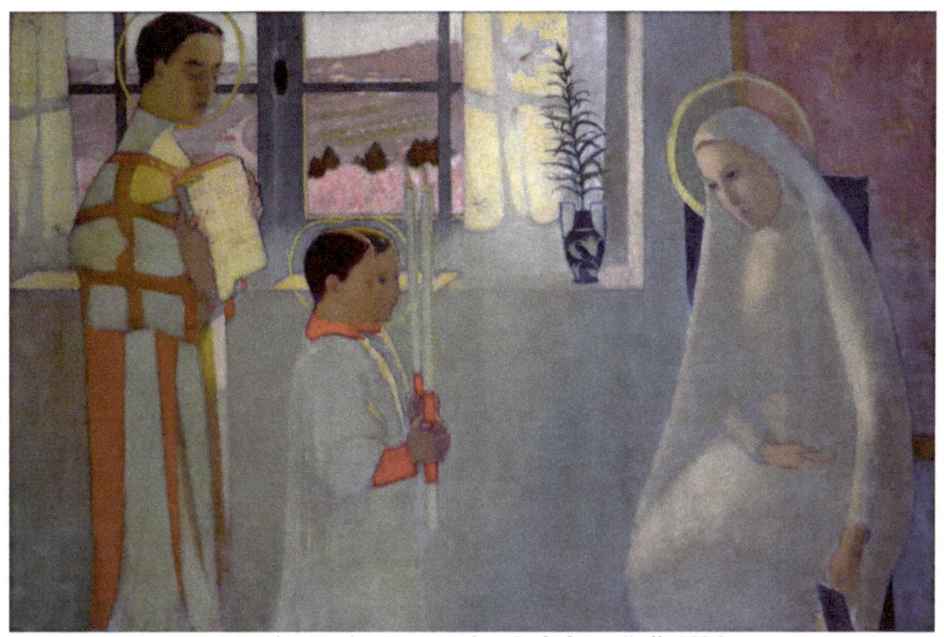

Maurice Denis, *"Le Mystère Catholique,"* oil, 1896

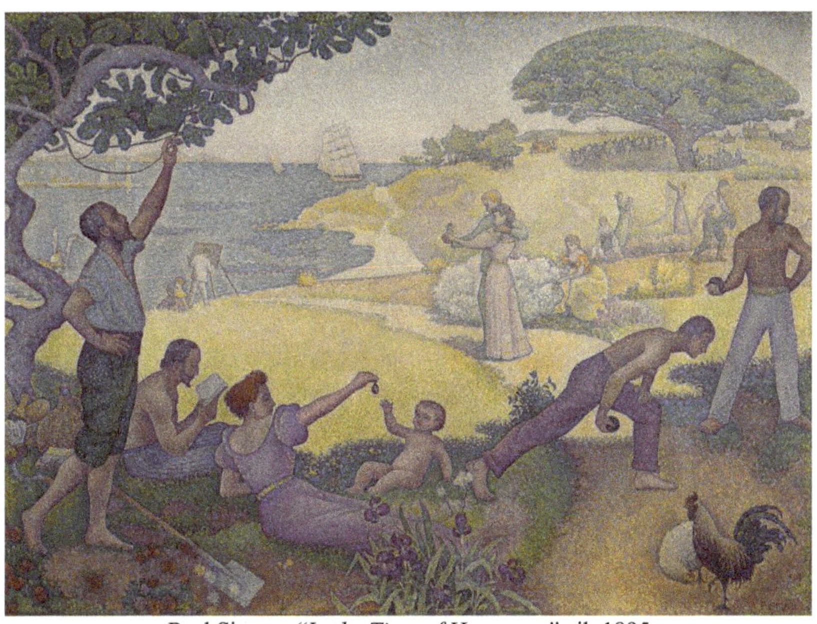

Paul Signac, *"In the Time of Harmony,"* oil, 1895

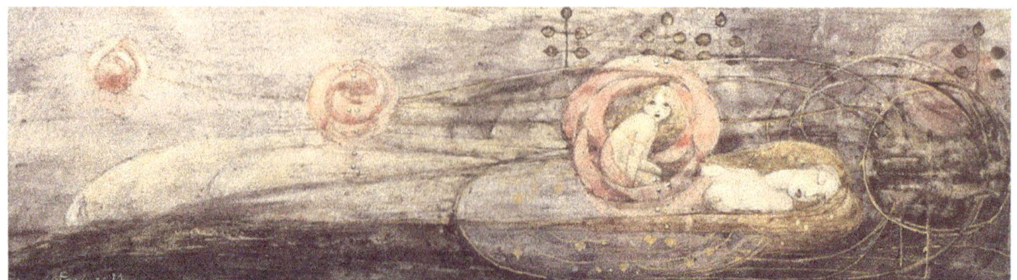

Margaret Macdonald, *"Oh ye that walk in Willowood,"* gesso on panel, 1902

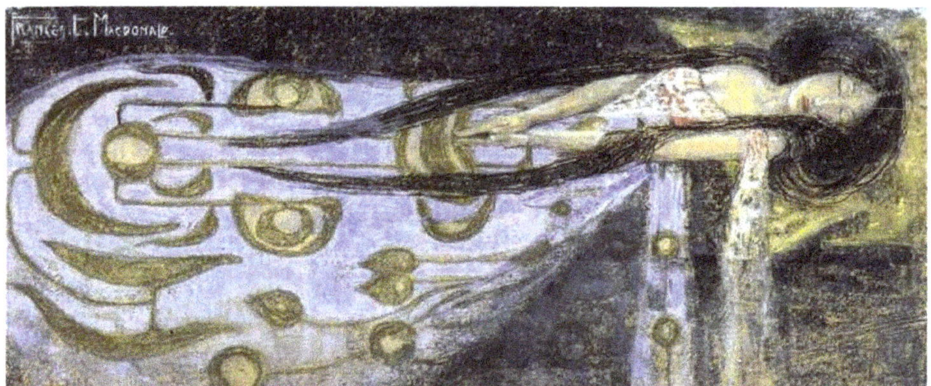

Frances Macdonald, *"The Sleeping Princess,"* watercolor, 1909

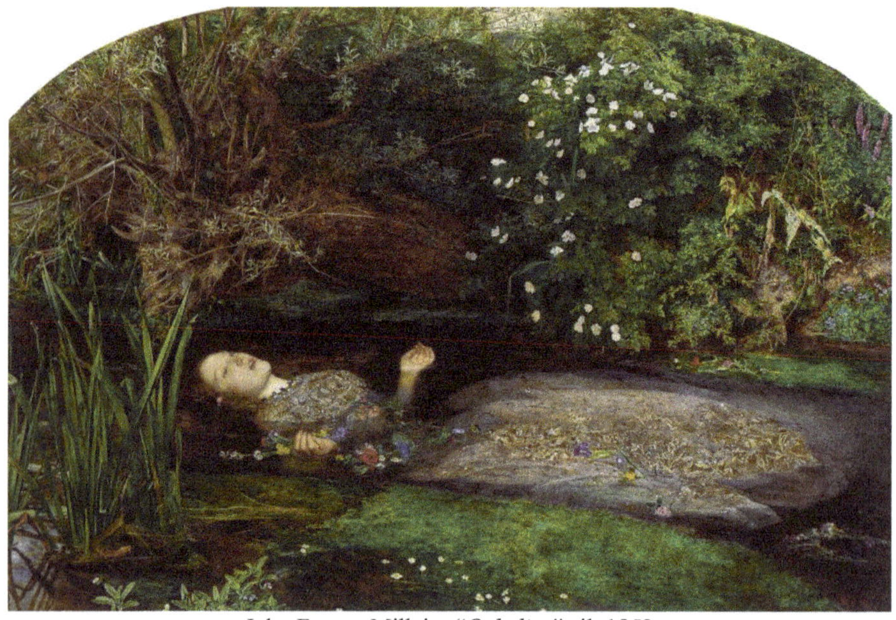

John Everett Millais, *"Ophelia,"* oil, 1852

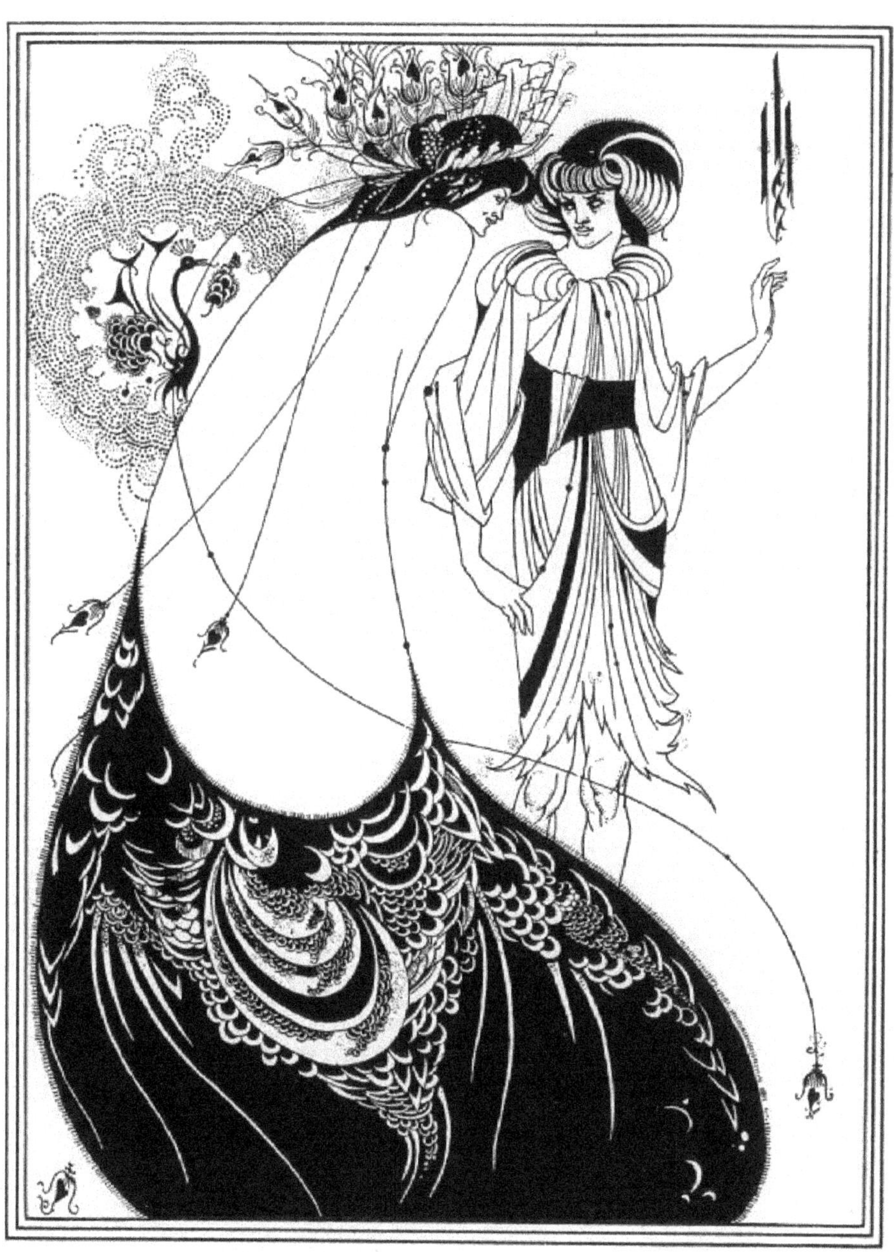

Aubrey Beardsley, *"The Peacock Skirt,"* ink, 1893

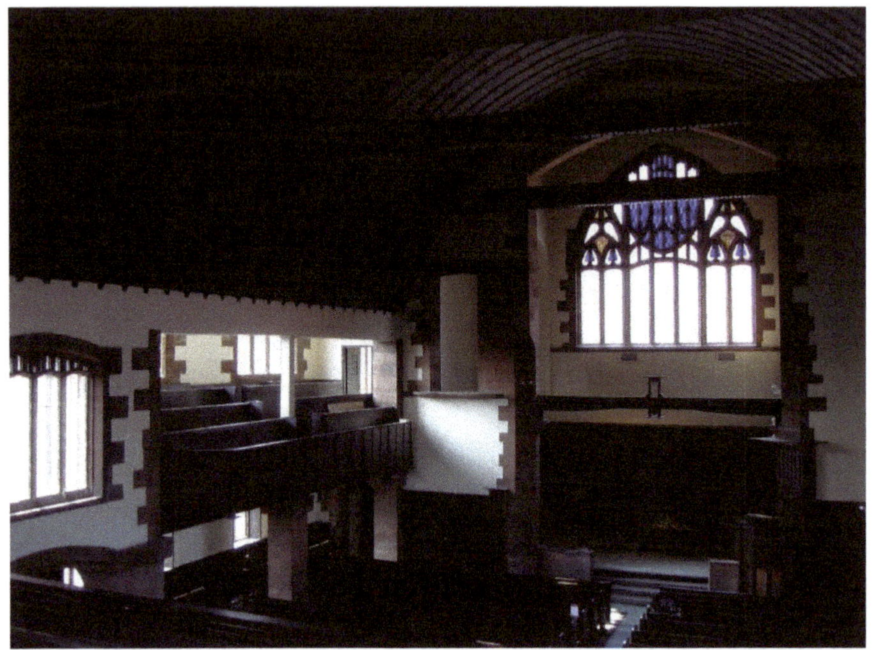

C.R. Mackintosh, *Queens Cross Church*, nave and "Blue Heart Window"

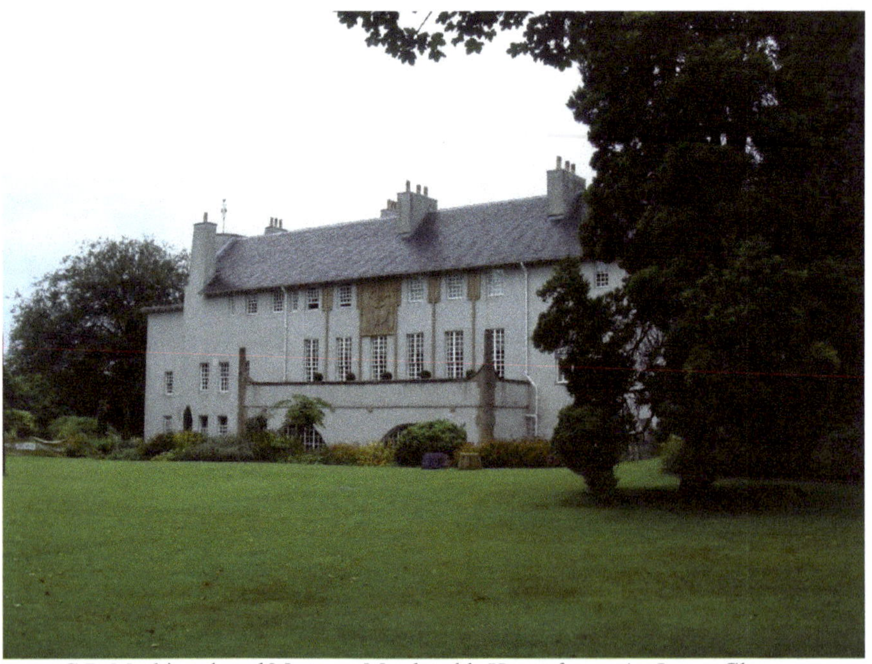

C.R. Mackintosh and Margaret Macdonald, *House for an Art Lover*, Glasgow

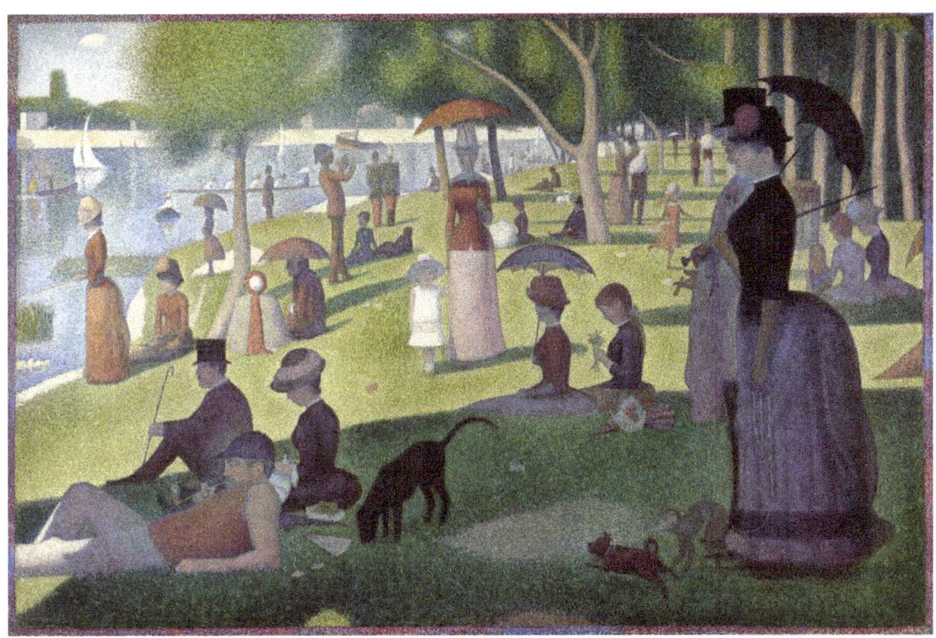

Georges Seurat, *‘L’Après Midi sur la Grande Jatte,”* oil, 1884-1886

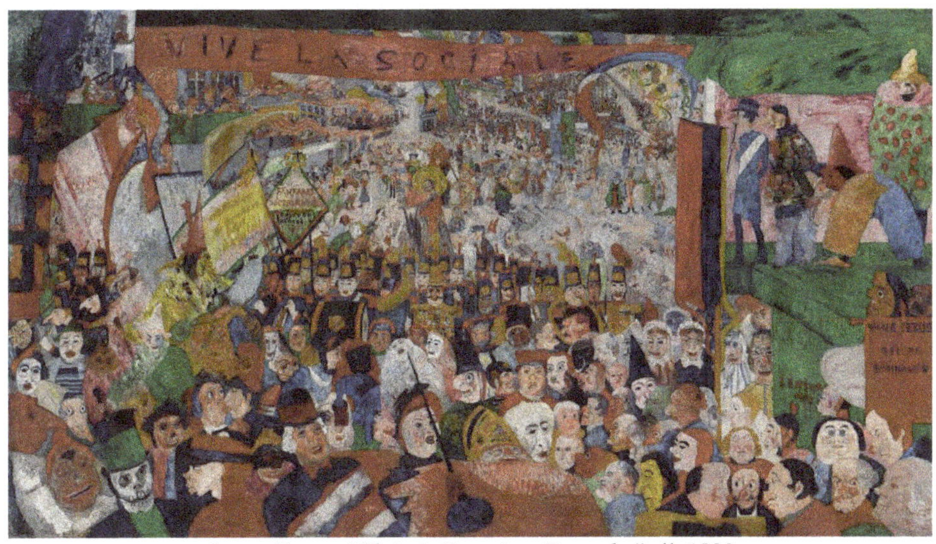

James Ensor, *“Christ’s Entry into Brussels,”* oil, 1889

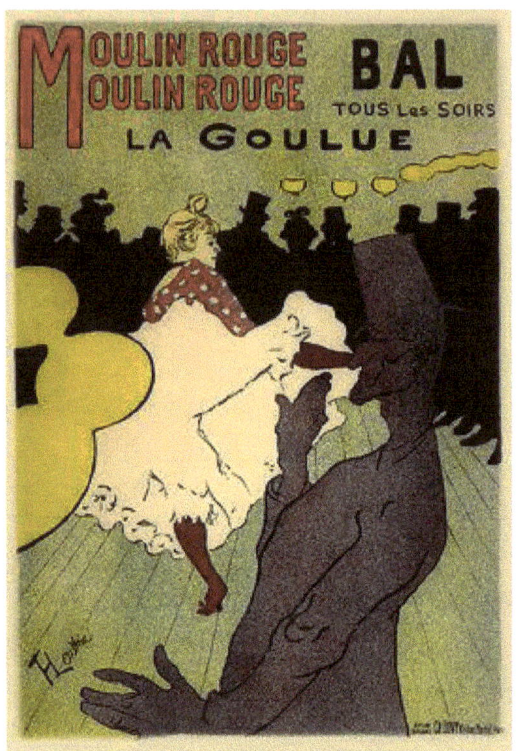

Henri de Toulouse Lautrec, *"Moulin Rouge, La Goulue,"* lithographic poster, 1891

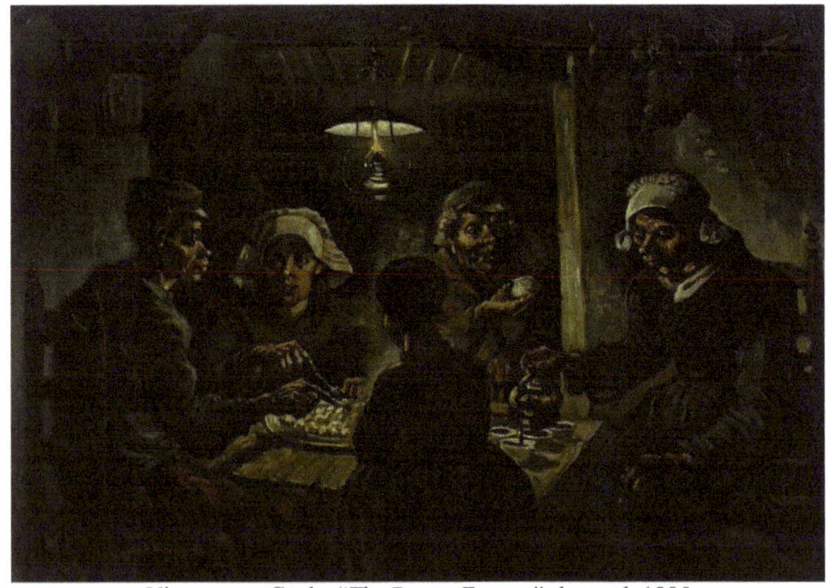

Vincent van Gogh, *"The Potato Eaters,"* charcoal, 1885

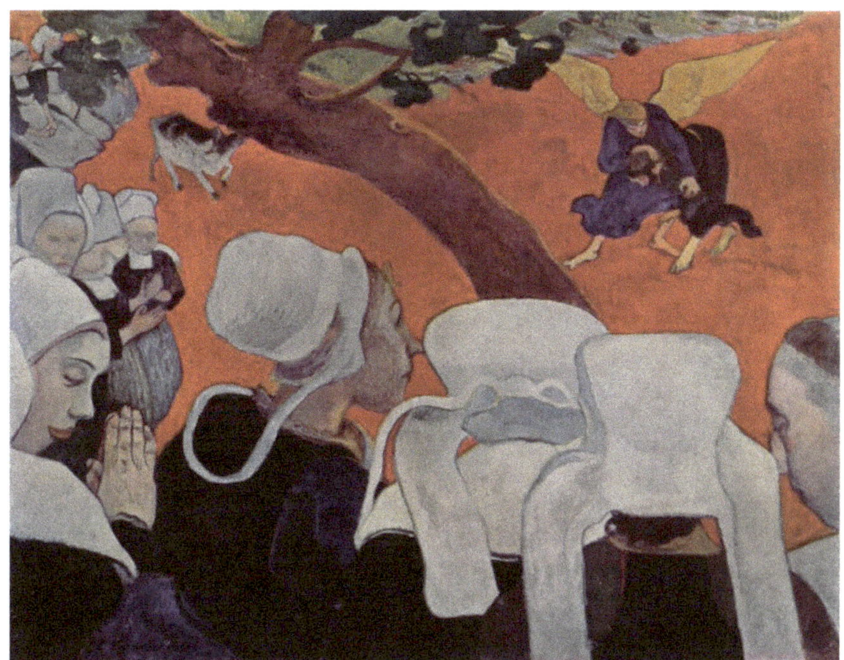

Paul Gauguin, *"Vision after the Sermon (Jacob Wrestling with the Angel),"* oil, 1888

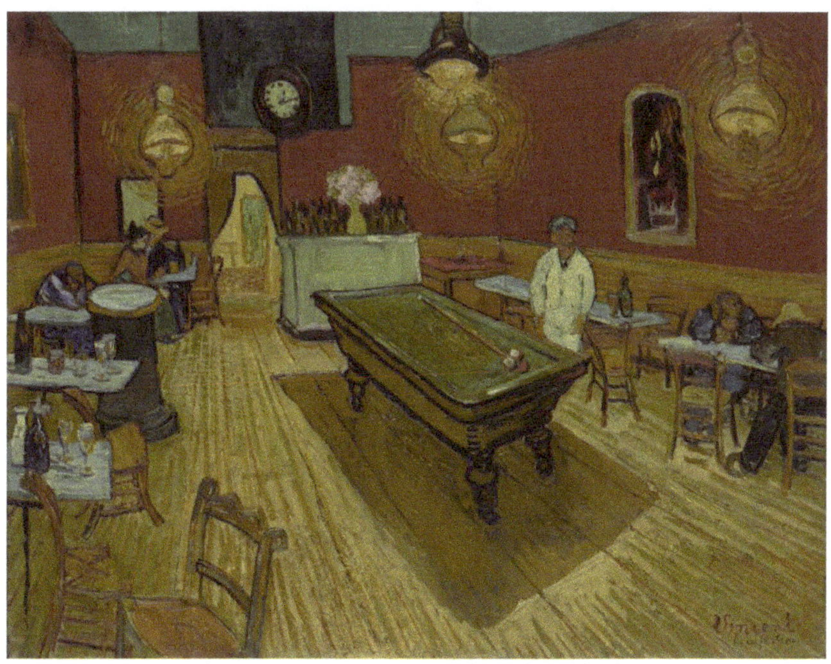

Vincent van Gogh, *"The Night Café,"* oil, 1888

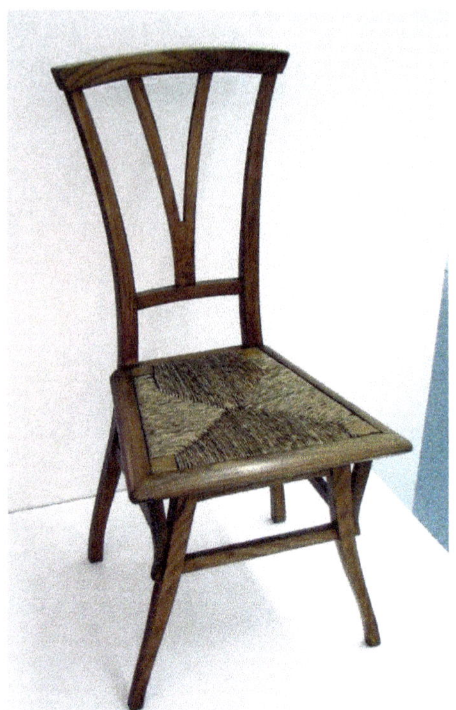

Henry van de Velde, *chair designed for Bloemenwerf*, Uccle, 1895-96

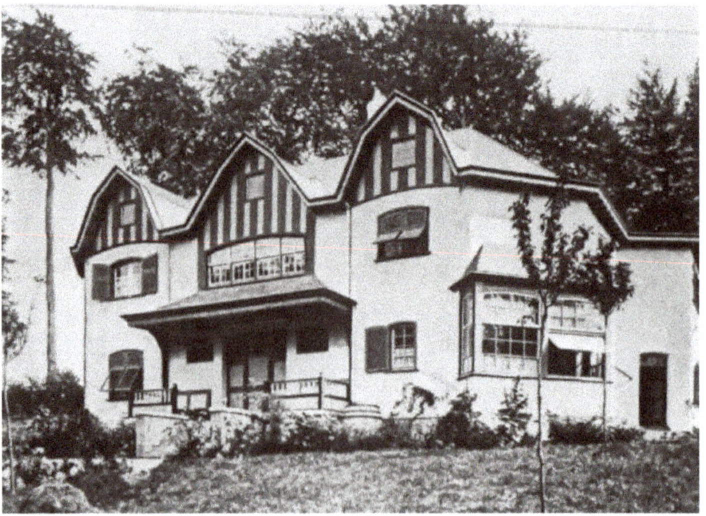

Henry van de Velde, *Bloemenwerf*, Uccle, exterior view, 1895-96

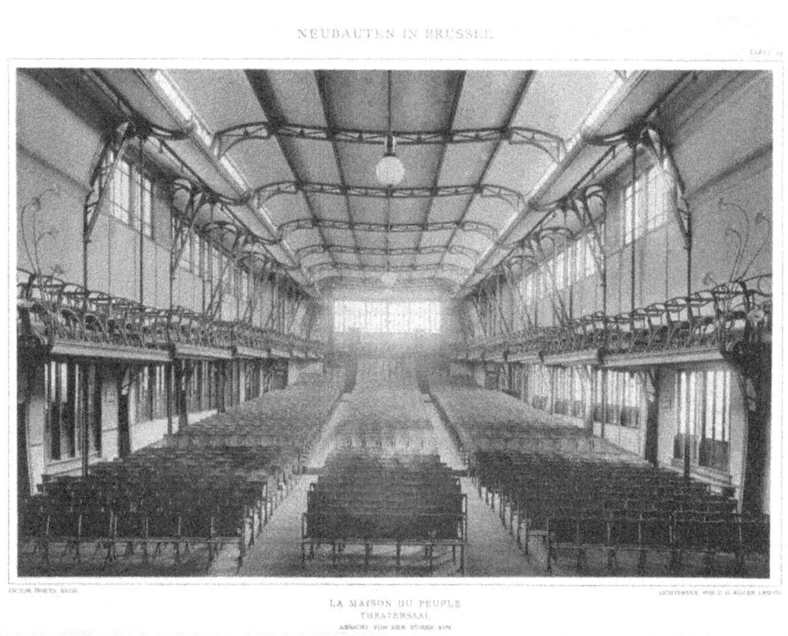

Victor Horta, *La Maison du Peuple*, theater hall, Brussels, 1896-09

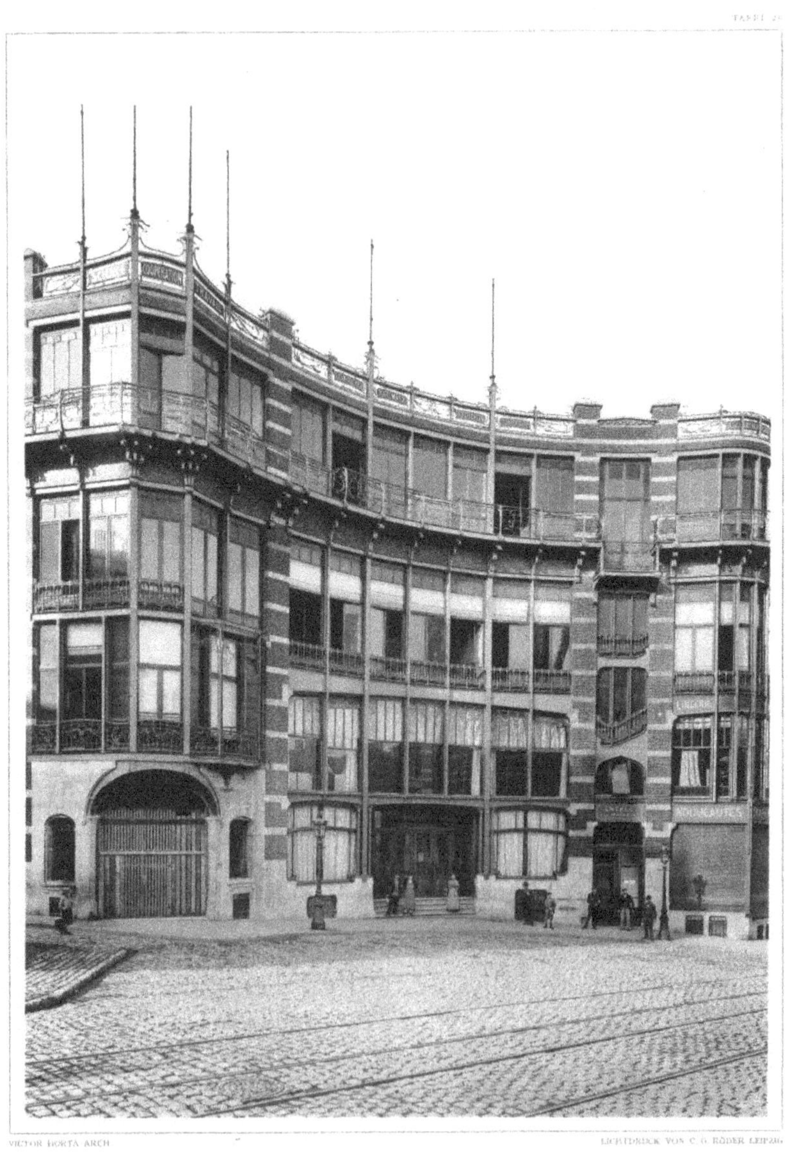

Victor Horta, *La Maison du Peuple*, exterior view, Brussels, 1896-09

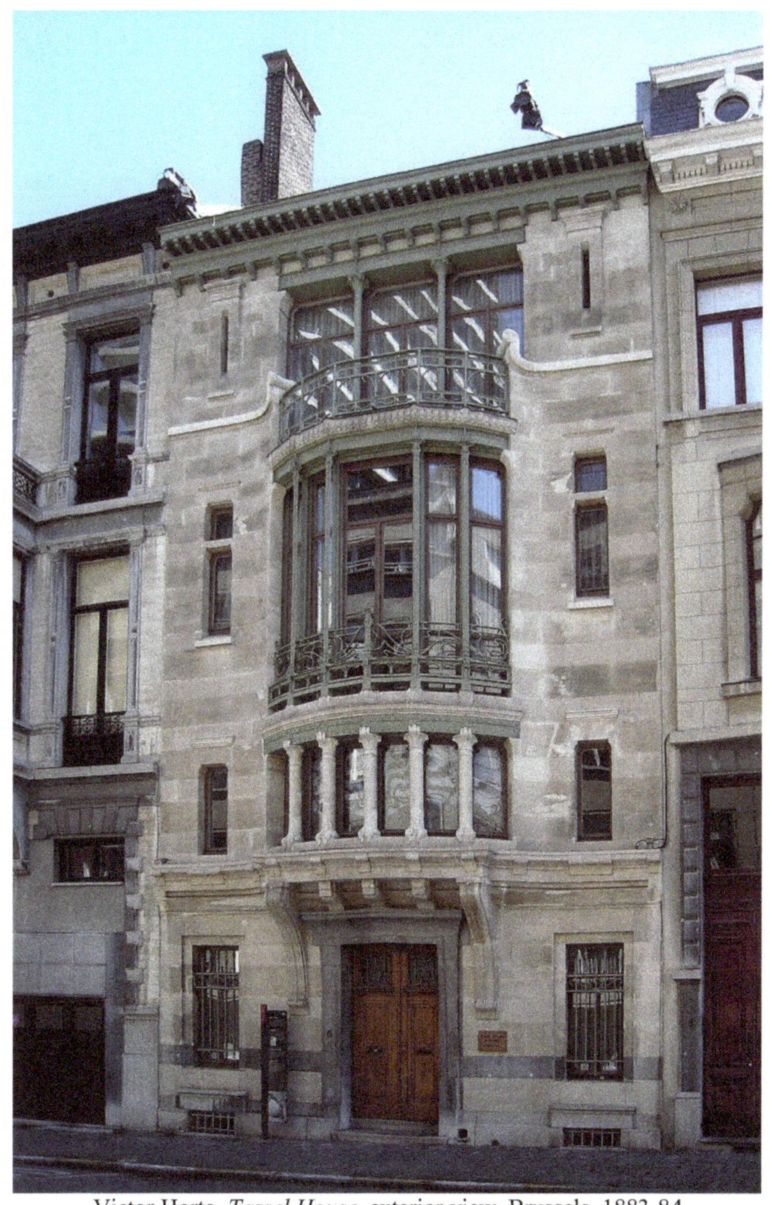

Victor Horta, *Tassel House*, exterior view, Brussels, 1883-84

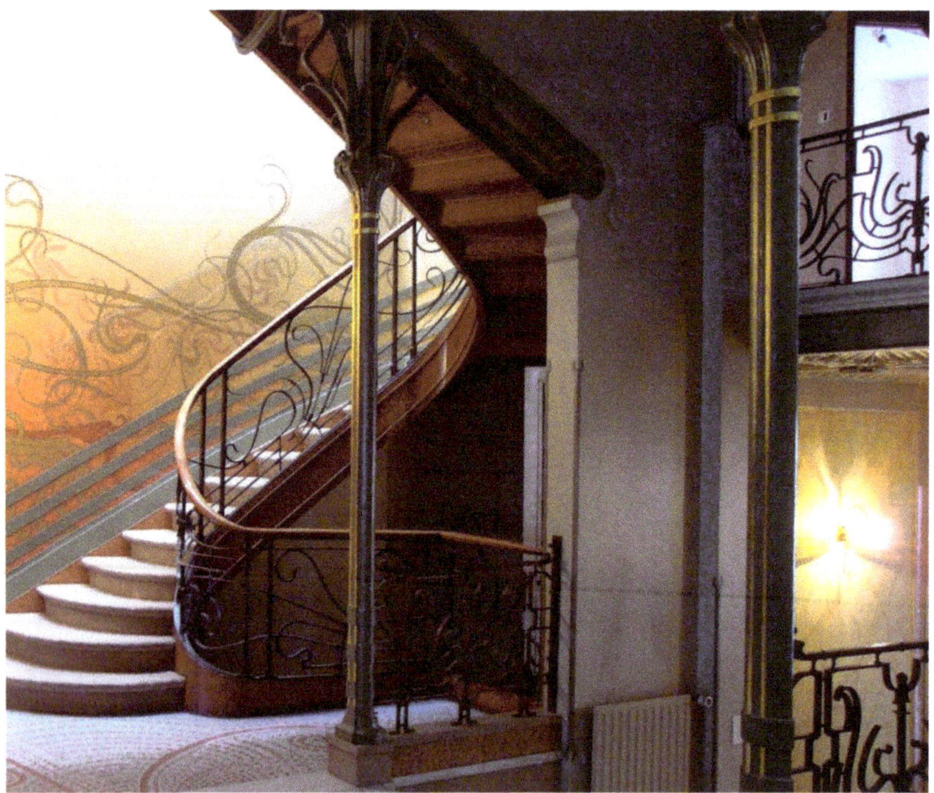

Victor Horta, *Tassel House*, staircase, Brussles, 1883-8

CHAPTER 4

Belgium and the Industrial Revolution

The emergence and consolidation of Belgium's avant garde art movement reflected the re-invention of its home city, Brussels, as a significant continental metropolis. In contrast not only with Belgium's major Flemish centers, but also with Paris, London, Vienna, and Munich, Brussels had, in fact, no history as a center of culture. Before 1830, the year Flanders and Wallonia joined forces to free themselves from Dutch control, Brussels had functioned solely as administrative center of the Low Countries. However, from the 1850s on, as the city witnessed an ever greater concentration of wealth in the private and public sectors, the trademarks of a true urban metropolis emerged: a thriving banking industry; flourishing publishing houses, dedicated to promoting fiction, poetry, and critical writing by Belgian *and* French authors; well-appointed art galleries; mansions custom designed for aristocrats and lawyers, physicians, and university professors with deep pockets. (Murphy and Strikwerda 24–25)

Brussels' newfound mid-19th Century centrality in cultural, as well as administrative, and financial terms, was an outgrowth of a more significant 19th Century phenomenon: Belgium's premier position in the vanguard of the Industrial Revolution. For Belgium, not, as is commonly believed, England or Germany, had been the European forerunner in the converging network of technological advances which culminated in the Revolution. Indeed, such a concerted effort in changing the means of production of material goods would have been difficult, if not impossible for the vast archipelago of German-speaking provinces until they were consolidated under Chancellor Otto Bismarck's leadership in 1871.

In the decades immediately following Belgian unification, when that small country was surging ahead industrially, the 16 German-speaking duchies were still divided by topography, religious affiliation, differences in dialect, and long-established protocols for social interchange. Moreover, as was true of small, culturally homogenous provinces elsewhere in Europe, the populations of the individual duchies retained a deep-seated attachment to local self-rule dating back to the feudal period. What ultimately overrode these differences, in what eventually became the German nation, was a overriding sense of *familial* loyalty, of membership in a larger German *volk,* intensified by the Prussian victory over France in 1871 and reinforced by the patriotic pronouncements of the Prussian Iron Chancellor and Kaiser Wilhelm I.

By the 1880s, when a unified Germany was steadily profitting from the advantages of centralized government, Belgium, the industrial forerunner, had moved backward into a period of recession. In the industrial heartland, populous cities like Liège buckled under labor unrest and strikes, which led to confrontations between workers and government forces, most destructively in the period 1873-1886. So, even as the German industrial juggernaut gained momentum, Belgian industrial hegemony declined precipitously on the continent, in large part a casualty of exploitative labor practices to which the engineers of rapid industrial growth had been indifferent Indeed, unrestrained *laissez-faire* capitalism was primarily responsible for Belgium's economic decline from the 1870s on. Importantly for the Belgian avant garde movement, Brussels itself, the nation's capital, suffered less from violent socioeconomic upheavals than other urban centers, at least until the mid-1880s.

This paradox can be explained in part by its sheer distance from the coal mines and metallurgy plants of Wallonia, and the farms, textile manufacturing centers, and glassworks of Flanders, areas where worker agitation, followed by often brutal government repression, was most pronounced. In this period, ca. 1870-1886, Brussels carried on its daily administrative and commercial business in relative peace, even as the city was in ascendence as a continental cultural mecca. It did so, that is, until 1886, the peak year in Belgium in terms of mass demonstrations, strikes, rioting, and often violent clashes between workers and the military.

Especially noteworthy, in the context of Brussels' rising cultural influence, is the absence of a ring of factories, operating full bore and spewing noxious fumes, surrounding its governmental and commercial inner precincts and its now-proliferating residential neighborhoods. This, in vivid contrast to the industrial necklace, or noose, encircling late 19th Century Glasgow, described in Chapter 2, albeit with a far less disruptive record of worker unrest in Glasgow than in Brussels of the 1880s and 1890s. Such class turmoil might very well have undercut Glasgow's status as Second City of Empire in that late 19th Century period.

Three symbiotic factors accounted for Belgium's vanguard position as Europe's leading major industrial power in the period 1830-1870. (Murphy and Strikwerda 19) The first was relative communal tranquillity, since the newly formed nation had, so far, no history of animosity, territorial aggression, or outright military conflict with other European countries. For that matter, communal calm was literally encoded into the Belgian constitution, which clearly stated a policy of political neutrality, so that government coffers would not be drained by war. Secondly, Belgium had the advantage of easily extracted natural resources, in the coal mines of the Borinage and the rich seams of iron ore in the Sambre-Meuse Valley, between Mons and Liège, where processing of the extracted ore was carried out on site.

A third critical element in Belgium's industrial primacy was the availability of human labor, a wide pool of men and women, particularly in Wallonia, needy of steady employment and not yet awakened to the possibility of mobilizing for higher wages and better working conditions. Together, "these factors prompted financiers to invest in Belgian industry decades before similar steps were taken in Germany." (Murphy and Strikwerda 19)

Easy to take for granted, but just as crucial to Belgium's economic leadership, was its small land mass and central location on the European continent. The Belgian population, comprising Flemings and Wallons, occupied a mere 11,000 square miles. Like its Low Country neighbor, Holland, the nation was easily traversed, with access to Great Britain across the Channel to the west, the Scandinavian countries to the north, Germany, Austria, and the Slavic countries to the East, and the Mediterranean countries to the south. This central location, in fact, goes considerable distance in explaining Flander's pivotal position in Medieval commerce as far back as the 12th Century.

By the 1840s, and of signal importance, the still-nascent nation had developed an elaborate rail system, linking major manufacturing, trade, and cultural centers within Belgium, which in turn facilitated access to valuable markets beyond its borders. (Murphy and Strikwerda 20) The efficient network of train lines provided outlets for Belgium's agricultural and industrial goods, including the fine wool, embroidered cloth and exquisite lace produced in the long-established textile districts of Ghent, Bruges, and Ypres Lastly, and critical for the nurture of the Belgian avant garde, the trains provided Belgian artists with convenient, affordable access to foreign cities, where liberating stylistic steps forward were taken, in the ferment created by an international mix of artists, with the support of their equally visionary patrons. Of course, for the late 19th Century Belgian painter or sculptor, Paris exerted the greatest attraction.

The Flemish textile districts demand particular attention in any study of Henry van de Velde's career, since his initial decorative art entries in the *Les Vingt* salons of 1892 and 1893 took the form of embroidery, sketches for tapestries, and the completed mural-size tapestry mentioned earlier. Van de Velde's reputation in Art Nouveau design rests on the entirety of his protean output: tooled leather book covers, gold and silver jewelry inlaid with precious jewels, voluptuous mirror frames, silver servingware and candelabras, and an impressive range of furnishings, all distinguished by his sinuous "whiplash" line. However, in the late 1880s, van de Velde stepped gingerly into the applied arts, *via* flat, 2-D, pictorial design: illustration of poetic texts by his friend Max Elskamp, ground breaking, abstract covers for the Flemish Movement's catalogue, *Van Nu en Straks*, and stylized imagery appliquéd on a cloth backing, i.e., tapestries.

Van de Velde's affinity with textile design can easily be ascribed to his upbringing in Antwerp, and to his hometown's proximity to the ancient Flemish cloth manufacturing centers, Bruges and Ghent. Both textile meccas could trace their roots to the Roman invasions in the 1st Century B.C.E., to subsequent incursions by the Germanic Franks in the 4th and 5th Centuries A.D, and to raids by the Vikings, in the 9th Century. These successive waves of ethnic intrusion contributed to an unusually eclectic linguistic and cultural mix in both cities, a diverse demographic similar to that encountered by van de Velde in *Les Vingt.*

Indeed, what followed from the 10th Century on, was a turbulent history of control won, lost, and won again by external continental powers: French, Burgundian, Spanish, Austrian, and Dutch. This constant jockeying for dominance in the region was owed, again, to the invaluable centrality of Bruges and Ghent on European trade routes, and to the growth of wool manufacture and export in both cities throughout the Medieval period.

Founded at the convergence of the Scheldt and Lys rivers, Ghent had the advantage of terrain characterized by "meersen," or "water meadows," whose periodic flooding was ideally suited to herding sheep. This unusual topographic feature, conducive to the production of wool on native turf, ultimately led to Ghent's position as the most important 12th Century European city for wool manufacture and trade, surpassing even its neighbor, Bruges Indeed, Ghent's mercantile trade in woolen cloth was so vigorous in this period that supplies had to be supplemented with imports from Scotland and England. By the13th Century, the bustling Medieval town, with a vibrant international population, had become an industrial metropolis in the modern sense.

These centuries of prosperity for Ghent *and* Bruges, both port cities, were accompanied by social tension and conflict predictably precipitated by socioeconomic inequalities. In Ghent, four chief textile guilds, the weavers, fullers, shearers, and dyers, comprised the majority of the city's working population, one increasingly bent on a stronger, more influential voice in communal affairs. Frequent strikes and insurrections in the late 12th Century culminated in the now-legendary Battle of the Golden Spurs (1302), waged by a citizens' army of Ghent guild members, and their counterparts in Bruges, against their wealthy bourgeois overlords. The uprising, the ancestor of strikes by workers in Liège in the1880s, was followed by violent clashes with ducal overlords and their troops. The guild members, driven by principle and economic desperation in equal measure, were victorious, and their role in Ghent's communal affairs increased substantially thereafter, although not without ongoing upper class opposition.

The city of Bruges' 300 year "Golden Age," lasting in loose terms from the 12th to 15th Century, rested primarily on wool cloth manufacture and trade. Bruges' economic dominance was further enhanced by its position as the cradle of Flemish painting in the 14th and 15th Centuries. Indeed, the Northern Renaissance Flemish School of oil painting, developed and refined by Jan van Eyck, Gerard David, and Hans Memling, can claim Bruges as its birthplace. Smaller than Ghent in population and geographic spread, Bruges saw a reawakening and re-energizing of town life and trade in the 12th Century, after a storm re-established its connection to the sea by clearing a passage through canals silted up in earlier centuries: "a wool market, a woollens-weaving industry, and the market for cloth all profitted from the shelter of [rebuilt] city walls, where surpluses could be safely accumulated under the patronage of the counts of Flanders" (Wikipedia).

As was true for Ghent, wool merchants in Bruges were dependent on English and Scottish wool to bulk up their inventory, to the extent that "The city's entrepreneurs reached out to make economic colonies of England and Scotland's wool-producing districts. (Wikipedia) A leader in the wool trade and in the higher reaches of the fine arts, Bruges was also in the vanguard in the realm of sophisticated finance. Bruges was the site of a bourse that opened in 1309, perhaps the first stock exchange in the world and an epicenter of financial transactions involving competing national interests and a somewhat confusing *mélange* of currencies.

The novelty and efficiency of a monetary clearing house was undoubtedly responsible for the flood of capital pouring into the city in the 14th Century. Moreover, in terms of goods alone, Bruges' English contacts brought its citizens grain from Normandy and wine from Gascony, while in 1277 the appearance of a merchant ship from Genoa in her port rendered Bruges the primary Flemish trade link with the Mediterranean region.

The application of this intricate, multi-faceted regional history to Henry van de Velde's growth as an artist, designer, architect, political activist, and educational reformer should be obvious. An intelligent, cultured native of Antwerp, always acutely sensitive to his environment, Henry van de Velde could not have ignored or dismissed the mercantile and cultural riches that formed his Flemish heritage. Bit by bit, that heritage infiltrated his painting, his initially hesitant, then more assured steps into the applied arts, his efforts in social reform, and his eventual program for improving applied arts education. While he left Antwerp and Flanders for good in his early 20s, the region's complex socioeconomic past, its cultural wealth, its tradition of independence at all levels, remained with him into his old age. One of the most visible areas of impact was that of tapestry design.

Design and fabrication of tapestry, contrived on a grand scale and devoted to depiction of historical and religious narrative, had been the pride of the Flanders for centuries. The tradition had its origins in the textile workshops of the northern Flemish cities, where, as was typical in the cloth trade, a majority of female artisans carried out exacting hand processes developed and refined since the Medieval period: carding wool, spinning and weaving thread, hand-stitching embroidery. Perhaps it goes without saying, that, in this collaborative enterprise, male designers most commonly conceived, draughted as "cartoons," and supervised the hand manufacture of detailed narrative images, assuming full control of composition, as well as delineation of figurative, natural, and architectural elements.

The tapestries adorned the walls of homes of aristocrats and the *haute bourgeoisie*; for that matter, their narrative specifics would only carry meaning for an elite, educated viewer. Familiar to van de Velde as well was the gradual, but inexorable infiltration of mechanized fabrication into the production of textiles, in what had long been small-scale, family-owned Flemish workshops. In 1800, a Flemish weaver, Lieven Bauwens, smuggled plans for a mechanized loom out of England, thereby introducing into his region the first mechanical weaving machine on the continent. The-long range impact of mechanization on Flemish textile fabrication is emblematic of the combined effects, salubrious and destructive, of mechanization on the applied arts as a whole. As one might expect, the virtual Gordian knot of contradictions inherent in mechanized production would preoccupy van de Velde throughout his long career.

The invention of the mechanized loom in England, and its eventual mobilization throughout the continent, did indeed accelerate the pace of textile production to an astounding degree. Fabric choices and purchases hitherto reserved for the elite, moneyed few, landed aristocrats, well-placed politicians, wealthy merchants, lawyers, physicians and university professors, were now options for mid-level craftsmen and tradesmen, even hard-working shop girls. Nonetheless, the recourse to mechanized textile manufacture, not yet reined in by concern for quality, led to the predictable inverse ratio: expanded production and lower price for the consumer, *both* sadly offset by a precipitous decline in durability and design sophistication. Needless to say, the one-of-a-kind bolt of fabric, tailored to the client's taste in color, pattern, even thread type, was out of the question.

Taking into account the downside of mass production of textiles, it is not so surprising that a steady domestic and foreign market for handcrafted Belgian textiles woven, sewn, tatted, and embroidered continued to sustain the traditional Flemish workshops, still owned and managed mainly by men, but "manned" by women, throughout the 19th Century. This healthy *niche* market for handmade goods, with Flemish towns as its locus, was, like its counterpart in industrial manufacture, both a blessing and a curse. While appreciation for meticulous handcraftsmanship remained high, the reliable, but greedy market also perpetuated the long hours, miserable working conditions, and bare subsistence pay defining the lives of lower class women in the textile trade, absent the controls eventually exerted by the organized labor groups that fought for and won reform. Industrial cloth manufacture proceeded apace; so, in tandem, did the hand fabrication of textiles in all their manifestations. But the living conditions of the textile workers remained abysmal.

Traditional Belgian male painters of genre scenes, trained in the "old school" academic tradition, often disguised the conditions in which female textile workers toiled, through persuasive illusionistic technique, a technique that skillfully omitted the more unsavory aspects of the situation portrayed. Women sewing, knitting, or embroidering were most commonly depicted through a window, from the outside looking in, peacefully at work in what appear to be comfortable domestic surroundings. As Sura Levine notes, these depictions "fail to do justice to the [often cramped, squalid] domestic space itself," and make no distinction between female piece workers earning a pittance and bourgeois housewives passing the time in an upper middle class diversion. (Levine 66-67) The stored-up frustration in female textile workers, the potential for voiced outrage whose outlet would be the demonstrations of 1886, are hidden from the viewer's eye in serene genre scenes that whitewash a cruel economic reality.

Several additional factors, all of the negative variety, must be noted in the discussion of Belgian economic dominance on the continent during the first half of the 19th Century, since these were the very factors that undermined that dominance in the second half. For one, during the period of greatest industrial growth, from1830 to the 1860s, the Flemish agricultural sector in the north remained the most densely populated in Europe, with little open space between or beyond the boundaries of family-owned farms. (The corporate agricultural enterprise, needless to say, lay far in the future.)

On the practical level, these crowded conditions inevitably intensified competition for what seem now miniscule plots of tillable land On the psychological level, the Belgian rural worker, witnessing the slow disappearance of the untenanted countryside, suffered as much from lack of privacy and peace of mind as did his counterpart, the industrial worker in Wallonia's crowded towns and cities. This very phenomenon would drive the novice landscape artist Henry van de Velde to Belgium's northern border, the shores of the North Sea, in the late 1880s. The sense of freedom and productive solitude experienced by Charles Rennie Mackintosh during his sketching tours of the countryside surrounding Glasgow were unavailable to his Belgian contemporary in the rural areas just beyond Antwerp.

Compounding the Belgian laborer's plight were two further ugly realities: (1) Belgian workers typically toiled for 11 hours a day, either on the farm or in the factory, as compared with a shorter, but still-daunting 9-10 hour day for workers in England or France; (2) Growing restiveness among Belgian laborers was fueled by appallingly exploitative wages, among the lowest in northwestern Europe, even in the booming metallurgy industry. (Murphy and Strikwerda 21)

Thus, while commercial opportunities for Belgium as a whole proliferated in these decades of vigorous international trade in raw materials and manufactured goods, quality of life deteriorated massively for the individual Belgian worker who had been indispensable in making it happen. Given this cumulus of dismal data, it is not surprising that empathetic Low Country artists, like Vincent van Gogh in the Borinage and Constantin Meunier in Liège, chose as their subjects miners, field hands, factory workers, and hand craftsmen, all grievously overworked and underpaid.

Tellingly, the salaries of the laborers, not to mention their status in *haute bourgeoise* or aristocratic society, more or less equaled that of the greater number of renegade avant garde artists, some of whom viewed the depiction of the "underclass" as a calling. Vincent van Gogh, is the inevitable case in point. Avid students of van Gogh's brief, but feverishly productive career know well the wrenching two- year period, 1878-1880, when the Dutchman lived among the miners and their families in the Borinage, unsuccessfully attempting a vocation as a lay preacher. Less well known are the statistical facts of the Borinage, the hard core, numerical realities that predate van Gogh's brief, stay by decades. The economy of the 30 municipalities in the Borinage was founded entirely on coal mining, from the late 18th Century to 1850. Between 1822 and 1829, coal production in that region doubled dramatically, from 602, 000 to 1,260,000 tones This statistic represented more than the combined production of French and German coal mining provinces in the same period. The Wallonian Borinage, with the city of Mons as its center, exported coal not only to France and elsewhere in Europe, but north to Flanders, before the two Belgian regions were united.

So, in fact, the Borinage had been a source of significant income not only for the Wallonian, but for the whole of the Belgian economy, through the early and mid-19th Century. Belgian coal mining continued as a lucrative source of income, at both the personal and governmental levels, well into the 1880s. Nevertheless, the poverty, rampant illness, and mood of fatalistic hopelessness van Gogh saw in the miners themselves gave irrefutable proof that the wealth had remained in mine owners' coffers. Van Gogh's despair at his failure to salve the miners' miserable lot through faith was ultimately transformed into full dedication to art-making. The redirection was slowly achieved through an emotional alchemy painstakingly documented in his letters.

From preaching, he turned to drawing using charcoal and conté to produce sheaves of powerful, uncompromising renderings of miners, as well as hand weavers, immersed in the grinding activities of their daily lives. The swift, decisive strokes that energized the drawings were eventually transferred to van Gogh's vibrant oils. In turn, following Henry van de Velde's exposure to van Gogh's work in the *Les Vingt* salons of 1890 and 1891, the decisive strokes were transferred to the drawings and paintings of Henry van de Velde.

One can argue that van de Velde was moved not only technically, by van Gogh's assertive stroke, but also by Vincent's subjects themselves, and the unflinching, but empathetic way in which he depicted them. Bodied forth in van Gogh's sketches, as in his intensely wrought oils, were the economically subjugated, disenfranchised members of the rural and urban working class who had peopled the canvasses of the French realists Courbet, Millet, and Daumier 30 years earlier. Van de Velde's response to the Dutchman's passionate humanity, fused with the impact of William Morris's more cerebral idealism, surely triggered the crisis of conscience that drove him to reject easel art altogether in 1892, and reroute his energies first to the decorative, then to the functional arts. Given the similarities between the two Low Country artists, relentless drive uncomfortably mated with profound insecurities, it makes sense to speculate on the sources of the psychological crises they endured, and the solutions they found to the upheavals.

While van Gogh churned his felt inadequacies as spiritual mentor into a visual record of the situation he was powerless to improve, van de Velde, whose upbringing had been as securely middle class as van Gogh's, sought a more pragmatic channel for his social concerns: well designed, affordable utilitarian goods. Both men were goaded by two, often conflicting forces: the first drew them outward, beyond the self, into the sphere of social betterment, hopefully with the added benefit of spiritual uplift; the second pulled them inward, into the very personal realm of creative satisfaction. In the end, van Gogh and van de Velde embraced the separate creative enterprises that best suited their gifts and temperaments. For van Gogh, who had been professionally weaned in Holland's fine art trade, the siren call of art-making could finally be answered in the Borinage, through drawings whose potency also made manifest his sympathy for the very subjects who had turned deaf ears to his preaching. For van de Velde, the shift into the applied arts rendered moot his ambivalence toward easel painting and harmonized what had seemed for so long a competing set of compulsions: the desire to create beautiful objects and the need to live a socially responsible life.

As Belgian industrial output positioned the young nation at the very epicenter of European trade, Brussels—its administrative core and commercial clearing house—sought to recreate itself as an important European cultural metropolis. In population alone, Brussels had grown from 140,000 in 1830, to 600,000 in the 1870s, taking into account the entire metropolitan area. (Murphy and Strikwerda 20) This astounding population growth resulted not from an increase in births, complemented by a decrease in deaths, but from immigration into the city of job-seeking blue collar workers, skilled craftsmen, commercial middlemen, and ambitious professionals, their hopes nourished by Brussels' word-of-mouth reputation for employment opportunity and a non-restrictive open door to newcomers.

As for living space, the progressive demolition of Brussels' 14th Century surrounding walls, begun in 1818 and completed in 1871, cleared the way for the city's geographic spread. Gradually, in the 1870s, new housing appeared to the east and southeast of the city, in areas adjacent to the administrative and financial districts of the old center. (Murphy and Strikwerda 20) The physical transformation of Brussels was spearheaded by King Leopold II, whose seemingly interminable parliamentary rule began in 1865 and ended in 1909. Hoping to raise the cultural status of Brussels to that of other European capitals through a process we would now term "urban renewal," Leopold chose as model Le Baron Haussmann's legendary radial restructuring of Parisian streets and boulevards, accomplished in the 1850s, for the updating of the Belgian city's center.

In addition, Leopold's planners and engineers transformed the hundreds of acres of agricultural land, woods, and fields surrounding Brussels' established center into blocks of houses on plots of land defined by newly paved roads. As the transformation was carried out, what had once been independent villages were gradually merged and bureaucratically absorbed into Brussels proper. (Culot: 79)

To this end, modest homes lining narrow, winding streets, those housing the families of shop owners, craftsmen, and skilled laborers responsible for maintaining Brussels' infrastructure, were for the most part cleared of their tenants and razed. Indeed, as the Haussmannization of Brussels progressed, three of the grandest boulevards were driven through several of the city's most established and picturesque districts. (Culot: 80) The boulevards at the city's center, in turn, were lined with massive stone structures and impressive monuments and parks, such as the *Palais de Justice*, the Sacred Heart Basilica, and the *Parc du Cinquantenaire.* (Murphy and Strikwerda 20) Impressive indeed, but for the greater number of Brussels' long term citizens, and even less so for newcomers settled on Brussels' outskirts, of little practical use in meeting the needs of daily life.

Nevertheless, mention should be made of two practical advantages for Brussels' populace in the construction of the broad boulevards: they allowed for the mobilization of initially horse-drawn, and later, in 1892, electrically-powered tramways; at the end of the century, they facilitated movement for the growing number of Brussels' privately-owned vehicles. (Culot: 74) Ironically, these would be the very vehicles that would hasten the departure of deep-pocketed homeowners from Brussels proper to its leafier suburbs, an "urban exodus" that would ultimately strip Art Nouveau architects like Victor Horta of their most avid clients. (Culot: 95)

Leopold and his advisors compounded the problems created by their misguided, ruthless demolition of traditional "inner city" neighborhoods with their unwillingness to acknowledge the distinctly Belgian tastes of the nation's homeowners. Unlike middle class Parisians, the Belgians favored adjoining houses, occupying small, narrow plots. (Culot: 79) So, starting in 1870, Leopold, in a spirit of extravagant hubris, commissioned the construction of imposing, Parisian-style family homes the size of apartment blocks, ignoring the principle of "little house" that had always held sway in Belgium. (Culot: 80)

One by palatial one, the imposing structures, their interiors sectioned into spacious, high-ceilinged chambers geared for wealthy tenants, made their appearance along Brussels' new, very broad avenues. Financed by English investors hoping for an immediate, healthy return, the Belgian construction companies responsible for their erection quickly went into bankruptcy when the buildings were soon abandoned by dissatisfied Belgian tenants, or occupied by crowds of impoverished foreigners.

(Culot: 79) The immense structures, already doomed to disuse in the period in which they were constructed, were destined to be broken up into apartments served by elevators, in the 20th Century. (Culot: 80)

The Belgian taste for the "little house" was by no means restricted to those of modest means, *la petite bourgeoisie.* Even Victor Horta's Art Nouveau townhouses, their elegant interiors custom-designed for the likes of the Tassels and the van Eetveldes, measured not more than 20 feet across and rose no more than three stories above street level. The typically narrow, elongated parcels of land available to Brussels' middle class challenged ingenuity. Indeed, the individualistic nature of the non-conforming Belgian householder accounted for his attraction to a style that allowed for daring and fantasy. Uniformity, even the lavish variety envisioned by Leopold, would have been impossible in Brussels, given the ingrained custom of private initiative that had governed home planning and construction in the villages that had been incorporated into Brussels proper after 1870, and swallowed up by the expanding city. (Culot: 94)

While Leopold targetted the staid *grande bourgeoisie* as future tenants for his grandiose "homes," Horta, the leading Art Nouveau architect of the 1890s and a *P.O.B.* supporter, depended primarily on close personal friendships with a more forward-looking clientèle to endorse and fund his design vision: university faculty, engineers, lawyers, a select group of successful, affluent artists. In many cases, the very nature of their professional activities rendered these men more receptive to design innovation, so that building itself "became a medium for the expression of ideology." (Culot: 92) Their stated allegiance to progressive ideas, they felt, would be visibly reinforced by their patronage of an "unashamedly modern young architect to design their homes." (Escritt: 77)

As Stephen Escritt points out, Art Nouveau "was the ideal aesthetic for dashing young bourgeois radicals who wished to pronounce their independence from the kind of historicist grandeur that characterized Belgian architecture at the time, without having to sacrifice style, artistry, and luxury."(Escritt: 77) Implicit, however, in Escritt's explanation is Horta's rejection of the Arts and Crafts ethos so embedded in Henry van de Velde's theory and practice, in which luxury, an entitlement historically reserved for a wealthy elite, played little part.

The Art Nouveau architect responded to two additional changes in the form and function of a private home for a clientèle that was well educated and comfortably well off, liberal in outlook, and culturally sophisticated. From 1880 to 1893, the venue for social affairs for this stratum of clientèle "found a new environment, moving from public areas to private space" (Culot: 96). Musical evenings, small scale theatrical performances, literary readings, and scientific lectures were now more commonly intimate occasions, held by social peers in their own homes, by invitation only. In addition, as Culot astutely observes, after "the bloody riots of 1886, the demonstrations for universal suffrage that followed, and the general strikes, it occurred to the wealthy that they should flaunt their riches less openly. (Culot: 98)

As a result, while Art Nouveau interior furnishings were subtly luxurious, exterior facades were left intentionally plain, giving no hint of the imported marble, polished exotic wood, fine fabrics, intricate mosaic floors and stained glass chosen by

Horta for the gracious entryways, grand spiral staircases, and elegant drawing rooms behind the closed doors of his clients' private homes. (Culot: 98)

The overhaul of Brussels' built environment, successful in some respects, woefully misguided in others, was carried out in tandem with Belgium's landmark achievements in public transportation, already noted in this chapter. By 1835, the nation had initiated the first railroad passenger service in Europe, with a train connection between Brussels and Mechelen. By 1870, Brussels had two railway stations, at the northern and and southern limits of the city, reflecting the development of an intricate intra-urban train system linking major hubs throughout Belgium. By the 1890s, public transportation had, indeed, been further improved by the introduction of the electrified tram, a more flexible mode of transport in what was by then a densely populated urban setting. (Murphy and Strikwerda 20)

In fact, Belgium's acknowledged superiority in railway engineering led to the selection of the nation's train car manufacturers for the underground system planned to accommodate visitors to Paris for the *Exposition Internationale* in 1900. While French cultural pundits marvelled at Hector Guimard's organically-inspired, wrought iron Art Nouveau structures marking *Métro* entrances at street level, income for the train cars themselves flowed back to Belgium. (Murphy and Strikwerda 25) The period 1874-1899 witnessed a four-fold increase in train and tram travellers in Belgium, many of them lower class workers spending long hours daily in rides from their homes in Brussels' poorer neighborhoods to factory jobs in outlying areas. As a result, in public transportation, as in so many aspects of the 19th Century Belgian industrial boom, the existential fallout for the lower class citizen was a classic "mixed bag": the trains and trams worked to his advantage in providing for a wider, if still underpaid range of job possibilities, but the slow commutes lengthened further an already exhausting work day.

In sum, the prime years of *Les Vingt*, the 1880s, coincided with an explosive social and political situation for all of Belgium, with Brussels as its administrative and cultural center. Starting in the mid-1870s and accelerating in the 1880s, the industrial behemoth generated and nourished by a powerful entrepreneurial class faced serious competition for its products, through expanding industrialization in France and, more importantly, in Germany. (Murphy and Strikwerda 21) Indeed, after 1871, a united Germany had rapidly become the industrial juggernaut to be reckoned with on the continent. Bismarck, a wily tactician as well as charismatic leader, had outmanoeuvered the forces of economic recession, eroding prospects for continental competitors like Belgium by banning foreign imports. At the same time, quite logically, he lobbied in the German Parliament for locating more global markets for German exports.

To further worsen Belgium's plight, its agricultural workers were increasingly undermined by American and Argentinian wheat farmers, whose enormous yields and inexpensive grain sales cut into established Belgian international markets. (Murphy and Strikwerda 21) And elsewhere in the political arena, an ongoing, highly contentious issue in 19th Century Belgian affairs demanded resolution, were the country ever to regain social or economic equilibrium: the franchise.

Puzzling, if not shocking for the modern observer is the percentage of Belgium's male population permitted to vote in the 1830s: 10% or 137,772 male adults, out of a total population of some 6.5 million. (Escritt: 66) More shocking still, this situation was perpetuated by the Belgian Parliament into the 1880s, a period in which both France and Germany had long since adopted universal male suffrage. While left wing Liberals, now renamed Progressives or Radicals, pushed for widening the franchise and bringing lower class workers into the political system, the conservative rear guard stood its ground, resisting both changes in voting rights and the argument for the secularization of education, a pragmatic move of long range value to the nation as a whole. (Murphy and Strikwerda 21)

Strengthening the reactionary grip on Parliament was the winning of majority rule by the Catholic Party in 1884. Fortunately for Belgium's future, however, was a second political phenomenon: while top-down control remained in conservative hands, the "closed political system and the hard times of the 1880s encouraged the spread of socialist ideas," (Murphy and Strikwerda 21) This expanding base of support for socialist principles was no doubt intensely gratifying to the split-off group of left-leaning Liberals who, with the lucidity of hindsight, perceived their own party's unqualified, unexamined encouragement of industrial expansion in Belgium in the 1830-1850 period as willfully blind to its potential social costs.

It bears repeating that the guiding forces in the creation of *Les Vingt*, the lawyers Octave Maus and Edmond Picard, consciously "fashioned the connection between *Les XX* and contemporary history." (Murphy and Strikwerda 22) What they emphasized in *L'Art moderne* polemic was the necessary connection between political and artistic upheaval, and the need for a concerted move- ment for progressive change, including the change in voting rights. Their objective was to persuade the invited artists themselves that they were "part of a vast social and cultural shift." (Murphy and Strikwerda 22)

Their leaders' avowed commitment to political reform generated a spirit of shared mission among *Les Vingt* member artists, a mood of righteous altruism that was certainly intoxicating. The artists' willingness to rally round a revolutionary political, as well as artistic flag spoke to the artists' need for solidarity in a cultural setting that had previously validated only the tried, the true, and the inoffensive in the arts, *via* the official Salon. Given the disparities in income and, more relevant to the issue of the vote, property ownership among *Les Vingt* members, one can safely assume that universal suffrage concerned as great a number of *Les Vingt* artists as it did the Belgian population as a whole. In Belgium as elsewhere, substantial property ownership guaranteed the citizen the vote. Universal male suffrage was finally granted by Belgium's government in 1893, six years after working class riots had reached critical mass in1886 and the very year in which *Les Vingt* disbanded, this latter no mere coincidence.

The riots of 1886, at their most violent in the Charleroi region, albeit as yet diffuse in their objectives, had been brutally suppressed by the army. The unprecedented brutality of the suppression, the "rank injustice of this action," compelled some Brussels intellectuals to abandon both their social milieu and the centrist Liberal Party, and join the Belgian Workers' Party, fully consolidated by

1885. Among this group were three articulate lawyers, Jules Destrée, Emile Vandervelde, and Max Hallet, whose move into *P.O.B.* ranks vastly improved the Party's chances of achieving its goals, and whose influence led to the selection of Victor Horta for the design of party headquarters, *La Maison du Peuple.*

The initially inchoate riots assumed greater focus in 1887, when 13,000 miners paraded through Brussels demanding universal suffrage. This impressive *manifestation* was exceeded in scope in 1890, when waves of demonstrators, 80,000 strong, surged through Belgium's capital, pressing for a right to representation that had long since been won by citizens of other continental nations. A final, decisive strike in 1893 forced Parliament to agree to the "principle" of universal suffrage. (Culot: 86) But wait. There were still two qualifications to this otherwise giant step forward in voting rights. One will be obvious to the observant 21st Century reader: *still* no women of any rank in Belgian society could cast a vote; Belgian women wouldn't have that option until 1948, a fact that defies credulity.

As to the second, an American, European or Brit of our time would doubtless look askance at a strange *caveat* in the suffrage guidelines: the granting of *extra* votes to the upper middle class, enacted into law by a united front of centrist Liberals and conservative Catholics. (Murphy and Strikwerda 23) In effect, the rich could stuff the ballot box. These drawbacks notwithstanding, however, the gift of the vote for the previously disenfranchised offered every Belgian man a voice in government: he would have a say in the election of his representatives, and by extension, in the legislation that would operate on his behalf.

By the mid-1890s, the political situation in Belgium "had been reduced to an electoral battle between heavily organized mass parties." (Murphy and Strikwerda 22) Ironically, the dominant Catholic Party, historically and logically a conservative stronghold, was overwhelmingly supported by the majority of Belgian workers, while the Socialists, who had gradually absorbed many Radicals and Anarchists into their ranks, only won votes in heavily industrialized Wallonia. (Murphy and Strikwerda 22) One might argue that the emotional respite that Roman Catholicism offered its adherents, through its moving liturgy, its consoling promise of heaven for the faithful, its impressive cathedrals, its priests in their gorgeous vestments, its wrenching images of Christ on the Cross, proved more seductive for the tired laborer than didactic Socialist theorizing.

However, unswerving religious faith, consolation in an afterlife, and gorgeous trappings alone hardly explain the Catholic Party's continued political dominance in Belgium until 1914. In real terms, it was the Catholic Party, not the Liberals or the Socialists, that held the governmental reins when Parliament had finally conceded universal suffrage, universal suffrage for Belgian men, that is, in 1893. In the 19th Century working class mindset, that concession alone might have been enough to keep the Catholic Party in power. Moreover, in the larger scheme, while the Liberals, traditionally the party of the urban middle class, had lost popular support during Belgium's transition to a "politics of the masses" in the 1880s, a pragmatic group of Catholic Party leaders had gradually formed a social middle ground. (Schaepdrijver: 63)

Having in the past "aimed its policies at preserving rural life," (Schaepdrijuer 63) by the 1890s, the Catholic Party had a complete hold on provincial life, including involvement in labor exchange, education, health insurance, and pension plans. The emphasis on improving mass education was of particular consequence for Belgium, given the low literacy level in its agricultural and industrial areas: 101 of 1000 Belgian military recruits were illiterate, as opposed to 5 Germans, 47 Frenchmen, and 23 Dutchmen. (Advantage to Belgium notwithstanding, be it noted that the drive toward literacy was accomplished through, and therefore limited by, the faith-based Catholic parochial school system.)

Further, the Catholic Party worked aggressively and effectively with an eclectic range of established provincial and urban organizations: craft guilds, student and women's associations, the Farmer's Union, insurance companies and mortgage banks, convents. (Schaepdrijver: 63) As social issues increasingly absorbed their attention, Catholic Party members to their credit, steadily forged bonds with progressive reformers whose own growing commitment to the Catholic Party was fortified, in turn, by the latter's zeal for societal reform. Ultimately, in the 20th Century, the widening scope of the Catholic Party's hands-on involvement in Belgium's economic affairs, those affecting the well-being of the country's least affluent citizens, led to the development of the Christian Democratic Movement.

In response, Socialist Party leaders, seeing the need for consolidation, tightened their organizational structure and threw themselves into the essential hard work of winning elections and more seats in Parliament, and pushing through more concrete social and economic reforms. (Murphy and Strikwerda 22) Indeed, in the late 19th Century, the Belgian Socialist Party was viewed as the best organized in Europe. (Schaepdrijver: 65) although the shift in the direction of greater pragmatism also served to marginalize the more visionary aspects of the movement, those aspects most pervasively represented in the Symbolist paintings, sculpture, and poetry of *Les Vingt* artists and writers. (Murphy and Strikwerda 22)

The stirrings of a Flemish movement in Belgium could be felt as early as the 1830s, in the nation's first years as an independent political entity whose borders encircled two historically distinct linguistic and cultural regions. The movement was spearheaded by bourgeois intellectuals mainly from Antwerp and Ghent, most of whom were bilingual and spoke fluent French. (French was, in fact, Henry van de Velde's first language.) Resenting their long-term exclusion from the higher reaches of Belgian military, governmental, educational, and professional life, the Flemings pressed for greater linguistic rights and championed the promotion of symbols of Flemish culture. By the mid-1880s, the movement was calling for equal use of French and Dutch in public schools in Brussels bi-lingual education, in fact as well as the use of Dutch in public administration, court proceedings, and the military, when Flemish soldiers and officers were involved.

By the final decade of the 19th Century, the movement had, in fact, attained modest legislative gains. (Murphy and Strikwerda 22) However, partisans of Flemish parity with the dominant Wallon culture were still struggling when *Les Vingt* came into being in 1883. For that matter, the avant garde movement itself, despite the large number of Flemish artist members, mirrored the general Belgian socio-linguistic and cultural hierarchy, in that its leaders, Maus and Picard, who determined the editorial direction of *L'Art moderne*, were French speakers and francophone in their administrative policies.

As the leaders of the two communities, Fleming and Wallon, marshalled their arguments for or against equal linguistic rights in Belgian society, Brussels became the site of impassioned debates focussed on the place of Dutch in Belgian public life. Ironically, despite growing dissension stemming from conflicting regional interests *and* regional pride, there is solid evidence of a still greater push in the Brussels community for the promotion of Belgian nationalism by *all* the citizens within the country's borders. "Many in the capital identified strongly with Belgium as a political/territorial unit and were concerned to strengthen a sense of national unity," (Murphy and Strikwerda 23) understandable given Belgium's growing economic vulnerability, as it saw itself outdistanced by other rapidly industrializing continental powers.

Initially, the artists of *Les Vingt*, whatever their regional or national origins, professed little involvement in linguistic or nationalistic causes. The greater number aligned themselves with the growing Socialist movement in Brussels, which was by definition internationalist. As an inherently progressive group, the artists could only sympathize with the Socialist agenda and with *P.O.B.* leaders, who argued not only for increased salaries and shorter hours for all Belgian agricultural and industrial workers, but for mandatory public education, subsidized housing for low income families, and the restriction of labor for women and children. (The Socialist party platform, in this early phase of its existence, was farsighted enough to propose that a 4-week maternity leave be legislated for working class mothers who had just given birth.)

These were all concerns reflecting an emphasis on *class*, not national identity. (Levine: 56) Moreover, in line with this internationalist stance, it should be noted that the mass demonstrations of March 26, 1886 paid homage to a landmark *French*, not Belgian revolutionary moment: the 15-year anniversary of the bloody Paris Commune of 1871. Furthermore, attempts to develop low income housing for Belgian factory workers would have necessarily derived their impetus from the *English* Garden City movement gaining momentum across the English Channel.

Nevertheless, ever more self-aware, Flemish activists within *Les Vingt*, including Henry van de Velde, promoted their regional identity through their work, and eventually through a journal. A symbol of opposition, *Van Nu en Straks* was founded in 1892 by a group of Flemish literary figures, impassioned in their quest for regional recognition. As did *L'Art moderne* for francophone members, *Van Nu en Straks* functioned as the Flemish critical voice, providing a forum for the discussion of specifically Flemish artistic and literary work Van de Velde himself was invited to collaborate with Lemmen and van Rysselberghe, the latter's French cultural leanings notwithstanding, in the design of the journal, which would accompany the 1892 *Les Vingt* exhibit. The Antwerp master took charge of layout. (Block 103) For this critical and heady obligation, van de Velde took his cue from his Arts and Crafts mentor, William Morris: he favored wide margins, headpieces, and tailpieces, legible text, and full page illustrations, so as to maximize readability, while minimizing ornamentation and avoiding visual fussiness. (Block: 105)

As to the illustrations, the more aggressive opponents of French hegemony in *Les Vingt*, chief among them Fernand Khnopff and James Ensor, entered specifically Flemish landscapes, buildings, and traditions, in drawings and etchings that glorified Flander's past and its unique character. Khnopff's depictions of the medieval cityscape of Bruges and Ensor's etching of the town hall at Oudenaarde exemplify their now intensified loyalty to their Flemish origins.

Movement leaders chose the Lion of Flanders, borrowed from the coat of arms of the medieval Count of Flanders, as their graphic symbol, and promoted literary, artistic, and dramatic work that, in their view, captured the "Flemish national soul." (Murphy and Strikwerda 23) Viewed in a larger context, this rise in consciousness of a distinctly *Flemish* identity in northern Belgium and Brussels provides an intriguing correlative to the Celtic Revival developing in Scotland in the same late 19th Century period.

While, at the same time, French-speaking Wallonian artists somewhat defensively directed *their* efforts at depicting the character of people and places of southern Belgium, (Murphy and Strikwerda 23) their goal, that of paying homage toWallon culture, was undermined by a landscape long since despoiled by mining and industrialization. In the end, then, the Flemish surge of creative energy directed at buttressing and/or enhancing Flemish identity did double duty: it served to highlight the specifically Flemish regional heritage, preeminent in both its cultural and its commercial achievements, while at the same time nourishing the prestige of Belgium as a whole, a national culture the movement promoted as "steeped in a splendid artistic and urban history." (Murphy and Strikwerda 25)

Increasingly vocal resentment of French dominance in Belgian governmental and cultural affairs revealed itself as well in growing Anglophilia, most visibly in Brussels. A single, but significant example of a larger trend, the celebrated English architect, Augustus Pugin, was commissioned to design the neo-Gothic House of Parliament. Pugin was popular not only in Brussels, but throughout Belgium, his impact widely visible in Gothic elements incorporated in other major municipal structures. (Murphy and Strikwerda 25) In broader social terms, perhaps even more important in the long historical run, Belgian legislators emulated British openness to immigration, welcoming into the country refugees, dissidents, and exiles from repressive regimes elsewhere on the continent. (Murphy and Strikwerda 25)

The result for Brussels was the influx of a dynamic group of left-wing social reformers and idealogues in the final decades of the 19th Century: Karl Marx and Friedrich Engels planned their collaboration on *Das Kapital* in Brussels; refugees from the devastations of the 1871 Paris Commune uprising found a haven in Brussels; German socialists "evaded Bismarck's spies by moving to Brussels and Liège." (Murphy and Strikwerda 25) The presence in Belgium's capital city of passionately idealistic foreigners, many of them political zealots, contributed to an already vital cosmopolitan environment, one likely to be receptive to the avant garde salon experience supplied by *Les Vingt.*

Added to Brussels' polyglot culture were the large numbers of British, French, and German representatives of their countries'' firms, along with savvy foreign investors who had made Brussels their home by the late 1880s. Their presence made itself known through the sizeable number of foreign language journals published and sold in the Belgian capitol. (Murphy and Strikwerda 25) This was the climate of freely, if sometimes fractiously expressed opinion and cultural cross-fertilization in which van de Velde was weened as a young artist, designer, lecturer, and social activist in the final decade of the 19th Century. Naturally, he could only assume that such artistic, intellectual, and social open-mindedness and vibrancy would be the norm throughout Europe.

For the mutually reinforcing bonds between *Les Vingt* and the *P.O.B.*, the year 1893 was indeed a turning point, notable again for two signal events: the one, the demise of *Les Vingt*, a cultural loss somewhat counterbalanced by the other, the franchise for all male Belgians. For the lower middle and lower classes, this was a major political gain. The achievement of universal suffrage, at least for men, had been hard won, through publicity campaigns, parliamentary lobbying, and strikes organized by an alliance of leftist political organizations. In the avant garde art realm, *Les Vingt* was swiftly succeeded as the reigning movement by *La Libre aesthéthique*, with Octave Maus as President. Maus now assumed a position of near-total control, his authority extending to the selection of artists and art work on exhibit. By contrast, in the larger political arena, 346, 000 citizen votes for the progressive *P.O.B.* resulted in the election of 29 deputies to Parliament in 1894.

Among the new *P.O.B.* deputies elected, four were lawyers who had been affiliated with *Les Vingt*: Edmond Picard, Jules Destrée, Émile Vandervelde, and Max Hallet, all highly educated, professionals, whose efficacy in promoting the interests of lower class workers (Culot: 90) was impressive, although initially regarded with ambivalence, even skepticism by the very constituency they represented. (What, the minimally educated factory technician might have asked, were their true motives?) The familiarity of these lawyers with parliamentary process, and with Belgium's intricate bureaucratic machinery, was obviously advantageous in gaining governmental support for the arts. Picard in particular had been editor and polemicist for *L'Art moderne* since its inception in 1881, so the journal had, as a matter of course, reflected his socialist views.

Moreover, he had long exhorted *Les Vingt* artist members to turn to the world of contemporary labor for inspiration, in the belief that by doing so, the artists would dissolve the barriers between the different segments of society, and create a more integrated, harmonious human community. This optimistic, if simplistic view of artistic clout assigned painters and sculptors the unprecedented role of *directors*, rather than marginalized observers, of social change. Now, as an elected member of Parliament, Picard could translate his vision for artists into concrete legislation and budgetary allotments.

Further expanding the productive reciprocity between the Brussels avant garde and left wing political figures of all stripes was the establishment of the *La Section d'Art*. Established in 1891 by the *Cercle des étudiants et anciens étudiants socialistes*, *La Section* was intended primarily for proletariat education: literary, artistic, musical, and scientific. Like their forebears in *Les Vingt*, *La Section* organizers presented exhibitions, concerts, poetry and prose readings, with the addition of lectures in the natural and physical sciences. *Section* administrators were unusually sensitive to the financial limitations of their target audience. Admission to a *Section*-sponsored event, for example, cost a mere 10 centimes, a pittance for the period. (Levine: 57) For artists, lecturers in all disciplines, and musicians, formal membership in the *P.O.B.* was not required for participation in *Section* activities, a strong inducement for those eager for exposure, but uneasy about overt political affiliation.

However, there did exist the unvoiced assumption that those participating in *Section* events would be sympathetic to the working class. (Levine: 57) Of *Vingtiste* member artists, Henry van de Velde and Georges Lemmen had the most extensive involvement in *Section* activities. The very titles of van de Velde's lectures suggest his ever greater interest in integrating his ethical concerns and social conscience with his training and experience as an artist: in 1894, he offered a talk entitled *"Les Arts d'Industrie et d'ornamentation populaire"*; in 1897, *"William Morris, artisan et socialiste,"* "each time making explicit the relationship between radical forms of art and the working class." (Levine 58) A more direct outgrowth of van de Velde's by now well-honed artistry were his designs for *Section* publicity materials, such as the program flyer for Pierre d'Alheim's *"Mussorgski et le peuple,"* a lecture and concert given in 1898. "He took the politics of this assignment very seriously, writing to *Deutscher* [the publisher] 'You can print my drawing in red. (Levine: 58)

And, logically, the sudden preeminence of the *P.O.B.* in national politics after 1893 demanded the design and construction of expanded headquarters. Since the 1880s, when its leaders had parted ways with a politically stagnant Liberal Party, the *P.O.B.* had carried on its activities for radical social reform in a former synagogue on the *rue de Bavière*, a workable, but now inadequate space. In fact, three years earlier, in 1890, the *P.O.B.*, with laudable foresight, had already commissioned new headquarters in three major centers: Ghent, Antwerp, and Brussels. Designed by Victor Horta, the Brussels *Maison du Peuple* was by far the most important in its time, and ultimately for architectural history.

Horta's purpose-designed building was begun in 1896 and completed in 1899, that is, in tandem with the first stage of construction of Mackintosh's Glasgow School of Art (1896-99). Horta's structure, as cutting edge for Belgium in the period as GSA was for Scotland, "was seen, by supporters and detractors alike, as the most explicit expression of a reciprocal relation between art and politics." (Levine: 59) Indeed, the Brussels *Maison du Peuple* was intended as a "visible reflection of the differences between the Catholic and Liberal parties who sought to represent the interests of the *status quo* and the party of the 'future,' the *P.O.B."* (Levine: 60)

Horta and his team of technical experts selected construction materials not only for their pragmatic, but for their metaphoric value. The *Maison's* strikingly non-traditional expanses of windows, for instance, allowed far more natural light and air into the structure's functional spaces its administrative and political meeting rooms, its cooperative store, and its spacious auditorium than in comparable older buildings. The tall glass panes also alluded symbolically to the light and air long denied laborers in their own windowless, claustrophobic homes.

Horta's heavy dependence on iron and steel, the trademark structural material of Art Nouveau architecture, also paid homage to the miners and laborers in the metallurgy industry who, like the glass blowers, had been instrumental in the formation of the *P.O.B.* in 1885. (Levine: 60) Horta himself described *La Maison* as a building "enjoying the luxury of air and light so long absent from the slum houses of the workers" (Escritt: 77) In this sensitive remark, he made clear that, for this commission, he had the interests at heart of a social stratum with which he had had little personal contact in the past. The *Maison*, sadly demolished in a surge of short-sighted "urban renewal" in 1965-66, was not uniformly modernist on its exterior, although its sinuous overall shape, strategically adjusted to its corner location, bespeaks a dominant Art Nouveau influence. For example, in photographs from the period, one can make out classical references in the columns on its edifice, as well as a decidedly conservative retreat into the past in the near-rococo typographic design of the lettering above the entrance. (Levine 60)

Nevertheless, in addition to honoring the industries responsible for the availability of its building materials, the *Maison's* inaugural festivities on "Red Easter" boldly broke with convention and risked Catholic reprisal in "transforming the holiest of Christian holidays into a two-day celebration of [intrinsically non-religious] socialism." (Levine 60) During this *Pacques rouges,* the Brussels public was treated to 48 hours of speeches and parades by members of the various syndicates involved in *La Section*, as well as concerts, fireworks, balls, and even the launching of a hot air balloon provided by the *P.O.B.* newspaper, *Le Peuple.* These rousing, celebratory events, strikingly prophetic of the *agitprop* organized by Russian Revolutionary leaders in Moscow twenty years later, were attended by thousands of Belgian workers and leaders of Socialist parties of France and Germany. (Levine 349)

Perhaps as provocative as the *Maison's* non-traditional architectural conception, and the extensive use of industrially fabricated materials in its construction, is the central paradox in the career of its designer, Horta. The Belgian architect most commonly associated with the emergence of Art Nouveau had won commissions primarily from wealthy, socially well-placed, moderate to conservative clients, among them the University of Brussels Professor Victor Tassel and Leopold's emissary to the Congo, Baron van Eetvelde. These patrons travelled in social circles unattainable for lower class workers, enjoying a comfortable, secure way of life utterly at odds with their own. In American college courses outlining the Art Nouveau movement, the paradox inevitably triggers two related questions: why was Horta chosen for the *Maison du peuple* commission, and why did he accept?

The most plausible answers seem, in retrospect, the most obvious: Horta was by far the most respected of innovative architects in late 19th Century Belgium. He was the designer most at ease with the hallmark structural components of the Art Nouveau style, through his extensive use of glass, iron, and steel in his domestic commissions. From Horta's standpoint, the project itself was substantial, intriguing, and certain to further enhance an already flourishing career.

Moreover, the three *P.O.B.* leaders who exhorted him to accept the commission, Destrée, Vander velde, and Hallet, were Horta's cultural and intellectual peers, none with family or community ties to the working class citizens whose interests they represented in Parliament. While in their zeal for reform, they even went so far as to advocate for women's suffrage in a decade where the very possibility seemed beyond the Pale, the lawyers' *modus vivendi* their dress style, their speech patterns, their reading habits, their cultural predilections was decidedly upper class, like that of Horta himself.

Horta maintained that he had been selected for the design of *La Maison* not for his sympathies with the *P.O.B.*, but because they [the lawyers] wanted a building in his aesthetic style. (Escritt: 79) Ironically, the immense project forced him not only to abandon the luxurious trappings of his domestic interiors, but to design a full scale, multi-use structure for the entire range of the *P.O.B.*'s activities. In doing so successfully, he proved, in fact, that Art Nouveau, should not only be viewed solely as an interior style. (Escritt: 77) Of equal importance, it "enabled him to demonstrate the modernity at the heart of his Art Nouveau vision by using mass-produced elements, as in the meeting hall, to produce a public building appropriate to its social function in both budget and flexibility of use." (Escritt: 79)

Interestingly, while Horta bore full responsibility for the design of the *Maison* shell, and for the meeting rooms, lecture hall, administrative offices, café, and bakery inside, Henry van de Velde shouldered the equally weighty burden of the many activities *Section* lectures, for example—for which the building was intended. And contributing further to the comparison between the two Art Nouveau masters, always bitter enemies, as legend has it, is van de Velde's design for the *Deutscher Werkbund* Workers' Hall, a genuinely modernist descendant of *La Maison,* similar in functional purpose. Conceived and constructed in conjunction with the 1914 *Werkbund* Exhibition in Cologne, van de Velde's sweeping, streamlined structure succumbed to a fate identical to that of *La Maison:* the wrecking ball. But much earlier and for radically different reasons.

CHAPTER 5

Henry van de Velde, The Master of Antwerp

> Line is a force whose activities are parallel to those of all natural elemental forces; several line forces, placed face to face, exert their activities in a contrary sense, provoking the same results as the natural forces opposed to each other given the same conditions. Line borrows the strength of its energy from the one who has traced it. (Canning, "The Symbolist Landscapes" 130)

The rather rarefied *dictum* quoted above constitutes Henry van de Velde's "essential contribution to modernist aesthetics," according to *Les Vingt* scholar Susan Canning. (Canning, "The Symbolist Landscapes." 130) In her 1985 monograph, Canning traces the development of van de Velde's theory of expressive line through ten critical years, 1883-1893, during which, she asserts, the Antwerp native deployed landscape painting "as an effective and powerful vehicle for expression of conceptual and emotive intent." (Canning, "The Symbolist Landscapes." 130) Since van de Velde is most commonly celebrated as prolific, versatile designer and reformer in applied arts education, Canning's investigation of his consuming ten-year commitment to easel painting is especially revealing, and of particular value in the study of the Antwerp master's emergence as a mover and shaker in modernist design in the mid-1890s.

Equally demanding of study are the links between van de Velde's efforts and achievements in the fine arts, his related forays into visual art aesthetics, and his pivotal role in the *Deutscher Werkbund's* primary goal the merging of aesthetically satisfying design with efficient, high volume industrial manufacture How, one might ask, does one reconcile the Belgian designer's metaphysical notions of the power of line with his embrace of industrial advances in production, both in his commercial enterprises in Brussels and Berlin and in his contributions to *Werkbund* objectives and *modus operandi.* A good, if knotty question good *because* it is knotty.

Henry van de Velde was born in Antwerp in 1863. He was the sixth child of a prosperous pharmacist, who was also a dedicated amateur musician.In fact, owing to this dedication, van de Velde's home environment was typically suffused with music, particularly that of the great Romantic composers, Wagner, Liszt, Berlioz, and Brahms. Scholars agree that van de Velde subconsciously channeled this lush, textured musical surround into dreams of a career as a composer, but that, bending to his father's opposition no doubt based on pragmatic "good sense" he was forced to adjust his fascination with musical structure and rhythmic pattern to the parameters of the visual arts and "the poetic possibilities of formal arrangement." (Canning, "The

Symbolic Landscapes" 130) (Admittedly, a hard look at this lateral move in the arts doesn't exactly indicate an awakened concern for a safe, profitable professional path.)

In 1878, in mid-adolescence, van de Velde met Max Elskamp, who would eventually become one of Belgium's most prominent Symbolist poets. Through Elskamp, he was introduced to the novels of Victor Hugo and the poetry of Charles Baudelaire, and, *via* these towering writers, the guiding assumptions of literary symbolism as played out in French literary circles. One must note as well that van de Velde shared with Elskamp a financially secure, middle class idealist's sincere, if uninformed, attraction to peasant life, that is, peasant life perceived at a distance and romanticized, but not lived.

In 1884, just past twenty and increasingly dissatisfied with the prescriptive style, rigid technical guidelines, and hackneyed content learned at the Antwerp Academy, van de Velde moved to Paris for a brief, but critical stay. The experience broadened his artistic frame of reference and brought his intentions into sharper focus. Predictably, like so many of his Belgian peers, he found in the French metropolis a more eclectic community of experimental painters and sculptors, and a more sophisticated cultural milieu overall, than any in his own country.

More specifically in terms of stylistic influence, in Paris, van de Velde fell under the spell of the French realist painter of rural life, J.J.Millet. In his admiration for Millet, the impressionable Belgian was in spiritual and aesthetic league not only with the Glasgow Boys, his counterparts in Scotland, but with Vincent van Gogh, whose assertive technique and stylistic ferocity would mark van de Velde so fully in the late 1880s. (With regard to van Gogh's affinity with Millet, *dévotés* of the Vincent's work are often bemused at his rough, vigorous take on Millet's "Reaper," only a true copy in composition, but a work clearly carried out as an *homage.)*

On his return to Antwerp in 1885, probably still clearer about the painter he wasn't than the painter he was, van de Velde turned to landscape and, in 1885, moved again to Welchel der Zande, an artists' colony near his home city. His stated goal was "to live among the peasants and record through his paintings their symbiotic relationship to the land." (Canning, "The Symbolic Landscapes" 130) The paintings van de Velde completed in the years 1885-1889 can be said to manifest his "resolve to penetrate beneath the surface of observation" (Canning, "The Symbolic Landscapes" 130), a sentiment that bears an uncanny resemblance to Vassily Kandinsky's voiced determination to reach artistically beyond the material realm, as the *Blaue Reiter* leader stated in his seminal tract of 1886 "On the Spiritual in Art."

Typical of van de Velde's work in this intense period are "Farmyard," "Potato Gatherer," and "The Washerwoman," all completed in that very year, 1886. Lovely to look at, the paintings are noteworthy for two reasons: the obvious impact of the quick, painterly French Impressionist brushstroke on van de Velde's technique in the mid-1880s, "when he allies his strident stroke to sunlight" (Canning, "The Symbolic Landscapes" 130) and the alternative names for the two latter paintings, "August Sun" and "September Sun." These double titles, referring to first the human and then to the natural element in the same scene, surely reflect van de Velde's hypothesis of an intimate bond, a shared identity, between the peasants and their natural surroundings, so that the farm laborers and the land they work form a single subject.

In addition, close scrutiny of the paintings reveals something else, something perhaps more important in van de Velde's approach to the canvas in the late 1880s: a growing preoccupation with order and cadence, combined with a "growing disaffection with Impressionist style." (Canning, "The Symbolic Landscapes" 131) Canning ascribes this palpable restlessness in van de Velde's Wechel der Zande paintings to his "search for a system to represent the universal aspects of nature," rather than "the aimless reproduction of nature's surfaces" (Canning, "The Symbolist Landscapes" 131)

For the sake of perspective, one might compare van de Velde's work of the late 1880s with the paintings of Claude Monet, the latter, in the minds of many, the quintessential Impressionist. If Monet cannot really be reduced to "just an eye," as Cézanne declared, at least we can be certain that the French master was far more attentive to the surface appearance of the phenomena he painted than any other aspect. (Here, one hastens to include the conclusion of Cézanne's paean to his friend's greatness, "but God what an eye") In contrast, as the final decade of 19th Century approached, Monet's Belgian contemporary gradually allowed his evolving bead on his favorite subject, the rural scene, to guide his stylistic address of the canvas. At this point, he increasingly apprehended the natural landscape, tenanted or not, as an aesthetic and philosophic foil, its surface qualities open to manipulation in ways that most Impressionists hadn't considered.

In 1887, Georges Seurat's Neo-Impressionist manifesto, *"L'Après Midi sur la Grande Jatte"* ("Sunday afternoon on the Great Jetty") was the centerpiece of the 1887 *Les Vingt* Salon. It would be two more years before van de Velde's acceptance as offical member of the group. However, long before becoming *Les Vingt* member, he did attend the Salon receptions, hobnobbing with Belgian and foreign artists and studying the work on show. Fortuitously for van de Velde, "*L'Après Midi*" offered him precisely what he'd been seeking since he'd been forced to abandon musical composition for the visual arts in the 1870s. In Seurat, he discovered a French painter who had adopted a quasi-scientific method for organizing perception, so as to create a rhythmic, patterned panorama similar in scale and complexity to a Flemish tapestry. Through his *divisioniste* technique, Seurat created an expansive image that "accented the harmonic and iconic aspects of nature," emphasizing what the painter construed as its inherent order, which in turn contributed to its expressive potential. (Canning, "The Symbolic Landscapes" 131)

The Great Jetty itself was no untouched rural site, but a structured slice of nature, a tamed and manicured urban park jutting into the Seine. In the painting, Seurat had systematically converted the multiplicity and variety of human presence on the Jetty into a serene, but haunting, surreal composition of geometric repeats. Moreover, his methodical application of adjacent "dots" of complementary color had succeeded in both flattening his figures and merging them with the Great Jetty trees, lawn and flowing river, all handled in the same manner. The socioeconomic reality of a recreational Sunday for a lower class, upwardly mobile Parisian population, newly fitted out in off the rack clothing, may have been lost on Seurat, a very young painter at the time, and perhaps on van de Velde as well. What counted for the Belgian artist most was the advance toward harmonious abstraction evident in Seurat's mural-size manifesto.

Van de Velde did not immediately take up the Neo-Impressionist technique in 1887; he was stll painting in fairly loose brushstrokes, not small, uniform dots, as much as a year later. However, 1888, while still preoccupied with the working-peasant theme, he completed "Peasant in the Orchard," in which "the figure assumes a pivotal position in the composition, even as the pointillist stroke effectively blends it into the total environment." (Canning, "The Symbolist Landscape" 132) Perceptible in "Peasant" is the reduction of forms, natural and human, to their geometric essence, unprecedented in the Belgian's painting up to this point. "No longer concerned with a naturalist description of a Realist-Impressionist world, van de Velde now [strove] to create a sensation of mood synthesized from observations found in nature." (Canning, "The Symbolist Landscapes" 132) Clearly, "synthesized" is the focal term here: no longer content to merely reproduce what lay before his eyes van de Velde was, from now on, intent on distilling and reordering that is to say, *designing* his perceptions.

Seurat's second solo exhibition with *Les Vingt* took place in February, 1889, giving van de Velde, now an elected member, the opportunity to discuss Neo-Impressionist theory with his Parisian colleague. One year later, in 1890, van de Velde himself exhibited a series of paintings entitled *"Faits de Village"* ("Village Occurrences") with the *Vingtist* Salon. In these tranquil paintings, Seurat's influence had been fully assimilated: *Pointilliste* technique fully informs his meticulous brushwork. Joining idiosyncratic color combinations with stylized, hieratic depiction of figures, van de Velde successfully imbues routine village activities with what Canning terms an "iconic flavor." (Canning," The Symbolist Landscapes" 132)

Indeed, in paintings like "Woman in the Window" and "Woman Who Sews," the female figures become, in effect, archetypes, the sensitivity in their portrayal reminiscent of Vermeer's female subjects intent on their work in Delft interiors. However, more importantly in these 1890 paintings, van de Velde had wed Neo-Impressionist divisionist technique, as developed and refined by Seurat and Signac, with Symbolist content. In this way, he visually underscored the close ties and shared values of the two movements, whose proponents had exhibited together at *Les Vingt* salons since 1887.

Received art historical wisdom notwithstanding, the theoretical and expressive aims of the Neo-Impressionists and the Symbolists were in fact not in all ways antithetical. Both groups sought "to record the essential, ordered, and harmonic aspects of nature." (Canning, "The Symbolist Landscapes..." 133) The Neo-Impressionists claimed to do so through simplified form and, in the case of Seurat and Signac, *pointelliste* technique. (According to the 1839 optical theories of chemist Michel Chevreul, opposite hues on the color wheel, placed side by side, in regular "dot" form, would intensify each other. As noted earlier, the pervasive application of dots of complementary color also served to flatten the entire image.) For their part, the Symbolists, Khnopff, Toorop, and Redon among them, "emphasized formal deformation in order to arrive at their intended expression of inner spiritual experience." (Canning, "The Symbolic Landscapes" 133)

Evident in the principles and practice of both groups is the rejection of the traditional obligation to draw and paint real world phenomena exactly as they appear to the eye. In the minds of many in the visual arts, 19th Century advances in photography had to a great degree taken over that role. So, for van de Velde, still motivated in part by his adolescent ambitions in musical composition, adopting Seurat's brand of Neo-Impressionism would permit him to represent "a reality whose color harmonies were analogous in his mind to music." (Canning, "The Symbolist Landscape" 133) As for Symbolist distortion and free-wheeling manipulation of external reality, all in the interests of achieving an expressive goal, that liberating process suited van de Velde's inclinations perfectly.

The technical and stylistic evolution in van de Velde's decade-long career in easel art can't be ascribed solely to theoretical shifts and changes in artistic circles. Indeed, awareness of our own emotional vulnerability tells us that personal upheavals can have as pivotal an impact on our actions as theoretical disputes among our peers, or, for that matter, disruptive events in the larger political cosmos. Such was certainly the case for van de Velde, whose beloved mother died in 1888, a loss which precipitated a long period of grief and depression. Added to an already acute sense of alienation from his urban, bourgeois upbringing, his grief was the final catalyst for a life-altering choice.

In late summer and autumn of 1888, through the winter of 1889, van de Velde made his home in Blankenberge, a resort town on Belgium's Atlantic coast. Given the population density of Belgium as a whole in the 1880s, the highest in Europe, the move to Blankenberge obviously allowed van de Velde the most solitude and the fullest exposure to unpeopled nature possible in his native country. While, in strict terms, the diminished human presence in the Blankenberge paintings reflects the area's sparse population, the relentlessly bleak images surely indicate as well the artist's extreme introspection in this period. But whatever the source, the Blankenberge landscapes and seascapes were indeed emptied of the human community, to a degree rare in the Welchel der Zande paintings that preceded them. "All human interaction has been placed at a detached and objective distance." (Canning, "The Symbolic Landscapes" 134)

The months of uninterrupted introspection by the sea brought to a head a long term internal debate, during which the conflicted van de Velde questioned his very professional direction. How could he, in good conscience, reconcile "the elitist practice of painting" with "the artist's [his] social responsibility"? (Canning, "The Symbolist Landscapes" 134) For some time, probably dating back to his year in Paris, van de Velde had been certain that such a reconciliation could be found in the work of Millet. His admiration for the French realist's *homages* to the dignity of the rural worker's day-to-day life, a life defined mainly by exhausting physical labor, was surely linked to his high regard for Millet's well documented humanism and his oft-articulated debt to the Old and New testaments.

Moreover, while van de Velde accurately perceived Millet's translation of a wide range of distinct individuals into universal types, he also understood that the "typing" in Millet's work was not meant in the negative sense, as a means of minimizing each individual's singularity. Rather, the creation of archetypes in Millet's work was intended to emphasize commonalities, what is shared in the human condition, in particular the *working class* human condition. Like van Gogh, van de Velde looked to Millet's oil and pastel portrayals of peasant life as models, albeit not rigid templates, for conveying honestly and sympathetically the rigors of rural life.

Ultimately, merely tinkering with the technique, style, or even the content of his painting seemed an inadequate, even irrelevant solution to van de Velde's ambivalence regarding the trajectory of his professional path. By the late 1880s, his ever more acute sensitivity to the conditions of Belgian lower class life, held at bay during his period of quietude on the North Sea coast, had begun to shake his creative moorings. He was starting to question the viability of painting at all, as an effective strategy for curing the pervasive social and economic inequalities in his native Belgium. His study of anarchist and socialist tracts by Kropotkin, Bakunin, Marx, and Engels, in which the very social value of the arts in general is called into question, only served to intensify his doubts. (Canning, "The Symbolic Landscapes" 134)

Nevertheless, up until 1892, van de Velde persisted in his search for "a pictorial form that would embody...his artistic and social ideals." (Canning, "The Symbolic Landscapes" 134) At Blankenberge, he had sketched, as well as painted the lonely beaches and ocean, his assertive charcoal and pastel strokes transferring directly to paper the relative formlessness, the absence of discrete volumes, in the desolate sand, surf, and skyline of the North Sea coast. While he occasionally included religious symbols in his sketches a church steeple, for example his overriding concern was with the elemental aspects of nature, expressed stylistically through lines and dashes. (Notable in these sketches is their resemblance to 20th Century Abstract Expressionist "mark-making" a vanguard process for which van de Velde may well have been an inadvertent pioneer.)

In the 1890 *Vingtiste* Salon, van de Velde encountered in van Gogh's muscular, expressive stroke a painterly approach totally at odds with Seurat's studied *pointilliste* dot. Effectively bodying forth, for example, the saturated yellows of sunflowers, the virility of van Gogh's technique, always disciplined and methodical, conveyed as fully as possible the clarity and brilliance of the Provence landscape. At this point, Van de Velde was riven by his dual attraction to the two opposing strategies and to the two distinct temperaments they represented, both no doubt inherent in his own: On one side, a technique hopelessly calm and slow, on the other, a fiery technique, representing a moment of extreme emotion. "I remained pulled between two techniques. Canvases patiently pointillist, pastels slashed with lines of dynamism in which I recognized after having practiced academic drawing for nearly ten years a true sense of drawing and of line." (Canning, "The Symbolic Landscapes" 134)

In paintings completed early in 1892, while moving inexorably away from a life dedicated solely to easel art, van de Velde nevertheless succeeded in melding van Gogh's energetic line with Seurat's methodical application of points of complementary color. It is a striking paradox, then, that the future Art Nouveau master abandoned painting altogether later in that very year. Doubtless, an additional spur to this radical creative shift was exposure to the theories of Arts and Crafts Movement leaders, William Morris and John Ruskin, *via* a lecture by Alfred William (Willy) Finch at the opening banquet for 1892 *Les Vingt* Salon.

Always inclined to sort out on paper his aesthetic, philosophic and ethical goals, not to mention his anxieties and triumphs, he attempted to articulate in that landmark year his struggle "to visualize nature's underlying structure," and, through the very movement of a line, to make visible "the rhythmic flow of life." (Canning, "The Symbolic Landscapes" 134) As he stated it, the patterns formed by sand dunes, the wave motion of the sea, and the contours of his fiancée's face simultaneously sprang from and led to the same metaphysical source: the presence and energy of their Maker, the spiritual essence behind it all. Line itself, van de Velde insisted, while lacking mass, volume, or density, functioned as a symbol of the elemental forces and energy in nature.

So, as Canning persuasively concludes, "Although van de Velde concentrated after 1893 on a career in design and architecture, that curving, forceful, meandering line, distilled from his long meditations on nature, served as the signatory emblem of his atelier and as the basic tenet of his artistic theory." (Canning, "The Symbolist Landscapes" 136)

Solitary introvert though van de Velde may have been, at least at Blankenberge, on his return to city life, he energetically churned his "long meditations on nature" and lofty ruminations on line into a variety of concrete decorative projects, all of them two-dimensional. His black chalk Blankenberge drawing *"Zon bij Zee"* ("Sun with the Sea"), ca. 1888-89, for instance, was the point of departure for the woodcut he designed for the cover of *Dominical*, Max Elskamp's first volume of verse published in 1892. That quite modest sketch was, in fact, "one of the first works in which the artist swept away the divisionist technique in favor of a purer abstraction," and "one of the first forays into the ecstatic organic forms that were to become the basis of art nouveau." (Goddard 350-51)

Van de Velde had, again, long profited from his bond with Max Elskamp, through their warm friendship and artist-writer collaboration. In his bond with Elskamp, van de Velde had also the advantage of easy access to the Japanese woodblock *ukiyo-e* prints in the poet's extensive collection Depicting the ephemeral "floating world" of old Edo (Tokyo), the prints offered stylistic visual norms not seen in Western art since the Medieval period: stylized figural, botanical, and landscape elements; clear outline of forms; flat planes of intense color, indifference to issues of depth or linear perspective. In addition, Japanese design instinct favored asymmetry and diagonal motion, lending the small prints an energy and potency less evident in their traditionally centered Western counterparts. The strong impression made on van de Velde by the Japanese prints would later be reinforced by exposure to posters by Jules Cheret and Toulouse Lautrec on display in *Les Vingt* salons of 1891 and1892. Both Cheret and Lautrec had been profoundly influenced by the Japanese woodblock images flooding into Paris from the late 1860s on.

In 1891, van de Velde submitted two mock-ups for tapestry projects to the *Les Vingt* salon, both entitled *"Paysage"* and both displaying "swaying forms, simplified shapes, and rhythmic, energetic line." (Canning, *Les XX* and the Belgian Avant Garde 353) While the mock-ups were never converted into full-scale cloth and embroidery tapestries, one can infer that they had been prepared for that purpose through the color notations van de Velde had methodically jotted in the sketched shapes. In addition, his choice and arrangement of complementary colors in the mock-ups closely resemble those in "Angel's Watch," a sweeping, gloriously curvilinear embroidered tapestry completed for the 1893 *Les Vingt* salon. Indeed, with the fabrication and exhibition of *"La Veillée des Anges"* ("Angels Watch"), a magisterial cloth masterpiece, van de Velde strode confidently into the realm of the decorative arts. The tapestry's pools of rich color, free-wheeling deployment of sinuous, pulsating organic forms, and sheer breadth, seven feet across, seem to merge the stylistic winds that had buffeted the ambivalent artist for over a decade of practice.

The tapestry indicated as well that van de Velde had finally surmounted the obstacle of ambivalence. The motif selected for the tapestry, one surprising in a pictorial designer with no overt religious commitment, was a group of angels in contemporary Belgian dress, seated on a lawn and watching over the infant Jesus. The heavenly grouping is framed by a swirling backdrop of trees whose trunks are bowed inward to form a protective canopy. The stylized shelter of tree trunks further illuminates the theme of maternal devotion and vigilance implicit in the image as a whole.

Three additional forms, angels as well, can be glimpsed to the far right of the picture plane, while the natural setting is handled so as to suggest neither an ancient Middle Eastern oasis, nor the lonely shores of a North Sea Beach, but a groomed Western European urban park. Indeed, it's evident that the memory of Seurat's "*L'Après-midi sur la Grande Jatte*" had insinuated itself into van de Velde's subconscious as he conceived the tapestry.

Observers at the 1893 *Salon* were struck by van de Velde's refusal to identify the angels through traditional haloes and wings. Controversial as well was his reluctance to differentiate the women's faces, so that only a range of prayer-like hand gestures distinguish them as individuals. In fact, as is common in Japanese *ukiyo-e* tradition, the women's faces seem nearly featureless, as absent of specificity as the deep green lawn and brown, the barkless tree trunks, the spreading red and orange folds of their loose fitting robes, and the whiplash curve of the path narrowing toward the horizon, its hue an eye-popping chartreuse.

The path winds vertically through the image, more like a pale crevasse than a solid surface for walking, while the sky, glimpsed through the trees rising above a high horizon line, is a brilliant cadmium yellow. (The saturated yellow sky, as well as the idiosyncratic depiction of the angels, may have been appropriated from the shocking palette and defiantly iconoclastic portrayal of sacred subjects that typify Paul Gauguin's visionary scenes of Pont Aven. Gauguin had, in fact, participated in several *Les Vingt* salons in the early 1890s.) And, again reminiscent of Japanese tradition, objects cast no shadows and volume is conveyed through contour, not tonal gradation.

So, in "Angels' Watch," van de Velde succeeded in making a traditional Christian motif, one constantly reworked through centuries of stylistic change, his own. Evidence of Seurat's impact is here, in those adjacent areas of color complements and in the designer's emphasis on 2-D pattern, rather than 3-D, fleshed-out narrative. Van Gogh's influence is apparent in van de Velde's bold, sensuous contour and near-feverish color choice, as is Gauguin's, in the Belgian's near-sacrilegious interpretation of a sacrosanct motif. The mark of Japanese stylistic strategies reveals itself in the tapestry's figurative stylization, in the cropping on the vertical and horizontal axes, and in the seamless harmony of its composition. Indeed, taken all in all, the tapestry represented for van de Velde both the culmination of past stylistic influences and a giant step into a career in decorative and functional design. It also permitted him a compassionate *homage* to maternal love.

Incidentally, the meticulous embroidery one can examine at close range in appreciating this bravura piece, one whose parts are so perfectly integrated in the whole, was accomplished by van de Velde's aunt, whose actual name, age, and circumstances are strangely missing from scholarly accounts of the tapestry's presence in the *Les Vingt* Salon of 1893.

Normally, a husband's need to house his wife and the children, is a serious concern. It is exceptional for it to raise great scruples, such severe scruples that they push someone who has never been involved in architecture before to build his own house. Even more exceptional is to see him build a house which is markedly different from those around it, and, in designing its interior, to create furniture whose very components differ so markedly from convention. What could be the motivation for such maverick behavior?

Culot quotes of van de Velde as follows: "The downfall of architecture and the general corruption of taste appeared to him in a particularly repellent light. There is no doubt that a vile infection has spread its ravages over everything we see before our eyes. It was necessary, at all costs, to protect the woman who had consented to share his life and the children who were to be born from their union. Ugliness corrupts the soul and the mind as much as the eye." (Culot: 79)

In this impassioned statement, van de Velde elected to voice in the third person his motives for designing, while still an untried architect, an innovative domestic environment for his wife, Maria Sethe, and his children, whatever the social ostracism in the neighborhood surrounding the structure he would name *Bloemenwerf*. Three objectives impelled him in this enterprise: the construction of a protective home for his family; a refuge from the architectural ugliness, the discordant *pastiche* historicism, he witnessed in late 19th Century Belgium; and the creation of a coherent interior setting, in which all the furnishings satisfied the demands of utility and aesthetic inclination, his own, combined. Ever the idealist, van de Velde went so far as to express concern for surrounding his children with beauty even before they were born. "I refused to allow the presence of any object in my home which was not as basically honest, genuinely straightforward and altogether above suspicion in design as the character of the friends we received there." (Marcus: 27)

Bloemenwerf, or Haven of Flowers, was built in Uccle, near Brussels, in the period 1895-6. In a blunt, negative appraisal of van de Velde's Art Nouveau peers, George Marcus points out that the house "does not display the typical turmoil of Belgian Art Nouveau architecture." (Marcus 27) Hardly an outrageous exterior from the 21st Century standpoint, *Bloemenwerf* displayed an English-style, half-timbered exterior, complete with mansard roof and "devoid of the customary ironwork of the 'bourgeois' villas in its vicinity." (Marcus 27)

Modest exterior notwithstanding, van de Velde noted in his memoirs that his custom-built home "offended the community and met with extreme derision." Sober and unobtrusive in both overall form and plain stucco surface, half-hidden in a leafy envelope of trees and bushes, *Bloemenwerf* was nevertheless shamelessly derivative of foreign architectural tradition. As a result, Haven of Flowers proved "offensive to onlookers" in the very qualities that "announced its modernity.": sobriety, along with vernacular, that is to say, lower class borrowings from beyond Belgium's borders. (Marcus 27)

Resolute in his resistance to not-so-neighborly ridicule, van de Velde steadily oversaw the construction and furnishing of his *Gesamtkunstwerk*, his "totally integrated ensemble" (Marcus 29), through the years 1895-96. Indispensable for this groundbreaking undertaking was the generous financial support of his mother-in-law and the unstinting support, practical and moral, of his wife, Maria Sethe. In sum, *Bloemenwerf* was the concrete manifesto of van de Velde's design principles. While his private home definitely served his family's needs; it also served as a showcase for "the most important icons of his revolutionary conception of art" (Marcus 27), whose avowed objective was aesthetic satisfaction, operating in concert with total functionality.

Students of the design ethic formulated by William Morris will recognize the underlying principles guiding van de Velde, a Morris disciple, in his plans for *Bloemenwerf*'s interior: honesty and reason. As to "honesty" both Morris and van de Velde felt strongly that the designer should make no effort to disguise either the structural materials or mode of fabrication in crafting a piece of furniture. If this guideline, revolutionary for its time, were followed, the product, be it a chair, a table, or a desk, would be "honest"; its designer and the craftsmen who carried out his plan would be operating with integrity. Of equal importance, the design should be "reasonable," that is, geared primarily for use, rather than for impressive appearance.

A concrete example of this somewhat high flown credo seems requisite here. Van de Velde devoted substantial time to fitting out the family dining room, an interior space in constant daily use, whose furnishings were inevitably subject to damage. Aware of the perils inherent in heavy, too-hot-to-handle platters, or spills of sauces and corrosive liquids, van de Velde solved the sticky problem of protecting the furniture's most vulnerable elements by cladding the sideboard and the center element of *Bloemenwerf*'s dining room table with brass plates. As a result, crockery filled to overflowing with steaming hot soups or casseroles might rest on them, without burning or scarring carefully applied finishes, and spills could be easily mopped up, without harm to organic, that is, wood surfaces. This solution may seem commonplace now, but for its time, the brass plates were innovative and pacesetting.

The "reductive principles of modernism" (Marcus 29) van de Velde applied to all of *Bloemenwerf's* furnishings take the most vivid and varied form in the types of seating he contrived for his home: armchairs, sofas, dining chairs, desk chairs, high chairs, chairs with arms and chairs without arms all devised so as to provide comfort and project visual harmony at the same time. In his choice of upholstery for his armchairs and sofas, Van de Velde's debt to William Morris again determined his selections.

The intricately patterned Morris fabrics, with their floral inspiration, were imported from Morris's London shop. (Three years earlier, van de Velde had used samples of Morris's textile design as examples of high end modernism in lectures he gave at the Antwerp Art Academy.) (Marcus 29) For his dining room and desk chairs, remarkably streamlined for the era, van de Velde opted for woven rush seats and lowly, "unpretentious" "serviceable" ash. These chairs also hark back to their vernacular English antecedents, and refer to Morris in their resemblance to his well-known line of Sussex chairs. (Marcus 29)

Also easily taken for granted, but representative of van de Velde's singular breakthrough in furniture design, are the outwardly curving lines of the lean dining room and desk chairs discussed above. According to Marcus, "they reveal van de Velde's interest in vitalizing forces and structural stresses at work," (Marcus 29), an interest that indicates a respect for engineers and their profession not shared by many in late 19th Century architectural circles. In that transitional period for design, even in heavily industrialized Belgium, the assumption prevailed that architects alone bore both the technical *and* the stylistic responsibility for buildings, while engineers, with *their* specialized expertise, bore the onus for infrastructural necessities, such as bridges, tunnels, and railroad tracks. Moreover, it was felt that there should be minimal overlap between the two professions, much less collaboration in what seem to us their obviously interdependent obligations.

Van de Velde was clearly the exception here. His fascination with the power of line, particularly curved, sinuous line, explains in part the outward bow of his chair's structural elements. But he was also no stranger to the physical stresses of mass and weight, the force of gravity, and load-bearing abilities of a variety of woods. The outward bow of a chair's legs, braced by horizontal elements front and back, contributed to the strength and stability of what appeared to be a spindly chair.

The stylistic consistency van de Velde intended for *Bloemenwerf* carried over to the flowing garments he fashioned for his wife Maria. Van de Velde designed for his loyal wife loose fitting robes and dresses that permitted far greater latitude of movement than did most women's clothing of the period. The couple's combined efforts in the design of modern clothing for women eventually resulted in a catalogue promoting a line of garments for retail sale. (Marcus 29) The catalogue , like so many aspects of the couple's shared life, was a joint venture. Henry was responsible for cover design, typography, selection of paper and page layout; he also contributed photographs of his elegant spouse wearing his robes, their collars and hems appliquéd in floral patterns.

The photos of Maria, whose blond beauty had also been captured in a *Pointilliste* portrait by Van Rysselberghe, were usually shot in profile or with her back to the camera, suggesing a contented middle class wife at work in her *Bloemenwerf* kitchen or drawing room and totally of a piece with her environment. Maria, for her part, wrote the catalogue text, supplying the details that clarified the images. Clearly, van de Velde's experience merging word with image for the covers of *Van Nu en Straks* served him well in the preparation of catalogues for his own designs.

One can argue that, at least during its period of construction, Bloemenwerf was intended as a private home first and foremost, certainly serving as exemplar of van de Velde's highly individual departures in utilitarian design, but primarily as a welcoming domestic haven for himself and his family. Its location, in a bucolic setting away but not too far away from Brussels' crowded, cacophonous center, rendered it a peaceful retreat for himself and his family.

However, *Bloemenwerf*'s untroubled natural setting also made it also an attractive draw for visitors. Facilitating the home's growing popularity among van de Velde's close friends and professional associates was Uccle's accessibility for Brussels' *bourgeoisie*, many of whom now, owned automobiles. And as automobile ownership increased, the widening and paving of roads on Brussels' outskirts took place at an ever-quickening pace, to accommodate the expanding numbers of travellers using them. The van de Veldes had many guests, most of them affluent and in a position to nourish further van de Velde's already burgeoning career in decorative and functional design. Notable among them were Siegfried Bing and Hermann Muthesius.

The scholarly emphasis placed on van de Velde's metaphysical ruminations, while entirely justified, tends to obscure two interrelated personal traits that accounted for the spread of his reputation in Belgium and elsewhere on the continent, from 1895 on: a shrewd business sense, working in tandem with a gift for self-promotion. Indeed, van de Velde's 1897 founding of his own furniture workshop, *La Société van de Velde*, in Ixerres on Brussels' perimeter, reflected an increasing demand for his designs, accomplished primarily through his skill in soliciting orders. Without doubt, his four-year experience with *Les Vingt* had driven home the crucial role savvy marketing plays in seducing clients. The success of his firm also indicates a third talent, that for selective delegation of duties, for mobilizing craft specialists and capitalizing on their technical expertise.

Van de Velde's promotional strategy was two-pronged. He produced a catalogue describing and illustrating his eclectic range of furniture designs, all of them integrating sinuous curve in surface ornament with overall form perfectly suited to purpose. He placed advertisements in journals that ambitiously, if not hubristically, claimed that his workshop could supply on demand, not only custom-designed furniture, but wallpaper, carpets, stained glass, and, of course, embroidered fabric. Record has it that none of the advertising was false: van de Velde's workshop, initially reliant on handcraftsmanship, then selectively on industrial manufacture, lived up to its promises.

In theory, the workshop was modelled on the cooperative template originated by Morris and later carried out in the Guild of Handicraft by Charles Ashbee: That is, as much as was feasible, every workshop participant had his say in the design and crafting of an object. In addition, and prophetically, van de Velde employed not only skilled technicians in the various applied arts, but also a painter, Curt Hermann, and an industrialist, Eberhard von Bodenhausen. These two men, with their complementary expertise, functioned as van de Velde's partners, in principle and practice his equals, in decisions regarding aesthetics or engineering. Their symbiotic roles in the highly productive *Société van de Velde* is, in fact, a clear harbinger of the goals and structure of the *Deutscher Werkbund*, and van de Velde's determining role in its creation.

The wealth of chairs and chair styles in *Bloemenwerf,* and van de Velde's resourcefulness in promoting them, provide persuasive proof of van de Velde's ever more refined commercial acumen. The dining room furniture he planned and executed for both family meals and lavish dinners for his *Bloemenwerf* guests again comes into play here. The suite was originally constructed in that eminently serviceable building material, ash. The wood was inexpensive, durable, flexible enough to adapt to many purposes, and fine-grained enough for a smooth, even satiny finish. It was also available locally in what was left of Belgium's forests. In selecting ash, van de Velde could, in good conscience, fabricate his decidedly upper middle class family's furniture in the very material lower class families attending his lectures at *La Section* might enjoy in their own, more modest homes.

The popularity of the dining room suite in particular was such that van de Velde was asked to duplicate the set for a growing number of new clients, all visitors to his home and guests at his dinner table. However, although initially satisfied with the unpretentious ash, his expanding clientèle eventually took seriously enough their upper-class status as to demand less mundane, more "exotic" woods, such as padouk, oak, or mahogany. These were luxury woods, heavy, dense and richly colored, woods that would have to be imported from other European countries or from Africa, that is, from King Leopold's mercilessly exploited African colony, the Belgian Congo. Van de Velde, principles aside, obliged.

He also obliged in the choice of seat covers for the chairs, when clients preferred leather or floral fabric over his original choice: woven rush. At this early stage in van de Velde's career in functional design, these concessions may seem minor, when one considers that expanding awareness of his technical and stylistic innovations, as well as sales to prestigious clients, were most critical for sheer commercial survival. Nevertheless, given van de Velde's expressed validation of "non-noble materials, like iron, those used for slaughterhouses, factories, and railway stations" (Pattemans: 62), his willingness to accede to his clients' insistence on materials suited to their patrician tastes does suggest a chink in his altruistic armor. One might expect as much of Victor Horta, but not of Henry van de Velde.

> "...is it not established that the middle class avant garde nurtures revolutionary ideas just as much as the avant garde of the proletariat?"
> Victor Horta, *re* the commission for *La Maison du Peuple* (Pattemans: 65)

While van de Velde's lectures and essays of the mid-1890s rail against the plague of "ugliness in architecture generated by the constant repetition of classical models" (Pattemans: 62), it is Victor Horta's fully integrated Brussels interiors, commissioned by well-heeled clients who were also his friends, that express most fully the motives and aesthetic of the Art Nouveau movement. Van de Velde may have inveighed against lack of control over the relationships of these models, architectural structures and interior furnishings, with the practical aim for which they were intended, and over the excessive use of ornament. (Pattemans: 62)

Townhouses designed for clients such as Eugène Autrique, Émile Tassel, or Baron van Eetvelde, it was Horta who actually succeeded in suiting form to function in the crafting of interiors for his clients, interiors said by some to express "the pride, arrogance, and comfort of the ruling class." (Pattemans: 62) "The great achievements of Art Nouveau, Horta's in particular, are to all those who see in this style more than a frivolous, merely ornamental art: its flowing spaces, the boldness of its composition, its structural motivation, its plastic unity at all levels, and the logic of its layout." (Pattemans: 67)

For this reason, the discussion of Horta's work begun earlier demands expansion in a chapter whose primary focus is the complex, sometimes agonizing shift in emphasis in van de Velde's career, from fine to applied artist. Vehemently opposed to the dehumanization and monotony brought about by industrialization, Horta brought all the factors Pattemans lists above together, in a custom-designed, unified interior. Feats of seamless integration, Horta's interiors of the 1890s combined three streams of influence, one oddly antithetical to the drive for design purification guiding all but the French Art Nouveau masters: (1) "the radical political influence of the English design reform tradition," (2) "the technological advances afforded by the use of iron and glass in architecture," and, (3) "the elitist aestheticism of the neo-Rococo style," (Escritt: 72) Horta's borrowings from the Rococo hardly coincide with Art Nouveau's drive for design reform, since, in most critical minds, the style was decadent, fussy, and frivolous, emblematic of the decadent tastes of an aristocracy headed for extinction by the end of the 18th Century.

However, the contrast between Horta and van de Velde lies in more than Horta's incorporation of Rococo stylistic elements in his otherwise streamlined interiors. Unlike the Antwerp master, Horta had set his sights on a career in architecture from the outset. His primary mentor at the Brussels École des Beaux Arts, was the architect Alphonse Balat. Balat's unusual gift for adapting his structural concepts to the availability of new technologies is most evident in his extensive use of glass for the cupola of the royal glasshouses in Laeken (1874-76). The long-range impact of this accomplishment on Horta would emerge in commissioned projects of the 1890s, including La Maison du Peuple. Also, nourishing Horta's taste for anti-historicist innovation was his friendship with Paul Hankar, a less well known Art Nouveau master, whose plans for his own home reflected the stylistic norms he discovered in his sizeable collection of Japanese prints. (Escritt: 72)

While initially Horta shared with van de Velde heightened concern for clean, unencumbered functionality, as proposed in house-cleaning spirit by Ruskin and Morris, his attraction to the teachings of the Arts and Crafts leaders diminished as he matured. As he aged, he was clearly governed more by his own innate taste for luxury without frills than by Morris's moralizing and high-sounding commitment to improving society through fine design. As his list of affluent, influential patrons grew, Horta increasingly viewed the group he scornfully labelled "the English School" with the same dissatisfaction he eventually directed at his staid Beaux Arts training, apprenticeship with Balat notwithstanding.

In fact, Horta's deep-seated sympathies had always been mainly francophone. So enamoured of the work of the medievalist Viollet-le-Duc that he owned all the French theorist's books, Horta had more direct links with Paris than with England. As a young man, he had spent over a year in Montmartre, "working as a stucco artist at a time when the Rococo was very much in vogue." (Escritt: 73) Interestingly in that regard, what he *also* shared with van de Velde was a transformative youthful encounter with the sheer variety of art, design, and architectural styles Paris offered to a provincial Belgian visitor, and with the city's virtual Tower of Babel of ardent, if doctrinaire stylistic voices. (Escritt: 73)

So, while van de Velde walked a wide circle around a profession dedicated solely to the applied arts for over a decade, Horta, operating under an array of influences, strode smoothly and successfully into his position as Art Nouveau architect and designer *par excellence*, a position he held through the final decade of the 19th Century. More intriguing still is Escritt's observation that "in keeping with the diversity of his influences, his projects embodied tensions at the heart of Art Nouveau." (Escritt: 73) While some of Horta's townhouses were commissioned by radical lawyers, others responded to the tastes and needs of conservative government ministers whose political outlook and policies echoed those of Leopold himself. In general, the homes were aesthetically progressive, but also "stunningly luxurious," and certainly beyond the means of "ordinary" people, those newly enfranchised citizens whose votes for the *P.O.B.* had given the Party its legislative clout. Ironically, Horta's own political affiliation was with the *P.O.B.* as well, as was that of many of his wealthy clients.

Horta's nominal association with the *P.O.B.*, while surely arising from genuine sympathy for the dismal lot of the Belgian working class, does seem at odds with his parallel membership in the Brussels Masonic Lodge, *Les Amis Philanthropes. Les Amis* provided a meeting place for the city's intellectual and cultural elite. The Lodge was, and still is, a charitable service organization with roots in the Medieval period, that nonetheless kept its social distance from the strata of Brussels' population it claimed to serve.

Moreover, as a kind of exclusive, upper crust men's club, *Les Amis* provided Horta with many of his crucial contacts. "'After joining the lodge to devote myself to the public good, I in fact only made friends there with people whose professions prevented them from taking public action or taking any interest in political matters and whose direct character led them more towards privacy and beauty than towards the masses and general vulgarity.'" (Escritt: 76)

Horta's collaboration with Émile Tassel in the completion of Tassel House allows us an excellent example of the changes in Horta's intentions after joining *Les Amis*. Tassel was a professor of mathematics at the University of Brussels, with a specialty in descriptive geometry. He was also an avid amateur photographer. Acting on an unapologetic elitist outlook, he requested a home that would provide a stylish retreat from a demanding public life. In his memoirs, Horta recalled Tassel's "brief for a house for 'a bachelor who took great pleasure in entertaining his close circle of friends, which only scholars and artists could join.'" (Escritt: 76)

The entrance to Tassel House, subtly, but unmistakably baronial, "was dominated by a curvaceous wrought-iron staircase, dramatically writhing wall decorations and vibrantly coloured mosaic floor," (Escritt: 76) The most important interior space, not surprisingly, was Tassel's study, while Horta also carved out of the traditional mezzanine area a laboratory for Tassel's photography equipment. Like so many of his well-educated professional peers, Horta's well-to-do patron held periodic *soirées* in his home.

During these genteel evenings for a select few, he presented scholarly lectures in the dining room, which he illustrated with slide images projected on the far wall. For these intimate occasions, he had asked that Horta include in his plans a guest bathroom, as well as a smoking room nearby, the latter presumably for the small group of *male* friends he'd asked to join him for the evening. It goes without saying that the content of these lectures and the socioeconomic makeup of their audience differed radically from lectures offered by van de Velde for *La Section,* and from the audiences who attended them.

Tassel was both a music enthusiast, with informed classical tastes, and inevitably it now seems, a collector of Japanese prints. In other words, like Horta, he was a cultured gentleman, in tune with intellectual and cultural advances of the times. So, one can comfortably conclude that Horta and his client were kindred spirits, progressive in their experiments with new processes - glass and wrought iron technology for Horta, photography for Tassel - but still quite conservative, or more accurately stated, reactionary, in their discomfort with the great body of Belgian citizens beneath their own social stratum.

On a final descriptive note, one delightfully inconsistent with his dismissal of the "The English School,' Horta agreed to cover the Tassel House drawing room walls with English wallpaper. The wallpaper, designed by Morris's London firm and obtained for him by van de Velde (of all people), was complemented by the upholstery for the drawing room chairs, a daffodil-patterned fabric created for London's Liberty Department Store.

Since Tassel House offered its owner an aesthetically harmonious, restful haven, similar in atmosphere to *Bloemenwerf*, it is tempting to push the analogy between the two Art Nouveau homes further than this shared purpose. But the analogy is, in the end, a false one: while Horta's structural, stylistic, and material decisions were limited by the demands and expectations of his client, van de Velde was testing *his* limits as his ideas for *Bloemenwerf* resolved themselves into concrete realities. Moreover, the planning for any domestic structure in Brussels proper would be literally boxed in by the very scale and proportions traditional for the city's domestic spaces, traditions reinforced by late 19th Century zoning regulations. Van de Velde, although targeted by his neighbors' derision, still had the advantage of a sizeable suburban plot of land, and consequently greater latitude in constructing his family's "model home."

Pattemans points out areas of shortsightedness in Horta's outlook and working practice that might accurately describe the limitations of the majority of European designer/architects in the *fin de siècle* period. He notes that Horta was unaware of or indifferent to the need to associate architecture with town planning and that he exhibited little interest in the relationship between interior and exterior space. (Probably, in this instance, as in others, Horta was respecting his wealthy patrons' wish to remain hidden from a politically restive and divided public.) Of equal significance, Pattemans observes that Horta had little knowledge of the productive potential for an architect in the use of manufactured "standardized parts" (Pattemans: 67)

Indeed, with hindsight, we can see that these areas of shortsightedness on Horta's part the importance of *contextual* urban planning, interior and exterior design coherence, the pragmatic value of standardized parts are the keystones of a modernism in design and architecture that would not take hold in Western Europe until the death knell for Art Nouveau had rung in the first decade of the 20th Century.

A further, pivotal factor in the contrast between Horta and van de Velde, in terms of the link between their achievements and the future of architecture and design, is the functional hitch in the visually coherent Horta interior discussed and applauded above. While Horta did, in fact, exhibit a "willingness to integrate all the component elements of display into architecture," he did so "to such an extent that the very shape of the rooms made it impossible to use furniture which had not been specially designed." (Pattemans: 72) As a result, while the component parts of a particular Horta-commissioned home fit together in a fluent, visually satisfying whole, one that offered the client privacy, comfort, and understated luxury, it ran the risk of becoming a fossil in its own time

In his planning, Horta implicitly posed obstacles to the reorganizing or repurposing of the customized space, to the introduction of new furnishings, and, more important still, to the introduction of modern, labor-saving domestic equipment. As Pattemans notes, Horta, in the 1890s, still had "a long way to go to the functionalist idea of *equipment* [italics mine], linking the composition of the plan to its practical and mechanical purpose; van de Velde was to become one of the first to discover this." (Pattemans: 72) The Horta *Gesamtkunstwerk*, while now a historical treasure, would soon become an architectural anachronism, a graceful, gracious relic geared specifically for a *fin-de-siècle* patron.

The contrast between the two leading Belgian Art Nouveau masters can be extended to the materials and working methods of their respective workshops, although surely there was considerable overlap between the two. Less inclined to participatory workshop process for his craftsmen than van de Velde, Horta employed an army of stone-cutters, wrought-iron workers, and cabinet-makers, "all working from innumerable drawings and plaster casts made in [his] own workshop." (Pattemans: 75) Unlike van de Velde, who was beginning to turn to semi-industrial products in the late 1890s and early 1900s, Horta turned a blind eye to the introduction of reinforced concrete and highly resilient steel for his projects.

Since his chief reference point was Viollet-le-Duc, Gothic Revival theorist and proponent of Medieval cathedral restoration, Horta strayed very rarely from his French mentor's precepts, Viollet-le-Duc's assumption that building would and could only be accomplished in stone, iron, and wood. These precepts lay emphasis specifically on Medieval Gothic functionality, a concept far distant from the radical modernist approach that would reach its apotheosis in Bauhaus experiments of the mid to late 1920s. While Horta had indeed proven his skill in designing and constructing with wrought iron and glass in his plans for the *Maison du Peuple,* his capacity for absorbing technological innovation into the entire range of his projects had been stretched to its limits in the completion of that supremely important public commission.

CHAPTER 6

The Orient and Art Nouveau: The Japanese Infusion

On display in a glassed-in corner of the Riverside Museum's vast, cluttered interior is a modest exhibit outlining Glasgow's commercial and cultural trade with Japan in the two final decades of the 19th Century. A controversial structure designed by Zaha Hadid and completed in 2011, the museum and its multitude of exhibits are intended to showcase Glasgow's singular history in land and sea transport. Alternatively known, in fact, as the Transport Museum, the building is, to a limited degree, a stylistic descendant of the Glasgow School of Art, at least on its exterior.

At once curvilinear and severe, both its imposing entrance and rather forbidding side and back walls are contrived to echo, in abstract form, the wave motion of the gray, choppy Clyde, the river that functions as *sine qua non* in explaining Glasgow's commercial vitality in the late 19th Century. The windows in the niche devoted to trade with Japan look directly on to the Clyde, whose seedy, long-abandoned banks are now undergoing rehabilitation. The renewal process is not directed at regenerating the river's once-critical importance in Britain's ocean-going commerce with Europe and the Commonwealth nations. That would be pointless. Instead, the urban planners focus on developing informational projects that celebrate the Second City of Empire's substantial contribution to Britain's preeminence in19th and early 20th Century world affairs.

The documentation for the Japan exhibit pinpoints the year 1878, during which two Scottish engineers, Henry Dyer and Robert Henry Smith, both teachers in Japan employed by the Japanese government, arranged for an exchange that would benefit both nations. Dispatched from Scotland to Japan was a multi-faceted program of scientific know-how, exported to newly-created Japanese technical colleges through envoys with specialized engineering expertise. These experts were recruited from as many as 20 Scottish companies. Sent, in turn, from Japan to Scotland were 21 crates of handcrafted works of art, resulting in a repository now held in Glaswegian public and private collections that far exceeds any other in Britain. Included in the collections are Japanese woodblock prints, scrolls, screens, ceramic objects, enamelware, and kimonos.

One can draw from this capsule datum three significant conclusions: (1) eagerness to modernize, in industrial terms, on the part of an ambitious Asian nation that had been closed to the Western world from the early 1600s to 1854; (2) the widespread reputation of the Scotch, in particular, for ingenuity in the realms of mechanized manufacture, infrastructural improvements on the urbanscape and, logically enough, shipbuilding. (3) the premium put on fine, handcrafted, exotic goods by a Western community sped willy nilly into industrial mass production, with rampant industrial growth's inevitable downside the production of cheap, shoddy goods in a matter of decades.

As the contents of one display case indicate, exports to Japan from Glasgow also included goods that probably seemed as "exotic," and therefore precious, to denizens of old Edo (Tokyo) as Japanese craft did to Scotch families in Edinburgh: homemade jams; hand-thrown or hand-built, glazed pottery; bolts of woolen cloth. Indeed, the frequent, rather puzzling appearance of plaid robes on figures depicted in late 19th Century Japanese woodblock prints testifies to the popularity of that unmistakably Western fabric in Japan. And to the full reciprocity in the Scottish-Japanese exchange itself.

The Museum's display of a few objects reflecting 19th Century trade relations between Japan and Scotland,is in fact, the proverbial tip of the iceberg in its account of interchange between a thriving British port and an awakening Asian nation whose eventual technological sophistication would render it a major world power, for good or ill, in the 20th Century. Unfortunately, however, the concise exhibit itself is most commonly given short shrift by visitors to Hadid's *magnum opus*, which is scaled to the size of an airplane hangar and crammed with bigger, far more seductive displays: a 10' model of a Cunard Line ocean liner, the Queen Mary; authentic vintage trolley and tram cars; exhaustive documentation recounting the deepening and straightening of the Clyde in the 1880s; the Scottish military's participation in World Wars I and II.

While the pocket reference to trade with Japan can be easily be bypassed in the Riverside Museum, not so commonly overlooked, in a very different museum setting, is the more extensive documentation outlining the impact of Japanese artistic norms on the painting of two Glasgow Boys, George Henry and Edward Atkinson (E.A.) Hormel, after their return to Glasgow from an 18-month stay in Japan. Their illuminating visit, running from 1893 to 1895 and equal in its impact to Mackintosh's 1891 journey through Italy, was jointly financed by the Glaswegian art dealer Alexander Reid and the omnivorous art collector William Burrell. Their generous patrons staked the "Boys" on the assumption that they "would return with new works in keeping with the current taste in Glasgow for paintings influenced by Japanese art" (wall documentation).

Certainly, business interests contributed to Reid's, if not to Burrell's, financial largesse. Reid had already shown and sold the work of French and Dutch painters well known on the continent, Millet and Joseph Israëls among them, at his Glasgow gallery. Fueled by those successes, he no doubt anticipated that the interest of the deep-pocketed, but self-consciously provincial Glaswegian public, for the sophisticated and exotic, i.e., the experimental and strange, would probably extend to paintings by Glaswegian artists clearly marked by Asian artistic norms.

The Glasgow Boys are given full and riveting exposure in the grand and unabashedly *pastiche* Kelvingrove Museum, a splendidly palatial, but nonetheless welcoming sandstone pile, all towers and turrets, a pleasant stroll from Glasgow University, in the city's lively, leafy West End. The curatorial statement introducing the Japanese influence on the Glasgow Boys notes that the fashion for Japanese art in Britain was actually initiated by James McNeill Whistler, whose enthusiasm fostered the spread of interest in England of all things Japanese during the American expatriate's long-term stay in London. (Perhaps of more than tangential relevance here is Whistler's own Scottish ancestry on his mother's side, well known to Scottish artists and their collectors.)

The Kelvingrove curators note that Japanese motifs and compositional influences can be seen in much of the Boys' work from the mid-1880s on. It reveals itself in flattened perspectives, high horizon lines, and decorative patterning on clothing. Further, many Glasgow "Boys," who were, of course, gifted, accomplished, determined men, themselves owned Japanese woodblock *ukiyo-e* prints, whose stylistic elements moved inexorably into their approach to the canvas. For that matter, the engraved depictions of old Edo's "floating world" of transient pleasures can occasionally be glimpsed, painted in miniature, in the backgrounds of their work. Typically half-hidden in the upper left or right-hand corner, the depictions serve as points of reference for the artists' stylistic innovation. In a larger sense, they indicate a debt owed by Henry and Hormel to their Japanese mentors.

The most blatantly *Japoniste* work in the Kelvingrove collection is the small, brilliantly colored "Japanese Lady with a Fan," completed by George Henry in 1894. The shape of the lady's hair, along with her kimono and fan, are accomplished with a freedom of brushstroke unprecedented in Henry's work of the 1880s, while the stylization of branches laden with cherry blossoms at the top left suggests nothing so much as Japanese calligraphy. The contrast between this vivid pictorial jewel, whose painterly handling verges on abstraction, and several paintings accomplished by Henry a decade earlier, is striking.

Already, midway between Henry's and Hormel's initial rejection of academic restrictions in the early 1880s and their sojourn in Japan in the early 1890s, the two were moving away from both Millet and Courbet-influenced naturalism *and* the Impressionist emphasis on the effect of light on perception of form. Indeed, both were moving toward their own brand of Scottish Symbolism. The increasing intensity of their palettes, diminished attention to naturalistic detail, and growing fascination with pattern emerged from a conflation of two complementary traditions: the Japanese and the Celtic.

In the late 1880s, dispensing with horizon lines and perspective altogether, they painted turbulent, outsize canvasses that "resembled nothing else painted in Britain at the time and when exhibited in Europe received great acclaim" (wall documentation), as the Kelvingrove curators state with admirable directness. For that matter, the vigorous, but, oddly claustrophobic pictures flanking the Kelvingrove's understated curatorial documentation would startle visitors to any cutting-edge New York venue even now. As collaborators, Henry and Hormel seem to have given each other permission to throw both academic convention and entrenched critical taste to the wind, and paint as they willed.

"The Druids: Bringing in the Mistletoe," a collaborative work accomplished by Henry and Hormel in 1890, is a dazzling exemplar of the bravado with which the two Glaswegians approached their painting in the late 1880s They depict an apparently slow, crowded procession down a hill, in a color scheme dominated by brilliant reds and turquoise. Little or no attention is paid to the relative size of each figure to the others as dictated by their position in three-dimensional space. Clothing is richly patterned, and gold leaf liberally applied throughout the image and on the frame. So as to drive home to the viewer the ancient Celtic experience informing the painting's narrative, Hormel, an amateur archaeologist, scoured the Galloway countryside for cup-and-ring marks in the earth or on ancient Celtic stone structures. At his, not Henry's, instigation, this ancient Celtic symbol found its way into the painting in the form of a crescent-shaped ornament (or *lunula)* applied pervasively to the canvas itself, and to the frame.

Since "The Druids" was completed, exhibited, and widely praised, at least on the continent, three years before Henry and Hormel departed for Japan, it would be illogical to search for signs of Japanese influence in this astounding work, which bears a strong resemblance to Ensor's in its let-out-all-the-stops flamboyance and surreality. However, the piece and companion pieces of the same year do make clear the readiness of the two Glasgow Boys to absorb novel stylistic elements of the art they encountered in Japan over an 18-month period, and then funnel the elements they found sympathetic to their own natural bent into their work.

From the nearest underground station, the approach to the Glasgow School of Art, for many the most important stop on the "Mackintosh Line," involves a steep climb up Renfrew Street for those on foot, an ascent demanding considerable physical stamina and determination. The punishing climb reinforces through first hand, breathless experience, the scholarly emphasis commonly placed on the challenge for Mackintosh, in adjusting his plans for the School to the topography of its new location. Admittedly, as well, the first glimpse of the Glasgow School of Art can trigger a conflicting set of reactions in a Mackintosh *dévoté* who has long looked forward to the visit.

Given GSA's reputation as "the first modern building," it is undeniably thrilling, even a bit uncanny, to see the canonic structure in the context of its own neighborhood, rather than isolated and enhanced in professional photographs. Undeniably thrilling, but somewhat disconcerting, since the Glasgow School of Art is a surprisingly small, unobtrusive edifice by twenty-first century standards. Also disconcerting is the degree to which this world-renowned, fully functioning center for design education literally merges visually with the unexceptional buildings that surround it on all sides.

And downright confounding, even off-putting, is the school's East Facade running along Dalhousie Street, a cobblestone road that presents another steep incline at right angles to Renfrew. The East Facade, dominated by a blank stone wall, presents so forbidding a face that GSA as a whole strikes one as uncomfortably prison-like when approached from that direction. One wonders: is the unlovely, utilitarian appearance of this architectural emblem of Scottish culture intentional, a reflection of its striving for modernity in the late 19th Century? Was Mackintosh, in carrying out his commission, determined to change the time-honored ground rules for architectural significance in public buildings? Or does the visitor's disappointment respond to aesthetic shortsightedness in the part of the great architect. An observation of this sort may amount to sacrilege for Mackintosh admirers, but the possibility is still there.

Thankfully, the frustrated expectations are dispelled, at least in part, as one mounts the stairs, framed by a slender, wrought iron arch, to the tall doors of GSA's main entrance on Renfrew Street, constructed in the 1896-99 period. The sheer act of entering GSA's precincts is a serious processional process. Moreover, the severity of the famed, and endlessly photographed, North facade entrance is, as Steele puts it, "both attenuated and endorsed by the wrought iron window brackets bracing the huge studio windows," (Steele 45) those brackets famously topped by stylized wrought iron roses. Those acquainted with Steele's impressive Mackintosh study, "Synthesis in Form," will also make note of the eight stanchions, rising 17' through clusters of wrought iron rose buds and ending in circular plates, each different, "whose motifs have been compared to Japanese Mon heraldic elements." (Steele 49)

Once inside, one's possible disappointment with GSA's exterior is further offset by the energetic presentations of the school tour guides, in this writer's case an enthusiastic young Scot named Andrew Houghton. Andrew offers explanation, if not justification, for many of the School of Art's troubling, or baffling features, of which the grim East Facade is just one. He informs us, for example, that the yellow sandstone cladding selected for the building's exterior reflects Mackintosh's determination *not* to distinguish the expanded Glasgow School of Art from the tenements, also clad in sandstone, that surrounded the new structure.

The idealistic young architect, having emerged himself from the "upper lower middle class" and not yet 30 when he won the commission, had after all been a GSA student himself in the 1880s. He had taken classes toward the end of the 50-year period (1845-1896) when the school's curriculum was solely intended to prepare students for draughting or design positions in shipbuilding and related industries. Indeed, in those decades, the student body had been drawn primarily from lower middle class families very likely housed in those very tenements next door, or in buildings like them, elsewhere in Glasgow.

Our guide's additional comments on the planning of the East Facade further succeed in softening its initial, rather chilling visual impression. The facade has a varied roofline, several different window types placed in no apparent pattern, and a centrally located tower. As noted earlier, these are key structural components of the Scottish Baronial Manor, an architectural tradition native to Scotland for centuries, and long a point of departure in Mackintosh's thought process as he carried out his commissions. In 1891, in fact, he had lectured on the Scottish Baronial style to the Glasgow Architectural Association, drawing on "The Castellated and Domesticated Architecture of Scotland (1887-1892), by MacGibbon and Ross. In his drawings for the East Facade, he had channeled his advocacy of Scotland's architectural vernacular into an imposing, if uninviting element in GSA's structure.

As we follow Andrew through what seems a labyrinth of narrow hallways, mounting and descending steep staircases with worn treads, our guide adds piquant data new even to Mackintosh afficionados familiar with the architect's work through scholarly accounts. He explains, for example, that the eight-year hiatus between the first stage, 1896-1899, and the second stage, 1907-1909, of GSA's construction was owed to baserock economics, a stumbling block rarely mentioned in scholarly texts. Headed by the visionary "Fra" Newberry, the School's GSA's Board of Governors, the School's commissioners, simply ran out of money in 1899, after two years' steady draughting and redraughting of plans on Mackintosh's part, and hands-on labor on the part of the engineers, infrastructural specialists, and handcraftsmen assisting him. Some of these specialists had been recruited directly from Glasgow's shipyards.

While the hiatus is common knowledge, not so commonly known is the source of the funds that enabled Mackintosh to complete the expansion of the school, albeit in more radical, modernist stylistic terms than those of the first stage. Those funds, and the project's rescue, were provided by Catherine Cranston, one of Charles' and Margaret's faithful clients.

So, there is some irony here, in that the income from a primarily commercial enterprise, Miss Cranston's tea rooms, should have been recycled into a municipal building whose *raison d'ètre* was fine and applied arts education, a purpose at once noble and practical in terms of Glasgow's future position on the Western world's cultural map. This was a goal in sharp contrast with the mundane provision of tea, cakes, and an agreeable setting for social interchange. A woman of high intelligence, enterprise, and determination herself, Cranston was certainly moved by the fact that a sizeable number of students admitted for instruction to the expanded GSA would be, like her tea room clientéle, women.

While our guide's informative narrative is both substantial and engaging, many of his comments cannot be verified through first-hand encounter with the rooms they describe, since much of GSA's intricate interior is off-limits to visitors. Newberry's elegant, luminous Director's Room, for instance, is out of bounds for us, its white wall panelling, round, unpretentious work table, deep arched window recess, and hanging light fixtures a reflection of the Director's progressive taste in interior design. The lamps, in particular, are noteworthy for those unmistakeable signs of Japanese influence: they are rectilinear and contrived of thin sheet metal, their sides perforated with geometric patterning. They hang and shed light unobtrusively, strikingly unlike the ornate, cumbersome chandeliers common to Victorian homes and public buildings of the period.

A further disappointment for the visitor is lack of access to the art studios themselves, those innovative, "purpose-built" Mackintosh studios, with their expanses of vertically-oriented windows and exposure to north light, indirect light which, as every artist knows, lasts the longest. These were structural elements mandated by Newberry, a painter himself, who introduced into the GSA curriculum the then-revolutionary Aesthetic Movement concept of "art for art's sake." The limits set on tourist entry to studios extend to Studio 58, located at the west end of GSA's top floor. Here, the roof of the studio is supported by wooden columns and beams, "rather than a system of roof trusses as used elsewhere in the building." (GSA documentation) As illustrated documentation in GSA's ground floor anteroom points out, the shape of the ceiling and wooden supports "suggest Japanese techniques."

Nevertheless, what our tour lacks in comprehensiveness, and, on occasion, coherence, it makes up for in valuable particulars, some enshrined in Mackintosh biographies, others, like the reference to Miss Cranston, quite unexpected. For example, plaster casts of classical figures those used by 19th Century students for figure drawing exercise, sit on pedestals lining the west corridor leading to GSA's library, the celebrated masterwork of the School's second construction stage (1907-

1909). The casts' pale classical presence seems oddly at home in a bare-bones interior that feels, at times, like the inside of a factory.

The corridor also features a skylight through which Glasgow's constantly appearing and disappearing sunlight pours, the windows' ogive-shaped wooden cross beams, with grain exposed, an allusion to the Gothic cathedral structural elements that appear frequently in Mackintosh's work. With regard to light sources, of special interest is Andrew's comment on GSA's all-important lighting system. He notes that, to supplement the architect's efforts at taking full advantage of natural light whenever possible, either through skylights or tall, story-spanning windows, the School did install electric lighting in the late 1890s. The system, a technological novelty at the time, served as further evidence of GSA's groundbreaking modernism. He goes on to note that the otherwise egalitarian Newberry could and did control its use from his central post in the Director's Office, a paternalistic behavior more in line with conservative Victorian attitudes than those one would expect of an educational reformer fresh from London's *avant garde* culture.

Somehow, some way, before actually entering GSA's near-sacred space, its library, we are led through the rarely discussed "hen run" a clear, if provocative reference to GSA's female student body, to the loggia, a wide, bright veranda-like walkway illuminated by a series of wide, arched windows, identical in curvilinear frame to those in the Director's Office. The loggia is a far more inviting space than any we've seen before on our tour. Most curious and exciting is the series of unfaced, supportive brick archways framing the walkway, their material makeup, in fact their entire mode of construction, undisguised, and yet in appearance aesthetically "right," as they would be in a vernacular Japanese structure.

Indeed, throughout our somewhat confusing, but delightful, breakneck tour of GSA's maze-like interior, I felt slight, but unignorable echoes of Japanese architectural norms. Now the echoes, the sense of *déjà vu* for this yearlong resident of Tokyo, are about to be intensified, as we follow our guide into the School's most celebrated space, the library. Steele articulates the libraary's charm in romantic terms: "The library is arguably the most complex space at the Glasgow School of Art and Mackintosh's most dramatic interior. Resembling a fantastical forest with its slender wooden columns, it has a dreamlike quality that transcends its restrictive boundaries." (Steele 65)

Sadly, however, the first impression of GSA's library for visitors primed by photos contrived to show to advantage elements new for the time is again one of disappointment. As promised, the library's windows are indeed three-stories high, but they allow in daylight through only *one* exterior wall. Moreover, depending on where one stands, the constantly shifting daylight is either interrupted or completely blocked by the profusion of those slender wooden columns.

As promised, the quality of a student's experience, as he works at one of the desk-and-chair combinations on the main floor, does resemble that of a solitary traveller through a dense forest. But the dark-stained posts that surround him, while protecting his privacy and ensuring steady concentration, emphasize both the library's verticality and the fact that this is, in fact a very modestly scaled, rather cramped space. (The load-bearing appearance of the posts is deceptive, as the room is actually suspended on two steel beams. The posts, for that matter,s don't reach all the way to the ceiling, as is the case for those in Miss Cranston's Oak Room.).

The Japanese influence on GSA's planning reveals itself here not only in the slim, dark-stained columns, strongly suggestive of quasi-tree trunks, but also in the light fixtures suspended on chains from the ceiling. The elegant, rectilinear hanging lamps "form a great sculptural cluster in the space," and "consist of pierced brass and zinc forms, inset with coloured glass. (Steele 64). The colors are blue, purple, and magenta, consistently favored by Charles and Margaret, and the muted, multi-colored light virtually poured from above serves to enhance the library's overall atmosphere of intimacy.

Cramped quarters notwithstanding, be it said that this is not the claustrophobic intimacy generated by heavy, ornately carved furniture, stuffed cushions, busily patterned carpets, fussy wallpaper, and windows curtained in silk or velvet, all tokens of Victorian taste, but the intimacy sensed in a forest grove, where one feels a soothing affinity with the natural world. This is the variety of intimacy sought, in fact, by the 16th Century architect of the traditional Japanese tea house and his descendants, in their design and construction of the Japanese private home.

In the introduction to her concise, but trenchant overview of Japanese art, Joan Stanley-Baker addresses the issue of influence from the Japanese standpoint. She pinpoints two "distinct ways in which the Japanese have reacted to foreign stimuli." The first she defines as "a spontaneous identification with and a rapid absorption of those new ideas which struck a responsive chord in the Japanese artist." (Stanley-Baker 8) This is the sort of identification that drove Henry and Hormel to integrate Japanese stylistic norms into their painting and Charles Rennie Mackintosh to incorporate Japanese structural, spatial, and stylistic norms into his commissioned projects of the 1890s.

Stanley-Baker then goes on to define a second, contrasting tendency in Japanese borrowings from foreign sources: "When required by self-conscious patrons, the mastery of styles and processes which might at first seem unbridgeably alien or mysterious." (Stanley-Baker 8) This determination to grasp in conceptual terms, and apply in practical terms, techniques of fabrication and stylistic approaches alien to Japanese tradition surely explains the two-fold effort made by Japanese officialdom shortly after the signing of the trade treaty with the United States in 1854: to import Scottish experts in engineering and shipbuilding, while same time sending Japanese students abroad, to apprentice in Glasgow shipyards and take engineering courses at the University of Glasgow.

The dichotomy in Japanese response to foreign influence defined above is, of course, common to all homogenous groups in their encounters with unfamiliar, but intriguing cultural, commercial, or technological norms: intuitive empathy on the one hand; pragmatic opportunism, larded with envy, on the other. But, for Japan in the latter half of the 19th Century, this dual response was intensified by the island nation's isolation from the outside world for 200 years. Later in her account, Stanley-Baker's insight into the creative mindset of traditional Japanese craftsmen carries us smoothly into a deeper understanding of Japan's legendary impact on most Art Nouveau masters, those who bucked both *pastiche* historicism and the decline of quality in the functional arts, a decline they perceived as linked to rapid, profit-oriented industrialization.

She notes that the "key to understanding the relationship of the Japanese artist or craftsman to his work lies in one word: union." (Stanley-Baker 13) The union she points to is exemplified by Japanese ceramicists, who incorporate the essence of the potting process, fingerprints in the clay or kiln accidents, in the completed vessel, or by woodworkers, who allow chisel marks or wood grain to remain visible in the finished piece. As a result, if we extend the principle of "union" to all the crafts, the marks of the artisanal process operate as an "integral and essential part of the finished work." (Stanley Baker 13-14)

Stanley-Baker elaborates: "The artist and his materials, clay, wood or ink-brush and paper, together create the work. This factor is of paramount importance. Considerations basic to other cultures, such as the obliteration of all traces of the creative process, such as chisel marks, exposed wood grain, or fingerprints, are often of no importance." (Stanley-Baker 14) Moreover, in a statement that resonates remarkably with both Celtic and Bauhaus design ethos she observes that "decoration and form are aspects of a single whole." (Stanley-Baker 14) And what qualities are unpalatable to Japanese sensibility? Among them are regularity, along with its partner, repetition, monumentality, equilateral symmetry, rigidly demarcated interior spaces in architecture, hard and shiny surfaces, and concepts of permanence and immutability. (Stanley-Baker 14)

Stanley-Baker's meticulous, brick-by-brick introduction to Japanese art, craft, and architecture has an unintended consequence. As she proceeds, she inadvertently lists a surprising number of stylistic biases that might easily inform a discussion of numerous Mackintosh achievements, the Glasgow School of Art and Charles' and Margaret's custom-designed Mains Street home among them. As for conscious intentions, Stanley-Baker is outlining a set of culturally-ingrained stylistic features that together inform the traditional Japanese tea house. (Any resemblance to the tea rooms designed for Catherine Cranston by Mackintosh and Macdonald is purely coincidental. Probably.)

The ritualized Japanese experience of drinking tea in quiet surroundings was instituted by the 15th Century tea-master Shuko. The ceremony was, and is, conceived as an art form, to be enjoyed in a small room contrived for the communal ceremony alone. In its early decades, the tea room displayed such rarefied items as paintings depicting the tea ritual, calligraphy scrolls, and fine Chinese celadon vessels. However, in the 16th Century, Sen no Rikyo, a distinguished and influential tea-master of the wealthy *sakai* merchant class effected an overhaul of the tea room interior, guided by his own Spartan views on the Way of Tea. For example, favoring rough-textured, irregular peasant ware, he rejected the jade-like perfection of the pale green celadons. (Stanley-baker 148)

In 1582, at the mature age of 61, Rikyu built the *Tai-an*, his own personal teahouse, in a modest hut in his native Yamazaki. The *Tai-an* was a simple, rustic, cedar structure, its overall conception guided by the principles of asymmetry and irregularity noted above. Its interior was characterized by rough-textured earthen walls and unpolished, exposed beams, while the ceilings of the bi-level structure were covered by cedar board, with wood grain fully exposed. Papered, as opposed to glass-paned, windows of different shapes were set at varying heights above the seated guests' heads, dimming and softening whatever available light filtered in from the outside. (Stanley-Baker 148)

Guests in the teahouse, all male and well-to-do, were invited to leave their worldly concerns behind when they gathered in the *Tai-an*, through the exclusivity of the experience and through their warm, dimly lit, intimate surroundings. In the *Tai-an*, friends were brought together to commune privately, at ease and in close proximity, led in the tea ceremony itself by a master, whose every move became their own. (Stanley-Baker 149)

In line with Rikyu's reformist agenda, his tea room guests now drank from *raku* cups. Indeed, the development of the famed *raku* pottery style emerged from Rikyu's rejection of Chinese celadon, *raku*'s conventional asymmetry echoing that of the teahouse as a whole. Moreover, irregularity characterizes both mouth and feet of the *raku* vessel, as does the absence of surface decoration, which is supplanted by a glaze of dull, matt black slip of irregular density. The *raku* vessel tapers slightly from base to mouth, with no effort made to disguise or hide the foot rim. (Stanley-Baker 149)
That is to say, the *raku* pot is one of those Japanese functional craft objects whose materials and fabrication remain visible in the finished piece. And contrary to expectation, in its very asymmetry, lack of ornament, dark, irregular surface and avoidance of other standard signs of finish, the *raku* vessel inevitably appears self-ratifying and perfect.

The style of architecture (*sukiya*) developed by Rikyu for his tea house, innovative for its time, was eventually extended into Japanese domestic architecture as a whole, and now constitutes a national tradition that reflects the "intense Japanese need for the preservation of the private self as distinct from the public face." Always a hallmark of the tradition is the emphasis on rusticity. Structural elements on the exterior and interior are exposed, but never lacquered, "echoing the effect of rusticity and airiness which harmonizes the interior and exterior space." (Stanley-Baker 149)

These statements may seem contradictory and raise further questions for some Western readers. One may wonder: if the Japanese domestic interior is geared for privacy, for escape from the larger community, then why the concern for harmony between exterior and interior? Why not play it the Belgian way: a plain facade masking an elegant, luxurious interior? The comments gain greater consistency, however, if one takes into account the heightened sensitivity to the natural world inherent in the collective Japanese outlook. This sensitivity, expressed in the tenets of the ancient Shinto religion, is manifested in the attempt to replicate that natural world, raw and untouched, in one's domestic haven, inside *and* out.

In addition to a general quality of rusticity - posts, cross beams, trusses and other wooden structural elements exposed, and stained, rather than painted, so as to leave grain visible; irregularly placed windows; an intimate, warm, dimly-lit interior; a gradual process of construction - each shift in plans reacted to the patron's changing needs. It is impossible for the student of Mackintosh's career not to correlate these Japanese architectural norms, conventional in teahouses and domestic structures, with similar stylistic elements in Mackintosh's *oeuvre*, particularly the Glasgow School of Art. Witness the apparently random placement of windows and irregular roofline of the East Facade, the exposed brickwork of the loggia, the dark-stained wood posts and railings of the library; the idiosyncratic relationship of each staircase, hallway, gallery, studio, administrator's room to the others.

Generally speaking, Mackintosh's design decisions are said to respond to the need for economy, in combination with his affection for the salient architectural characteristics of the Scottish Baronial Manor. Less frequently, scholars note as well the mark of the strictly utilitarian tenements and factories defining Glasgow's cityscape. However, by the time he began work on GSA, Mackintosh had already internalized and made his own an understanding of Japanese design and architectural principles acquired mainly from his and Margaret's collection of Japanese ceramics and woodblock prints. And clearly, his assimilation of those "exotic" principles would not have been so profound, had they not resonated so fully with his own.

Pamela Robertson identifies three *ukiyo-e* prints in Mackintosh and Macdonald's collection, all shown in views of the couple's Mains Street apartment. Two of the three, both *surimono,* were a wedding present from the ubiquitous architectural reformer and *Japoniste* Hermann Muthesius. (Robertson email of 4/2/13) In addition, Mackintosh had easy access to a wealth of photographs brought back from Japan by fellow artists Henry and Hormel, as well as those taken by engineers and shipbuilding experts sent to Japan to pass on their expertise.

Robertson further emphasizes the likelihood that Mackintosh absorbed information on Japanese architecture published in English language texts of the 1880s and 1890s. In that regard, she notes that "the connection between the southwest transept gallery of Queens Cross Church, which projects into the body of the church on deep, closely-set joists, may have been influenced by the illustration of an Old Inn at Mishima in E.S.Morse's *Japanese Homes and their Surroundings.*" (Robertson email of 4/2/13) As a result, it's probable that the young architect borrowed stylistic traits consonant with his own taste for simplicity, easy functionality, and "honest" use of materials from prints and photographs of Japanese domestic structures. If those traits echoed and reinforced Scottish influences noted above, and were in keeping with the tenets of the Arts and Crafts Movement he so admired, all the better.

It is hard to square what we take for granted in our time, the pervasive commercial, technological, and cultural presence of Japan on the international landscape, with the island nation's near-240-year enforced isolation from nearly all other communities on our planet. But such is the historical reality. Until March 31, 1854 and the signing of a treaty between representatives of the United States government, led by Commodore Matthew Perry, and its Japanese counterpart, the ethnically homogeneous Asian archipelago had been closed to all but a small number of Chinese and Dutch traders for over two centuries.

The United States initiated the negotiations that put an end to Japanese isolationist policy, *sakoku*, long kept in place by the implacable Tokugawa shogunate, in hopes that the Japanese would agree to opening several of their ports to foreign ships, first and foremost, American ships. Two pragmatic objectives drove the American mission, a mission which should be defined as ambitious and optimistic, but still exploratory: (1) growing interest in a potential Japanese market for Western manufactured goods; (2) the opportunity for the wide-ranging American commercial whaling fleet to replenish its energy source, coal, as well as supplies for survival on board ship, in Japanese harbors. The final signing of the March, 1854 treaty was the culmination of a lengthy, exhausting process for the Americans, involving two separate expeditions to and from Japan, in 1853 and 1854, each simultaneously naval, that is, aggressively military, and diplomatic, that is, strategically civil.

The actual signing of the agreement, in fact, reputedly followed weeks of lengthy, exhaustive, and exhausting talks. As for the treaty itself, the First Article states, somewhat vaguely and generically, a promise of peace and friendship between the United States and Japan. However, the Second, Third, and Fourth Articles move swiftly into more concrete areas and issues, all three of major concern for the Americans: the opening of the ports of Shimoda and Hakadute to American ships, specifically for purposes of trade; help for any American ship wrecked on the Japanese coast; permission for American ships to buy coal, fresh water, and necessary provisions in Japanese ports.

For Japan, the signing of the treaty represented the first documented, mutually agreed-upon relationship with any Western nation other than Holland, since the start of the isolationist period centuries earlier. The treaty provided few specifics regarding import and export for commercial purposes, specifics regarding tariffs, for example. Nevertheless, and of far greater long term importance, it marked the beginning of the modern era in Japan. So, given the exceptional productivity of Glasgow's shipyards in the final decades of the 19th Century, and given the exceptional nature of Scotland's trade with Japan in that period, there is profit in recounting the dramatic entry of Commodore Perry's American flotilla into Edo (Tokyo) Bay on July 8, 1853.

Perry commanded four black-painted ships, led by the USS Powhattan. As yet ignorant of the existence of steam-powered vessels, both Japanese officials and crowds of onlookers were shocked by the sight of mighty black ships spewing clouds of grey smoke, which they naïvely misconstrued as "giant dragons puffing smoke." More shocking and fearsome still were the number and size of guns on board each vessel. Needless to say, the reaction was the one Perry intended. However, while the appearance of the intimidating Western ships, with their load of weaponry and noisome power source, at first generated a mix of awe and terror among the Japanese. Those emotions were rapidly supplanted by admiration, envy, and the desire for emulation. Moreover, this mix of emotions would ultimately be translated into productive action in Japan's shipbuilding sector later in the 19th Century.

Matthew Galbraith Perry, age 60 in 1853, could boast a long and distinguished career in the military. Certain of success, he had brought to Japan a letter from the American President Millard Fillmore addressed to the Japanese Emperor. Both Perry and the American Supreme Commander had naïvely assumed that the Emperor's political clout equaled that of the President of the United States. Self-confident and stubborn, Perry waited in his private quarters on board ship, refusing to see any of the lesser dignitaries sent by the Japanese and insisting on discussing terms of agreement only with the Emperor's highest emissaries.

In contrast, the official Japanese response to the imposing Western naval force occupying its home waters was ambivalent. Hostile and suspicious, the Japanese authorities nevertheless realized that they could no longer maintain their isolationist position without risking invasion and war, one in which they would surely be outgunned and defeated. The message sent to the Japanese by Perry and his officers, through the menacing nature of their steam-spewing ships and arsenal of modern weaponry, was unmistakable: if they were refused diplomatic contact with Japan's highest dignitary, they would very likely bombard Tokyo, as well as Japan's other major port cities.

The Americans, however, made one serious error in their calculations, tough and intransigent as was their stance in Tokyo's harbor. This error arose from their misunderstanding of the relationship between the Emperor and the Tokugawa shogunate, the latter long dominant in the isolationist period. Indeed, in the larger sense, the Americans were ignorant in general of the inflexible nature of Japanese class divisions as a whole. Admittedly, one would be hard put to find a society, East or West, that has been at any point free of class distinctions, whatever the basis for the stratification. Nonetheless, those distinctions in isolationist Japan had been uniquely unbreachable for centuries.

Essential to grasp here is the position of the Emperor in Japan when Perry arrived, an ironic position that remained in place until the Meiji Restoration of the Emperor to political primacy in 1868. Although still the nation's religious leader, the Emperor had, in the 1850s, none of the political control Perry assumed he owned. Instead, the traditional leader was habitually confined to the palace grounds in old Edo, now Tokyo, where he spent his time studying and reading poetry. Spied upon continually, he was permitted no visitors without the presiding *shogun*'s permission. While revered as a deity, he was nonetheless, in real terms, treated as a prisoner.

As a result, Perry had unwittingly set his sights on the wrong person in his insistence on meeting with the man at the top. That man was *not* the impotent Emperor, but the power behind the throne, the reigning Tokugawa *shogun.* The latter ruled Japan in the *de facto* sense, generating laws covering all aspects of communal and family life, and concocting intricate rules of personal conduct. Not surprisingly, given the Tokugawa shogunate's wide scope of control, this reigning social entity, whose hegemony lasted for an amazing 700 years, was rarely subject to the laws and rules of conduct it devised and mercilessly enforced.

A brief overview of Japan's traditional social stratification is helpful here, as its singular nature bears significantly on the Asian nation's commercial and cultural trade with Western countries both before and after the 1854 treaty. One rung below the shogunate, a larger class of *daimyo* comprised landowners, an economically secure group nonetheless regulated by the *shogun*'s laws. These laws determined, for example, such minutiae as the number of laborers the *daimyo* could own and/or employ, and the size of the castles they could construct. Allowed to socialize only within their own districts, as a hedge against possible alliances and plotting against the shogunate, the landowners paid for castle, road, and fortress repairs. These were measures designed to prevent the *daimyo* from becoming too wealthy or powerful.

Obviously, the clamp on this otherwise comfortable *daimyo* class was uncomfortably tight.

One rung below the *daimyo* were the *samurai* warriors, employed by the *daimyo* and probably the most romantic figures in what can only be termed a feudal socioeconomic hierarchy. The *samurai* are familiar to Western audiences through Japanese films of the 1950s, typically shown in urban *cinémathèques* and on American college campuses. In fact, the classic films of Akira Kurosawa draw plot, characters, and setting from the period called the Era of the Warring States (ca. 1340-1540). During this period, numerous *daimyo*, strikingly similar in rank and ambition to Medieval European "lords of the manor," took possession of their fiefdoms through the disciplined, ferocious military prowess of their retainers, the *samurai*. The only caste allowed to carry swords, these warriors operated through a rigid code of honor and were expected to give up their lives for their lords, the *daimyo*, without hesitation. In turn, the *samurai* exerted limited control over the three classes beneath them in social status: farmers, artisans, and merchants. All this, while dependent on the *daimyo* for a small salary.

The emergence and ascendancy of the *samurai* warrior class can be traced as far back as the Kamakura Period (1192-1333), a period roughly corresponding to the height of the Medieval period in Europe; that is, to the Crusades and the construction of the great Gothic cathedrals. A mere 140 years witnessed the displacement of the Emperor and the aristocracy by an alliance of *daimyo* and *shogun*, led by the military dictator Minamoto Yoritomo. From 1192 on, the deposed Emperor and his court were isolated on a remote seaside village named Kamakura. (Interesting to note, Kamakura is now a suburb of Tokyo and a tourist hotspot, notable for an enormous bronze sculpture of the Buddha and private homes that served as models of domestic design for Frank Lloyd Wright in the first decade of the 20th Century.).

In light of their singular relationship to the fine and applied arts, the *samurai* merit further discussion in a study of the Japanese impact on Western culture, including design movements like Art Nouveau. The consolidation of combined *shogun, daimyo,* and *samurai* power in the late 12th and 13th Centuries, along with the political stability that resulted, permitted far greater attention to refinement in all the arts, attention that extended to the fabrication of weapons and armor. Universally celebrated for its light weight, flexibility and protective properties against the elements *and* against enemy attack, Japanese armor is distinctive in its effective use of a lightweight organic material, leather, rather than the rigid, suffocating metal plating and chain link traditional in the West.

Moreover, the lethal nature of a sharpened Japanese sword blade is proverbial. That is to say, as early as the Medieval period, even in the fabrication armor and weaponry, the Japanese were gaining maximum advantage from minimal materials, and integrating practical function with elegant form. The Japanese warrior in his armor could fight with surpassing speed and agility, while his appearance still suggested fearsome power. In addition, unlike most of their Western peers, many *samurai* were painters, poets, and men of learning, a radical split in intellectual and psychological focus that indicates equal emphasis on two opposing realms, the art of war and the peacetime arts. This extreme split in focus, in the same individual, was surely not lost on Western artists, architects and designers, who were accustomed to viewing military heroes merely as effective, but artistically insensitive warriors. Moreover, in light of that split in focus, it is useful to outline here the introduction of Buddhism into Japan in the 19th Century.

Originating in India, Buddhist philosophy was later introduced into China and Japan, rapidly attracting large numbers of adherents in both nations. The philosophy rests on the linked tenets of mental and physical discipline. These tenets, so appealing to the honor-bound Japanese *samurai*, were clearly as applicable to the peacetime arts as to the art of war, so that a meticulously crafted poem resounded to one's capacity for disciplined action as fully as a victory in battle. So the adoption of the Buddhist outlook may very well have played a role in the unique ability of the *samurai* to fight ferociously on the battlefield at one point and create exquisite lyric poetry at another. (Importantly, in terms of numbers, when Perry and his men sailed into Tokyo Harbor in the mid- 1850's, 250 daimyo had a virtual army of 35, 000 multi-gifted samurai knights in their employ.

One final Japanese social class remains for examination, this one an enterprising group whose members comprised both merchants and artisans. In status alone, both artisans and merchants had for centuries been perceived as lower class, unworthy of the respect and deference accorded their social betters. However, by the time Perry sailed into Tokyo Bay, the two groups, pooling their skills, constituted one of the wealthiest in Japan, although their ever more manifest economic advantage was still, to some degree, undercut by the restrictions placed on them by *shogun* and *daimyo*. Spied upon like the Emperor, these unlikely bedfellows, were forced to carry on their fine artisanal manufacture and profitable trade within and without Japan, the latter with the assistance and mercantile skill of Dutch traders,, with caution and guile. If they appeared too prosperous or flaunted their wealth too openly, the shogunate would be quick to confiscate their businesses.

The emergence of Japan's vigorous merchant class can be traced to the late 15th Century. Its fortunes lay in money lending and the brewing of beer (Stanly-Baker 152), the former doubtless as indispensable to the economic survival, and the latter to the high spirits of their Japanese clientèle as to their counterparts in urban centers on the European continent. The emergence of the Japanese *commerçant* runs parallel with that of the shogunate, the class of "dictator-warlords" who would swiftly replace an increasingly impoverished aristocracy as Japan's dominant social order, and eventually close the nation's ports to the outside world.

Events in this late 15th Century period then followed an unprecedented course. Forming a *de facto* league, in which economic need trumped traditional social barriers, aristocrats and merchants perforce became allies. "The aristocracy often depended on the merchants to bail them out of financial difficulties and the latter, through frequent contacts with the court, soon developed similar cultural preferences." (Stanley-Baker 152) So, in Japan, the productive bond between enterprising traders and skilled artisans had its origins in another kind of mutally profitable exchange: financial support supplied to the displaced aristocracy by prosperous traders in exchange for refined aristocratic taste in art, poetry and all aspects of the applied arts.

What we see in 1854, then, at the end of Japan's long years of communal xenophobia and enforced insularity, is a peculiar system of socioeconomic checks and balances, in which one social stratum, the shogunate, held sway over all the others, to the extent that none - not the *daimyo*, not the *samurai*, not the combined energies and skills of craftsmen and merchants - posed any threat to the shoogunate's domination. Nevertheless, through a strategy merging stunning productivity in the applied arts, ingenuity and aggression in domestic and foreign trade, and sheer guile, a "dark horse" socioeconomic group did emerge, one whose growing wealth allowed them a steady climb up the socioeconomic ladder and expanding political clout.

In the early years of the isolationist period, both nobility and the merchant class "paid a heavy price in power and influence." (Stanley-Baker 159) However, 100 years later, the aristocracy and the tradesmen, working together in what may seem incongruous alliance, "had also launched the last and most glorious reincarnation of Japan's classical tradition." (Stanley-Baker)In 1715, Hon'ami Koetsu, a member of a distinguished family of sword connoisseurs, was granted a large tract of land in Tokagarmine, northeast of Tokyo, by the Tokugawa *shogun* Ieyasu. Established on the donated land and directed by Koetsu was a colony of craftsmen whose output of "unparalleled quality and diversity" was animated by Buddhist spiritual principles. (Stanley-Baker 159) Tellingly, the range and variety of enterprises carried out in the colony, all subsumed under the rubric "craft," speaks to the Japanese unwillingness to stratify the fine and applied arts, or to erect barriers between creative pursuits. Indeed, the distinctly Japanese tendency to position the fine and applied arts, and creative activity in general, on an unbroken continuum would make an indelible impression on Art Nouveau impresario Siegfried Bing, during his initial visit to Japan in 1882.

The Tokagarmine "craftsmen" engaged in calligraphy, lacquer painting, gardening (in the spatially attentive Japanese sense), paper-making, ceramics, and the writing of poetry. Significantly, however, none of the artists and artisans participating in this charmed 18th Century artistic utopia had the "common man" in mind as client for his work. Nor did the content of paintings and poems reflect any aspect of lived experience but that of the aristocracy, the *daimyo*, the *samurai*, or the *shogun* himself. Subject matter was both hallowed and restricted by classical tradition. Nevertheless, the meticulous fabrication and stylistic refinement that characterized the colony's output rendered their products precious commodities for Western merchants sailing into Japanese ports in search of exotic artisanal treasures after 1854.

By the mid-18th Century, the new, upstart city of Edo, now Tokyo, had replaced Kyoto as political and military seat for the Tokugawa shogunate. At the same time, Edo had emerged as a center for both Chinese and "Dutch," read "Western" learning. While the light in this chapter is, in part, trained on Western influence on Japanese intellectual and cultural advance during the isolationist period, a brief appreciation of historic Japanese cultural ties with China is essential here as well, given the taste for *chinoiserie* among European, British, and American designers and their clients in the late 19th Century.

Responsive to a growing awareness among his subjects that ancient China had been the source of their own civilization, the Tokugawa shogunate had, by the mid-

17th Century, established Confucian centers of learning throughout Japan, which "produced a new class of esteemed but powerless confucianists." (Stanley-Baker 172-173) Thus was introduced into Japanese cultural consciousness "the ideal of the Chinese scholar-amateur-painter" with the Chinese painting tradition, always carried out in water-based media, defined rather vaguely as "the free expression of lofty ideals." (Stanley-Baker 172-173)

The quiet, introspective Confucian scholar-painter in his study was there to be admired and emulated, his wisdom absorbed by the thoughtful student, as were his skill and sensibility in painting and poetry. However, unlike Christianity, with its emphasis on non-rational faith in a non-corporal divinity and its potent political center in Rome, Confucianism, focused instead on learning and the delicacies of appropriate behavior, and so posed no threat to Japan's dominant classes. So, the Confucian presence and its contribution to Japanese cultural life was welcome.

The mid-18th Century relocation of the Japanese political and cultural epicenter to the city of Edo (Tokyo) marks the start of the Edo Period, one during which "diversity and elegance in the fine arts was easily matched by the robust humour and virile self-confidence of the rising mercantile class." (Stanley-Baker 184) In a productive ferment that similarly characterized Brussels, Paris, Vienna, and Berlin in the late 19th Century, anonymous Edo craftsmen, sponsored by enterprising merchants, turned their expertise to a variety of everyday items habitually spurned by their artisanal counterparts in earlier periods.

Catering to mass, rather than aristocratic tastes, they turned out metal cookware and ceramic tableware, textiles and home furnishings for daily use by an expanding tradesman population, as well as a range of tools for farmers and illustrated books for a citizenry whose literacy level was increasingly high. Moreover, the printing business in Edo flourished in the late 18th Century, in a restless urban setting, a social crucible, in which a newly empowered, mainly mercantile populace demanded text and illustration responsive to their not-so-rarefied interest and concerns. (Stanley-Baker 184)

The visual arts in Edo took three forms in the 18th Century, genre painting, the illustrated book noted above, and the *ukiyo-e* print, this last evolving rapidly in size, multiplicity of colors, and image sophistication in the hands of woodblock print masters. While the media were distinct, the image content in both moved steadily in a single, market-oriented direction: initially toward the depiction of "popular recreations and amusements" and ultimately toward "the more down-market activities of low grade prostitutes or bath house attendants," or "entire city blocks: street dancing, festival floats, interiors and exteriors of every kind." In short, the demi-monde of Edo, "at its most extravagant" received the ardent attention of artists who, in the past, would very likely have deemed that world beneath their notice. (Stanley-Baker 185)

By the mid-19th Century, both craftsmen and merchants had long since shed the constraints imposed by the shogunate, a consequence of the financial aid they were able to offer to the *shogun* and *daimyo,* who still comprised the ruling class, but were now nearly as impoverished as their aristocratic predecessors had been. Indeed, it is generally believed that the pooled financial solvency of the artisans and merchants, and the clout wielded by this "joint venture" in governmental affairs, were instrumental in Japan's decision to negotiate with the United States in the opening of its ports to Western trade.

Most discussions of late 19th Century cultural interaction between Japan and the West highlight the changes wrought by Japanese imports on the fine and the applied arts in Europe, Britain, and the United States. The discussions address the influence of Japanese norms on the work of of specific individuals, like Henri de Toulouse Lautrec, or on entire art and design movements, like Art Nouveau. This scholarly bias is certainly understandable. We are Westerners, after all. However, the emphasis does overlook the substantial impact of imported Western art and craft, as well as advances in the physical and natural sciences, on an eager, receptive Japanese public, especially during the extended period of isolation. This influx of European and British pictorial and verbal data, as exotic to the Japanese as their own cultural artifacts were to the West, was made available from the 16th Century on, primarily through illustrated books brought to the Asian archipelago by European traders who followed Christian missionaries in their proselytizing efforts. By 1580, there were 150,000 Christians in Japan, and by 1630 the number had doubled to 300,000. (Stanley-Baker 153)

The Western mercantile invasion (if you will) of Japan was launched by four major trading nations, countries whose vessels had plied the seas for decades: Spain, Portugal, Holland and England. However, only two mercantile groups were actually preceded by missionaries, Spain and Portugal, both staunchly Catholic. Portuguese traders followed their missionaries to western Kyushu in 1543, while Spanish merchants reached Japanese shores in 1593, following the arrival of the Spanish Franciscans. (Stanley-Baker 153) The appearance of Dutch and English traders in Japanese ports actually dovetailed that of the Spanish and Portuguese. but both the Dutch and English traders represented commercial interests in Protestant countries more concerned with profit than religious conversion. The former set up trading posts in Hirado in 1590; the English joined them in 1613. (Stanley-Baker 153)

In Japan, the link between Western religious and commercial outreach in the 16th Century took a further significant turn in the early 17th, when Protestant merchants, bent on undermining the competition, convinced the Tokugawa *Iemitsu* that "foreign trade did not depend on missionaries and that allegiance to God above all posed a potential threat." (Stanley-Baker 153) The persuasive force of this argument was so great that, in 1617, Christianity, in *all* its manifestations, was banned in Japan and the Spanish and the Portuguese were expelled. Oddly, so were the less conversion-minded Protestant English missionaries and merchants. Clearly, the expulsion responded not only to the dire Protestant warning, but also to the uneasiness already felt by ruling Japanese powers in response to the injection of an alien, monotheistic belief system into Japanese society.

Moreover, with some justification, the Japanese associated spiritual infiltration with Western nationalist expansionism. Xenophobic suspicion directed at Catholicism in particular was intensified by rumors of the Pope's control over *all* his followers, control that straddled national boundaries. Twenty years later, in 1636, the Tokugawa *Iemitsu* further decreed that no Japanese citizen was to leave the country and, in the same year, the shogunate declared that the thousands of Japanese colonials living abroad in Southeast Asia could never again set foot on Japanese soil. (Stanley-Baker 153)

This draconian set of directives would have weighed even more heavily than it did on Japanese economic stability and cultural advancement for hundreds of years, had there not been one exception to the Tokugawa broad-brush prohibition against Western presence in Japan. Unable to halt commerce with other nations entirely, given Japan's resource-poor condition, the *Iemitsu* did permit Dutch ships right of entry into the thriving port of Nagasaki. Indeed, the closing of Japanese ports to all but Dutch (as well as Chinese), vessels in particular, had important consequences for the evolution of Japanese art and craft as it developed in Edo-era Japan, since it was through the decidedly non-spiritual Dutch merchants that the Japanese had access to Western artistic and scientific advance.

Before their expulsion, the Spanish and Portuguese missionaries had for years whet the Japanese appetite for Western knowledge with gifts of illustrated texts and religious icons, restricted in artistic and intellectual content by Church doctrine as those "gifts" were. However, after the closing of Japan to all but Holland's merchants, the Dutch brought to the Japanese public, its hunger for Western cultural artifacts and scientific learning now exacerbated by deprivation, a far wider, more sophisticated range of printed material in astronomy, medicine, and the natural sciences. (Stanley-Baker 153) In fact, the content of these imported texts was naïvely labelled "Dutch learning." And since the books, bound or in loose *quarto* form, were written in foreign languages, primarily Dutch, English or French, the Japanese were compelled to learn those languages, with their alien characters, diction, and syntax, as well.

The Dutch imports, often bringing together in one volume reproductions of Western painting and advances in the natural sciences, exposed Japanese artists, and artisans to strategies for image-making not seen before in Japan: closely observed renderings of flora and fauna, accompanied by verbal observations in the precise, descriptive mode of Dürer and Da Vinci. (Stanley-baker 153) Revelatory as well for Japanese draughtsman was the use of point perspective in drawings and paintings of the Italian landscape, a technical advance doubly illuminating in an Asian culture for which rendered or painted depth itself had never been a concern. (Stanley-Baker 153) Consequently, Japanese artists, excited by approaches to image-making utterly at odds with their tradition, recycled those pictorial strategies into their fabrication of screens, scrolls, and *sumi-é* ink painting.

When the *ukiyo-e* woodblock print made its appearance in the early 1700s, eventually moving into full, polychrome flower later in that century, Western advances in realism generated by the Renaissance infiltrated the Japanese master printer's conceptions as well. One of the best examplars of that process is the frequently reproduced *ukiyo-e* perspective print entitled "A Large *Uki-e* Depicting the Kabuki Stage at Nakamura-za during the Kaomise Performance of 1740" (Admittedly, a very lengthy, if fully informative title.) The print's creator, the innovative *ukiyo-e* master, Okumura Masanobu (1686-1764), takes advantage of Western point perspective technique to depict the entirety of the Kabuki theatrical experience. The comprehensive image includes the stage and a moment in the performance itself, a crowded spectators' gallery, and even a glimpse of stagehands in the upper right and left corners, those Edo-era light technicians who produced light or darkness on stage by opening and closing sliding panels (Kobayashi 12-13).

Masanobu, played a major role in the emergence of a new type of *ukiyo-e* artist, "the self-conscious professional who took great pride in the originality of his own work" (Kobayashi 40). Indeed, his insistence on identifying and, more to the point, celebrating the author of an original, skillfully accomplished work of art very likely had its source in his familiarity with famous Western artists, for whom anonymity was out of the question. Masanobu's versatility extended to the invention of the "pillar print," a tall, narrow print suitable for display on load-bearing wooden posts in Japanese homes.

"A Young Dandy on a Horse," a lacquer print of *oban* size also familiar to Western audiences, "depicts two young women, attracted by a young gallant on horseback, peering excitedly through the spy window of the wall surrounding a stately *samurai* mansion." (Kobayashi 9) Published in the early 18th Century, the stylized depiction includes a *haiku* in the upper right-hand side, a horse whose head is impossibly twisted toward its rider, severe image-cropping on the right and left vertical axes, most appealing to late 19th Century Western artists, and *no* reference whatever to Western perspective principles. Most intriguing of all, the dandy sports a Scotch plaid robe.

This particular print virtually embodies the Japanese attitude toward foreign influence outlined by Stanley-Baker in her account. On the one hand, Masonobu has integrated into his seamless image one outstanding element in the wealth of Western goods exported to Japan in the 1700s: a textile of strictly rectilinear pattern, woven in Scotland. On the other hand every other pictorial element in this compelling composition remains fully Japanese, indicating that Masonobu only borrowed Western norms for his imagery when he felt them advantageous for the result. The surprise appearance of plaid fabric, incidentally, gives evidence of the exchange of goods between Scotland and Japan in the isolationist Edo Period, thanks to the efforts of Dutch traders, who played the part of cultural intermediaries.

While relishing the novel patterns and color schemes in Western textiles Dutch traders brought to their own *négoçiants*, the Japanese were perhaps most fascinated by the "curious" Europeans themselves, burly, hearty, and forthright, with their "waisted garments," "plumed head gear" and "sharply chiseled features" (Stanley-Baker 153). These flamboyant foreign adventurers, at once welcome and kept socially at arm's length, would be portrayed in quasi-caricatural form by Japanese artists, often painting the Europeans aboard their galleons that outstripped in scale and bulk, number of sails, variety of fittings, load capacity, and durability on the high seas any vessel seen before in Asian waters.

Entertaining as these pictorial records of European traders are, however, it is the Western influence on the Japanese draughtsman's depiction of the natural world that should most interest students of East-West cross-fertilization. Paradoxically, the illustrated books, folding screens and hanging scrolls, textiles and kimonos, ceramics, lacquerware, and strange, but dazzling *ukiyo-e* prints that inundated European and British art and design circles from the late 1860s on had already been stylistically altered by the European academic tradition they are said to have undermined.

By the 1880s, travel to the Orient in general and to Japan in particular had become almost commonplace for curious Western tourists, at least those who could afford it, as well as for enterprising businessmen. Siegfried Bing, at that point a respected Parisian entrepreneur and connoisseur of *japonaiserie,* embarked on his first, year-long trip in 1882. Later in the 1880s, the German architect, architectural reformer, and theorist Hermann Muthesius spent three productive years in Tokyo. Both men, of course, accomplished this lengthy, arduous journey on commercial ocean going vessels manufactured by their home country's shipbuilding industries.

Significantly, however, the Scotch were in the vanguard of European and British arrivals to Japanese shores, after the opening of Tokyo's port in 1854. The Scotch merchant Thomas Blake Glover, for example, reached Nagasaki as early as 1859, charged with managing the local office of the Hong Kong-based trading company, Jardine, Matheson and Co. Once settled in, Glover set up his own business in this long-established Japanese trading center. In this capacity, he sold armaments imported from the West, contributed his technical knowledge and experience to the development of Japanese coal mines, and, most notably, was a key figure in establishing the Nagasaki shipyard that would ultimately mushroom into the Mitsubishi Corporation of Japan. Glover used his long-distance contacts with nautical engineering experts in Glasgow to import, primarily *via* instruction manuals, the required technology directly from the Clyde to Nagasaki.

The equally famed Scot Henry Dyer is credited with the shaping of education for engineers in Japan, having been appointed head of the newly established Imperial College of Engineering in 1872. For his Japanese students, Dyer set about creating an innovative curriculum that would combine theory and practice in a way that anticipated Henry van de Velde's applied arts curriculum for the *Kunstgewerbeschule* in Weimar by 35 years.

In Glasgow itself, the Scottish shipyards received many orders from the Imperial Japanese Navy from the 1860s on, requests that were filled through contracts facilitated by British intermediaries. By the early 1880s, the ambitious Japanese government had shifted its emphasis in naval matters from the purchase of ships constructed in Western shipyards, including those in Britain and Scotland, to the transfer of Western shipbuilding skills and technology of the West to Japan. The obvious goal was to acquire shipbuilding expertise that would render the Imperial Japanese Navy self-sufficient, no longer requiring the advice of the British Royal Navy.

To this end, the Japanese government proceeded to export shipbuilding apprentices to Western ports, chiefly that of Glasgow. It should not be assumed that the Japanese visitors were inexperienced technical or theoretical novices in the design and construction of seaworthy ships Emerging mainly from *samurai* families, the greater number were well educated, university trained engineers, naval cadets, naval engineering officers, and high ranking naval officers. Although the subject does hover in the realm of conjecture, it is nevertheless logical to assume that the Japanese apprentices themselves brought to the situation their own savvy *vis-à-vis* tools, materials, and techniques of construction, while working side by side with their Scotch mentors. In this way, there would have been technical reciprocity between the two groups, Western and Asian. And conceivably, some of this Japanese *modus operandi* made its way into Mackintosh's design methods, through the shipyard craftsmen he commandeered to carry out his commissions.

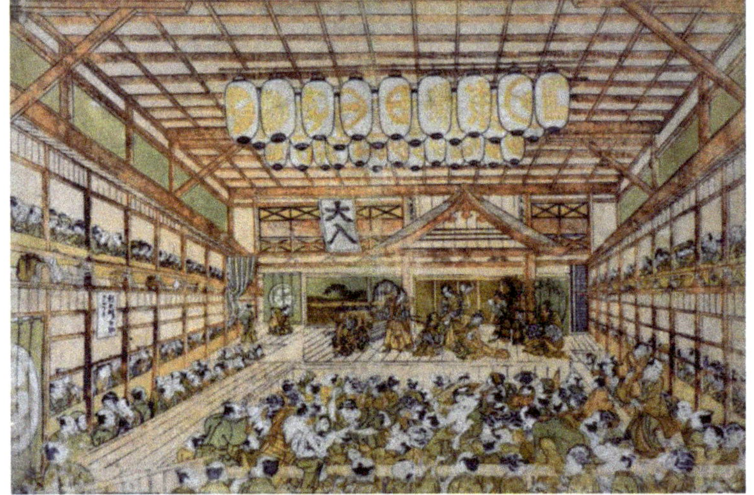

Okumura Masanobu, *"A Large Uki-e Depicting the Kabuki Stage,"* woodblock print, 18th Century

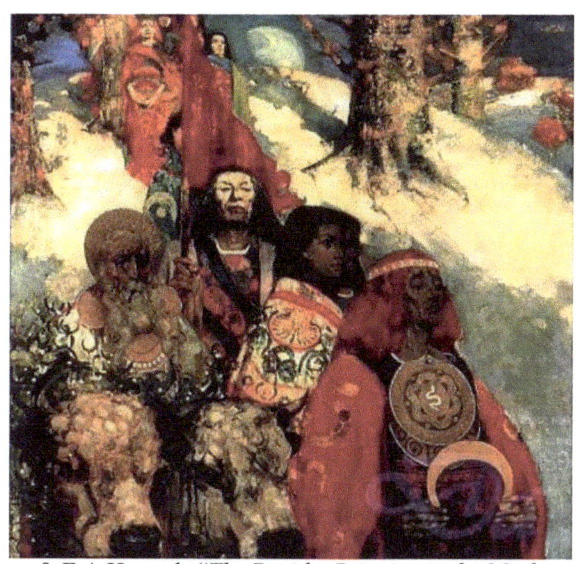

George Henry & E.A.Hormel, *"The Druids: Bringing in the Mistletoe,"* oil, 1890

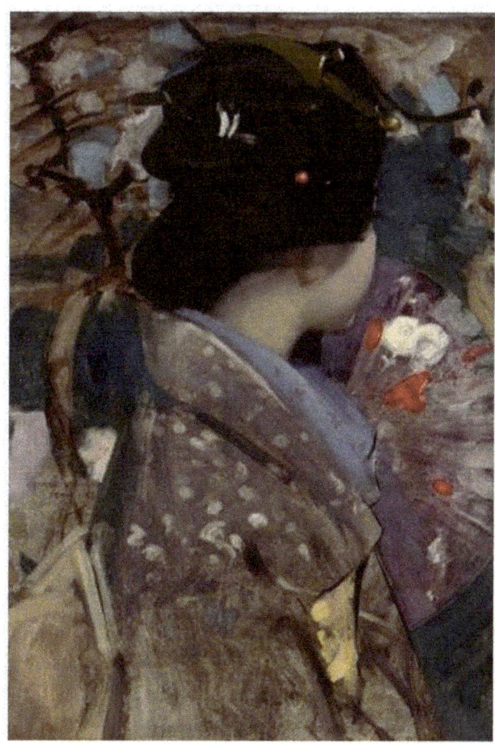

George Henry, *"Japanese Lady with a Fan,"* oil, detail, 1890

Japanese Tea House (Chashitsu)

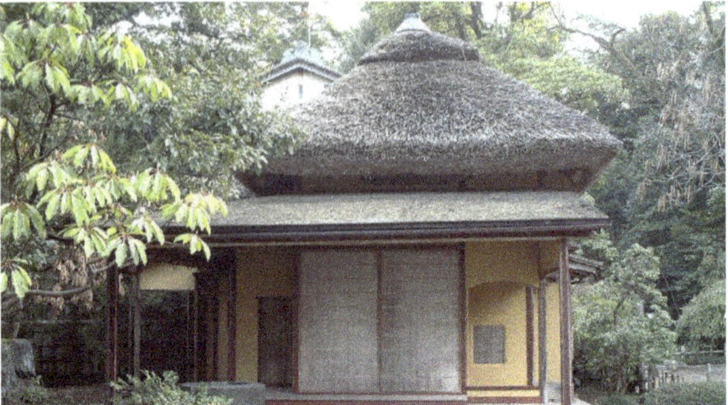

a.*Yagao-fei in Kanazawa, Ishikawa* (exterior)

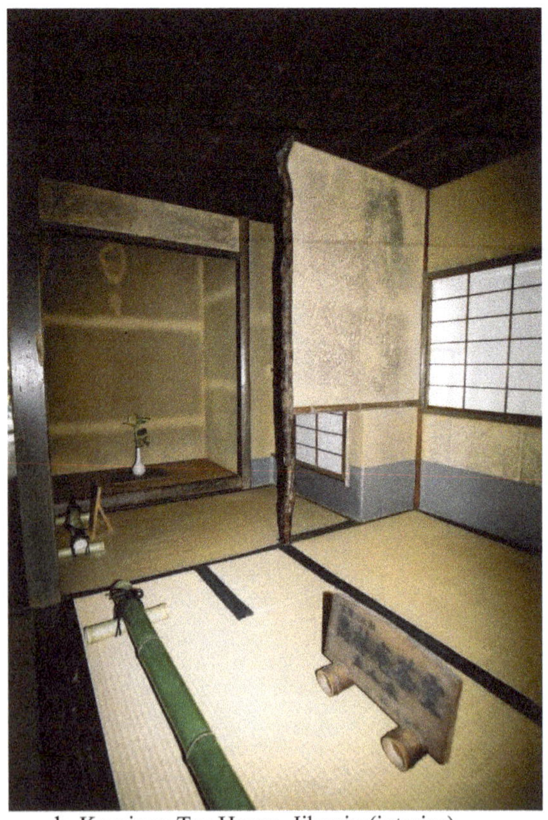

b. Kourinen Tea House, Jikouin (interior)

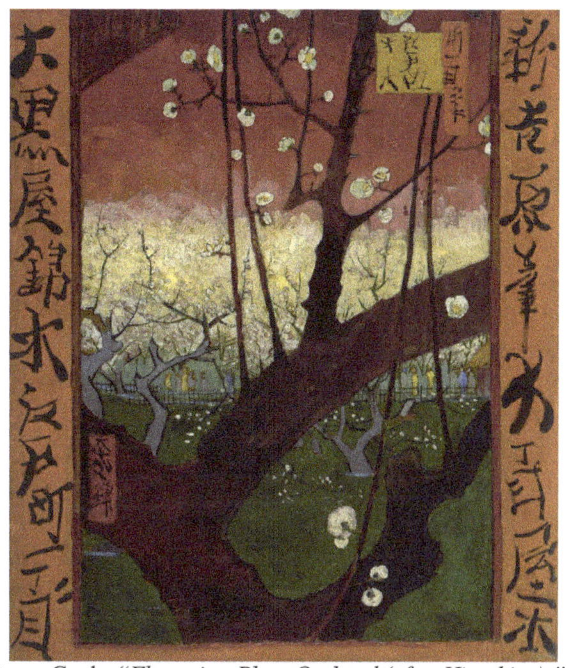

Vincent van Gogh, *"Flowering Plum Orchard (after Hiroshige),"* oil, 1887

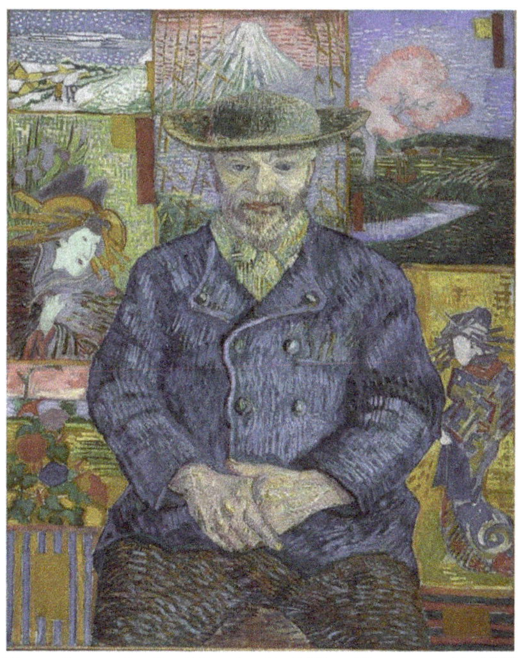

Vincent van Gogh, *"Portrait of Père Tanguy*, oil, 1887

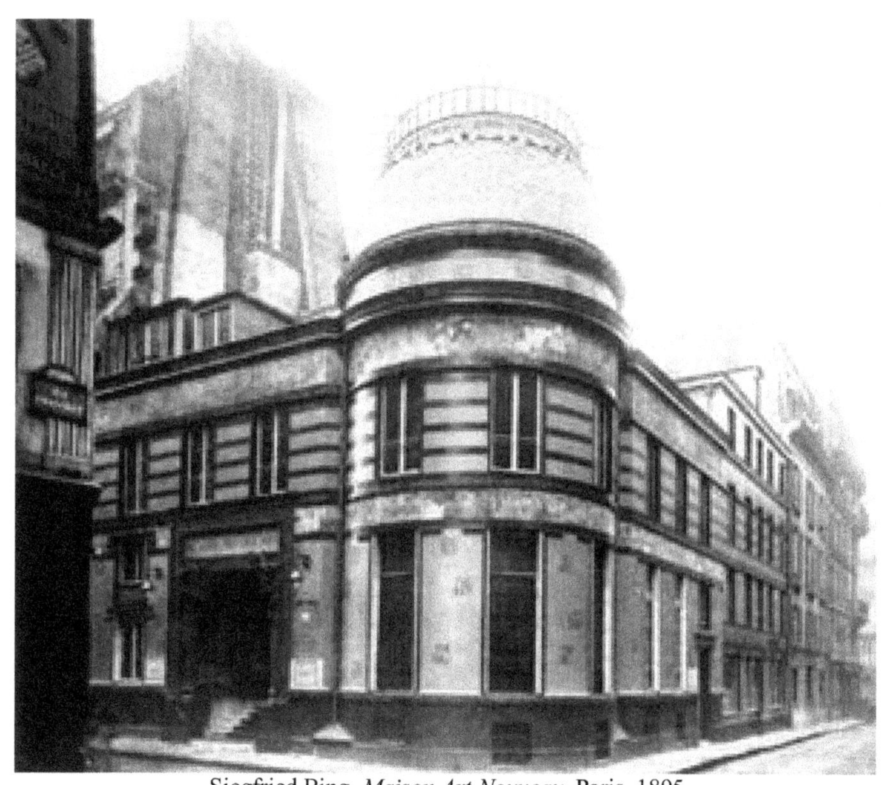

Siegfried Bing, *Maison Art Nouveau*, Paris, 1895

CHAPTER 7

Japonaiserie in France: Enter Siegfried Bing

> "He firmly believed that a new design could be stimulated in Europe simply by applying Japanese aesthetic principles to everyday objects and by adapting the Japanese attitude of making no distinction between the major or minor fine or applied arts." (Weisberg 9)

The commercial and cultural links between the Scotch and the Japanese from the 1860s on may not be familiar, in rough outline or specifics, to the student of 19th Century East-West trade. But the same student, particularly one steeped in French Art Nouveau arcana, will be quick to recognize the name of Siegfried Bing, for the latter's entrepreneurial efforts in promoting *japonaiserie*, through objets d'art he acquired both in Paris and during his journeys to Japan, and for the innovative showrooms that comprised his Paris gallery.

It is something of a paradox that Bing, so closely associated with French culture at its best, was not a native Frenchman. Bing was, in fact, born in Hamburg in 1838, the second of three sons in a family of merchants. The family firm, *Bing Gebrüder*, was established by Jacob Bing, an enterprising *pater families*, with the goal of importing treasured French porcelain and glass to Hamburg. In order to smooth the border-crossing, import-export process, Jacob opened a branch of the family business in Paris as well, creating a second base of operations where he was often joined by all three of his sons. (Weisberg 12)

In 1854, Bing *Père* expanded his French base of operations, through the purchase of a small ceramics factory outside Paris. The purchase allowed for direct involvement in the manufacture of porcelain objects, for a rapidly increasing trade in luxury items. "With the purchase of the firm also came a patent for the firing of hard porcelain in a coal-burning kiln, which was extremely efficient for its day and increased production markedly." (Weisberg 12) This series of related events in Siegfried's childhood and adolescent life contributed in three important ways to his preparation for the entrepreneurial work that would consume him for more than 40 years: (1) he was already conditioned, at a very young age, to the pragmatic realities of international trade; (2) he had early exposure to an innovative fabrication process that would increase production, while maintaining high quality; (3) he was already acclimatized to French manners and mores, a comfort level that extended to fluency in the French language from late adolescence on.

When Jacob retired in 1868, Siegfried took over the family interest in manufacturing and selling decorative objects. The ceramic factory now defuncts, he purchased a second, again specializing in porcelain, so as to provide fine tableware for the Bing retail outlet on *rue Martel*. Indeed, by 1869, his client base had become primarily French, rather than German With Michael Bing now handling the firm's business end, Siegfried could devote all his time to what would become a thriving Parisian hub for a variety of high end art objects, some functional, most decorative. Initially focussed on porcelain and glass, Bing eventually diversified his store's inventory to include lamps and some bronze sculpture. And, to unburden himself of full responsibility for sales, as well as reinforce his available stock, he also allied himself with another porcelain manufacturer, Jean Baptiste Ernest Leuillier. (Weisberg 13) That Bing declared himself *chef d'atelier* in this collaboration between peers gives evidence his native self-confidence, or some might say to his native vanity and opportunistic tendencies.

Bing's prosperous Parisian gallery suffered a serious, albeit temporary, setback in 1870, as the rising political tension between France and Prussia exploded into full-scale military conflict: the Franco-Prussian War. Unable to hold his business together in this tumultuous period, the German-speaking Bing, doubtless viewed with either suspicion or real hostility by many Parisian colleagues and clients, fled Paris for Brussels with his family. In May, 1871, he returned to his adopted country, now defeated and humiliated, to find his firm in disarray and most of his former employees conscripted. Chief among the obstacles to rebuilding his once-flourishing *affaires,* however, was the decline of the decorative arts business in general, in a cultural epicenter now physically in shambles, with a population far more concerned with survival, than luxury. (Weisberg 14)

Nevertheless, in the period 1871-1873, through a series of moves typical of the resourcefulness, tenacity, and methodicity he would demonstrate throughout his career, Bing waged a campaign of retrenchment. He began by revitalizing the manufacture of porcelain he'd carried on first alone, and then in partnership with Leuillier. Then he established cordial relationships with several major French importers of foreign craft objects, functional and ornamental. Finally, he took a step in an uncharted, but very promising direction: he started to collect Oriental crafted ware, with an initial focus on ceramics. (Weisberg 14)

This adventurous step hardly constituted an impulsive leap. For one thing, Bing had long nourished a personal interest in fine ceramics. Looking eastward to Asia was a natural extension of that interest. For another, his seasoned businessman's sense of the decorative arts market had "led him in the direction of the mania for Japanese curios then sweeping France." (Weisberg 14) The market, while quiescent in the aftermath of war, was in reality a sleeping giant, and Bing cannily anticipated its awakening. By 1874, his reputation as a prominent collector of Japanese art had spread so far as to generate an invitation to join the East Asian Society in Tokyo. Not coincidentally, in that same year, he was prosperous enough to pay rent on three commercial Parisian establishments. Finally, two years later, in 1876, he was sure enough of his welcome in France to submit a request for naturalization. (Weisberg 14)

Bing's attraction to the Orient and to the singular qualities of its craft traditions may have stemmed in part from genetic predisposition, but his fascination was certainly informed and intensified by the availability of Asian art and craft in Paris from the 1860s on. He routinely paid visits to Oriental exhibitions sponsored by the *Union Centrale des Arts Décoratifs*. In addition, he went out of his way to view displays of ceramics "that replaced traditional [Western] motifs with designs lifted, often quite directly, from Japanese prints and albums." (Weisberg 14) His visits to small vendors of decorative art objects located off the beaten track for that market took him to shops that sold Oriental wares exclusively, such as *La Porte Chinoise*, where he discovered woodblock prints, ceramics, and bronzes. As Weisberg points out, "not one to ignore an entrepreneurial opportunity, he actively dealt in *japonaiserie* by the 1870s, if not before." (Weisberg 14)

Bing built his collection of Oriental *objects d'art* slowly and in secret for a few years, in part because his name was still associated with *Leuillier,fils* and in part because he still viewed the acquisition of Asian craft as a sideline. However, in March, 1876, he sold a sizable number of Oriental pieces at public auction at the *Hôtel Drogue* and netted 11,000 francs. The sale represents the first record of his public involvement with the Asian market. It suggests as well "an already developed eye for buying objects of high resale value." (Weisberg 14) The cohesiveness and high quality of the collection, not to mention Bing's impressive profit from the sale, serve as indicators of his skill at functioning on two tracks simultaneously, as tasteful perceptive *connoisseur* and as shrewd businessman.

What Weisberg terms the "raging mania for Japanese art" in France was "reinforced and disseminated" by the dazzling Japanese Pavilion on the grounds of the *Exposition Internationale* of 1878. (Weisberg 16) Crammed with fine craft, the pavilion was a magnet for an avid Parisian audience, whose viewing experience was enhanced by English-speaking Japanese experts "who provided data on artists and history of a specific place where a particular kind of ceramic [and other crafts] was produced." (Weisberg 16) That the Japanese installation brought together, in the same display examples of both art *and* industry revealed to the French public an aspect of Japanese culture previously unknown to the West: the harmonizing of the values of fine design with those of efficient, qualitatively high industrial production.

With one voice, the critics for the Paris press extolled the variety of objects on display in the Japanese Pavilion, calling attention to their "importance as models for Western designers." (Weisberg 16) At the same time, astute businessmen like Siegfried Bing observed in the splendid trove of Japanese *objects* goods that would meet the Western consumer's expectations for "exotic" Japanese art. (Weisberg 16)

The opening of Bing's shop at *rue Chauchat* in 1878 coincided, surely not by chance, with the *Exposition* and its popular centerpiece, the Japanese Pavilion. Having successfully displayed and sold items from his own collection from the outset, he was bent on cornering the Japanese market, fully aware that, to do so, he had to establish personal ties with Japanese sources, unmediated by French or Japanese middlemen. In this approach, he would depart from the methods of other French dealers in Japanese goods, who either chose their art *objects* from goods regularly shipped to French ports from the East, or actually lived in Japan for several months "to make the business contacts needed to obtain a larger and more varied stock." (Weisberg 16) Bing distinguished himself from the others in his effort to establish personal relationships with private Japanese collectors of antiquities, whose holdings were "still out of reach for foreigners." (Weisberg 16)

In addition, Bing had an important advantage over other merchants in his quest for Japanese fine craft in the person of his brother-in-law, Michael Martin Baer. Baer actually lived in Tokyo, where he held the position of Acting Consul for the German Legation in the periods 1870-74 and 1877-81. Baer was not only wealthy and well-placed, but also a connoisseur and collector himself. His diplomatic status gave him access to Japanese high society, and, with it, the opportunity to view the rarefied contents of collections unavailable to other Westerners. Items he bought, but didn't keep for himself, found their way into Bing's stock and, ultimately, into his *rue Chauchat* exhibition cases. (Weisberg 16-17)

In 1880, Bing took his first trip to the Far East, leaving his family behind in Paris. He covered an astonishing amount of territory in his year-long journey, travelling through large areas of India, China, and Japan in a century when overland travel in Asia was inevitably slow and arduous. A quote from Bing's journals, expressing the intrepid adventurer's unabashed excitement, his genuine wonder at the singularity of Japanese art and craft at all levels, strikes us as at once childlike and prescient.

"Once arrived in Japan, I beat the drum in order to procure from one end of this remarkable Island Kingdom to the other all the artifacts that money could buy. I crossed the country in all directions and let it be known anywhere that a wild man had come ashore to buy up everything. That brought forth from underground hiding places treasures of which one had never dreamt before. Well, I bird-dogged the art of this nation of artists down to their most modest products which previously no one had found worth the trouble to stop and consider. The things that were utilized for the most common daily use toilet articles which women of the lower class used, combs, hairpins all seemed to me to be marked by such a special and enchanting character that it provided material for collections, and the time that followed did, in fact, prove that, in this instance, I was not the victim of self-deception." (Weisberg 18)

The eclecticism that characterized Bing's voracious buying spree in Japan from the homely and commonplace to the classical and refined extended to his enthusiastic acquisition of work by contemporary Japanese artists and craftsmen. (Weisberg 19) And, to reinforce and complement his own prodigious efforts, he sent for his brother Auguste Bing, a canny businessman himself and, like Baer, nearing retirement, "to join him in Japan to ensure a steady supply of imports for the Paris shop." (Weisberg 20) Involving as many family members as possible in his growing Japanese enterprise obviously provided Bing with the dependability and trust he needed in what was still a dicey mercantile venture.

On his return to Paris in 1881, in a spirit of self-confidence bordering on bravado, Bing opened two additional outlets, one on *rue de Provence* and one on *rue Bleue*, the latter an especially fashionable location. Both were spacious shops, equipped with opulent rooms that served as private parlors for meetings with favored clients, as well as areas where pieces awaiting receptive buyers or reserved for distinguished clients could be safely stored. (Weisberg 20) The selective display of Japanese decorative objects in his shop was a strategy Bing had learned from the Japanese collectors of antiquities he had met in his travels.

The opening of Bing's trio of posh, high-end retail shops dovetailed conveniently with the general rise of popular and scholarly interest in Japanese art and its history in

Paris, and in France as a whole. One particularly stimulating event, an enormous asset to Bing as a dealer, was an extensive exhibition of Japanese art organized in 1883 by Louis Gonze to benefit the *Union Centrale.* (Weisberg 20) To fill the exhibition galleries, Gonze, an art critic and collector of Japanese art himself, relied on the *japonistes* among his friends for loans. Bing reputedly lent over 650 objects to the ceramic portion of the show (Weisberg 20), quantitative proof of the sheer scope of his holdings.

The exhibit, which displayed an almost overwhelming array of paintings, sculpture, prints, ceramics and other decorative arts, was a popular and critical success. Critical comment in newspapers, journals, and scholarly articles emphasized that "Gonse, by placing Japanese art in a historical and aesthetic context, had changed the Western attitude from *fad* [italics mine] to serious inspiration." (Weisberg 20) Gonse supplied historical and aesthetic context, through the scholarly volume, *L'Art Japonais*, he prepared to accompany the exhibit, an informative tome expressly calculated "to inspire a serious French interest in the tradition and antiquities of Japan." (Weisberg 20)

It is likely that both exhibition guests and critics for the city's multitude of news dailies and periodicals marvelled at the show's emphasis on craft, an emphasis in sharp contrast to the Western salon tradition, where painting and sculpture held sway. To clarify and fortify the focus on craft, essays in *L'Art Japonais* examined the origins of "minor" Japanese arts from the 9th to the 19th Century, while the works on display gave proof positive of the superlative skill of Japanese artists and artisans in combining painting with lacquers, or ceramics with metalwork, sculpture, and prints. (Weisberg 20) As Bing and other Western visitors to Japan had discovered for themselves, boundaries or walls between the fine and applied arts, or between types of applied art, were non-existent for the Japanese.

Moreover, Bing's personal participation in Gonse's landmark show moved beyond the simple loan of ceramic treasures: in an essay for a separate exhibition catalogue, he outlined in detail the traditions and the techniques of Japanese ceramic art, one of the first such educational documents published in the West. The essay, a landmark in itself, "secured Bing's place as a connoisseur and scholar in the field." (Weisberg 21)

What must seem by now the feverish quality of Bing's activities as scholar/entrepreneur in *japonaiserie* continued into 1883, when he renovated his core outlet on *rue Chauchat*, and opened two more, a second on *rue Bleue* and another on the *rue de la Paix*. Scholarly pursuits notwithstanding, Bing—ever the sagacious businessman—now catered to "two distinct levels of clientèle who had opposing tastes and expenses," always at separate retail locations. For the well-heeled, he dealt in fine objects of superior quality that he could count on selling at high prices. For the middle-class consumer, with "a monetary taste for *japonisme*," he dealt in what he deemed ordinary Japanese art and craft, which he sold at affordable prices. (Weisberg 22)

Needless to say, Bing depended primarily on his own instincts, informed as they were, in determining quality and value in *japonaiserie.* The Doubting Thomas among readers will be interested to learn that, on occasion, expensive art and craft objects

Bing labelled "antique" were not reliably so. There are two possible causes for the inauthenticity: some apparently antique pieces were actually made in the 19th Century either "in response to the rising Western demand." or "as a way to honor ancient styles in Japan." (Weisberg 22) "Whatever the reason," Weisberg notes, "Bing's sponsorship of ancient pieces was not always infallible." (Weisberg 22) A passionate *dévoté* of Japanese art and craft at all levels, Bing nonetheless lacked the requisite caution, the inclination to reserve judgement typical of scholars of our day.

Bing suffered a brief period of declining sales in the mid-1880s, perhaps the consequence of a Parisian market now glutted with Japanese art. Closing the outlet on the *rue de la Paix*, he shifted his mercantile energies to Japan itself, opening offices in Yokohama, in 1886 and Kobe, in 1887. As alert to Japanese eagerness to industrialize as had been Glaswegian merchants and shipbuilders a decade earlier, and eager to expand his own business, Bing, the connoisseur and collector of *japonaiserie*, responded to the Japanese demand for industry-related products "by importing diverse trade items for the country, including heavy machinery, munitions, dynamite, and gas and oil fixtures." (Weisberg 24)

Through the diversity of his mercantile efforts, in which he handled deals for French firms whose products bore no relation to his own private interests, Bing became a major figure in the Far East trade. (Weisberg 24) By 1888, with new and larger offices in Yokohama, the addition of Japanese staff, and trade relations reaching into China and Indochina, *Bing et Cie.* had become "the general import-export agent for the *Syndicat L'Industrie Française au Japon*." (Weisberg 24) And while the import-export trade in manufactured goods now became a major source of income for *S. Bing et Cie.*, Bing himself continued to deal primarily in Japanese *objects d'art.,* using the profits from the more pragmatic enterprise to support the more culturally rarefied.

In 1888, Bing published the first in a series of journals devoted exclusively to Japanese art: *Le Japon Artistique.* The publication featured articles printed in three language editions, French, English and German, as well as illustrations of Japanese art and craft from Bing's own collection. Generated with the intention of showing "that Japanese articles were both beautiful and a good investment," (Weisberg 25) the journal was itself a full-scale commercial venture. *Le Japon Artistique* was innovative in the commercial art world of the period, "since its ultimate purpose was to seduce the nonspecialist, through word and image, into buying Japanese art." (Weisberg 25) Ironically, however, while Bing targeted a less well informed and less affluent middle class client in the planning and layout of *Le Japon Artistique,* than similar journals of the period, the publication itself, with its handsome color plates, was expensive to produce. As a result, it was abandoned three years later, in 1891.

In the first issue, Bing identified Japanese art as an *art nouveau* that would have lasting impact on European creativity a comment that proved to be, as Weisberg notes, "overwhelmingly prophetic." (Weisberg 26) Strategically selected illustrations provided models of Japanese style and technique for Western artists, and study examples for Western scholars and students. Of significance for specialists and laymen alike was Bing's inclusion of the work of Japanese artists not yet familiar to the European public. He thus presented a more rounded view of the Japan's painters, printmakers, and craftsmen than had previously been available. (Weisberg 26)

The journal's broad range of illustrations, its pictorial array of bronzes, textiles, furniture, prints, sculpture and with a nod to the *samuari* tradition, sword guards, elicited mixed reviews. The British Art Journal, for example, pronounced *Le Japon Artistique* a great success, while, in more cynical quarters, Bing's elegant journal was as frequently denounced as "just another mechanism by art dealers to inflate the market for Japanese art." (Weisberg 26)

Most disturbing for Bing, in its combination of *hauteur* and barely concealed xenophobia, was the barrage of critical comment launched by the Japanese Weekly Mail, an English-language publication whose appeal was to travellers and businessmen. The Mail attacked the scholarship of experts in *japonaiserie* commandeered by Bing for journal articles: "Its letterpress is the work of men who substitute enthusiasm for knowledge. Instead of information we have rhapsodies; instead of research vapouring." Equally as ferocious was venomous criticism levelled at Bing's own contributions: "Mr. Bing touches only the hem of the garment, and we doubt if the work of weaving the whole is possible for anyone except a Japanese as deeply versed in the social and political history of his country as he is closely in touch with the spirit of art inspiration" (Weisberg 27).

The Japanese critical assault, however justified in its skepticism, simply missed or ignored the avowed goal of Bing's journal: his appeal was to a popular audience not yet conversant with the particulars of Japanese artistic tradition, rather than to Western or Japanese experts in *japonaiserie.* From a specialist's standpoint, the journal articles may very well have been somewhat simplistic in fact and concept, overly extravagant in their praise of Japanese art *objets,* and overwrought in tone. However, the essays did succeed in their aim of opening the door to a world of art and craft hitherto closed to most middle-class Europeans, Englishmen and Americans.

Of signal importance in its relevance to Bing's career as a whole is the blatant chauvinism evident in the Mail's dismissal of Bing's own credentials as champion of Japanese art. Conservative Mail critics seemed reflexively to write Bing off as a pretentious, "wannabe" foreigner, an ignorant *gaijin* on the outside looking in. Similar hostile attacks by the French press would greet the opening exhibition of Bing's Art Nouveau gallery in Paris, in December, 1895. For his show-rooms, Bing had invited foreign designers like Henry van de Velde to create *Gesamtkunstwerken* featuring their own work and, in many cases, that of their non-French countrymen. Of course, Bing himself, who had conceived, supervised and financed the installation of the sometimes overstuffed, but always exciting, interiors, was seen as a subversive intruder on the Parisian cultural scene, since, although long a naturalized French citizen, he had been born a German Jew in Hamburg.

A welcome ray of sunlight in the hailstorm of negative comment directed at *Le Japon Artistique* was the praise of one anonymous critic for Bing's editorial efforts at elevating the *unkyo-é* print to 'the domain of serious art' (The critic further observed, on a more practical note that the widespread public enthusiasm evoked by the prints, stimulated mainly by Bing's journal, had "enabled the wily dealer to raise prices by a factor of twenty") (Weisberg 28). Good sense tells us that Bing was by no means the sole purveyor of Japanese woodblock prints in Paris, given their ever-increasing popularity. However, it may surprise some to learn that Vincent van Gogh, who drew immense inspiration from the prints in his own painting, actually worked for Bing, selling prints on commission to fellow artists.

Van Gogh's correspondence with his brother Theo makes clear that, despite his family's disapproval, Vincent "had no intention of cutting himself off from the largest supply of Japanese objects in Paris." (Weisberg 28) While the young Dutch painter sold the greater number of prints Bing gave him, he did keep some for himself, as the scope of the *ukiyo-é* collection on display in Amsterdam's Van Gogh Museum makes clear. Indeed, the prints often seen in the backgrounds of Vincent's paintings may very well have originated with Bing.

The alliance between intense Dutch Post-Impressionist and the shrewd Parisian dealer took more than one profitable form. Van Gogh encouraged his artist colleagues to study *ukiyo-é* images on display in Bing's shops or stored carefully in cabinet drawers thereby attracting more customers for his employer. Yet another kind of profit, in this case for van Gogh, lay in "the many hours Bing willingly spent educating him to really look at Japanese prints." (Weisberg 28) Moreover, the collaboration between the two *devotés* of Japanese art extended into the realm of the decorative arts. Through exposure to the *ukiyo-é* prints, Bing introduced younger avant garde painters, many of them Vincent's friends, to the "doctrine of the decorative style in painting" (Weisberg 28-29).

Admittedly, by no stretch of the term's definition can van Gogh's texturally rich, expressively potent paintings be described as "decorative." However, the Japanese influence *is* immediately visible in the Dutch master's deployment of brilliant, saturated colors, strong, defined contours, aggressive cropping, and indifference to established protocols for anatomy and perspective. Having assimilated so many Japanese stylistic norms into his work, van Gogh, in turn, through the vehicle of his painting, influenced many avant garde Belgian artists, when he participated in *Les Vingt* exhibitions of the early 1890s. In this way, his near-evangelical passion for *ukiyo-é* art left its imprint on the work of both Belgian artists *and* designers, Henry van de Velde chief among them

In addition, van Gogh may have inadvertently assisted Siegfried Bing in the dealer's effort to spread appreciation for Japanese art beyond the limits of Paris. In Brussels, Bing organized an exhibit of prints by Utamaro, Hokusai, Sharaku, and Kiyonaga, which, with the help of enthusiastic press reviews, "generated considerable interest among Belgian artists and the general public alike" (Weisberg 29). Indeed, so heartening a response in a nearby European capital, a French-speaking cultural hub to boot, no doubt contributed to Bing's decision, in 1890, to mount a comprehensive *ukiyo-é* print exhibition in Paris, one "that would firmly anchor the genre as a legitimate artistic tradition" (Weisberg 29).

Oddly, by 1890, only the landscapes of the *ukiyo-é* masters Hiroshige and Hokusai had become sought-after treasures in France. Although familiar to dealers in Oriental goods, connoisseurs, collectors, and *avant garde* artists like Monet, Cassatt, Degas, and Toulouse Lautrec, a host of other Japanese printmakers were unknown to the general public. To this end the introduction of the French public to hitherto unknown, significant Japanese printmakers, Bing organized a show unprecedented in European exhibition history in that year. Intent on an all-inclusive exhibit, he borrowed heavily from both private and public collections. Among the lenders were the art critics Edmond de Goncourt and Roger Marx, and Louis Metman, Director of the *Musée des Arts Décoratifs.* The greater number of objects, however, was drawn from Bing's own vast collection. Predictably, Bing wrote the introduction to the catalogue (Weisberg 29).

The *École Nationale des Beauz Arts* served as venue for what must have been a visually exhausting array of 725 woodblock prints, complemented by 421 illustrated books, drawn from all periods of *ukiyo-é* development. (Weisberg 29-30) The show was definitely the largest survey of Japanese prints France had ever seen and displayed the work of Kiyonobu, Kiyonaga, Toyonabu, Harunobu, Toyokuni, Sharaku, Utamaro, and Hiroshige, some of whom are obscure names even now to casual students of the *ukiyo-é* print genre. This was obviously not an exhibit for the impatient viewer and was probably visited piecemeal, a few hours at a time, by those concerned with taking in its riches, varied in detail, motif, and theme as they were.

While distillation was not among its merits, Bing's landmark exhibition served its purpose for its ambitious curator. Not only did it open up a new cosmos of exotic image-making to the French public, but it also paved the way for Bing's winning of the *Légion d'Honneur,* accomplished *via* the nomination of his friend Charles Gillot, fellow editor of *Le Japon Artistique.* This was an honor rarely bestowed on a naturalized citizen and "indicated that he was recognized as a major tastemaker in France whose exhibitions and publications had greatly furthered the arts of the Far East"(Weisberg 30). If Bing dependeded the memory of a moment of triumph to help him weather the storm of withering criticism that greeted the opening of his Art Nouveau gallery in 1895, the recollection of the award of the *Légion d'Honneur* in the early 1890s certainly satisfied that need.

The early 1890s witnessed an accelerated pace in the number of Japanese art exhibitions Bing personally sponsored. His ardor for Japanese art, at this point, approached missionary zeal. In addition to organizing shows for his own firm, he encouraged other collectors to mount exhibits of their holdings, "with the promise of generous loans from his company stock or from his own private collection" (Weisberg 32). In addition, in this febrile period, he originated the practice of opening an exhibit at his firm's galleries and then sending it on the road. These travelling shows were innovative in their mingling of Japanese *objets d'art* with the work of European decorative designers he'd begun to represent. All objects were for sale: collectors, private dealers, and museum curatorial staff in each city visited were courted and won over with the promise of a potentially valuable purchase (Weisberg 32).

The ferocious energy Bing invested in his exhibition activity by no means marginalized his devotion to scholarship in matters of Japanese art. In 1894, he completed an article on "The Art of Utamaro" for the London journal, "The Studio." In it, he drew parallels between Utamaro's near-exclusive focus on elegant women and, conceptual stretch though it may seem, the art of the ancient Greeks. Bing was not the first among French *japonistes* to draw an analogy between Classical Greek and Japanese art. Earlier writers had already emphasized the "similar harmonies of their compositional designs" (Weisberg 35).

Although the depth of Bing's undertstanding of Japanese art, past and present was profound, and his scholarly skills impressive, "The Art of Utamaro" was not intended as a neutral meditation on the work of an *ukiyo-é* master. His real purpose in writing the article was to launch an assault on the views of Edmond de Goncourt, "a rival collector of Japanese objects, a firm believer that he had begun the *japonisme* craze in the 1860s, and an anti-Semite with whom Bing had been feuding for years" (Weisberg 35). In other words, underlying the meticulous reasoning in Bing's argument was a seething personal grudge.

Strictly in terms of art criticism, Bing's analysis took exception to Goncourt's emphasis on the eroticism implicit in Utamaro's depictions of women, as Goncourt saw it. Avoiding direct attack on his antagonist's opinions, Bing went to great lengths to explain the prints differently, in language that bears a striking resemblance to the formalist critical stance formulated by the American critic Clement Greenberg in the 1950s: "The Japanese artist, he said, created a designed image that had as its 'sole aim to combine grace of outline and harmony of brilliant colors.'" (Weisberg 37) Bing was implicitly suggesting, then, that the eroticism Goncourt perceived in the "large head prints" of Utamaro may actually have been a projection of the French critic's personal biases and, conceivably, base desires.

The roots of the simmering feud between Bing and Goncourt clearly lay deeper, however, than a theoretical difference in interpretation. And, in light of those roots, the eruption triggered by Bing's essay in 'The Studio" did considerable damage to Bing's success as a purveyor of the "new art" when his *Maison de l'Art Nouveau* opened in December 1895. While Bing had tried to veil his animosity through restrained, analytical language, his article in "The Studio" was still perceived as a mean-spirited, personal assault on Goncourt by many Parisian critics, and a crass "bid for publicity for his [Bing's] new enterprise" (Weisberg 37).Further, since Goncourt "was recognized as both promoter of Japanese art and a major collector," "The Art of Utamaro" was dismissed as a disrespectful affront to a superior scholar and connoisseur (Weisberg 37). Goncourt died shortly after the argument started, but the scandal triggered by Bing's article "cost Bing dearly in his hopes for an *art nouveau*" (Weisberg 37). His vision for an innovative approach to interior design, in which all elements would cohere in a unified *Gesamtkunstwerk*, was either ridiculed or ignored in the Parisian daily press; only specialty art journals outside France "greeted *art nouveau* with undiminished approval." (Weisberg 37)

Vindication came to Siegfried Bing in other ways, however. By the end of the 19th Century, more European museums had started collecting Japanese art, in part "to illustrate a cross-fertilization between East and West in contemporary Western art" (Weisberg 37). Having contributed so much to this curatorial wave, Bing persisted in his relentless efforts to encourage the East-West connection. If, for instance, a museum's curators purchased glassware by Louis Comfort Tiffany, with Bing as intermediary, he would capitalize on the transaction by sending them an exhibition of Japanese prints or ceramics. Age and the aging process, in fact, did little to diminish his vigor in accomplishing a deal that would be both nourishing culturally and financially lucrative.

In the final years of his life, having weathered a stunning number of mercantile and personal storms, Bing finally achieved the status of elder statesman in France. On the governmental level, he served on commissions to strengthen ties with the Far East, while in the private sphere, as the need arose, he provided expertise for major Oriental art sales when collectors died or sold off their holdings. (Weisberg 39) In 1900, in addition to assuming full responsibility for a pavilion on the grounds of the *Exposition International Universelle*, Bing was invited by Japanese officials to select pottery for the ceramic section of the Japanese Pavilion, a rare honor for a Westerner (Weisberg 40).

The Japanese Pavilion, shaped like a Buddhist temple, displayed both modern works and traditional Japanese art drawn from the imperial treasure, as well as private and temple museum collections that had never before left the country. Bing, who had devoted so much of his youth to developing expertise in the design and manufacture of ceramics, chose the pottery of Miyagawa Kozan, a porcelain artist who ultimately received the *Exposition* grand prize. (Weisberg 40)

Moreover, now lionized in France, Bing also maintained close ties with the Japanese government. The ties that were responsible for his participation in the Japanese Pavilion display also played a central role in the choice of Bing's galleries for the installation of the Nihon-Gwakei exhibition in 1901.

Sponsored by the Japanese Ministry of the Interior, the exhibit was initially "intended to reveal the continuity of [Japanese] traditions in modern Japanese painting." (Weisberg 40) However, as selection of work proceeded, the show became instead "an adventurous display of contemporary Japanese art that showed a distinct Western influence on space and composition." (Weisberg 40) Landscapes, animal studies, sketches of flowers and fruit all forcefully suggested a growing fusion of Oriental and Western concepts. In the words of the critic for 'The Studio,' the show demonstrated a stage between that which is no more and that which is to come (Weisberg 40). In other words, the cross-fertilization that had begun in isolationist Japan centuries earlier had reached fruition, as was evident in the galleries of the impresario Siegfried Bing.

Although Bing's efforts, and those of numerous other connoisseurs and collectors, were directed at impressing the European public with the stylistic excellence of Japanese art and craft in *all* media, in no medium did those efforts succeed as visibly as in the medium of the woodblock print. There were several reasons for the exceptionally enthusiastic response to the prints, reasons seemingly at odds with their artistic worth. For starters, until the mid-1890s, when recognition of their intrinsic value spurred a substantial rise in price, the prints were both easily accessible and affordable. In addition, unlike larger or less easily replaced Japanese craft objects, like screens or ceramics, they were lightweight and portable, while their pictorial content, at once exotic and oddly childlike, was provocative of lively, open-ended debate. So, given their widespread popularity and their influence on significant numbers of late 19th Century painters and designers, it makes good sense at this point to outline, in broad terms, the birth and development of the *ukiyo-é* woodblock print in Japan. Such an outline must also perforce look at the wood-block print medium's ancestry, beginning with the early years of the period in which the *ukiyo-é* style emerged and evolved toward ever greater sophistication. That would be the Edo Period.

The Edo Period more or less corresponds with Japan's long period of isolation, when the island nation was dominated by the Tokugawa shogunate. Although opinion regarding Edo Period start and end dates does vary, , the majority of scholars settle on the years 1615 to 1868. (In 1868, the imperial Meiji dynasty was restored to power, formally, if not in concrete political terms. The restoration took place a full 14 years after the official opening of Japan's ports to the West.) Ironically, the development of what many consider Japan's most important contribution to the world of 2-D art-making, *ukiyo-é* prints and paintings, coincides with the years when Japanese artists had little contact with other nations or cultures. Moreover, *ukiyo-e,* while a primary art form in historical terms, was not the only pictorial art practiced during the Edo period.

Students of the impact of Japanese art on 19th Century European artists commonly assume that the *ukiyo-e* woodblock prints flooding European capitals from the 1860s on represent the only form of picture-making carried on in Edo-era Japan. And it is certainly true that the *ukiyo-e* "pictures of the floating world," whose tradition-flouting content also appeared in one-of-a-kind genre paintings, comprised the primary channel of expression for Edo artists by the mid-18th Century. Originally associated with the Buddhist world view, the *ukiyo-e* outlook "subsequently came to suggest a hedonistic preoccupation with the present moment." (Kobayashi 33) It was this preoccupation, along with the vigorous realities of city life itself, that drew ambitious artists to the depiction of ephemeral pleasures typical of an urban culture whose prosperity rested on the relentless enterprise of its merchant class.

Nevertheless, it is critical to point out that *ukiyo-é*, the depiction of fugitive pleasures, initially found its place on a spectrum of classical traditions that, in most cases, predated it. The *samurai*, for example, patronized the Kano school of painting, a nation-wide organization of artists specializing "in a sumptuous style that combined Japanese and Chinese elements." The Emperor's court in Kyoto favored the *yamato-e* style, a tradition preserved by the *Tosa* school of painters, which traced its origins to ancient times. By the 17th Century, however, these official schools, "while maintaining their aristocratic patronage, gradually declined in creativity and fell into a pattern of conservative formalism" (Kobayashi 33). Hard to ignore here, and telling, are the parallels between entrenched stylistic traditions in Edo-era Japan and those of conservative art academies in Paris, Brussels, London and Edinburgh, whose gradual ossification and related decline in influence began in the mid-19th Century.

Furthermore, a necessary focus on *ukiyo-e* prints and genre painting shouldn't so absorb our attention that we overlook three other styles that rose to prominence in Edo in the 18th Century, all of them marked by exposure to Western or "Dutch" art: *bunjin-ga*, a proto-Impressionistic approach practiced by educated amateurs; *shasei-ga*, a type of naturalistic painting taken from direct observation; *yofu-ga*, a style of painting based on Japanese studies of Western art, mainly available to Japanese artists in reproduction (Kobayashi 33). Indeed, the thirst for Western knowledge during the

Edo period noted earlier, including close observation and analysis of flora and fauna, had infiltrated the visual arts as well. While the *ukiyo-e* image hardly qualifies as a literal expression of the phenomenal world, there was no doubt some seepage of Western naturalistic style and technique into the *ukiyo-e* artist's *modus operandi.*

Again, Masonobu's panoramic depiction of *Kabuki* theater, in which he employs two-point Renaissance perspective to suggest depth, gives clear evidence of this seepage. Like the three Western-influenced forms defined above, *ukiyo-é* definitely qualified as "new" in relation to classical Japanese art, but the revolutionary "floating world" emphasis, with its radical shift in content, actually materialized somewhat earlier. When Edo was elected seat of the Tokugawa shogunate's military government, *ukiyo-e* genre painting, whose emergence antedated that of *ukiyo-e* prints, was created by and for Edo's mercantile townsman class, not for the shogunate's military aristocracy or the now-marginalized court nobility. Indeed, with the advent of *ukiyo-e* genre painting, an art form that records the mundane activities and occasional delights of so-called "ordinary people," Edo citizens "gained virtually their first opportunity to enjoy the art of painting," (Kobayashi 33) accessible to them at least in terms of what it depicted, if not always in cost.

So, one may conclude that the change in pictorial content reflected, to some extent, the change in artistic patronage. From the classical period (645-1192) through the medieval period (1192-1573), the Japanese artist had been supported financially by an eclectic range of patrons: Shinto shrines; Buddhist temples; the imperial court in Kyoto; the military governments of the Kamakura and Ashigawa shogunates. Naturally, the work he produced "served the interests of these various religious and political authorities, or appealed to the tastes of the aristocracy." Therefore, he minimized or avoided altogether a significant realm of subject matter, that is, the "harsh realities" of the lives of common people who comprised the bulk of the Japanese population. (Kobayashi 33)

By the end of the Muromachi period (1392-1573), however, for an intricate web of related reasons, all forms of traditional political, social, economic, religious and cultural authority in Japan were collapsing. And, as both mirror and consequence of the collapse, the quotidian experience of the less privileged made its appearance in Japanese art. While the manners and mores of the aristocracy, a social stratum composed of court nobility, the *samurai*, and the priesthood, had to this point provided the content of Japanese painting, late 16th Century genre artists began to direct their attention elsewhere: to peasants planting rice in fields or to artisans and merchants "engaged in the occupations that gave the urban cultural centers their vitality." And those occupations "assume[d] a leading role for the first time as artistic subject matter" (Kobayashi 33).

Unfortunately, the 16th Century shift in thematic material was not accompanied by innovations in media that would have reduced the price of the work. Consequently, "even while artists were beginning to seek themes in the daily lives of the common people, the paintings themselves were still available only to an established class, by this time composed mainly of powerful *samurai* and wealthy merchants." (Kobayashi 33) This glaring disparity, between the experiences of those depicted in the paintings and the experiences of those who bought them, demanded resolution. As a result, as the 17th Century neared, the very century in which Japan closed its ports to the world, Edo townsmen artists made their first attempts "to respond to the rising demand for paintings that could be produced in quantity and at affordable prices." (Kobayashi 34) Their solution to the problem of cost was the development of the *shikomi-e* or "readymade pictures," monochrome paintings with simple compositions and popular motifs, easily manufactured in relatively large quantities.

As young Edo artists churned out "readymade pictures," they also gradually displaced time-honored subject matter by focussing on Edo's pleasure quarters, on its theaters and bathhouses, and on the seductive charms of prostitutes and beautiful, "loose" women, thereby increasing the work's profitability. While certainly more affordable than their more refined predecessors, *shikomi-e* themselves, readymade pictures had limited "potential as a mass-produced, inexpensive art form." In the end, then, the quest for the ideal technical means for large-scale production led artists and publishers to the medium of the woodblock print. (Kobayashi 34) And given Japan's rich woodblock print heritage, one reaching back to the 8th Century, it is not surprising that this option for high volume, low-cost production was exploited by 17th Century Edo artists, whose interests lay mainly in expanding their clientèle.

The single sheet *ukiyo-é* print familiar to Western art historians did not emerge immediately when 17th Century Edo artists and publishers began to capitalize on the advantages of the print process. Instead, early printed images, hand colored, were generally paired with narrative or poetic text in illustrated books that were printed and published in the Kamigata region, an area dominated by Kyoto, Japan's ancient capital and the site of the imperial court. (Kobayashi 34) As in so many areas of Japanese art and craft, the two expressive media, printed image and poetic or narrative text, appeared in integrated form.

This innovative medium then found its niche in Edo, Japan's new political center When the shogunate moved its headquarters from Kyoto to Edo in the mid-17th Century, the authorities shrewdly grasped the opportunity for a complete transformation of the new cpital in "self-consciously modern style." The opportunity presented itself in the horrendous fire of 1657 that destroyed Edo castle and most of the city. The subsequent construction of new municipal buildings and thoroughfares brought with it a vibrant new urban culture that borrowed from Kyoto, but was at the same time distinctly its own. It is surely no coincidence that the first illustrated book aimed at a mass market, "A Tale of Manly Love," was published in 1657 as well, in a rebuilt Edo proud of its modernized architectural face and its prosperous culture. (Kobayashi 35)

From then on, Edo-era publishers, their sights trained on an expanding middle class market, covered a eclectic range of dependably seductive topics: fabulous deeds of heroism; erotic narrative; information and critical comment on well-known courtesans and Kabuki actors. (Kobayashi 35)(The uncanny resemblance to present-day media exploitation of down-market public taste, in Europe and the United States, is hard to miss.)

Hishikawa Moronobu is the master generally thought to have first liberated the woodblock print from its secondary role as illustration of Edo poetry and prose. Moronobu is thus viewed as the inventor of the *ichimai-e* or "single sheet print" "the independent format in which a single print could be displayed for viewing." (Kobayashi 35) Moreover, while the *ichimai-e* he designed could stand alone as independent entities, they could also figure as pictorial elements or stages in a series linked by a single theme. With this development in mind, the Western reader's thoughts might move laterally to the Impressionist Claude Monet, both to Monet's impressive collection of *ukiyo-e* prints and to his longstanding, habit of working in series. Monet's serial depictions, such as those of haystacks, poplar trees and the facade of Rouen Cathedral, accomplished at different times of day, weather conditions, and seasons, are obvious cases in point. Surely then, this serial aspect of the prints in his collection had a strong impact on Monet's *modus operandi.*

The son of an embroiderer, Moronobu appeared in Edo during the feverishly creative years, 1658-1673, when publishers were mobilizing their efforts for the mass market. Gifted and ambitious, he played a role in the tumultuous competition "that prevailed among illustrators of popular literature." (Kobayashi 35) The enterprising Moronobu, in fact, was "first" in a variety of ways. In terms of celebrity, he was the first Edo illustrator "to achieve such prominence as to be able to sign his own work," whereas, in the past, creators of printed images had remained anonymous. In terms of style, "Moronobu turned the as yet unrefined techniques of early woodblock printing to his own advantage, deliberately emphasizing the contrasts achieved by rough-hewn lines and stark black and white compositions. [His] prints suggest the aesthetic consciousness of the Edo townsman, who was fond of frank lucidity" (Kobayashi 35-36).

The road to the liberation of the woodblock print from its subordinate role in the illustrated book was indeed paved by Moronobu's own publications, 150 illustrated books addressing "every conceivable theme" in which "illustrations predominated over textual commentary." (Kobayashi 36) Attuned to the eclectic tastes of Edo townsmen, Moronobu avoided restricting himself thematically: heroic deeds, erotica, famous women, the hedonistic life of Edo in general, all were grist for his incisive pictorial mill. With each new publication, the role of the printed image became more dominant, so that eventually the "page" itself could be extracted from the book, purchased separately, and displayed as an independent entity. (Kobayashi 36)

Not all of Moronobu's achievements were accomplished through the print medium. The protean master also paintied on silk, as evidenced by one of his masterpieces, "A Standing Woman." This stylized figure, with its sinuous contours, intricate patterned surface, and muted brown background, impresses us at first as anything but erotic. As is typical in Japanese depictions of women of any class, and in contrast to the Western preoccupation with nudes in expressive figuration, Moronobu presents us with a fully clothed woman, enveloped in her gorgeous robe.

Rather than defining the seductive curves of her body and the qualities of her skin and flesh, Moronobu concentrates his efforts instead on the woman's striking *kimono*, her ghostly white makeup, her delicate features, and her modest, but coquettish pose. The red ground of the *kimono* is covered with tiny, closely arrayed flowers and 11 shells, scattered randomly over the folds of the *kimono* fabric.Within the contours of the shells, the artist has painted scenes from the ancient Heian (Kyoto) court described in the11th Century novel, "The Tale of the Genjii," a legendary tale notable, in part, for having been written by a woman.

In his description, Tadashi Kobayashi emphasizes the classical restraint in Moronobu's depiction: "Like the shellfish matching game itself, which was popular among the ladies of the Heian court, the subject's S-shaped posture and suggestion of graceful movement lend a gentle, classical elegance to Moronobu's image of the beautiful woman." (Kobayashi 6) One might justifiably add that, in the multi-layered symbolism of his full-length portrait, Moronobu, like other *ukiyo-e* masters, would also present to Western artists and designers an alternative strategy for bodying forth erotic appeal, one that was subtle and allusive, rather than direct and blatant.

While Moronobu established the Hishikawa school, named, not surprisingly, after himself, his most celebrated disciples, Kiyonobu and Ando were not official school members. However, both artists drew from their mentor a heightened concern for "the beauty of human form itself," (Kobayashi 37), Kiyonobu in printmaking and Ando in painting. The disciples took Moronobu's figural concern further, in discarding the elaborate backgrounds that often characterized his work and tended to distract attention from the Kabuki actors and stunning women that formed their creative focus Ultimately, the artists favored subjects, Kabuki actors for Kiyonobu and beautiful women for Ando, would emerge as the two central motifs of the *ukiyo-é* repertoire (Kobayashi 37).

The Kabuki actor depicted by Kiyonobu deserves particular attention, given the marked resemblance between the Japanese printmaker's kinetic, assertive, self-assured line and that of Henri de Toulouse Lautrec, an artist closely allied with the Art Nouveau movement. Equally noteworthy are the similarities in their chosen medium, printmaking woodblock for Kiyonobu, lithography for Lautrec and in their shared attraction to the gaudiness and glitter, the escapist deceptions of urban night life and theater. Kiyonobu's actor is anything but a composed, elegant stage presence. The Japanese master exploits the actor's trademark strategies, his "gourd legs" and "earthworm lines," to convey his "flamboyant *aragato* style of acting," (Kobayashi 39) clearly the dramatic style Kiyonobu himself found most riveting. While the "gourd legs" exaggerate the actor's leg muscles, to suggest the strength demanded by his performance, the "earthworm lines" convey the shifts in rhythm and intensity in the actor's gestures and movements (Kobayashi 39).

The brilliant, caustic Lautrec was in many ways Kiyonobu's Western counterpart. Equally at home with Parisian prostitutes and the city's cultural elite, Lautrec was in many minds the Post-Impressionist most instinctively in tune with *ukiyo-e* style and content. Importantly, Lautrec was also a frequent participant in *Les Vingt* exhibitions, as both exhibitor and designer of installations. Certainly then, Henry van Velde, a full *Les Vingt* member by 1889, had by that date noted Lautrec's swift, incisive contour, as well as the close cropping and asymmetry in his composition, both strategies operating in concert with his vivid, penetrating depiction of Montmartre's *demi-mondaines.*

Evidence points clearly to Seurat and van Gogh as major influences on Henry van de Velde's landscape painting of the late 1880s. Less obvious is is the impact of Toulouse Lautrec's graphic work, such as his promotional posters for *Le Moulin*

Rouge, on van de Velde's landmark 1893 tapestry, and on the Belgian master's eventual achievement in the decorative arts. In turn, Lautrec's reductive approach to form, his impatience with superfluous detail, and most of all the emphatic quality of his draughtsman ship can be traced to Kiyonobu's strategies for conveying the energy and volatility of his adored Kabuki Actors. Ironically, these strategies were passed on, through Lautrec, to a Belgian designer of radically different temperament and intention.

Japanese art historical tradition describes Kaigetsudo Ando, Kiyonobu's colleague and contemporary, as "a true son of the Edo townsman class." Indeed, an enterprising urbanite, Ando was, for a time, a licensed broker for the Tokygawa shogunate. While primarily an *ukiyo-e* printmaker, Ando applied equal energy to the workshop production and promotion of art. In the late 17th Century, he organized and operated an atelier that specialized in the fabrication of original paintings, "by this time a rarity in the world of *ukiyo-e*." (Kobayashi 37) Taking Moronobu's efficient atelier process a step further, Ando "developed an even more effective system of mass production by strictly limiting and stereotyping pictorial subjects and the range of expressive techniques" (Kobayashi 37).

We can instantly recognize the prototypical "Kaigetsudo beauty," in reality a courtesan of Edo's pleasure quarters, through her standardized characteristics: inevitably voluptuous, at least in Japanese terms, she is presented standing against a blank ground, her stomach thrust forward and her shoulders bent back from the waist. Every Kaigetsudo beauty wears the same type of *kimono*, with bold flower and grass pattern (Kobayashi 37).

The colors in a painting produced in Ando's atelier are bright and unmodulated, strong, seductive hues emerging, however, from the use of cheap, inferior pigments. Naturally, as Kobayashi observes, the "repeated mechanical duplication of these simple compositions by the artists of the atelier made it possible to turn out paintings in large numbers." (Kobayashi 38) However, the downside of this pre-industrial solution to the linked problems of limited output and high cost of manufacture is obvious: an expressively bland, predictable image accomplished with inconsistent, non-durable materials. The question arises: would a 19th Century Western collector of Japanese *ukiyo-é* painting recognize the degraded image as easily as his Japanese counterpart?

In the very period when Ando's sacrifice of sophisticated pictorial quality and fine craft to easy profit resulted in a second-rate painting, revolutionary advances were being made in the woodblock print color use elsewhere in Edo. As one might expect, the Edo townsman's heightened interest in color coincided with the establishment of the single sheet print as an independent genre. This innovative step was closely followed by the emergence of the large oban print, often more than 50 cm.(h) by 30 cm. (w). This larger print, initially produced only in black and white, was developed with a view to enhancing expressive potential through simple expansion in size, potential that would then be further enhanced with color, the lighter, brighter, and more varied the better. Color *per se* was introduced into the *ukiyo-e* printing process in the late 17th Century, followed by greater subtlety and variety in the early to mid-18th Century. Initially, mineral pigments, derived from red lead, sulphur and saltpeter, enlivened the well-known "orange print," whose range of hues ran from orange-red to mineral green or yellow, applied with a rough hand.

In the decade 1720-1730, *ukiyo-e* "rose prints" supplanted orange prints in popularity, the rose-colored medium, with its translucent quality, now extracted from the petals of the safflower. A definite advance in delicacy, the hand-painted rose print "represents a general transformation of color composition toward lighter, crisper colors," (Kobayashi 39) an advance complemented by greater attention to the quality of the lines defining the color areas and the strategic use of evocative hues to emphasize selected details in the overall design. In other words, by the mid-18th Century, Japanese printmakers and their technical collaborators were now capitalizing on the inherent power of color to trigger or intensify emotion.

The creation of the "lacquer print" signals a further stage of sophistication. The lacquer print technique involved the use of black ink with an unusually high glue content, producing "a lustrous effect suggestive of traditional Japanese lacquerware" (Kobayashi 39). Indeed, the lacquer print provides still another example of the permeable membrane between the fine and applied arts in Japanese tradition. The glossy medium accentuated the lustre of black Japanese hair and the black sashes for *kimono* fashionable during the period. The ebony sheen proved all the more effective through its contrast with the lighter, translucent colors used elsewhere in the prints. The strategic use of glossy black in the prints would have been especially liberating for Western artists long inhibited in the use of gleaming, pitch black areas in their work by Renaissance strictures.

The next step in the evolution of Japanese printmaking was indeed a "giant step": the invention of techniques for creating high quality images in high volume that were all exactly alike. Oddly for a Westerner, the development of an effective method for producing identical polychrome prints in high volume in Japan can be traced to the popularity of picture calendars. For the makers of the calendars, the objective was to complete "a single print in which the correct order of long and short months [in the Japanese year] was represented in the most ingenious fashion possible." (Kobayashi 41) Publishers offered lavish commissions to established *ukiyo-e* artists, each of whom "seized this opportunity to pursue to the limits the expressive potential of the woodblock print." (Kobayashi 41) In this competitive ferment, the first polychrome *ukiyo-e* prints to be produced entirely through the woodblock printmaking process emerged.

For this process, which permanently replaced hand painting, the printer inked a series of colors onto separate blocks, one by one, over a black outline of the image, also printed from a separate block. (Each inked block carried one pictorial element of the entire image.) The challenge for the printer was to line up or "register" each successive overlay of color area on the others, so that the final image would be seamless and coherent.As to impact on Western artists, the richness of the printer's colors, their consistency oilier than that of traditional, water-based Japanese paint, their hues unmodulated by tonal gradation, ultimately opened to Western artists a means to a stylized depiction of the phenomenal world that had long been supplanted by Renaissance advances in realism

Edo publishers were quick to recognize the marketing potential for the polychrome prints produced from ateliers employing the breakthrough color printing process. And since the brilliant colors of these new *ukiyo-e* compositions - the brilliant indigo and saffron shapes on scarlet backgrounds - suggested the Shuchiang brocades (*Shokko nishiki*) imported from China in the period, the publishers, taking their cue from the textiles' popularity, promoted their innovative products as "brocade pictures" (Kobayashi 42).

Critical as well to a discussion of Edo era woodblock printing is a second 18th Century phenomenon: collaborative production. Indeed, the multi-color print owes its birth as much to a symbiotic collaboration between a wealthy connoisseur, an artist, an engraver and a printer as it does to the invention of the polychrome woodblock technique (Kobayashi 42) While later in the 18th Century, the skilled engraver and printer were relegated to anonymity, and the connoisseur replaced by a publisher driven mainly by a fickle market, the collaborative nature of *ukiyo-e* printmaking process remained in place.

The first brocade prints offered for sale to Edo townsmen were actually inexpensive copies of picture calendars, their pages altered so as to suggest a bit of benign chicanery. Publishers bought the calendar woodblocks from connoisseurs, and then had engravers obliterate both the connoisseurs' identity and explanations regarding the individual months. Images printed from the calendar blocks, original owners' names and clarifying descriptions now removed, were then sold as single-sheet brocade prints (Kobayashi 42). In this way, the picture calendars of the celebrated *ukiyo-e* artist Suzuki Harunobu (1725-70), sought after by learned connoisseurs and merchant townsmen alike, reappeared on the open market.

Of the artists profitting from technical advances in the creation of polychrome prints, Harunobu (1725-70) was the first to achieve widespread popularity, accompanied, of course, by financial success. In the initial phase of his relatively brief career, Harunobu did indeed deploy his sure grasp of the new polychrome technique in the fabrication of picture calendars. However, far more noteworthy in his artistic legacy, for both Japanese and Western art historians, were his efforts in regenerating the lyricism of classical Japanese painting, achieved through the restraint manifest in his depiction of the human figure. (Kobayashi 42) Consequently, Harunobu injected a gentler, more refined quality of experience into modern, frenetic Edo culture than was commonly seen in *ukiyo-é* prints produced for an expanded buying public. In Harunobu's pictorial cosmos, slender, fragile men and women inhabit an ethereal realm, their refinement at odds with the unambiguous eroticism defining the greater number of *ukiyo-é* prints designed by his contemporaries.

Preferring the smaller *chuban* to the larger *oban* size sheet, Harunobu opted for subtle, dulled or "broken" colors, rather than the saturated hues of his artist colleagues. His compositional strategy depended on the oblique directional line, with the viewer looking down on the events portrayed. (Kobayashi 42) Conceivably, the immense popularity of Harunobu's work reflected a subconscious longing in his clients, a repressed nostalgia for a less hectic, clangorous environment than that of 18th Century Edo, prosperous and energizing though the city was. Nevertheless, while Harunobu exercised classical restraint in his depiction of figures, fascination with the intricacies, intrigues, and occasional deceits inevitable in affairs of the heart governed his choice of narrative motifs as commonly as it did those of his less tasteful peers. The frequently reproduced brocade print "A Story of Love on the Veranda" (1767-68) is perhaps most emblematic both of Harunobu's distinctive stylistic tendencies and his thematic inclinations.

In this iconic work, we see a young man in *kimono* and *obi*, seated on a veranda, his feet dangling over the edge. (Admittedly, the delicate young man might easily be mistaken for a young woman, to a Westerner unseasoned in the ways of Japanese figuration.) As Kobayashi suggests, "the older woman who has put her arm around him and, grasping his wrist, is whispering into his ear must be a lady in waiting or the nurse of the young woman peeping through the sliding panel." In fact, we are not sure, since Harunobu, here as elsewhere, leaves the puzzled viewer in a state of uncertainty. Is this very attractive older woman merely a go-between, or is she a seductress herself, with "her mature, erotically bewitching [for a Japanese viewer] manner" (Kobayashi 10).

The provocative, "entangled drama of love," in whose expression Western advances in anatomy and perspective play no part, is "enacted in the natural, familiar setting of an autumnal garden in which bush clover is flowering." (Kobayashi 10) In this intimate scene, the commercial energy and hurly-burly of contemporary urban life in Edo seems distant, *unless* we are actually witnessing a moment in the development of a commercial relationship between a young businessman and a pretty courtesan, just as young, whose "go-between" is actually a brothel Madame. But, once again, as a result of Harunobu's reversion to classical modes of depiction, we can't be sure.

The oblique line, the diagonal motion one commonly associates with Japanese design sensibility is the dominant structural factor in "Love on the Veranda." For that matter, the composition as a whole develops obliquely from the fence at the lower left toward the upper right, while the dark colors of the wall, garden, and fence set off the lighter, more vivid colors of the central scene, "creating a beautiful pattern of shade and light." (Kobayashi 42) Thus, in linking Japanese stylistic norms to 19th Century art and design developments in the West, we can be justified in assuming that artists like Lautrec and Edgar Degas were thrilled by the heightened visual energy generated by the diagonal thrust. For the Japanese masters, the diagonal motion was a natural pictorial outgrowth of the pervasive sloped stone wall, an architectural requirement in an earthquake-prone environment, while the French masters adopted the device for expressive purposes instead, to enormous effect.

The ongoing focus on women in genre painting and woodblock prints, be they courtesans or respectable townswomen, intensified further during the so-named Golden Age of *Ukiyo-é*, starting with the important innovations of Torii Kiyonaga during the short-lived Tenmei era, 1781-89. Returning the beautiful women, he depicted to current day urban Edo, Kiyonaga expanded the standard dimensions of the single sheet brocade print from *chuban* (ca. 28 x 20 cm.) to *oban* (ca. 39 x 26 cm.) size.

Kiyonaga's panoramic narratives, more ambitious in scope and complex in content than those of his predecessors, spread across two to three *oban*, arranged horizontally and integrated thematically in a single composition. These generous surfaces, similar to those of Renoir ("The Boating Party") or Georges Seurat ("Afternoon on the Great Jetty"), permitted the artist unusually expansive descriptions of favorite outdoor recreation spots for Edo's newly prosperous population, such as the banks of the Sumida River or the seashore near Shinagawa. (Kobayashi 43)

In marked contrast to "the poetic, dreamlike setting of a previous age" and the subtle expression of group dynamics that typify Harunobu's work, Kiyonaga's women and men, while still somewhat idealized, enjoy their fashionable amusements in contemporary Edo settings chosen for their natural loveliness. In the three-panel visual saga, "A Moored Pleasure Boat beneath the Bridge" (1784-85), a group of women *and* men, in a variety of naturalistic, uninhibited positions standing, sitting, kneeling, reclining, enjoy the fine weather and each other's company in a manner that seems spontaneous and unforced. Bound to rivet the attention of *avant garde* artists in Paris of the 1870s to 1890s a city then enjoying equivalent prosperity and loosening of traditional social restraints, Kiyonaga's women display a refreshingly clear, eloquent expression of the human form unusual in Japanese painting (Kobayashi 43).

In terms of composition, Kiyonaga's line of vision is direct and frontal, a departure from Harunobu's more remote overhead view. Landscape features and human figures rise perpendicularly from the horizontal, "in direct contrast to Harunobu's oblique angle of vision." (Kobayashi 44) The figures are tall and svelte, in contrast with the smaller, roly-poly figures of the mid-18th Century, the comfortable conviviality of their quite modern, urban relationships revealed in their individualized responses to the overall recreational experience and to their companions (Kobayashi 44). One would be hard put, for example, to find in the work of earlier artists a seated woman with fashionable *kimono* hiked up above her knees to keep it dry, like the unself-conscious figure in the foreground of the middle panel. Demure she isn't. Sensible she is.

Apart from landscapists Hiroshige and Hokusai, Kitagawa Utamaro is arguably the best known of *ukiyo-é* masters to Western students of woodblock prints. Utamaro emerged from the "turmoil created in Edo's art and literary circles by the Kensei Reforms, sumptuary edicts formulated by Matsudaira Sadanobu and carried out during the Kensei era (1789-1801)." Taking Kiyonaga's daring innovations in realistic female portraiture even further, Utamaro's habit of depicting only the upper half of the figure's body allowed him exclusive focus on the subject's face. His "large head" *oban*-size portraits of women form the core of his body of work, and account for his virtually unrivalled popularity among European and American collectors, beginning in the early 1870s (Kobayashi 44).

Before embarking on the development of his mature work, brocade prints of "large head" women, Utamaro, from 1782 on, honed his skills in naturalistic rendering through illustrations created for a popular variety of "picture book" featuring, oddly enough, comic verse. To complement the verse, publishers demanded "naturalistic representation of landscapes, as well as detailed depiction of insects, shellfish, birds and plant life." (Kobayashi 44) The Japanese artist could, of course, work from "live models" right before his eyes; or he could take advantage of the precision with which Western artists conscientiously depicted the wealth of plants and animals in their distant and radically different European natural world. No doubt, Utamaro, during his apprenticeship in realistic visual description, did a little of both.

Moving from the preparatory experience of accurate reproduction of the observed natural world, Utamaro then devoted the bulk of career to capturing the differences in character and temperament of women of every class and background. As Kobayashi remarks, "Utamaro's 'large-head pictures,' based as they are on the artist's own careful observations of feminine beauty, constituted a sharp criticism of existing approaches to the genre of female portraiture, which had traditionally produced a succession of stereotyped, ideal images of women completely without expression or individuality."

He further notes: "Utamaro achieved his greatest expression of the nuances of feminine psychology, capturing fleeting emotional states that could be revealed only in a close study of facial expression and expressive gesture" (Kobayashi 45). Kobayashi's comments reflect the received wisdom regarding Utamaro's portraits of women, portraits whose swooping, curvilinear contours, patterned surfaces, and minimal description of facial features undoubtedly had critical impact on depictions of women in Art Nouveau design.

Admittedly, however, given the disconnect between what Japanese scholars tell us about Utamaro's departures in portraiture and what one actually sees in his "large head pictures," it is difficult for a Western appreciator of Utamaro's elegant, strangely quiet and remote portraits to feel "fleeting emotional states," in the Western sense, of any kind. Perhaps the cultural chasm *is* the culprit here. A slight tilt or turn of the head, a slight opening of the mouth, a barely perceptible lift of the eyebrow may signify a strong shift or change in feeling for the Japanese viewer of Utamaro's portrait heads.

But such minute indicators in Utamaro's portraits may escape the Westerner acclimatized to a more generally emotive culture, traditionally depicted in less minimal ways. Utamaro's sympathy with a gamut of emotions in his female subjects, and his effort to portray them, are undeniable. But what may have moved Art Nouveau artists and designers more is his appreciation, in aesthetic terms, of the delicate female form *enclosed* in its draped kimono, the dignity of an elegant woman's stance, and the near-opacity of the *ukiyo-e* female face, politely disguising, as much as revealing, the powerful emotions behind it.

CHAPTER 8

France: Where Were the Women?

Among the many ironies one encounters in the study of Art Nouveau is the disjuncture between the centrality of the stylized female face and figure in French Art Nouveau design and the accelerated access to higher education and the professions gained by flesh-and-blood French women from the 1860s on. In French Art Nouveau jewelry, serving ware, and interior furnishing, the stylized female face and form remained an intriguing, sometimes suggestive, but still decorative element, while, by the end of the 19th Century, the educated Frenchwoman had become a potent social and economic force. In the 1860s, that signal decade, French women were finally admitted to first rank French universities; twenty years later, in the 1880s, the Ferry Laws extended secondary education for women throughout the country. In 1885, French female physicians won the long-sought-for right to practice medicine in public, state-supported hospitals. (Escritt: 86)

Indeed, by the 1880s, the seemingly inexorable progress of women in gaining a more substantial role in French public life had been accompanied by the coining of the term *la femme nouvelle.* This was, in truth, an ambiguous label whose connotation depended on the political leanings of the speaker and the listener. For those with socially progressive attitudes, a "new woman" was a woman unfettered by outdated notions of female inferiority. But for the more conservative Frenchman, the steady upward mobility of *la femme nouvelle* in French professional life, her path smoothed by greater access to higher education, threatened the stability of long-immutable social structures, as well as artistic traditions that had held sway for centuries.

The emergence of French women, particularly those of the middle and lower middle classes, from their traditional, restrictive place in the home was not the consequence of a newfound egalitarian driving their male peers in education, the professions, or government. The opportunity to learn at an advanced, sophisticated level, and apply that learning to meaningful work in hitherto male-dominated professions such as medicine, owed much to energetic agitation by members of the well-organized 19th Century French Feminist Movement. This was a national movement that had, in turn, had gained wide recognition as an effective agent for women's rights through its vigorous participation in the first *Congrès International du Droit des Femmes*, which met in Paris in 1878 (Escritt: 86).

The *Congrès*, no doubt a source of unprecedented personal affirmation for delegates from many European countries, had seen its initially dominant moderate wing superseded by radicals like the French activist Hubertine Auclert. Auclert, a leader and ardent voice in the campaign for women's voting rights, was also instrumental in the founding of *La Citoyenne*, a weekly newspaper whose aim was, in unequivocal terms, "to claim the equality of woman and man" (Escritt: 56). Auclert's campaign for equality for women in both the legal and the day-to-day practical sense, an agenda disseminated through the written word, easily matched in intensity that of

Siegfried Bing, advocating for the importance of Japanese art and craft for Western designers, or Henry van de Velde, celebrating Flemish culture, in journals of their making in France and Belgium.

Stephen Escritt notes that conservatives in France, "viewed all such changes as a rejection of women's traditional roles and linked them to France's declining birthrate, which was seen as particularly worrying while Germany's population boomed" (Escritt: 86). It is indisputable that women aspiring to rewarding professional lives were also bound to opt for smaller families and reduced the amount of time spent maintaining, not to mention decorating the home. Nevertheless, it is likely that the anxiety expressed over Germany's expanding workforce and growing industrial might was but one factor in the complex matrix of unsettling changes Frenchmen perceived in their nation's feminist ferment. Indeed, in view of that looming destabilization, numerous French and other continental biologists and anthropologists invested considerable energy in concocting what now seems dubious "scientific" justification for an exclusively domestic role of women.

An especially preposterous pseudo-scientific pronouncement by Carl Vogt exemplifies this line of defense by anti-feminists. Vogt, Professor of Natural History at the University of Geneva and an avowed Darwinist, used his supposedly "objective" study of skulls to declare that "the female skull approaches, in many respects, that of the infant, and, in a still greater degree, that of the lower races.' "(Escritt: 86) Equally as persuasive, for those already convinced of female inferiority, was the theory of masochism propounded by Richard von Krafft-Ebbing in his 1886 treatise "Psychopathia Sexualis." According to Krafft-Ebbing, voluntary submission, or more accurately put, subjection to the opposite sex. was a clear form of psychological perversity in a small number of men. However, for women, such willing subjection had its source in genetic endowment, and was therefore normal (Escritt: 87).

Krafft-Ebbing and other (but not all) 19th Century scientists, took their examination of sexual behavior, normal and abnormal, into a wider social realm, that is, into modern European cities, which they condemned, in hyperbolic purple prose, as "venues of squalid inequity." "Where poverty and luxury were concentrated, so degenerative neurological disorders would eventually prosper." (Escritt: 87) This notion gained currency in Paris as early as 1857, when the poet and critic Charles Baudelaire published his canonic "*Fleurs du Mal*," a lean volume of exquisitely crafted poems that paid perverse reverence to decadence and spiritual exhaustion. Indeed, for many poets and painters of the latter half of the 19th Century, the Symbolists among them, neurotic personality traits, sexual perversion, social degeneracy, and a condition of fatalistic *ennui* were inextricably bound together, their merged thematic centrality in the visual arts and literature perversely more magnetizing for a devoted public than more upbeat motifs of spiritual and physical health and wellbeing.

Without question, then, anti-feminist attitudes were especially deep-rooted in the 19th Century Parisian art world, where upper crust fashion had long favored images of women in states ranging from elegant passivity to physical and/or spiritual depletion. Notable exceptions to this general rule, of course, were the Impressionist painters, who found their female subjects in "the real world, at cafés and galleries, at home and in shops" (Escritt: 88). Women depicted by such leadingImpressionists as Manet, Degas, and Renoir carried on independent lives in the here-and-now Parisian milieu, their individuated faces and figures, mode of dress, manner and gestures, their range of activities in the contemporary urban setting, taken directly from life, Their Impressionist creators had , in fact, had largelyliberated themselves from academic Beaux Arts conventions.

Edouard Manet's "scandalous" nude models and mistresses immediately come to mind here. A haughty, boyishly angular Victorine Meurand, for example, boldly stares down the viewer as "Olympia," in the painter's revolutionary 1863 take on the traditional odalisque. So does the model-mistress relaxing with her fully clothed companions in *Le Déjeuner sur l'Herbe* (1863). For that matter, the pensive young woman tending bar at the Folies Bergère, in Manet's expansive masterpiece of 1881-82, may earn a pittance for her efforts, but she is nonetheless her own woman.

As for Edgar Degas, suspicions of the polymath artist's misogyny are offset not only by his close, collegial friendship with Mary Cassatt, but also by his rigorously honest, yet sympathetic depictions of milliners, laundresses, and adolescent, gawky female ballet students, practicing or at rest on the sidelines in a Parisian dance studio. Admittedly, Degas' female subjects are not, in the main, women working or preparing for work at the highest levels of Parisian professional, cultural, or commercial life. Nevertheless, in light of Degas' legendary high intelligence and wide ranging, probing curiosity, we may assume that he's chosen to draw and paint them not only for their potential as arresting forms on the picture plane, but in appreciation of the sheer strain of their daily efforts as self-supporting women.

Moreover, the plump, pink cheeked, conventionally pretty young women who people Pierre-Auguste Renoir's lively outings at the *Moulin de la Galette* (1876) or by the Seine ("The Boating Party," 1881) appear at ease, self-possessed, and as likely as not on their own in their respective recreational settings. They dance, converse, and flirt on an equal social footing with their male peers. The woman in the yellow hat near dead center in the background of "Boating Party," for example, leans comfortably on the railing as she receives the attentions of the young man with his back turned to us. We sense that, at any moment, she can easily turn *her* back and walk away, alone.

Renoir's women, with their fine, fair complexions, unfailingly sweet, some say saccharine expressions, and ever-fuller torsos and limbs, are ultra-feminine in the conventional way. However, even this most mellow of Impressionists was clearly marked by the militant feminism of his period. His women, like those of Manet and Degas, move freely, alone or in company, in the hurly burly of the Parisian throng, strolling along the city's wide boulevards and apparently at ease hobnobbing in its cafés and urban parks. Certainly, nothing of the sort can be said of the standard issue nymphs and sirens who pervade French Art Nouveau design.

From the late 1860s on, the Impressionists persisted in realistically depicting contemporary French women, in all their variety, against a resistant critical tide. Victor Jozé, for example, cultural critic for the journal *La Plume,* deplored the "'illusory emancipatory ideas which are unrealizable and absurd. Let woman remain what Nature has made her, an ideal woman, the companion and lover of man, themistress of the home .let there be no androgynes'" (Escritt: 87). Essential to note, however, is that virulent anti-feminist rhetoric like Jozé's increasingly stimulated equally strong reactions by articulate standard bearers like Maria Deraismes. Writing for the moderate weekly *Le Droit des Femmes* in 1869, Deraismes clarified the feminist stance "What women want is not to be brought up, educated, moulded according to some conventional image, an image conceived in the brain of poets, novelists or artists and therefore unreal" (Escritt: 87)

While cultural critics and artists of all stripes, reacting to the expanding presence of *la femme nouvelle* in French society, hotly debated the appropriate model for depicting women in the expressive fine arts, those concerned with restoring French leadership in the applied arts looked to women's traditional homemaking role as a lever for attaining that goal. In 1892, the *Union Centrale des Arts Décoratifs* staged an exhibition titled "*Les Arts des Femmes*," a show of small, primarily decorative craft items, most with minimal essential function in the bourgeois home. Much of the craft on display bore the mark of stylized, curvilinear Art Nouveau design. Louis de Foucard, writing for the *Revue des Arts Décoratifs*, pronounced the exhibit "a prophetic manifesto for the relationship between Art Nouveau and women, as both consumers and subjects" (Escritt: 88).

In clear denial of or blindness to the rising swell of feminist political activism all around him, Foucard continued, "What a woman suggests is worth more than what she conceives. Technically a woman excels at small tasks. She is a born upholsterer, seamstress, refined decorator of intimate space, an inexhaustible orchestrator of worldly elegance. For everything else, her lofty function is to be an inspiration, even when she does not know it" (Escritt: 88).

Even when she does not know it? In the end, fortunately for succeeding generations of designers male *and* female, the exhibit contributed little to the regeneration of French craft in the minds of other European nations. Instead, it served to solidify the resolve of French feminists to maintain their newfound gains in French professional and political affairs.

The determinedly anti-feminist Edmond de Goncourt, a far greater force than Foucard in Parisian cultural circles, carried further the virtual crusade by social conservatives against the inroads made by the *femme nouvelle* on French cultural tradition. The *femme nouvelle*, he observed, was proving so unsatisfying to the French male that he had shifted his interest to "pretty inanimate objects, with a passion charged with the nature and character of erotic love." (Escritt: 88) "According to this logic," Escritt observes, "the aesthetic desire to covet objects with a kind of erotic zeal previously reserved for women was an inevitable result of female emancipation" (Escritt: 88). What is more, in a dubious conflation of interior decoration with "the arts" in general, Goncourt, the self-same Goncourt who served as *bête noire* for Siegfried Bing, went on to fulminate that the impact of the *femme nouvelle* on the arts could only be destructive, as she was now out studying or working, rather than beautifying the domestic environment (Escritt: 88).

Meanwhile, against "a background of such commentary and debate, the female figure joined plant tendrils and dragonflies as an embodiment of nature in Art

Nouveau object." (Escritt: 88) Not surprisingly, these stylized emblems of the natural world, the female form inclusive, were incorporated in French Art Nouveau jewelry, fine metal and ceramic servingware, glassware, and lamp bases created primarily by male designers. Their depictions of women suggested either a long established ideal for feminine beauty, one abandoned even by some academic artists exhibiting in the Salon, or barely disguised fears regarding *la femme nouvelle*. Two predictable stereotypes, poles apart in symbolic weight, prevailed: the fragile nymph, metaphor for innocence and purity, and the femme fatale, emblem of evil and temptation, possibly a stand in for *la femme nouvelle* herself. (Escritt: 90)

Coincidentally, these stereotypes, pervaded 19th Century Symbolism in the fine arts realm, their reductive view of the female persona extending even as far as some late 19th Century Glaswegian studios. An enamel and silver brooch, set with opals and coral pearls and fashioned by Henri Ernest Dabault in 1901, typifies one strand of French Art Nouveau in featuring a recognizable biblical figure. The brooch deploys the familiar motif of Eve's temptation by the snake, to give proof of the weakness of will, vulnerability, and degeneracy not only of the Old Testament mother of us all, but of womankind in general. Biting into the forbidden fruit picked from the Tree of Knowledge, Eve is the unwitting instrument of humankind's expulsion from Paradise into a world of sin and evil. (Escritt: 90) The implicit, if far-fetched parallel the designer may very well suggest, between the biblical Eve and the well-educated *femme nouvelle*, assertively claiming her rightful place in medicine, law, business and the arts, is hard to ignore. Both women, in upsetting the "natural" order, God-given peace and harmony on earth, generate instead disruption, conflict, and social chaos.

Intimate scale and delicate fashioning barely disguise the erotic charge of two pieces by the famed French Art Nouveau jewelry and glass designer René Lalique. In one, "The Siren" (1897-8), the intersecting curves of the antique bronze framework encircle the head and nude torso of a central figure, who is actually an unnamed seductress from a second Art Nouveau source: classical mythology. While her identity is unknown, the siren's fearsome nature is suggested by the transformation of her legs into scaly, powerful extensions reminiscent of Medieval dragon tails. These flexible limbs wrap whip-like around inset emeralds and opals far exceeding in scale the siren's slim torso and upraised arms, telling us that, loveliness aside, Lalique's siren is a dangerous predator.

More ambiguous in content, and thus more tantalizing for the well-heeled client, is Lalique's "The Kiss" (1904-6). This tiny brooch (2 3/4" in width), crafted of silver and luminescent moulded glass, depicts two lovers of indeterminate gender, the soft curls of their hair "bedecked in laurel wreaths" and their faces almost mirror images. (Escritt: 94) Are we observing a homoerotic encounter in Lalique's miniaturized romantic moment? If so, then the encounter would have surely challenged the conventional values and staid lifestyle of the designer's clients. As a result, we may then surmise that challenge to convention itself lay in both the designer's intention and the client's attraction to the piece.

Nevertheless, the impact of the possible homoerotic hedonism implicit in "The Kiss" is definitely diminished by the small scale of the brooch, so that a wealthy middle class woman, one most likely dependent on her spouse for financial support, might freely sport the expensive ornament in public. The brooch, closely observed, might provoke comment, but its delicacy and function as mere ornament would preclude real scandal.

So, unlike the adventurous Impressionists, French Art Nouveau designers tended to play it safe. Selecting their decorative female forms from a familiar arsenal of mythological or biblical subjects, they might tinker with their traditional depiction. But artistic acknowledgement of the *femme nouvelle* in the positive sense, that is, recognition and expression of her expanding influence and success, both her economic success and her *succès d'estime* in contemporary French affairs, lay outside their pragmatic interest. Indeed, such acknowledgement lay as well beyond their creative powers. How would one depict a robust Degas laundress, yawning and stretching her brawny arms, much less a female medical practitioner healing a sick patient, in the facture of a silver brooch inset with fine gems, fashioned to clip on to a rich woman's ermine wrap?

There is ironic justice in the fact that the most effective agents in the mobilization of the French Art Nouveau stylistic agenda for promotional goals were neither men, nor fully French. French, that is, in ways that would meet the rigid criteria of diehard chauvinists. Moreover, neither of the two great female icons of French Art Nouveau, neither the revered actress Sarah Bernhardt, nor the dancer, choreographer, and wizard of stage lighting, Loie Fuller, measured up physically to the tall, willowy ideal for Art Nouveau beauty. Small in stature, Bernhardt was notoriously thin and angular until middle age; Fuller, short and stout.

Escritt sums up the paradox at the heart of Bernhardt's and Fuller's shared position as both model for the ambitious, enterprising *femme nouvelle* and epitome of the Art Nouveau feminine ideal: "In a contradiction typical of Art Nouveau, Bernhardt and Fuller embodied elements of the '*femme nouvelle*' in their working careers, while at the same time providing critics and artists with raw material with which to reassert the dominant ideal of natural female grace and beauty." (Escritt: 102) Be it said, however, that the provision of "raw material" involved considerable misrepresentation of the facts of their appearance on the part of both women, alert as they were to importance of publicity tailored to common expectation, no matter how deceptive.

Bernhardt was the eldest of three illegitimate daughters of a Dutch Jewish courtesan, Julie or Judith, or Youle Bernard, a woman who, once at home in Paris, demonstrated an impressive gift for insinuating herself into elite cultural circles. Fuller was an American performer, transplanted to Paris from Chicago, who had honed her onstage skills in burlesque, vaudeville and circus shows in her home country. Certainly, foreign or "exotic" origin accounted in large part for their immense popularity in the late 19th Century Parisian theater world. However, one can also identify three additional sources of their popular success: bold theatrical innovation, exceptional personal charisma, and the audience's sense that what was taking place onstage was an unprecedented mix of the exotic and the erotic.

Sarah Bernhardt, the "Divine Sarah," had long since found her place on the Parisian stage when she began her collaboration with the Czech painter and designer, Alphonse Mucha, in 1894. While nearly 50, she was still playing, and would continue to play for many years, a range of leading roles good sense would deem more appropriate for actresses decades younger. Moreover, owing to her apparently ageless stage presence, she got away with it. Again and again, she enthralled her public by virtually inhabiting the personalities of passionate female characters whose demise, through murder, suicide, or simple heartbreak as frequently resembled that of young, doomed Shakespearean heroines, Ophelia, for example, as more mature figures of classical tragedy, such as Phèdre, one of her most celebrated roles.

Already a steady patron of Lalique, Bernhardt recognized in Mucha's "intricate and detailed linear style," (Escritt: 97) a means for visually defining her dramatic persona that would further enhance what had become a near-mythic reputation in fin de siècle Paris. Mucha's depictions of Bernhardt as Gismonda, *La Samaritaine*, or Marguerite Gautier in *La Dame aux Caméllias*, in images whose subtly hued open areas or "voids" set off richly detailed surfaces, would also, she rightly anticipated, bulk up ticket sales. Bernhardt was definitely the dominant player in the collaboration with Mucha: "neither a waif nor a submissive figure, Bernhardt was far from being Mucha's passive aesthetic plaything. She was already the most famous actress in Paris when he was introduced to her in 1894. It was Bernhardt who enthusiastically approved Mucha's first poster 'Gismonda.' In doing so, she plucked him out of obscurity, overriding the skepticism of her printer, and throughout their patronage, she retained the power of veto" (Escritt: 101).

Bernhardt's soft, but resonant "golden" voice and exceptional grasp of psychological motivation a grasp informed by disciplined insight into her own psychological mainsprings, so riveted audiences that they remained indifferent, if not blind to her physical limitations in playing impassioned, suffering, but always authoritative characters. Unlike her model and mentor, Rachel, also beloved by the Parisian public and also Jewish, Sarah concerned herself with feeling each part, rather than imitating the tried-and-true, histrionic gestures of older, established actresses. "There was a touch of hysteria, perhaps even of danger, in her willingness to expose her emotions, to impose them on her audience. Yet her elegance of carriage, the charm of her voice, her consummate taste in the delivery of her lines protected her from appearing uncomfortably aggressive." (Gottlieb 186)

Her face was not the problem: at her behest, the photographer Nadar preserved for us Bernhardt's decidedly un-French, but lovely features, all the more seductive for a Frenchman in their exoticism. Robert Gottlieb pays eloquent homage to the now-classic photographs of a pensive young woman whose face was hardly suited to simple, boiler plate Art Nouveau depiction: "Fortunately for posterity, a series of astoundingly beautiful portraits of the young Sarah was taken by the great photographer Félix Nadar. (She may have been sixteen, or perhaps a year or two older.) She posed calmly, meditatively, with a mantle of cloth draped carelessly around her shoulders. Her untamed hair bursts out around her face, looking darker than the red-gold that was its natural color. The eyes are startling and enigmatic. A number of observers noted that, depending on her mood, they changed color, from gray to green to blue. The forehead is high, the nose just slightly irregular (Jewish, they said.) The effect is mysterious, intense, yet withheld, closer to tragic than assertive. She looks like no one else in the world." (Gottlieb 27)

The loveliness of her face a given, it was rather Bernhardt's slight stature and tight auburn curls that ill fit the image she sought to project in posters advertising her performances. What is more, by the time her collaboration with Mucha began, Bernhardt was in full middle age. The slim figure of her youth had finally given way to what we now crudely term "middle age spread." Mucha tactfully compensated by adding Bernhardt's head to drawings of tall, lithe models done in the studio, and softening those tight curls into wavy, flowing locks that formed the central framing device of the seven promotional posters the actress commissioned over a decade's collaboration

Mucha's "Gismonda" poster, created in 1894 and his first for Bernhardt, is probably the most familiar to both Mucha and Bernhardt *dévotés*. The Czech artist presents the title character as a statuesque, idealised, figure, "bathed in muted colours, her head framed by a halo," (Lipp 13) a halo which, incidentally, records the name of the actress. What set Mucha's poster apart from those of Lautrec and Chéret were its proportions narrow in width and two meters high, exceptional for the period and its presentation of a nearly life-size, somewhat geometricized Gismonda/Sarah. Moreover, to further heighten its impact, the poster was everywhere strategically displayed so that Gismonda's commanding figure engaged the viewer at eye level, as though she were a flesh-and-blood woman encountered on the street. As to information, Mucha give us only essential data for the production, albeit in bold Art Nouveau lettering: the name of the play, the name of the theatrical venue, the name of the actress.

Ronald Lipp attempts to convey the poster's impact on the Parisian public in the context of *fin-de-siècle* Paris, a setting in which promotional efforts for the arts may seem restrained, even genteel, in comparison with our own: "In our media-saturated age, ever more inured to ever more outlandish pitches in high-decibel stereophonic sound and high-density fluorescent colour, it is perhaps difficult to comprehend 'Gismonda's' impact. By all accounts *La Divine* was enchanted, Paris was astonished and Mucha found himself an overnight celebrity" (Lipp 13).

"Gismonda," a four-act play by Victorien Sardou, had already premiered in Autumn, 1894 at *Le Théâtre de la Renaissance*, when Bernhardt asked Mucha to contrive a new promotional image for an expanded production to open in January, 1895. Under Sarah's unequivocal direction, Mucha portrayed Gismonda as she was conceived by Sardou: a Greek noble- woman enveloped in splendid gown and robe, with an orchid headdress and a palm branch in hand. However, one might justifiably go on to say that, while the title character, an Eastern empress in her finery, would represent the far distant and exotic in time and place for Parisian audiences, the regal, golden-haired woman, lavish dress notwithstanding, could have stood as well for the Parisian *femme nouvelle*, indeed Sarah herself: imposing, uncompromising, and always in control. After all, tolerating little advice from colleagues, Sarah alone chose her roles.

Mucha's core effort for Bernhardt lay in poster design, but the Czech artist also had a hand in the creation of her costumes and sets. Among his best known contributions was a snake bracelet the lethal, if apocryphal asp for her performance in "Cléopatre." This broader participation in Bernhardt's productions was inevitable, given the Czech artist's apprenticeship in set design in Vienna, in 1879.

In his essay on Mucha's "complete vision," Petr Wittlich expands on this biographical moment, pointing to theater at the end of the 19th Century as "the obvious model for a complete work of art [the *Gesamtkunstwerk*] which combined in itself all different art forms to make the most powerful impression possible on audiences." (Wittlich: 8) Here, again, we see the late 19th Century embrace of the "total work of art," an embrace originating with the operas of Richard Wagner, in which all elements are fused in a single cohesive entity. In theater then, both Mucha and Bernhardt found a multi-faceted enterprise that would give full play to their shared versatility and unembarrassed, often unbridled taste for the sumptuous.

Like Bernhardt, who found time to paint and sculpt, (quite skillfully, albeit in an academic style appropriate to the Salon), and write her own biography (albeit more fictive than factual), Mucha was a polymath. From 1895 to 1905, "le style Mucha" expressed itself in posters, book and magazine illustrations, screens, decorative panneaux, stained glass and jewelry, as well as theatrical accoutrements for his generous, but demanding patron. And like Bernhardt, who was Jewish by birth, but Catholic by conversion and convent school education, he had been deeply affected by the "total theater" of the Catholic mass during his childhood in Eastern Europe: "the sensuality of the theatrical illusion was tempered by his childhood experience of the Catholic masses in which he participated for many years, as a member of the choir at St. Peter's Church in Brno in Moravia" (Wittlich: 8).

What was clearly an inborn taste for drama, nurtured in childhood by the Catholic Church, was reinforced not only by a year in Vienna, but by a second year of study at the Munich Academy of Art, in 1885. These years in Munich, by then a magnet for European avant garde artists, led Mucha "by way of the contemporary cult of history painting to his own particular vision of history as a series of dramatic and fateful scenes" (Wittlich: 8). Dramatic and fateful scenes, of course, constituted Bernhardt's stock-in-trade: "her finest skill was projecting her emotional poses into unforgettable *tableaux*." (Shapira online)

By 1887, Mucha, gratis his generous patron, Count Khuen-Belasi, had migrated further west to Paris, Europe's cultural capital, and been absorbed into a circle, whose members included such now-canonic figures as Paul Gauguin and the Swedish playwright August Strindberg (Strindberg's brand of stringent realism would revolutionize the theatrical arena in which Bernhardt had long held sway, and render her own, once-revolutionary approach to acting "dated.") In this high voltage environment, in which flouting of tradition was the norm and French the *lingua franca*, Mucha was introduced to the theory and practice of Symbolism, whose impact on his achievements in painting and design was significant and lasting. This impact shouldn't be surprising, given the trajectory of Mucha's youth in rural Eastern Europe.

Born in 1860 in a backwater Moravian village of the Hapsburg Empire, Mucha had daily acquaintance with poverty and suffering, the latter at an intensely personal level: he lost three of his five siblings to tuberculosis. Mucha's mother, seeking consolation for her grief in religion, enfolded her young son in her embrace of

Catholicism and enrolled him in the St. Peter's Church Boys' Choir at age 11. The Brno church choir experience was an intimate, provincial one, far removed in spirit and purpose from the wide-ranging, energizing cultural sophistication Mucha later found in Vienna, Munich and Paris. Nevertheless, the chanting, the symbolic décor and pageantry, the mystical ambience of the Catholic mass, a theatrical experience, if there ever was one, left a permanent stamp on the Czech artist's sensibilities and work. He was prepared for Symbolism's strategic deployment of coded signs, emphasis on spiritual essence underlying earthly materiality, its belief in the efficacy of visual pattern in stirring the emotions - years before he encountered the Symbolist painters in cosmopolitan Paris.

The French capital Mucha discovered in 1887 was hardly a haven for mystics, religious or otherwise. Still on the rebound from its devastating defeat by Bismarck's Prussian army in 1871, France had invested heavily in economic recovery in the years that followed. The nation had aggressively encouraged industrial growth at home and welcomed technological innovation from abroad, both with substantial financial support by the French government. The evidence for this phenomenon was manifest in Parisian day-to-day life.

In Paris, as in Brussels, sputtering "internal combustion vehicles" plied the city's network of narrow streets and wide avenues, roadways as often illuminated by electric as by gaslight from early evening on. Indeed, given the prioritizing of technology over time-honored tradition in the 1880s, it seems entirely reasonable that a towering iron structure, nearly 1000' high, conceived by an engineer, and looming like a colossus over the *Champs de Mars*, should have dominated the attention of visitors to the 1889 *Exposition Internationale*.

The Eiffel Tower was an elegant, almost lacy structure, but its mode of fabrication, via the use of standardized parts produced on an assembly line, represented not so much artistic or architectural as industrial.progress. Most importantly for our purposes, ever more sophisticated developments in the communication media, in voice recording and in "moving pictures," stimulated stage luminaries like Bernhardt and Fuller to widen their audiences and preserve their preformances for posterity through experiments in early cinema, primitive as those experiments seem to us now. So, taken all in all, the struggle to reassert French primacy in European affairs seemed destined, in the minds of many Frenchmen, to move in the direction of cutting edge technological ingenuity.

In other Parisian quarters, however, opposing tendencies held sway. As was true for late 19th Century Glasgow, large numbers of *fin-de-siècle* Parisian artists and cultural pundits, uneasy with what they perceived as industrial soullessness, found the lure of spiritualism and the occult irresistible and psychologically reassuring. The Symbolists, Mucha among them, were not alone in "their preoccupation with a wide range of theosophies which expanded or supplemented Christian mysticism with spiritual messages thought to originate in Buddhism, the Jewish Kabala, and Egyptian, Greek and other ancient faiths." (Lipp: 12)

For the Symbolist movement in particular, idealism and mysticism admittedly abstract, gauzy terms as opposed to let's-get-the-job-done pragmatism, provided a conceptual framework for the creation of paintings, drawings, and prints intended to bolster and uplift, rather than crush, the human psyche Feeling alienated and diminished by the seeming ruthless dehumanization inherent in industrial mass production, the Symbolists turned to alternative, non-rational world views for both conceptual guidance and concrete visual symbols.

Ronald Lipp explicates, in terms the precision-minded might find frustrating, Mucha's absorption of an array of mystical world views in the formulation of his own: "The spiritual systems that influenced Mucha believed that man is engaged in a long and painful struggle to raise himself toward a divine state." A man's journey is "supported by a divine presence, the 'great soul of the world,' who mediates a higher wisdom to man, linking heaven and earth, the visible with the invisible, the eternal and the mortal." (Lipp: 13) For Mucha, the mediating agent was not Jesus Christ, or any other semi-divine *male* being, but woman, at her lovely, gentle, benevolent, but still seductive best. In line with this thinking, the Czech artist attempted, throughout his career, to express in his art the ideal woman's unique gift for joining "the visible with the invisible."

The so-named "Mucha woman" forms the focal motif not only in Mucha's posters, including the seven he prepared for Bernhardt, but in all of his decorative work, since she "embodies in anthropomorphic form the great soul of the world." The archetypical Mucha woman, is "wholesome, alluring, uplifting and erotically vulnerable." (Lipp: 13) Her appeal is intensified by her inevitable trademark, her hair, that luxuriant, dishevelled mass of golden hair forming a halo around her face. "She is," Lipp opines, "the antithesis of the morbid, effete and diabolical females who populate the contemporary works of Toulouse-Lautrec, Redon, Denis and Gauguin" (Lipp: 13). Displaying this oddly assorted *mélange* of innocent and come-hither traits, she is clearly the antithesis of *la femme nouvelle* and the imperious, resourceful, sexually profligate and financially savvy stage actress who commissioned Mucha's work for a decade.

One cannot avoid taking issue, however, with Lipp's negative branding of the "morbid, effete, and diabolical females" depicted in the work of Mucha's contemporaries, all of whom occupy far more space and critical attention than the Czech artist in current art historical scholarship. Toulouse Lautrec, in particular, contributed significantly to Art Nouveau poster design, after legislation passed in France in 1881 eased censorship of poster display in public places, allowing the medium was to expand rapidly. Some viewers do find off-putting Lautrec's uncompromising, generally unflattering, but incisive depictions of female performers in his posters for Parisian cafés, music halls, and popular theater. The master of linear definition seems to stop just short of caracature... or not. Indeed, the famous actress Yvette Guilbert, who commissioned an album of prints from Lautrec in 1894, felt compelled to complain that the Post-Impressionist painter of urban life had made her look far too ugly.

Nonetheless, Lautrec's record of *fin-de-siécle* Parisian nightlife in all its explosive energy, variety, joie de vivre and seaminess—its can-can dancers, chanteuses, scenery-chewing actresses, and prostitutes—plunges us with merciless *honesty* into the heart of the electric experience itself. Unlike Mucha, Lautrec drew and painted in direct response to what he actually lived as a denizen of Parisian nightlife. That is, he committed to paper, canvas or cardboard what he witnessed firsthand, although through a lens no doubt distorted by disappointment and bitterness. For that matter, unlike those of Mucha, his female subjects were mainly cabaret entertainers like Guilbert and Jane Avril, performing for raucous audiences in tawdry settings, not serious tragedians in more formal theatrical settings.

Still, taking into account the contrast between the two artists in nationality and socioeconomic origin, in creative impulsion and desired end, in stylistic bias and personal predilections, there is no sidestepping the greater visual clout of Lautrec's portrayals of Parisian demi-mondaines for the tough-minded modern audience. As a result, one wonders: supposing, aware as she must have been of Lautrec's expanding pool of wealthy patrons Sarah Bernhardt had looked to Lautrec, rather than Mucha, for her promotional posters? Would the result of that collaboration have been a little less florid and decorative, a little less stylistically generic, than the seven lithographs Mucha produced, gorgeous as they were?

Would Lautrec, of the savage, piercing eye and facile hand, have produced images of Bernhardt's stage persona that were more accurate to the riveting female presence the actress was, even when she took on androgynous roles? Or did Bernhardt, in fact, consciously avoid Lautrec, reacting to a degree of distortion in his work that approached, in brutal anti-Semitic satire, the cartoons that appeared regularly in the right-wing Parisian press whenever she appeared on stage?

The American Loie Fuller was a pioneer in two related realms: modern dance and theatrical lighting techniques. Unfortunately, her reputation as a crucial agent in choreographic innovation has, until recently, been overshadowed by those of two other groundbreaking American dancer/ choreographers: Isadora Duncan and Ruth St. Denis. Important to bear in mind, then, is the unstinting encouragement given to Duncan and St. Denis, both innovators in "free form" dance, by their then-more celebrated compatriot, Fuller.

In appearance and temperament, Fuller, like Bernhardt, was hardly a likely choice for the expression of the French Art Nouveau feminine ideal. The pragmatic American performer Marie Louise "Loie" Fuller was born in 1862, in what is now the Chicago suburb of Hinsdale, and began her professional life as a child actress. She has been described as an "ingenious and plain-spoken descendant of American Revolutionary warriors." (Aloff New Republic) Certainly, the social restrictions that placed obstacles in the professional paths of her female counterparts in Europe raised none during Fuller's steady ascendance in American popular theater.In fact, she turned a blind eye to social restrictions.

Gradually and persistently developing and performing her non-balletic, improvisational "free dances" on American vaudeville and burlesque stages, Fuller attained some degree of fame in the United States through works such as the famous "Serpentine Dance." Audiences for the "Dance" were urged to believe that the whirling, swooping, apparently spontaneous quality of her movements was never the same from performance to another. The excitement generated by Fuller's non-traditional choreography was further intensified by her choice of costume: loose, floating, overlapping veils of multi-colored silk - and by self-invented, revolutionary lighting techniques that illuminated the swirl of fabric from below. Multi-colored electric light was, in fact, literally projected upward through a glass stage floor.

Fuller made her debut on the stage of the *Folies Bergère* in 1892. The experience was the high point in a European tour, during which she enjoyed far more appreciation for her expressive choreography than in the provincial American Midwest. Thus, Fuller's decision to remain in Paris and continue performing for enthusiastic French crowds seems the most sensible, in both pragmatic and emotional terms. Indeed, Fuller thrived on Parisian stages. Creating "an undulating, ever-changing visual display" (Escritt: 102), she twirled, dipped, and swayed to the compositions of Schubert, Chopin, and Debussy, varying her pace and gestures to suit the music and responding intuitively to the melodies and harmonies that informed her movement. The kinetic apparition she presented onstage was multiplied by a surround of sheets of mirrored glass.

If hard facts were all that mattered, then one would be quick to point out the inherent duplicity in Fuller's "act." The mesmerizing quality of her performance, a *Gesamtkunstwerk* enhanced by the swirl and swoosh of translucent silk fabric lit from below and by reflections on all sides, disguised the mundane truths of the dancer's short stature and stocky build. However, another truth holds sway here: the illusion Fuller created was total; the mundane reality all but invisible to both audience and critics.

Fuller's dazzling performances, combined with her autodidactic ventures into light technology, made her a magnet for avant garde artists and writers, as well as their scientific peers in physics and chemistry She was depicted in posters by such diverse masters as Lautrec, Jules Chéret, and Kolomon Moser. In his poster for Fuller's star turn at the Folies Bergère, Chéret presented Fuller as a cheerful, chubby cabaret dancer, flamboyantly dressed in turquoise and flame-color silk veils. Her muscular calves and bare feet exposed, Fuller arches her back in ecstasy, her upraised arms and flying red hair bodying forth her joyous abandon in the dance.

Lautrec, on the other hand, in a more subtle portrayal, skillfully reduced the shifting lift and flutter of Fuller's veils to a near-abstract network of sinuous lines. And in sharper contrast, the Viennese Moser came close to transforming the American dancer into a golden butterfly on a black background, the layers of her costume raised and spread like mammoth wings. In the future *Wiener Werkstätte* master's hands, Fuller seems to have undergone a metamorphosis: from vibrant, flesh-and-blood performer to elegant, but flattened design motif.

Depending on the scholar one consults, either Fuller or Bernhardt most completely embodied the Art Nouveau movement in its Parisian incarnation. However, competition for the title between the two female luminaries seems irrelevant, given their shared rejection of outdated stage tradition, gift for attracting and entrancing audiences, and insistence on total control not only of their own performances, but of costumes, lighting, and the intricacies of effective staging. Moreover, both women, by instinct stubbornly independent and resentful of unsolicited advice or direction, proved themselves canny strategists in promoting their productions, looking to advances in cinematic technology, as well as conventional media, to broaden their audience.

The filmed version of Fuller's trademark "Serpentine Dance," a commission carried out by the brothers Auguste and Louis Lumière in 1896, gives clear evidence not only of her willingness to gamble on untried new media, but of her foresight. (NOTE: the svelte dancer in this short, landmark film is not Fuller herself, as is commonly believed. No doubt Fuller was aware that, while the speed and motion of an onstage performance might distract attention from her rather pudgy face and chunky physique, those attributes would be unignorable on film and would undercut the impact of a "Serpentine Dance" preserved on celluloid for posterity.)

As for Fuller's involvement in the complexities of chemical compounds, the sometimes grudging, sometimes ardent flirtation Art Nouveau architects and designers carried on with scientific and technological innovation is echoed in her successful efforts to develop chemical substances intended to intensify further the excitement generated by her performances. Fuller, always ardent, moved far beyond flirtation. In fact, she held several patents related to stage lighting. These included compounds used in the creation of colored gels and chemical salts designed to render her garments luminescent.

It is not easy to tell, in reading hagiographic accounts of Fuller's "discoveries," how much the self-taught dancer/choreographer really understood, at the molecular level, of the chemical substances she played with in the lab. That said, what clearly matters more than a grasp of scientific fundamentals is her wholehearted attempt to marry science and art, in order to bring to fruition her hopes for a "total" dance experience. Very likely, she commandeered a number of knowledgeable chemists to assist her in the details of laboratory work. Very likely as well, they found her vision a seductive scientific challenge. And while Fuller's lust for the limelight may have unfairly relegated these unsung cultural heroes to the wings, it's unlikely that her marvelous theatrical events would have taken place at all without her personal vision.

Fuller's sweeping, gestural choreography and floating veils were memorialized for posterity in a range of media: in posters by diverse graphic masters, in photographs, such as a photo of the dancer appearing in the 1900 *Exposition Universelle*; in a motion picture created when cinema was in its infancy. However, perhaps the best known representation of Fuller as the emblem, if not the very essence of Parisian Art Nouveau, is a table size (17 1/2") bronze sculpture of the dancer in full, floating silk regalia, created by the popular 19th Century sculptor, François-Raoul Larche. Fittingly, given Fuller's affinity for light, the piece was intended as a lamp base. No doubt at the behest of his patron, Larche took considerable license with her figure, slimming down and elongating her torso and limbs to accord with the Art Nouveau ideal.

More significantly, however, the small sculpture captures the excitement of Fuller's performance, in focussing attention on the quasi-baroque swirl of billowing fabric above her head. Larche may have fudged the facts of Fuller's real-life appearance, but, through the skilled manipulation of what is by nature a static medium, he suggests the evanescence, the fugitive quality of motion itself. The dancer becomes the dance.

CHAPTER 9

Scotland: Where Were the Women?

By the final decade of the 19th Century, Glasgow, universally touted as the British Empire's "Second City," was indeed one of the richest cities in the world. Its population had ballooned to 750,000, an impressive figure for Western urban centers of the time. Moreover, Britain's Second City, while still no match for Edinburgh and London in cultural sophistication and political clout, had all the components necessary for industrial pre-eminence: "a ready supply of skilled, cheap labor and technological expertise; a great river for steam power and transportation; easy access to both raw material and imports." (Kinchin and Sharples 28) By 1900, textile production, for centuries Scotland's leading sector in manufacture and trade with other countries, was competing in economic importance with the growth of heavy industry, particularly the manufacture of locomotives and shipbuilding.

Not surprisingly, however, Glasgow's remarkable industrial expansion, from the mid-19th Century on, had its downside: unchecked urban sprawl, accompanied by poverty, overcrowded living conditions, and rampant contagious disease. "With little in the way of planning, environmental or fiscal constraints, prodigious growth and congestion continued unabated, creating staggering extremes of wealth and poverty." (Kinchin and Sharples 11)

The solution came early, in this vigorous city on Scotland's west coast. In 1859, the Loch Katrina Scheme, devised by Glasgow's municipal authorities, brought the pure water of the nearby Trossach mountain streams into the city's heart. Of interest to students of political theory put into practice, this mid-century example of beneficial public intervention "both presaged and accelerated the city's rapid rise to fame as a world model of municipal socialism." (Kinchin and Sharples 11) The Katrina scheme was followed by an impressive program of improvements in sanitation, health care, and housing. Indeed, by 1909, the Glasgow Corporation had planned and executed the construction of 2000 new homes. While the additional housing by no means eliminated overcrowding, it went some distance in alleviating the problem.

As a result, the mushrooming of Glasgow's population was accompanied by a perceptible rise in standard of living, at least for a segment of its citizens. The citywide infrastructural improvements noted above, as well as a highly efficient public transportation system—those gleaming trolleys on view in Zaha Hadid's Transportation Museum!—went hand in hand with increasing separation of home from workplace for a burgeoning middle class. As soon as they could afford it, upwardly mobile Glaswegian families fled the slums and factories in the city's eastern districts to residential areas west and south of the Clyde, generally regarded as locales "of greater amenity." (Kinchin and Sharples 28)

Successive waves of urban relocation in the 1880s and 1890s, involving the transplantation of entire households to newly constructed, look-alike dwellings, demanded in turn, "visual differentiation through fashion and domestic furnishings." Consequently, "whole hosts of mutually supporting specialised trades contributed to the Glasgow interior. Even the more modest tenement flats had elaborate plasterwork, with stained glass and decorative tiles in the close (the common stair). Still more prestigious was the purchase of art." (Kinchin and Sharples 28) The latter phenomenon, the purchase of fine easel art to raise social status, explains the success of gallery owners like Alexander Reid in attracting buyers not only for paintings by French and Dutch masters long validated by foreign critics, but also for homegrown artists like the Glasgow Boys. In sum, the need to distinguish oneself and one's family from the common run of Glaswegian homeowners, through the display of worldly taste, drove the surge of interest in upgrading domestic interiors.

The refurbishing of the interior in the domestic realm was carried out in tandem with the construction of new municipal, commercial, and recreational buildings imposing stone structures for government offices, museums, railway stations, theaters, and pubs in the public realm. Morever, from the late 1870s on, Glaswegians witnessed a dramatic growth not only in the sheer number of buildings in their home city, but also in their scale and height. Two factors accounted for these changes: the introduction of steel and reinforced concrete in the construction process and the invention of passenger lifts or, for Americans, elevators.

Most impressive now for the 21st Century visitor are the Glasgow University complex on Gilmorehill (1878), the grand, or grandiose, Municipal Chambers (1888), and the gracious, expansive Kelvingrove Museum (1902). As Kinchin and Sharples point out, the "lavishly appointed" Municipal Chambers on George Square "offered a tangible expression of civic authority, administrative control, and economic recovery after the bank crash of 1878, which had temporarily slowed Glasgow's otherwise prodigious expansion." (Kinchin and Sharples 12)

The palatial Kelvingrove deserves special attention, as its design and construction was financed by profits amassed from two International Exhibitions held in Glasgow in the late 19th Century. Mounted in 1888, the first International Exhibition effectively expressed "the city's industrial maturity and vigorous municipal government as well as her imperial status." (Kinchin and Sharples 20) International displays of traditional craft, counterbalanced by industrial machinery and products indicating Scottish technological advance, were brought together in a spatious Main Hall only half-facetiously labelled "Baghdad by Kelvinside." The dazzling 1888 Exhibition drew not only local and regional crowds, but legions of tourists from abroad. Competing for visitors' attention during the day were sporting events, concerts, and rides on a roller coaster or, more exciting still, a switchback railway. In the evenings, audiences thrilled to firework displays and to a Main Hall that transplanted bit of exotic Baghdad whose exterior walls were illuminated with electric lights.

Note bene; A close look at photographs taken of exhibition sporting events reveals an apparently inconsequential, but nonetheless critical detail linked to a significant aspect of Scotch feminism: clothing designed for freedom of movement for women in the late 19th Century. In a few of these photo images, young female athletes wearing simple, lightweight sporting costumes leap, swoop, and lunge at tennis balls on fairground tennis courts. These are decidedly non-Victorian costumes.

Indeed, they are the loose, unembellished, short sleeved, and short-skirted outfits one would expect to find in photographs taken decades later.

The stunning success of the 1888 International Exhibition was a prime factor in the municipal authorities' decision to stage a second world's fair in 1901. This turn-of-the-century extravaganza, which reputedly attracted 11,000,00 visitors, was installed in the wake of the more celebrated *Exposition Internationale* held in Paris in 1900. The latter was, indeed, the very *Exposition* in which Siegfried Bing introduced Art Nouveau designers Georges de Feure and Edouard Colonna to a continental audience that had, in many cases, travelled great distances for the event. The dovetailed mounting of the two world fairs was,in fact, no mere coincidence.

The Kelvingrove Museum, which owes its very existence to Glasgow's two international exhibitions, is a stately, expansive red sandstone pile for which two Southern European stylistic models served as templates: Spanish Baroque on the exterior, Italian Renaissance on the interior. While the magisterial edifice clearly manifests the historicism against which architects like Mackintosh railed, the building itself, theoretical carping aside, is undeniably welcoming and aesthetically harmonious.

On the Museum's interior, the galleries display both fine and applied art in permanent and temporary exhibits that are installed side by side (almost) seamlessly with archaeological and anthropological artifacts on show in adjoining rooms. Added to the eclectic mix are organ recitals, offered free and frequently to appreciative audiences seated on folding chairs in the museum's cavernous main hall. Unlike its counterparts in major urban centers throughout the globe, the Kelvingrove's interior conformation, in particular, its enormous, resonant central hall, is "purpose built" for musical performance, so that the museum functions as a *Gesamtkunstwerk* to a degree that do few museums, even to this day.

Important to note, however, was the absence of fine and applied art created by the Macdonald sisters, C.R. Mackintosh, or Herbert MacNair in either of the two International Exhibitions. Nor, for, for that matter, did their work figure in the Kelvingrove's inaugural shows. Nevertheless of importance to their creative development was the backdrop of international cultural wealth the Exhibitions, as well as the newly opened Kelvingrove, provided the central proponents of the Glasgow Style, as they completed their plans for the Eighth Secession Exhibition in Vienna (1900) and the International Decorative Arts Exposition in Turin (1902).

In the male-dominated realm of shipbuilding, a "heavy" industrial enterprise which accounted for Glasgow's prime position in global commerce, the more precise fit-out of ship cabins, was crucial to the development of Glasgow's furniture industry. The craft and spatial ingenuity invested in preparing cabins for leisure class passengers on luxury liners are especially pertinent here. Alluding to the link between artisanal work by Scottish men in the shipbuilding trades and the centrality of Scottish women in domestic interior design Kinchin emphasizes both the exacting nature of cabin fit-out *and* its impact on Glasgow's furniture industry. "They [the ships] had close fitting, odd-shaped compartments which required high quality joinery work." (Kinchin and Sharples 26)

Many yards, in fact, had their own cabinet and upholstery works. The floating palaces built on the Clyde helped to disseminate the reputation of Scottish firms for well-made, stylish furnishings all over the world." (Kinchin and Sharples 28) The high quality of Scottish furniture, at once stylish and sturdy, was clearly not lost on female patrons charged with selecting and purchasing chairs, tables, side-boards, cabinets, and *armoires* for their parlours, dining rooms, and bedrooms.

The stylistic influence of male-dominated ship's cabin fit-out on established female turf, the furnishing of the home interior, is indesputable. Nevertheless, women did ultimately retain control over the domestic setting. They selected the furnishings and had the last word in the design of each room. Further, in larger sociological terms, the surge of socioeconomic change in late 19th Century Glasgow still "expressed itself," as Kinchin states it, "in the creation of two types of social space. One was the public world largely peopled by men, the other was the private or domestic sphere inhabited by women and children." (Kinchin and Sharples 29)

For the seasoned student of Western cultural history, there are no surprises here. And while one might not require scholarly proof to verify a familiar home truth on gendered roles in 19th Century Glasgow, following Kinchin's overview of the situation for women in Scotland, surprising or not, helps us understand the cultural climate in which the Glasgow Girls and the Macdonald sisters made their determined way.

Focussing initially on the arts, Trinchin notes that the "ways in which art and design of the period were both purchased and consumed reflected this dichotomy [between spheres of social domination]." (Kinchin and Sharples 29) She adds that the time-honored divide between men and women in the control of social space extended also to rigidly maintained territoriality in the making of art: oil painting, sculpture, and architecture comprised the male domain, while artistically inclined women applied themselves to watercolor, drawing, decorative design and handicraft, which together comprised the so-called "lesser arts."

With near-total control over important artistic media, men also controlled the commercial sphere "The main artistic institutions were run by and for men and the growing public support for the arts in the municipal institutions did not change the gender balance." (Kinchin and Sharples 29) The resounding statement by Kinchin that follows sums the situation up: "The places of exhibition and display, the social venues for fine artists and the sources of patronage and support, all centred on networks, which were almost exclusively masculine." (Kinchin and Sharples 29) *Plus ça change, plus c'est la même chose.*

However, in Glasgow, Britain's Second City of Empire the familiar litany of gendered societal roles took a new, unprecedented turn from the mid-19th Century on. Things actually *did* change, particularly in the field of the "lesser" applied arts and *didn't* remain the same for many gifted, ambitious women, owing chiefly to the founding of the institution that would eventually become the Glasgow School of Art.

From its inception as a Government School of Design, the School of Art geared its curriculum to the training of industrial designers whose skills were considered vital to Glasgow's economy. While the city's utility-centered manufacturers were initially "more interested in technical facility than artistic originality," farsighted merchants "increasingly came to recognise the selling powers of artistic product design and marketing." (Kinchin and Sharples: 29) The source of the recognition lay in a clear-eyed awareness of Scotland's remote location, its insularity and cultural provincialism. The nation's urban centers, Glasgow among them, stood in sharp contrast to London, as well as urban meccas on the continent, such as Brussels, Amsterdam, and Paris, where elegant, well-crafted objects were visible to their denizens daily as they walked their cities' streets and entered public buildings.

Aware of this disparity and acknowledging "the selling powers of artistic product design and marketing," Glasgow manufacturers agreed that the design process was "too important to leave to the whim of a machine-operative." (Kinchin and Sharples: 29) Moreover, "they realised that they would need trained designers and qualified teachers to replace traditional methods of handing down knowledge." (Burkhauser: 63) What resulted was a merger of odd bedfellows in mid-19th Century Glasgow, a joining of forces built on a shared understanding between Glasgow's industrial elite, its civic authorities, and its merchant class. According to this understanding, Glasgow's industrial products would bring the city to the world's attention only if they pleased the consumer in appearance, as well as utility.

Founded in 1840, the Glasgow Government School of Design was initially placed under the control of the South Kensington Science and Art Department in London in 1852. (The Department, an arm of the British government, would later oversee the development of the vast treasure chest of applied art masterpieces we now know as the Victoria and Albert Museum Museum.) That the administrative control of the Glasgow Government School of Design emanated from London, rather than residing within the School itself, had its obvious drawbacks. Nonetheless, "the prestige and publicity surrounding its [South Kensington's] annual National Competitions undoubtedly drew public attention both to the institution and to talented individuals such as the prize-winning Frances Macdonald." (Kinchin and Sharples: 19)

Nevertheless, bureaucratic jurisdiction aside, the ancestor of GSA in faraway Scotland was largely funded and administered from the outset by Glasgow's industrial elite, a far-sighted, energetic group, who providentially placed no obstacles in the way of lower class young women eager to enroll in its classes. A paradox emerges here, in that *only* women of the "artisan class" had the benefit of this government-funded education, since presumably only they had the requisite craft skills, those commonly acquired in small town domestic settings. (Burkhauser: 63) This educational opportunity, made available *only* to lower class women, is especially noteworthy, given that university education for all women in Scotland was denied until 1892, nearly a decade later than in France.

By 1885, the policy of accepting women for courses at the Government School of Design, now renamed The Glasgow School of Art, was firmly in place. Moreover, in the 44 years between the School's founding and the arrival of Francis Newberry as Director in 1884, increasing numbers of middle class women had enrolled in its courses, once administrators opened the School's doors to women of every class. Seeing a route out of full-time domesticity and into an interesting, fulfilling means of livelihood unavailable elsewhere in Glasgow, women rushed to sign up.

Newberry, while essentially an authoritarian, was also a confirmed socialist, with strong convictions about the role of the arts in society, convictions reinforced and amplified by his friendship with William Morris in London. Art schools, Newberry believed, existed not to produce designs, but designers, and were not primarily commercial, but artistic institutions. Their purpose was not to satisfy, but to lead public taste. (Burkhauser 65) With this groundbreaking, admirably idealistic goal in mind, he set about to nurture independent vision and originality in his co-ed student body.

From 1885 on, Newberry appears to have encouraged male and female students with an even hand, "and set the pace for a continuing broadening educational opportunity for women." (Burkhauser: 66) With life drawing classes involving nude models the most conspicuous exception, women were permitted to enroll in most day school courses and drew, painted, and sculpted side by side with men in GSA studios. While so egalitarian an outlook and policy is now the norm for British, European, and American art schools, Burkhauser notes that this "was not the case in all art schools at the time, when timetables, curriculum and architectural space often segregated male from female students." (Burkhauser: 66)

The emphasis on "vision" and "originality" once established, the canny Director, familiarly known as "Fra" Newberry, went on to develop the more pragmatically oriented Technical Art Studios in 1892. The stated intention was 'to offer a complete cycle of Technical Artistic Education applicable to the Industrial Arts in the City of Glasgow." (Burkhauser: 64) Innovative for the period was Newberry's insistence on hiring craftsmen in each technical area as instructors, a sensible practice that would be repeated in 1907, in Henry van de Velde's *Kunstgewerbeschule*, in Weimar, and again in 1919, at the Bauhaus. The selection of experienced, hands-on craftsmen for its instructional staff was also standard policy for the Applied Arts Studios, initiated by Newberry in 1895. That most of the teachers hired for such classes as embroidery, textile design, metalwork and stained glass were women was a standout breakthrough as well.

All Glasgow School of Art students began their education with a traditional base of fine art courses: sculpture and modelling, drawing, and painting. The resort to traditional academic methods for teaching these disciplines is manifest even now in the many plaster casts of classical sculpture dispersed throughout the School of Art. The second level course of study at GSA could be pursued in one of four sections: Drawing and Painting; Modelling and Sculpture; Design and Decorative Art; Architecture.

Newberry's goals were not limited to the development of a broad, inclusive, discipline-straddling curriculum that wove together the fine and applied arts. By the mid-1890s, he was fully engaged in involving his students, both men and women, in significant design exhibitions abroad, sending them, with their crafted ware, to expositions in Turin, Vienna, and Liège. By the mid-1890s, he had also envisaged a new building for the school that would provide a theater for his planned expansion of GSA's program. For this project, he sponsored the competition that would be won handily, as we know, by C.R. Mackintosh.

At this juncture, one would be remiss in omitting one questionable aspect of Newberry's other-wise progressive view of gender parity. At heart, still a Victorian Englishman, he believed that there existed for the sexes "separate spheres of ability" (in essence, "separate, but equal") and that women were, as he put it, "to needle and thread as the peasant to the plough, or the writer to the pen." (Burkhauser: 66) Indeed, while committed to open admissions and course offerings that prepared men *and* women for teacher certification and work in industry, Newberry did, in fact, "track" GSA's students by gender. As a result, while the decorative arts classes were dominated by women, albeit with offerings in metalwork, stained glass and gesso painting that ventured far beyond the needle arts, courses in architecture were closed to women until1905.

How many women at GSA, one wonders, did in fact resent their exclusion from courses in architecture, when their options in the decorative arts curriculum were so varied, and opportunities for future employment as teachers or industrial designers so secure? The studios were indeed hotbeds of applied arts innovation; the sense of camaraderie, of shared creative adventure between students, and between students and instructors, intensely stimulating. In no area of design does this creative ferment so satisfying for ambitious women reveal itself more fully than in women's fashion, in clothing contrived *by* women *for* women, and designed and worn by GSA students and teachers themselves. Conceivably, then, for many women enrolled at GSA, being barred from classes in architecture mattered not so much, when the officially sanctioned chance to improve on the comfort and convenience of clothing they wore, day by day was so easily obtained.

Establishing a historical link between the Artistic or Rational Dress Movement in Glasgow and the Art Nouveau movement as a whole seems, at first glance, a stretch, primarily because the Artistic Dress Movement weighed so heavily in favor of comfort, as opposed to elegance, in women's wear. The advocate of Artistic or Rational Dress rebelled against fashion that "would limit her [woman's] activities, participation, or enjoyment of life, and affirmed her individuality and creativity through her dress." (Burkhauser: 50) Obviously, in Glasgow, the rejection of confining clothing, not to mention suffocating underclothing long sleeves with buttoned wristbands, ribbed bodices with high-necked collars, layers of petticoats, rigid corsets, and laces pulled tight to create unnaturally small "wasp waists" was but one element in a larger social reform agenda. This comprehensive agenda advocated access to university education, more humane working conditions and higher pay for female textile workers, and, perhaps most importantly, the franchise.

The issue of radical change in women's dress is further complicated by the existence of not one, but two unprecedented trends in women's fashion that came to the fore in *fin-de-siècle* Great Britain. The dominant trend, the Aesthetic Dress Movement, emerged from the studios of such Arts and Crafts eminences as Walter Crane and William Morris. Adapting or "quoting" women's clothing from classical and medieval costume, they followed the path laid out by the Pre-Raphaelite painters (Burkhauser: 50), one which led to visually lush, but physically inhibiting garments, fashioned of floral-patterned fabric. These were voluminous, downright heavy dresses and cloaks far more suited to a sedentary than a physically vigorous lifestyle.

The influence of the Aesthetic Dress Movement on women's fashion throughout the British Isles was widespread So, for that matter, was its emphasis on "a totality of approach which decreed that clothes be in harmony with interiors." (Burkhauser: 50) William Morris himself had occasionally translated his fabric designs for upholstery into dress fabric (Burkhauser: 50), while across the English Channel, Henry van de Velde had contrived robes and gowns for his wife that were intended to merge, in overall curvilinear form and appliquéd surface pattern, with his Art Nouveau interior at *Bloemenwerf.*

Indeed, the Aesthetic Dress Movement left its mark on clothing styles for women, particularly in progressive circles, not only in London and in van de Velde's carefully calculated home environment, but also in Vienna, some years later. Midway through the first decade of the 20th Century, Viennese designers took the movement a step further. Guided by the concept of "dress-as-art" they "produced clothing which considered dress one aspect of an artistic whole." (Burkhauser: 54) (For the 21st Century observer, a nagging question arises here: would the female wearer in this theory-driven context function primarily as mannequin for the male designer's fashion vision?)

Pertinent to the link between Glasgow's brand of Art Nouveau and the Aesthetic Dress Movement is an article that appeared in "The Studio" in 1906. Entitled "Modern Decorative Art in Glasgow," the piece focussed on Catherine Cranston's Argyle Street Tea Rooms, which opened in 1878 and was the first of Kate Cranston's four tea room ventures. Referring to the collaboration between Mackintosh and Margaret Macdonald in the refurbishing of the now-expanded tea room interiors the writer notes that "Even feminine attire has not escaped the attention of the modern artist; with some recent schemes of decoration he has indicated the design and colour of the gowns to be worn, so that no disturbing element might mar the the unity of the conception.'" (Burkhauser: 54) So, with the folding of waitress's uniforms into the overall scheme, Cranston's teashop qualified as a true *Gesamtkunstwerk.*

The Artistic or Rational Dress Movement was the more pragmatic trend in *fin-de-siècle* fashion, onc that was both groundbreaking and adapted to contemporary social change. Sensitive to the needs of an ever more independent, socially mobile modern woman, it promoted the "freeing of women's bodies from the restrictive laces of imposed fashion." (Burkhauser: 51) The style, which dispensed with ribs, stays, bustles, corsets, and other rigid, confining, often stifling garments and undergarments, emerged in part from "women's adoption of formerly male only sports, such as cycling and tennis, and the resultant need for sensible, functional and healthy dress." (Burkhauser: 51) (Those photographs on view at the Kelvingrove, of young women on International Exhibition tennis courts, exultant in their newfound athletic opportunities, give evidence of this also-newfound modernization of women's dress.) The breaking down of a gender-related barrier in one realm, it was hoped, would lead to the breaking down of barriers in the others.

In the vanguard of the Artistic Dress Movement in Glasgow was Jessie Rowat Newberry, initially a GSA student, then the wife of the school's Director. Finding popular fashion "constricting, inartistic, and ugly," Jessie rejected mass-produced wear for herself, her children, and her colleagues at GSA, while affirming Arts and Crafts ideals. She designed, embroidered, and sewed her own and her children's clothing, determined to release the craft of embroidery from its time-honored taint, that of trivial, fussy "woman's work." (Burkhauser: 54) Her embroidery designs in particular, with their inventive, simplified geometry, echoed in the realm of needlework the stylized geometric furnishings, light fixtures, and cutlery that characterized Mackintosh's and Macdonald's interiors. This was inevitable, given the day-to-day proximity in which Mackintosh, Macdonald and the Newberrys lived and worked.

The cutting-edge direction that hand embroidery took at GSA, in the hands of Jessie Newberry, Anne Macbeth, and their colleagues, found an audience beyond GSA's workshops. The Applied Art Division of Glasgow's 1901 International Exhibition featured examples of tapestries and art embroidery conceived and accomplished by Jessie and others that were praised by *The Studio* for their "distinctly modern feeling." (Callen 124) Moreover, Jessie Newberry refused to restrict her innovations in needlework to clothing for her family and textiles for her home, created in the privacy of her studio. She was responsible for the inauguration of GSA's first needlework class in 1894 and continued teaching at the School until 1908, carrying her trademark individualism and zeal into classroom education, as well as theoretical articles written for the progressive periodical, *The Studio.* The following statements, with their unmistakable undercurrent of rebellion against tradition sum up her ethos regarding both design education and design itself:

"I believe in education consisting of seeing the best that has been done. Then, having this high standard before us, in doing what we like to do, "that" for our fathers, "this" for us. I believe that nothing is common or unclean; that the design of a pepper pot is as important, in its degree, as the conception of a cathedral. I believe that material, space, and consequent use deserve their own exigencies and as such have to be considered well. I like the opposition of straight lines to curves; of horizontal to vertical; of purple to green; of green to blue. I specially aim at beautifully shaped spaces and try to make them as important as the patterns." (Callen 124)

Jessie Newberry encountered two hurdles in her efforts not only to bring embroidery design into the modernist arena, but to promote the innovative embroidered pieces themselves to a skeptical public. As Anthea Callen points out, Newberry was designing for a craft "considered essentially feminine in character." In her 19th Century Scottish cultural setting, Glaswegian feminist activism notwithstanding, woman's art was viewed as 'distinct from man's because of all that society attributed to the sex in terms of softness and sentimentality." (Callen 124) In addition, in terms of promotion, even the most open-minded writer for well-respected journals like The Studio was "constantly faced with the problem of a double standard of criticism, since traditionally women's work was criticised by more lenient standards than those used for men, as they were felt to be incapable of equal quality." (Callen 124)

With admirable persistence, Newberry acted on the set of creative principles outlined above, simplifying her embroidery patterns beyond any Morris and his followers had contrived. In doing so, she effectively released the craft from its time-honored role: the time-consuming, spirit-dampening fabrication of tea cozies and ladies' pillowcases. As one astute Studio commentator pointed out, Newberry's embroideries "may take their place as examples of well-applied art, with no question of sex, and no attempt to evade criticism by a spurious chivalry which is often but a covert form of insult." (Callen 124)

The reform of women's dress, with an eye to greater comfort and freedom of movement, was one aspect of the political activism carried on by GSA staff and students, reluctant to divorce their educational lives from the surge of social reform efforts outside GSA's doors. In concert with Anne Macbeth, Jessie Newberry mobilized other instructors in lobbying for universal suffrage, for men *and* women, temperance a particularly inflammatory issue for women in Glasgow, and shorter hours and better pay for female textile workers. The latter formed an artisan class generally perceived as a cheap source of labor that was excluded from trade unions "as they were considered a hindrance to obtaining better pay and working conditions for men" (Burkhuaser: 46)

So, realizing that collective action was the only effective tool for social change, Newberry, Macbeth, official head of the Embroidery Department, and other female GSA staff became active members of the Women's Social and Political Union, mobilizing their needlework skills to create banners for WSPU rallies and demonstrations. (Burkhauser: 46)

A *caveat*. While Jessie Newberry's energy and versatility can only earn her high praise, it is difficult to ignore an inbuilt inconsistency between her ideals for women's clothing and her *modus operandi* for carrying them out, both harnessed to her passionate political activism. Indifferent, if not antagonistic to the meshing of her mode of dress with someone else's broader interior scheme, the overriding concept of the Aesthetic Dress Movement, Newberry nevertheless shared with Arts and Crafts theorists distrust of industrial mass production and scorn for its shoddy products.

Logically, the flexible, loose-fitting garments she advocated for the "New Woman" would be sewn by hand, one at a time, according to Arts and Crafts protocol. This high level piecework would leave the wearer, or her patient, painstaking dressmaker, little time left over for the rewarding career the New Woman in Glasgow, Paris, or any progressive urban center had long sought. Jessie herself, while disciplined in her work habits, a skilled craftsman, and a natural leader, was also Fra Newberry's wife. The latitude she could count on in professional affairs at GSA and in Glasgow as a whole, not to mention bedrock economic security, were guaranteed by her marriage to the School's headmaster. She could easily afford the extra hours required not only to design, but to sew her own and her children's Rational garments, reduced in needlework complexity as they were, without concern for the source of her next meal.

As to the heady issue of Glaswegian "gender dichotomy" as it applies to patrons and collectors of art, that is, the "spheres of acquisition" mentioned earlier, Liz Bird examines the situation in depth. As one might expect in an industrial boom town with few blooded aristocrats, those collectors were most commonly drawn from industrial or commercial ranks. Indeed, they were *nouveaux riches,* mainly male patrons, more fully equipped with business savvy than aesthetic sophistication. In the fine arts realm, their tastes initially ran, rather snobbishly, to imported paintings accomplished by French Barbizon School painters or Dutch artists from Amsterdam or Delft. Fortunately for these novice collectors, work by these continental masters could be found in Alexander Reid's appropriately named *La Société des Beaux Arts,* the exhibit venue the prescient dealer had opened *ca.* 1889, shortly after his return from an apprenticeship at Goupil's in Paris. (Bird 31)

Reid, an enterprising dealer with a taste for risk, deserves credit for pushing beyond the aesthetic boundaries set by his Glaswegian clientèle. It was Reid who financed the transformative trip to Japan taken by Glasgow Boys Hormel and Henry. It was Reid who, far more aggressively other Glaswegian art dealers "forged connections with comparable businesses in other European and North American centers, and played a crucial role in showcasing contemporary European and Scottish art to [an ever more] discriminating Glasgow audience."(Kinchin: 29) And it was Reid who, in 1895, had exhibited the controversial poster designs by Frances and Margaret Macdonald, with their attenuated, "spooky" female figures, alongside graphic work by Toulouse Lautrec and Aubrey Beardsley.

A further, gender-related distinction in Glaswegian habits of purchase should be emphasized here. It was true that, for the newly affluent patron, art "clearly cost money and conveyed social prestige whether consumed by men or women. What differed was the type of capital investment and form of art considered appropriate to each." (Kinchin and Sharples: 32) So, men alone bought those landscapes, still lifes and genre paintings by sanctified foreign masters. A prized and pricey painting by Corot, for example, was a "commodity which was likely to retain or increase its market value and was sold and exhibited in the public sphere." (Kinchin and Sharples 32) In contrast, the wife of the inevitably male industrial magnate, excited by her recent financial empowerment, bought art solely for use, display, or both, in the privacy of her family's home.

Women spent fortunes on modish clothing and tasteful home furnishings in Glasgow from the 1870s on, but, fas Bird notes, from the point of view of investment, "such expenditure was difficult to recoup." (Kinchin and Sharples 32) Moreover, while men browsed in upscale galleries in search of potentially lucrative masterworks by foreign, or, on rare occasions, Scottish artists, "women's art was consumed through the agency of department stores and furnishing shops," (Kinchin and Sharples 32) lively mercantile and social centers indeed, but also decidedly lower in status. Middle class women, dubbed, with unmistakable condescension, "Angels of the Hearth," were expected to be arbiters of taste only *within* the family, where they would show "refinement and an artistic, cultured temperament." (Kinchin and Sharples 32)

Useful here is a comment on British retail culture in the late 19th Century, since, by 1900, Glasgow and Liverpool, the latter home to the MacNairs for a decade, were among the biggest shopping centers in Britain. Both cities played prominent roles in the rise of a commercial entity whose pervasive presence we now take for granted: the department store. As is the case now, the department stores of the period were more than just markets for consumer goods. They were "complex concerns that combined manufacturing, retailing and subcontracting, with agents and outlets around the world." (Kinchin and Sharples 16)

In Glasgow, the largest and most popular of these stores, Wylie and Lochhead and Fraser's, had developed from small firms of cabinet-makers and drapers established in the 1830s and 1840s. Their popularity as social, as well as mercantile centers played a major role in the proliferation of cafés and restaurants in their vicinity. Miss Cranston's tea rooms are the best known examples. And all of this vigorous, profitable urban hustle-bustle was in turn enabled by Glasgow's elaborate transportation system of trolleys and trams initially developed by privately owned companies and taken over by the municipal Glasgow Corporation in 1894. Obviously, the system smoothed the conveyance of raw materials, finished goods, and people. Not so obviously, "trains and trams not only facilitated movement, but brought about a new mixing of social classes." (Kinchin and Sharples 13)

Ironically, while women of means most commonly profitted, through their menfolk, from large scale, assembly line industrial production, they were at the same time implicitly entrusted "with resisting the erosion of traditional skills in an increasingly industrialised society." (Kinchin and Sharples 32) In light of this implicit obligation, Scottish women were enjoined to take an active role in maintaining or, where necessary, reviving craft traditions in their home country.

The Scottish Home Industries Association, founded in 1889, was run almost exclusively by and for women The Association focussed its energies on rural craft-workers alone, "rather than trying to alleviate sweated labour of women in the urban textile and clothing industries."(Kinchin and Sharples 33) This exclusive focus clearly reflects a blind spot in the thinking of otherwise well-intentioned Association leaders drawn mainly from the middle class, since, in terms of working conditions, the "dividing line between cottage industry and industrial homework [or piecework] was a thin one." (Kinchin and Sharples 33) And while the Association "drew on the language and philosophy of the Arts and Crafts Movement," a sure sign of cultural sophistication in urban centers like Glasgow and Edinburgh, "the system of production they encouraged was little different from industrial piecework in the cities." (Kinchin and Sharples 33) As one might expect, in both cases, this "system" entailed grueling manual labor, long hours, and meager pay.

The inequities for women in Scotland's textile and clothing sectors reflected those of women at all socioeconomic levels in Scotland throughout most of the 19th Century. Scottish women "rarely owned a substantial income in their own right," (Kinchin and Sharples 33) even after the passing of the Married Women's Property Act in 1882, which enabled wives to own land and keep their own earnings. (That the passage of a law was required to ensure such rights will very likely baffle modern women, particularly those in First World countries where the right to vote, as well as access to higher education and the professions, have long since been taken for granted.)

As to legal documentation specific to the visual arts, names of women bequeathing or lending paintings for public display appear only in their capacity as widows administering their late husbands' collections. For that matter, Scottish women were, more often than not, legally invisible in records such as financial ledgers, sequestrations and bankruptcies, wills and inventories of estates, all of which were usually constructed in the names of men. (Kinchin and Sharples: 33)

So, in the end, women of the Scottish *bourgeoisie* relished their sole cultural outlet, the single source of influence or control reserved to them. It was women who selected and purchased decorative and/or functional art applied art for their homes, in glittery department stores or the refurbished warehouses that were being steadily divorced, geographically, from gritty factory districts. Magazines, manuals of household taste, and newspaper ads of the period directed their appeals to a female clientèle, for whom a "visit to the shops and a break for tea was regarded as a legitimate means of socialising in public." (Kinchin and Sharples: 33) And while women were excluded from key areas of production, such as managerial posts in factories, they were still the primary arbiters of the "look" of home interiors through the "exercise of choice as consumers." (Kinchin and Sharples: 34)

But wait! A cautionary afterword is required here. While many women thrived in their role as arbiters in domestic design, that otherwise satisfying arena of choice and purchase often exposed them to the mockery of conservative male critics. For example, Neil Munro, popular novelist and journalist, ridiculed the social and artistic aspirations of the Glaswegian middle class housewife. Citing her "susceptibilities to the vagaries of fashion," (Kinchin and Sharples 34) he dismissed her shopping expeditions as frivolous, essentially feminine activities. Read "trivial and insubstantial" in Munro's use of the adjective 'feminine," since that was indeed Munro's understanding of the term.

"A break for tea." From the outset, a distinction should be made between the concept of "tea room," as understood by readers who reflexively link soft-spoken female gentility with the taking of afternoon tea in quiet surroundings, and the reality of the commercial tea room in late 19th Century Glasgow. In that clangorous metropolis, the tea room was more commonly the site of serious business transactions, carried out in tandem with lively, sometimes raucous conversation and, among male customers, some gaming.

Moreover, in Glasgow's teashops, food and drink, non-alcoholic drink, that is, were occasionally served in surroundings that provided a venue for experimental art and design, most noteworthy those established by the legendary Catherine Cranston. The tea room was definitely not, then, a haven for "amateurish, faded gentle-women.," but rather an "institution through which women strongly affected taste and social habits." (Kinchin and Sharples 35) Moreover, the tea room "flourished at a time when the women of the Temperance Movement were exerting powerful pressure on society." (Kinchin and Sharples 35)

Given the presence of both men and women in 19th Century Glaswegian tearooms, it should not surprise us that the founder of the city's first tea room was the tea dealer Stuart Cranston, brother of "Kate" Cranston, universally celebrated as one of C.R. Mackintosh's most generous, loyal patrons. Stuart Cranston began his tea room enterprise in 1875, offering his customers free sample cups of tea on newly fitted out commercial premises. He then went on to build a thriving business, so that, by 1901, he was running three lively eateries, specialising in tea, but serving coffee and other beverages. (Unfortunately for his patrons, Stuart's enterprise offered little more than sandwiches to eat).

Stuart's innovative, alcohol-free restaurant started a trend, so that, by the 1890s, Glasgow was seeing a great boom in tea rooms. In high power commercial areas, the tea shops were "little places" which satisfied cheaply and conveniently the businessman's coffee habit and need for a quick lunch (Kinchin and Sharples 35), while tea rooms located in fashionable shopping areas catered primarily, as one might expect, to women. However as noted above, by no means were any of these modest establishments segregated by gender. They could be entered freely by both men *and* women, the ladies unescorted, a welcome perk for women of the period bent on independence. (Kinchin wryly notes that men equally bent on maintaining *their* independence "could bolt to the female-free zones of smoking and, in the larger establishments, billiard rooms." (Kinchin and Sharples 35)

Egalitarian approach to patronage notwithstanding, the increase in the number of tea rooms in a city already well provided with restaurants added a "distinctively feminine accent" to the mix. Typically, the tea shops, usually owned by men, but managed by women, were basement spaces, refurbished for appealing style and comfort by an "Artist Decorator." The Decorator's decisions guided those of an additional interior design specialist, an "Artist Upholsterer." Importantly, in this singular mercantile context, Glaswegian men welcomed female taste without sneers, feeling gratitude instead for the contrast between their city's tea rooms and tea shop chains that had sprung up elsewhere in Scotland. (Kinchin and Sharples 36)

The centrality of the tea room in Scottish design history is inexorably linked to the entrepreneurial Catherine "Kate" Cranston, a champion of vanguard design, was as crucial for the emergence of the Scottish strain of Art Nouveau in Glasgow as were Sarah Bernhardt and Loie Fuller for the promotion of Art Nouveau stylistic norms in Paris. Taking the initiative as an unmarried woman, Catherine opened her first tea room on Argyle Street in 1878; the second, on Ingram Street in 1886. Fortunately for design history, her marriage to John Cochrane in 1892, rather than short circuiting her professional life, allowed her instead to expand her premises, since Cochrane contributed his own funds to her enterprise. And if that weren't sufficient proof of an exceptionally egalitarian marriage, Kate retained her maiden name in her business affairs without Cochrane's opposition, a rarity for the period. (Kinchin and Sharples 36)

Kate played it safe in her selection of an architect for the construction of a new building for her tea rooms, so that the building's exterior would ruffle no municipal or critical feathers. But in selecting designers for the all-important interiors, she trusted her own instincts in opting for non-traditional style. In 1888, she commissioned George Walton, an Art Nouveau adherent, for the furniture and fittings of the Argyle and Ingram Street teashops, Mackintosh for the large-scale murals she had in mind for those drab basement walls. Nine years later, with Walton's departure in 1897, Mackintosh was given freedom to experiment with furniture design as well, ultimately producing his first signature tall-backed chair, among other trademark innovations.

Indeed, with Walton gone, Kate turned every new job over to Mackintosh, most notably the building of the famous Willow Tea Rooms on Sauchiehall Street in 1903. The collaboration between Kate Cranston and Charles Rennie Mackintosh, by then wed to Margaret Macdonald, was a symbiotic meeting of shared design sensibilities. As leader of the now consolidated "Glasgow Style," Mackintosh spoke openly and ardently of his desire to transmit "instinct," "emotion," and "poetry" in his work, qualities associated with a prototypically feminine persona, rather than that of a sober, all-business male practitioner.

In addition, the Arts and Crafts impact on Mackntosh's *modus operandi*, which favored the hand over the machine, had long identified Mackintosh with high quality craftsmanship in the public mind. In the end, all of these factors coalesced to make a strong impression on Kate Cranston, a tough-minded female restaurateur whose own persona could seem, at times, decidedly masculine.Steadfast in her faith in Mackintosh's aesthetic judgment, Kate allowed him a free hand in the production of her tea room interiors. So "his work for her evolved through all periods of his interior design, from heavy oak and organic forms, through white paint and squares to the brilliant zig-zag of a new style seen in the last project, the underground Dug-Out at the Willow Tea Room in 1917." (Kinchin and Sharples 36) Given the bitterness with which he and Margaret departed from Glasgow in 1914, with few return visits thereafter, it is a measure of Kate's trust in the crusty designer that she sought him out for this final project three years after he left the city.

The control of tea room decoration and furnishings by Mackintosh was virtually total. He had responsibility for color schemes, carpets, curtains, metalwork, lighting, furniture (of course), menus, and what was misleadingly termed "incidental works of art." As to the designer input in the Cranston tea room interior, it was not limited to the spare, elegant chairs, tables, light fixtures, and textiles planned and executed or farmed out to craftsmen by Mackintosh alone. Margaret Macdonald's gesso panels adorned the walls, while she, Frances Macdonald, and Jessie King, the latter a guiding force in the eclectic group of Glasgow Girls, were all commissioned for what seem even now strikingly modern menu cards. (Also striking is the absence of prices for the dishes listed on the menus.)

Margaret's gesso panels, like those Mackintosh prepared for the Buchanan Street Tea Rooms, hardly qualify as "incidental," given their scale, rich, intricate surface, and visual power. Most celebrated among them is actually the first she designed and executed. "The May Queen" was created for the Ladies Luncheon Room of Miss Cranston's Ingram Street Tea Rooms in 1900. Depicting the crowning of the May Queen at the ancient Celtic festival, the panel is surprisingly modern in its deployment of non-traditional materials, as well as the crude quality of its fabrication, for which the artist apparently felt little embarrassment.

Margaret prepared three panels, identical in size and proportions, for the panoramic May Queen image. She began by stretching coarsely woven hessian or scrim over three wooden frames, then coated each surface with several layers of gesso, a white ground composed of gypsum or plaster of Paris mixed with water. This created a thick, resilient ground for the application of a variety of media, as well as an unusually heavy completed piece. Rather than defining figures and plants with traditional drawing or painting tools, Margaret instead outlined her forms with lengths of brown string, secured to the panels with long steel pins. Then, with insouciant bravado, she integrated glass beads, thread, mother-of-pearl, shapes of modelled plaster, and tin leaf to the rich, if unruly pictorial surface, so that the visual narrative, with its near-relief surface, was best understood at a distance. (Fortunately, "The May Queen,' along with its companion piece "The Wassail" was hung high in the tea room, as if part of a theatrical stage set, rather than a picture on the wall. Viewed at that height by tea room patrons, the pieces made visual sense.)

Given the scale of "The May Queen," it is puzzling that the dominant color is a dull beige or dun, while the vivid pinks and greens we associate with the "Merry Month of May" appear only in the halo-like crescent that frames the May Queen's head and torso. Perhaps, in avoiding brilliant, saturated colors, she was intentionally avoiding visual competition with Charles' muted design palette. The May Queen's facial expression, by the way, is as fierce as those Aubrey Beardsley created for the imperious women depicted in his graphic illustrations. Beardsley's well-documented impact on Margaret is palpable here.

The end product of Margaret's rule-flouting studio process is a provocative, riveting portrait of a mythical female quasi-deity, discovered deep in Scottish history. She is flanked on either side by two, nearly identical women regarding, with *hauteur* equal to her own, the crowned queen at the center of the composition. "The May Queen," and its companion, Charles' "Wassail," were probably all the more seductive for Scottish tea room clients in that their appearance coincided with the Celtic Revival, spearheaded by Patrick Geddes, that had animated Glaswegian cultural circles for more than a decade.

Before being installed in the Ingram Street Tearooms, both "The May Queen" and "The Wassail" were transported to Vienna, where they were displayed in the Eighth Exhibition of the Vienna Secession, in December, 1900. The exhibit's acclaimed Scottish Room, with its lean, clean, white-painted furnishings, established Mackintosh and Macdonald as leading British designers in the eyes of a mainly but not entirely ecstatic Viennese public and critical establishment.

The cutting edge look of Cranston's tea rooms might seem, on the face of it, a counter-productive choice for an ambitious businesswoman catering to a middle class clientèle. However, Kate was not only following her own predilections in choosing Mackintosh and his female collaborators for her rooms; she was also heeding her fine-tuned business sense. In her assumption that people who would not live with avant garde design would find the strangeness exciting as visitors, she was ultimately vindicated. So, in fact, a visit to any Cranston tearoom became, for Glaswegians and travellers from abroad alike, a theatrical experience. (Kinchin and Sharples 36) The stylistic divergence from the norm on display in wall hangings, light fixtures, dining room chairs and tables, staircases and bannisters, and even waitresses' uniforms became a feature unique to Glasgow.

In zeroing in on the Cranston-Mackintosh collaboration, it is tempting to marginalize Kate Cranston's singular independence as a female entrepreneur, as well as her resolute support for the Temperance Movement. In her proto-feminist attitudes, Cranston, a non-artistic "Glasgow Girl," had always been "acutely aware of the potential role of women in the commercial world almost exclusively a man's world in Glasgow of the 1880s." (Howarth: 37) While her husband, John Cochrane, contributed substantially to the expansion of the tea rooms in the 1890s, Kate's own family had actually opposed her initial enterprise on Argyle Street eight years before her marriage. Lacking the anchor of family support, she had, however, persevered.

In her dedication to the Temperance Movement, Kate's investment in the tea rooms was tied both idealistically and pragmatically to her perception of daytime drunkenness as a major problem in her home city. Rampant alcoholism not only undermined the city's attraction for potential visitors, but also seriously undermined the productivity of its workforce. Obviously, Kate was not alone in this view as evidenced by the sheer number of participants in Temperance Movement street protests.

Further informing Kate's tea room plans was the absence of lunch-time venues for out-of-town workers, commercial travellers, and foreign tourists in a city where only rough-and- ready taverns serving beer, wine, and hard liquor opened their doors at midday. (Howarth: 37) Perceiving the void in inviting lunch hour eateries, Kate rushed to fill it. Primarily committed to an alcohol-free menu for her teashops, Cranston was also, from the outset, bent on satisfying the needs of both her male and female customers. So, with impressive business acumen, Cranston "decided to set an example by turning her tea-room into a miniature social center where, at lunch-time, her male patrons could not only enjoy good food, but relax over a game of dominoes, draughts (checkers) or even play billiard and smoke." Indeed, all that was missing from the stereotypical "smoke-filled room" geared for male comfort, was the requisite bar. And for women, Kate carved out a "ladies' corner," providing privacy and escape from male attention. (Howarth: 37)

Positing an analogy between the efforts of the formidable Kate Cranston and those of Sarah Bernhardt and Loie Fuller, her counterparts in Paris, makes good historical sense. All three women were innovative and dauntless in their respective professions. In their shared resistance to the undertow of established cultural convention, all were significant agents in bringing Art Nouveau design, increasingly geometric in Glasgow, curvilinear and conventionally decorative in Paris, into the public eye.

But the analogy, while sustainable, is clearly limited. Bernhardt and Fuller, in their self-presentation on stage and in promotional media, unabashedly reinvented themselves in the elegant, sylph-like Art Nouveau mode. In contrast, Cranston deliberately developed for herself an image that ran counter to the Art Nouveau feminine ideal, Scottish, French or otherwise. Short and stout, with famously bright eyes, she favored old-fashioned, bulky outfits that emphasized her rotund figure. The dowdy dresses she wore in public reinforced the dependable, conservative tea room image she sought to convey to her customers. Escritt notes that, until her death in 1934, Cranston dressed with a "sartorial sobriety that was reflected in her support for the Temperance movement." (Escritt: 305)

This "branding" process, one Kate engaged in long before the concept was articulated and the term coined, extended even to her cutlery, which she customized with her name imprinted on the back of each handle. In fact, some of the cutlery fashioned by C. R.Mackintosh, the fiery young designer she commissioned for her tea room *Gesamtkunstwerk*, clearly draws on 18th Century servingware patterns. One can only assume that this was a compromise Mackintosh was willing to make to remain in his patron's favor, even as he was steadily assuming a position of leadership in the emerging Glasgow Style.

Finally, be it duly noted that Catherine Cranston, while legendary for endorsing and financing the shocking and unprecedented in design for her tea rooms, was reputedly less than fair-minded and considerate in her management of a staff composed entirely of women. Meticulous to a fault, some would say simply domineering, she oversaw and corrected when "off" her waitresses' dress, demeanor, and even voice quality. Working 12-hour days at very low wages, Cranston's female staff members remain unsung heroines in an avant garde setting in which there was only one star, unprepossessing as she might have appeared to the casual observer.

What, then of Frances, the other Macdonald sister, nine years Margaret's junior and even now a dim figure, all but obscured by her more assertive sibling's long shadow? While by no means as familiar to students of *fin-de-siècle* Art Nouveau as the much discussed Margaret, beautiful Margaret, tall and striking, with her trademark mass of auburn hair Frances nonetheless won more in-house awards than her sister during their years at the Glasgow School of Art. Added to those was an impressive array of prizes Frances garnered in local and national art and design competitions. For that matter, it was Frances, not Margaret, who was given a full scholarship to GSA when the two first began their studies in 1891.

The Macdonald sisters were born not, as one might assume, in Scotland, but in England, in the town of Kidsgrove, near the county of Stafford. The family identified itself as Scotch, however, since *pater familias.* John Macdonald, was a Scotch born and educated engineer. Unlike the four older children, Frances, the youngest of the Macdonald brood, is recorded as receiving no formal education, except, possibly, home schooling in art. (Robertson 31) In 1890, the family moved to Glasgow, where Margaret and Frances enrolled at GSA as day students.

Initially, the sisters followed the traditional path for art students, taking classes in composition, still life and figure drawing, and sculpting in clay, with classical casts as models. But in 1892, when Newberry instituted the Technical Art Studios, they were given access to courses in a wide range of applied art techniques, including stained glass, textile design, graphics and metalwork. Indeed, the integration of the fine art skills Frances had refined earlier at GSA with the metalwork and textile design expertise she acquired in the Technical Art Studios, defines much of Frances's contribution to the rooms she and Herbert later created together for exhibitions in Vienna and Turin. One of Newberry's shrewdest educational innovations, the Technical Art Studios provided the Macdonald sisters as well with "role models of capable, successful women artists, notably Jessie Newberry, and a stimulating artistic environment" (Robertson 33)

Also in the mid-1890s, through the intervention of Fra Newberry, Frances and Margaret began at first collegial, then romantic relationships with Herbert MacNair and Charles Rennie Mackintosh, respectively. As matchmaker, Newberry had accurately perceived the similarities in stylistic bent shared by the four young artist/ designers. That said, however, one must also highlight one critical *caveat* in tracing the evolving professional relationships between MacNair and Mackintosh, MacNair and Frances Macdonald, Mackintosh and Margaret Macdonald, and between all four members of the group.

To begin with, Herbert and Charles had already become friends by the late 1880s, through sheer proximity as employees of the architecture firm Honeyman and Keppie. Herbert had been taken on as apprentice in 1888; Charles, as a junior draughtsman in 1889. The two soon formed an artistic alliance that took them on sketching trips to

Iona and Linlithgow in Scotland and to rural areas in northern England. As novice architects, they urged each other on, working on competition drawings side by side in Keppie's home in Preswick and attending evening classes together at GSA, starting in 1889. (Robertson 31). The men studied building construction, perspective, geometry, and architectural design. Outlining the evening school coursework Herbert and Charles engaged in before joining forces with Frances and Margaret is no mere academic exercise here. These were all disciplines unavailable to their female companions in GSA's day school. (Robertson 33)

So, while Newberry was correct in perceiving the affinities between the four young artist/designers, who became, in fact, the Glasgow Four - their shared attraction to continental Symbolism, their shared interest in both their Celtic heritage and Scottish vernacular design, their shared efforts in melding easel with applied art - the Director's schedule of courses made an implicit, but firm distinction between the eventual professional responsibilities of Herbert and Charles, and those of Frances and Margaret. It was expected that the men would eventually take charge of the planning and construction of private and municipal buildings, while the women would design and orchestrate their interior elements. There would be some overlap in decision-making and practice, of course, but the more significant obligation, the edifice itself, would remain a male responsibility and, when completed, a male achievement. (As we now know, Newberry was only partially on the money in this regard where Mackintosh and McNair were concerned, since Herbert's career in architecture was short-lived and abortive.)

The Macdonald sisters shared a studio in the GSA precincts until their graduation in 1894. They then continued their partnership in rented quarters aptly named The Macdonald Sisters' Studio on Glasgow's Hope Street, dividing their energies between graphics, textile design, book illustration and metalwork. Versatile to a degree rare in our time, both women pursued their work in painting as well, mainly in gesso and watercolor. In 1899, Frances married Herbert MacNair, whose own commercial efforts on nearby George Street had failed, and in 1900, Margaret married Charles. After their marriages, the Macdonald sisters never collaborated again. Instead, they adjusted their creative talents to those of their husbands and their professional paths, to some extent, diverged.

In contemplating the divergence of the Macdonald sisters' creative paths in particular, it is useful to consider three pictorial narratives developed in the period 1895-98, during which Frances and Margaret integrated their drawing skills with their proficiency in metalwork: "The Christmas Story" (1895-6); "The Defense of Guinevere" (1897); "The Four Seasons" (1907-08). Pamela Robertson notes their choice of more conventional subject matter than in the past for these projects, perhaps in response to a client's brief, perhaps reflecting a wish for wider commercial and/or critical acceptance. (The sobriquet "Spook School" must have stung, despite the women's apparent insouciance. On the practical level, it probably drove away many of their more conservative clients.)

Of the three narratives, "The Four Seasons" most invites scrutiny, since it suggests an early parting of the ways in the sisters' perception of themselves as women, a perception expressed in their joint depiction of seasonal change. While there is no indication of personal friction between the two, the contrast in content and mood between Margaret's expression of "Summer" and "Winter," and Frances's expression of "Spring" and "Autumn," is unignorable and telling.

In the panels for "The Four Seasons," each season is represented by a single, full length female figure, presented in a narrow, upright format. The symbolic figure for each season is thematically supported by motifs worked into the panel's lead frames. In Robertson's words, Margaret bodies forth "Summer" as a "fertile, light-filled subject attended by angelic putti," while "Winter" takes the form of "a snowdrop princess watched over by snowflake infants" (Robertson 36), portrayals very likely too glutinous for jaded 21st Century sensibilities, but no doubt appealing to the sisters' female customers.

Frances, on the other hand, presents "Spring" and "Autumn" with a subtext of foreboding that may have repelled her more sensitive clients, but would surely offer the modern observer a provocative ambiguity worthy of serious consideration. In "Spring," we see a naked figure encircled by white blossoms, suggesting a conventional Flora. But, as Robertson notes, Flora's "unnerving eyes stare out from the nebulous background," her gaze "compelling, enigmatic." (Robertson 36) A second shadowy figure stands behind her with downcast eyes. In the panel for "Autumn," there are two naked figures, one wreathed in roses, symbolizing fruitfulness, the other, Eve, the very emblem of fatal temptation. Deepening the mood of pessimism, Frances delineates skulls in the lower section of the painting, and weeping female heads in the metal frame.

What conclusions should we draw in our attempt to fathom this collaborative work accomplished by two women bound together by blood, gift, and training, but clearly divided by temperament? "It has been suggested that the series is a meditation on women's life cycle. The differences in the sister's interpretation may simply have reflected their stylistic differences, or they may have been deliberately incorporated to illustrate more powerfully the range of choices/ opportunities facing women." (Robertson 36) (Men, by the way, are conspicuously absent in all four pieces.)

Until recently, scholarly convention has described Margaret as not only the more forceful and pragmatic of the Macdonald sisters, but also her younger sister's superior in both easel and applied art. However, when we examine Frances's contribution to "The Four Seasons," as well as the seven haunting paintings completed toward the end of her life, we see that it was Frances who was on to something regarding the destabilizing complexities, the often mutually exclusive demands on a woman's time, energy, and emotional involvement that the American Feminist Movement would articulate more fully in the 1960s.

While MacNair had snagged few commissions during his brief, solitary foray into the architectural profession, his joint ventures with Frances late in the decade netted far more positive critical comment and commercial success. "By the end of the 1890s, Macdonald and McNair had emerged as distinctive and impressively varied artists, whose work had been noted by leading critics at home and abroad." (Robertson 39) The couple fit the profile of progressive artist-designers of the late 19th Century. Most importantly, they clearly subscribed to the Arts and Crafts precepts of hand craftsmanship and diversity of output. In addition, their work in narrative watermedia painting and decorative design drew thematically from the common well of much mainstream 19th Century art, avant garde upheavals in Paris notwithstanding: the cycles of the year and human life; Christian values; romantic love. Moreover, their habit of selecting imagery from a familiar academic glossary—flights of birds, fruit-bearing trees, roses, children—ensured ongoing popularity. (Robertson 39)

It should be noted, however, that Frances and Herbert, feverishly productive and commercially solvent as they were in the 1890s, stood apart from their peers in a number of ways. Some looked askance at their "often willful transformation of form," their "frequent disregard for conventional motif," the introduction of personal symbolic references into their work, references mystifying and opaque to many viewers, and their focus on the feminine. (Robertson 39) Indeed, it seemed to some that Herbert, knowingly or not, took a stylistic and expressive back seat to his wife.

Ironically, the most intense, if not the most lucrative period of collaborative activity for Frances and Herbert coincided, in part, with the ten years they spent in England In 1898, the couple left Glasgow for Liverpool, where Herbert had landed a teaching position in the Applied Art section of the newly founded (1894) School of Architecture. He had been hired as instructor in an ambitious program linked administratively to the University of Liverpool. The post, the mood of optimism informing the new program, and progressive attitudes in Liverpool as a whole all boded well for the MacNairs. Liverpool was a thriving port city with international reach similar to that of Glasgow, and a sizeable population of Scottish merchants and engineers.

Sited on England's west coast and far distant from the country's other major urban centers, the city now known primarily as the birthplace of the Beatles, had a "long tradition of civic idealism, led by the Unitarian Rathbone family, who included Arts and Crafts [Movement] enthusiasts among their number." (Crawford 74) Richard Rathbone, had, in fact, taught applied arts locally, with the assistance of the sculptor C.J. Allen and the decorative artist Robert Anning Bell. The wedding of the fine and applied arts in this educational setting seemed a perfect fit for Herbert, who, like Charles, Margaret, and Frances, had always moved comfortably between easel painting and functional craft as though the two disciplines formed a an organic whole.

The newly founded School of Architecture and Applied Arts provided architectural training in Liverpool for the first time. Feeding the School's reputation for daring was its offer of instruction for the would-be architect prior to hisapprenticehip in an architectural firm, a strategy that had been already adopted in the United States. (Robertson 40) Also groundbreaking was the its attempt to link architectural training to design and fabrication in the applied arts, a process that Newberry had initiated, *de facto*, through the opening of Technical Art Studios to male *and* female GSA students in 1892.

In the theoretical realm, the establishment of the School of Architecture and Applied Arts "reflected one side of a debate which had been smouldering in the profession over the past few years: was architecture a profession or an art?" (Robertson 40) In this heated discussion—or was it an argument?—the School weighed in on the side of art. This pedagogic direction was reinforced by the School's administrative link to the University of Liverpool and tandem independence from the

Science and Art Department in South Kensington, "with its rigorous curriculum and examination schedule." (Robertson 40) Reflecting the focus on architecture's artistic aspect, the applied arts curriculum presented students with a set of courses strikingly similar to those at GSA: modelling, sculpture, drawing, painting, design, woodcarving, and ironwork.

With his fellow instructors, MacNair offered an broad set of options for interested students. By 1899, under his direction, the Applied Arts program had generated work in stained glass, tiles, posters and book illustrations, fabric, and stencilled wallpapers. (Robertson, Doves and Dreams 41) Obviously, MacNair brought an impressive range of technical skills to the program, given his exposure to a wealth of craft tools, materials, and technical processes at GSA. He also brought with him considerable experience in architectural design, albeit of the theoretical variety, and a portfolio of drawings and watermedia paintings, albeit much of it overly sentimental by 21st Century standards. Both in concert with Frances and alone, he had racked up a substantial record of exhibitions in Glasgow, Liverpool, London, and Paris.

So, given MacNair's widespread reputation and array of fine and applied art achievements, it surprises us to learn that his teaching obligations in Liverpool were carried out in makeshift buildings called the Art Sheds. These wooden enclosures were *literally* sheds, low-slung and protected from the elements only by corrugated iron roofs. (Robertson 41) Equally frustrating for both instructors and students, the requisite hand tools and machinery MacNair had come to take for granted in GSA's Technical Art Studios were either missing altogether, or damaged and barely functional in the Sheds. For seven years, MacNair, his fellow instructors, and an ever-smaller number of students soldiered on, improvising when necessary, until 1905, when the Applied Arts section was detached from the School of Architecture and merged with the municipal School of Art and Design. (Robertson 49)

The decision to eliminate the Applied Arts Section was justified on administrative and financial grounds. In the end, the applied arts department hadn't become an integral part of the architecture curriculum. The two sections "had neither premises or staff in common," the income for the former was stagnant, and, from 1901-1905, while the architecture students had all taken painting and drawing classes, only two had signed up for applied arts courses (Robertson 50), a startlingly low and rather questionable statistic.

The architecture component, however, under the direction of Charles Reilly, flourished. As Crawford suggests, perhaps "this was because classical architecture and traditional easel painting counted for more in nineteenth-century Liverpool than decorative art," (Crawford: 74) in a city where popular and municipal support for design that was both functional and elegant had never approached that of Glasgow. Reilly himself, who had been named Professor of Architecture in 1904, professed himself puzzled both by the widespread emphasis on crafts in the 1890s, and "the need of adding 'artiness' to architecture." (Robertson 50) Conceivably, the creative independence MacNair fostered in the Art Sheds was ill-suited to Reilly's more methodical, pragmatic direction.

The loss of the Liverpool teaching position, along with the sudden disappearance of what had been dependable income from MacNair family wealth, left Frances and

Herbert financially stressed and demoralized. Up until then, they had been able to count on some assets, at least in the realms of creative versatility and social connectedness. They had a small son, Sylvan, born in 1901, and a home on 54 Oxford Street in Liverpool, where they had pooled their Glasgow Style tastes and applied art expertise to generate an "arty" environment totally at odds with the stodgy home interiors of their English neighbors. Frances had explored two new fields, jewelry design and embroidery. She had also taken an active role in university life, helping Herbert stage productions of Greek and Shakespearean tragedies for which he created sets and costumes in the Art Sheds.

However, by 1905, the couple had seen a significant drop in income from their work. The few sales they made were to "a well-informed elite of artists and art-lovers," (Robertson 51) such as Newberry, the wealthy Austrian Art Nouveau patron, Fritz Waerndorfer, Anna Muthesius, and, irony of ironies, Charles Reilly. The termination of the Art Sheds delivered the *coup de grâce*. Out of options in Liverpool, the couple returned to Glasgow in 1908.

Back in her home city, Frances taught design in GSA's metalwork and enamel studios, profitting from the school's 20-year tradition of hiring female instructors. Margaret, on the other hand, like her prodigiously talented, mercurial husband, never followed the default path followed by artists, designers, and architects, then and now, that is, teaching in her areas of expertise. Rather, she spurned the steady salary, job security and camaraderie educators in established institutions have always taken for granted. Instead, Margaret parlayed her strong organizational skills and financial savvy, not to mention her considerable natural charm, into a kind of vocation: she helped find, manage, and bring to fruition her husband's commissions.

The demands on her time as GSA instructor did not detract from Frances's commitment to painting, which seems, on re-examination, perhaps more deep-dyed than that of her sister. Moreover, the emotions that propelled Frances in her painting, especially later in her life, may have been not only more intense than Margaret's, but of an altogether different order, In the final years of her relatively brief life-she died prematurely in 1921, some say by her own hand-Frances completed a series of watercolor and pencil images now viewed by feminist scholars as comments on the difficult choices facing all women, even those enjoying a modicum of financial security. Here is the central bind many see informing the pieces: if a woman chooses to dedicate herself only to her career and remain adamantly single, she risks losing the economic anchor and emotional fulfillment marriage and childbearing can ensure; if she opts instead for marriage and motherhood, she may be forced to sacrifice personal independence and professional advancement.

Obviously, Frances had faced these choices herself. The Turin Decorative Arts Exhibition, held in 1902, provides one, perhaps minor but still significant case in point. To the delight of Frances and Herbert, critics reviewing the interiors developed for the Turin exposition described the harmonious Macdonald-MacNair Writing Room as the product of a "united brain." However, the birth of Sylvan meant that the couple was unable to savor firsthand the initial display of their combined efforts and "united brain" on the European continent. It is a measure of Herbert's loyalty to his wife that he elected not to travel to Turin alone. Charles and Margaret, on the other hand, then and always childless, attended the Turin exhibition.

So the pale, melancholic watermedia images Frances painted mainly for herself, as either a rumination on her loor an exorcism, suggest anything but an optimistic bead on the fate of gifted women in *fin-de-siècle* society. Of the seven paintings, only one, very moving visual hint of her despondent outlook is available to the public at the Kelvingrove: "Truth Lies at the Bottom of the Well" (ca. 1912-15). According to Kelvingrove wall documentation, the image illustrates an ancient proverb describing truth as a symbolic female figure, confined or imprisoned at the bottom of a well. This picture, the comment continues, "may have a wider significance as an allegory on the restrained role of women in Edwardian society."

At the top of the image, three emaciated young women, their features identical, appear half-submerged in the well, whose walls are transparent. Through the brick outlines, we see the faint forms of the lower portions of the women's bodies, starting just at the pelvic level. All three maidens, barely pubescent, are depicted with index fingers raised to their mouths, as if to ward off intrusive noise of any kind. A fourth lies prone at the bottom of the well. Her eyes are closed and her index finger is also raised to her lips, which are reddened.

This is the only touch of color in a painting whose overall surface is a uniform, mottled grisaille. All the women, their limbs and torsos attentuated, their flesh translucent, seem not only dematerialized, but de-energized and forlorn. For the 21st Century viewer, admittedly hard to accept is the cloying, even kitsch quality of their features as Frances has defined them, in her effort to express the helplessness and vulnerability she was no doubt feeling herself at the time. However, cynicism aside, there is no denying the emotional authenticity of her rendering.

Less ambiguous in meaning, and not on display at the Kelvingrove, is "The Choice" (1909). For this more unambiguous expression of the female bind, Frances has placed two overlapping, again emaciated female figures on the right. Like the figures in all her paintings, the women are nude, their faces blank and their breasts so small as to render them virtually non-erotic, even sexless. Most tellingly, gold coins fall from the hands of the figure further to the right. At the center of the painting, by contrast, Frances has depicted a romantic couple in profile. The male figure at the left seems to at once embrace and protect his lover, who seems, in turn, to stare, at the women described above.

A transparent swirl of fabric, strewn with roses, envelops the lovers just below their torsos and, to reinforce the message. The woman in the center holds, not coins, but a rose in her hand. Since Frances left no art gallery statement of the motives for, or meaning of, her final paintings, interpreting their import in strictly late 20th Century feminist terms would be presumptuous and intellectually irresponsible. However, those gold coins, clearly emblematic of commercial success, set against those roses, the time honored floral symbol for romantic love, surely suggest a lifelong conflict in Frances's psyche, one she felt insoluble.

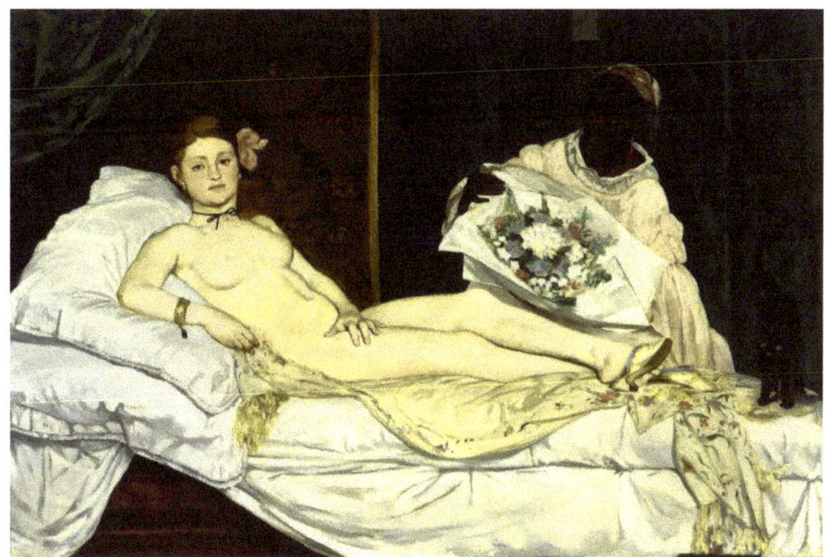

Edouard Manet, *"Olympia,"* oil, 1863

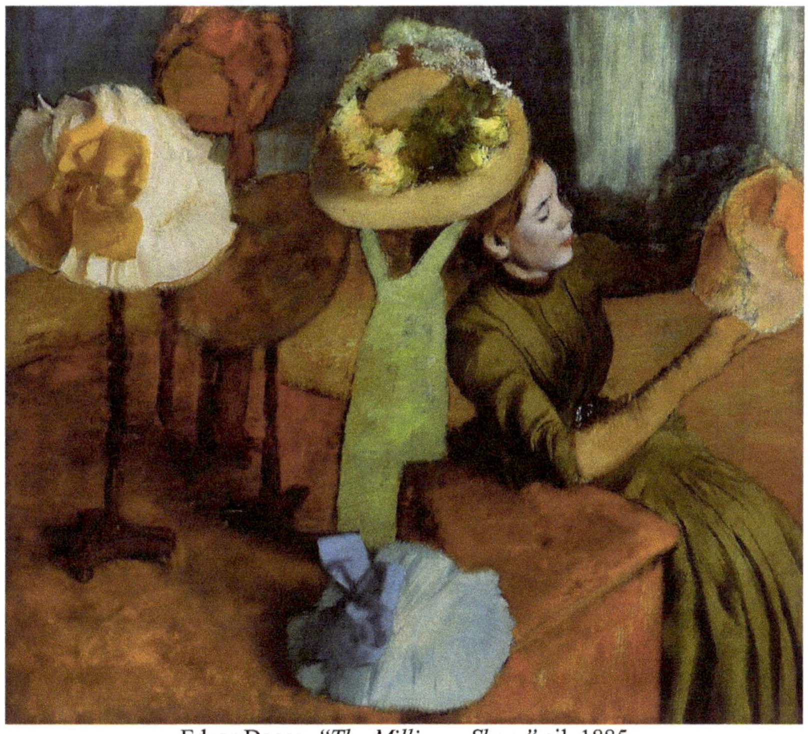

Edgar Degas, *"The Millinary Shop,"* oil, 1885

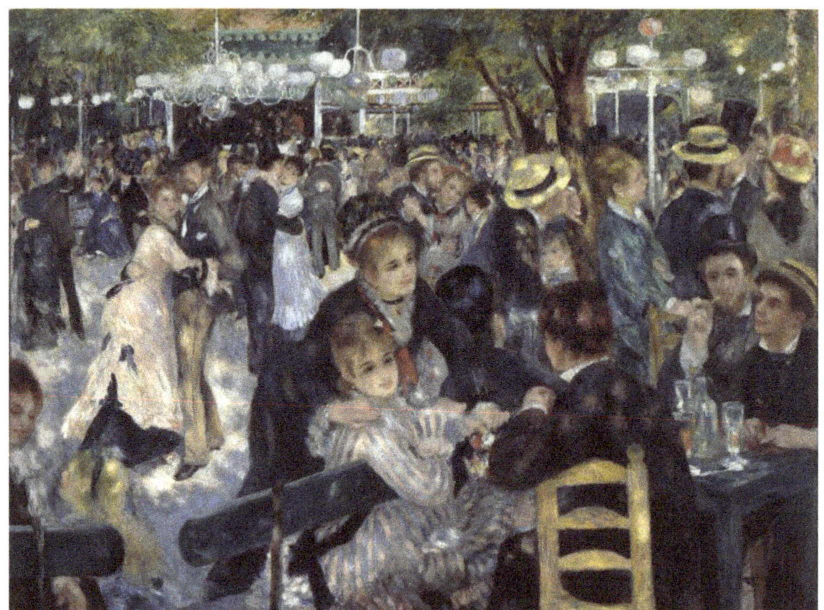

Auguste Renoir, *"Dance at the Moulin de las Galette,"* oil, 1876

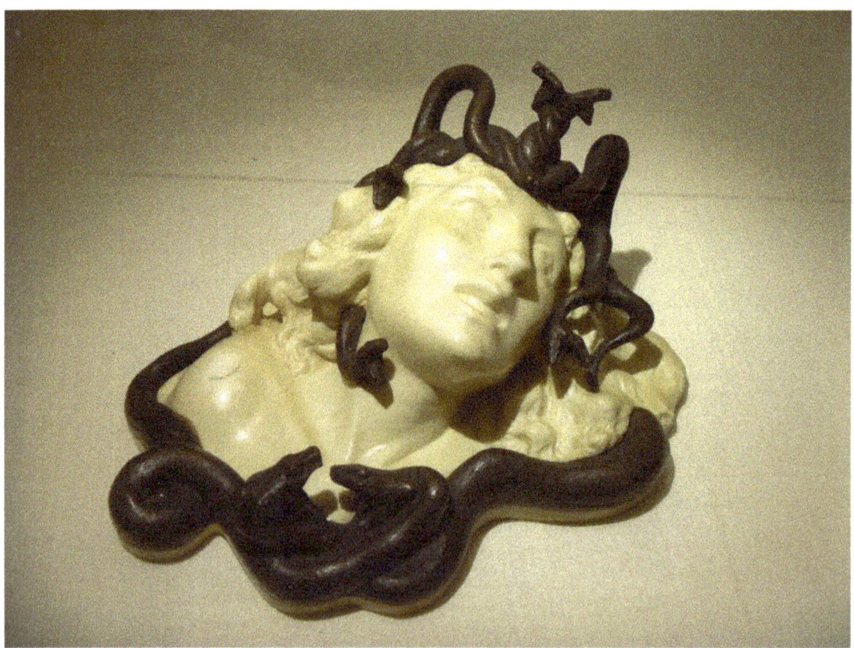

René Lalique, *"Medusa"*

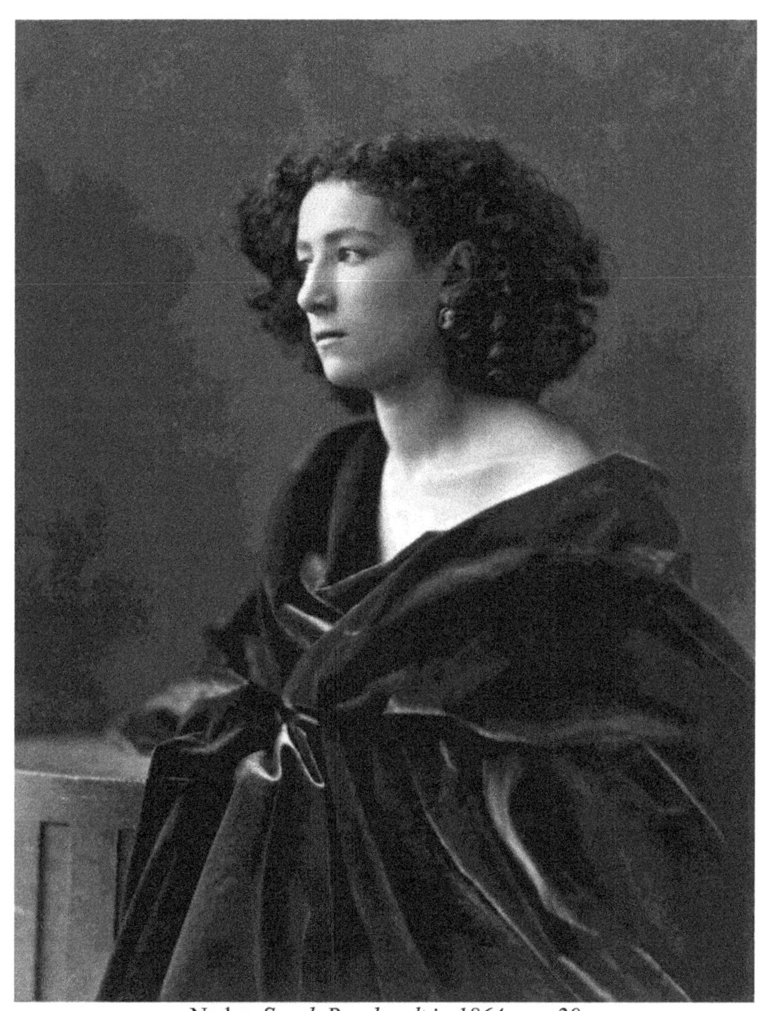

Nadar, *Sarah Bernhardt in 1864, age 20*

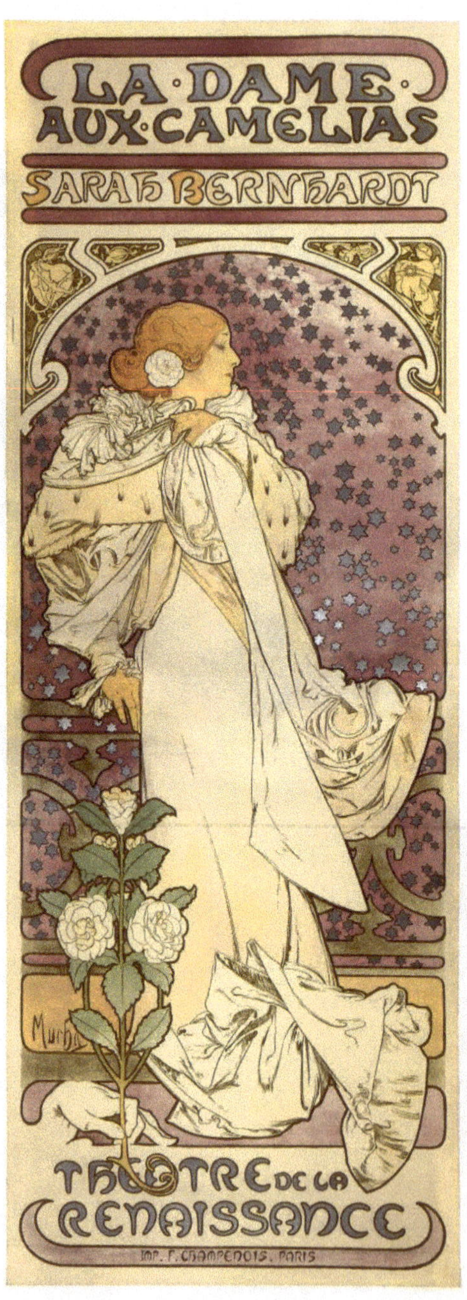

Alphonse Mucha, *Sarah Bernhardt as "La Dame aux Camellias,"* lithographic poster, 1896

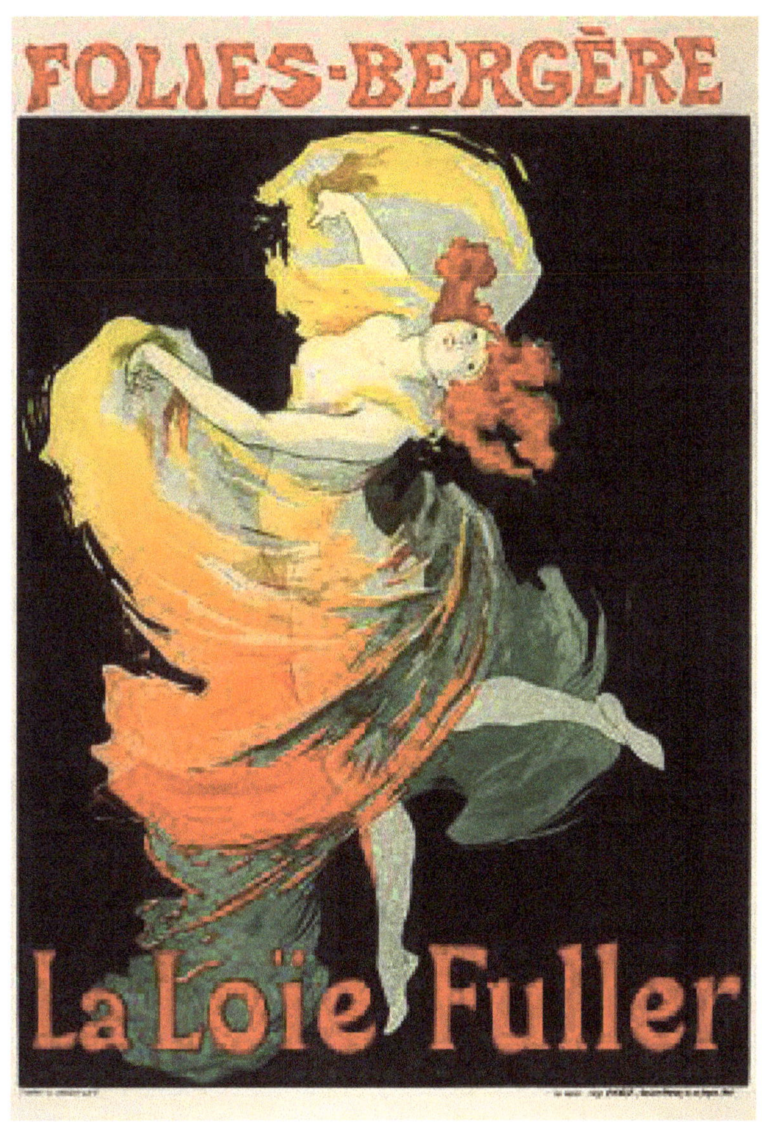

Jules Chéret, *Loie Fuller at the Folies Bergère*, lithographic poster, 1901

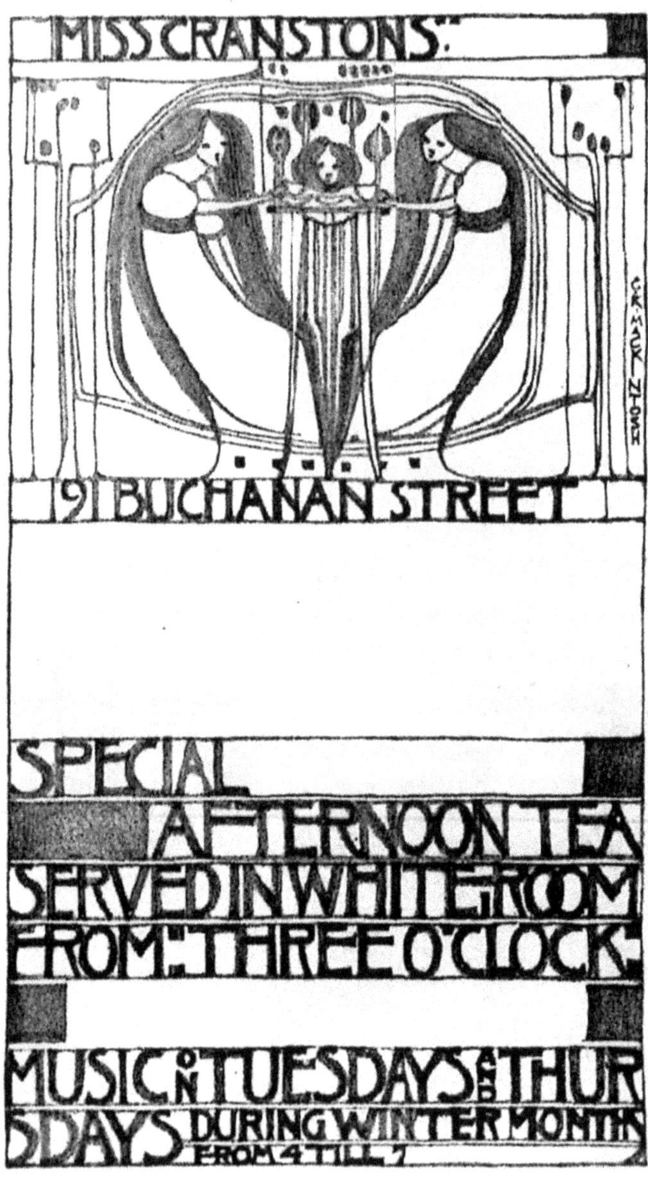

Charles Rennie Mackintosh, *poster design for Buchanan Street Tearoom*s

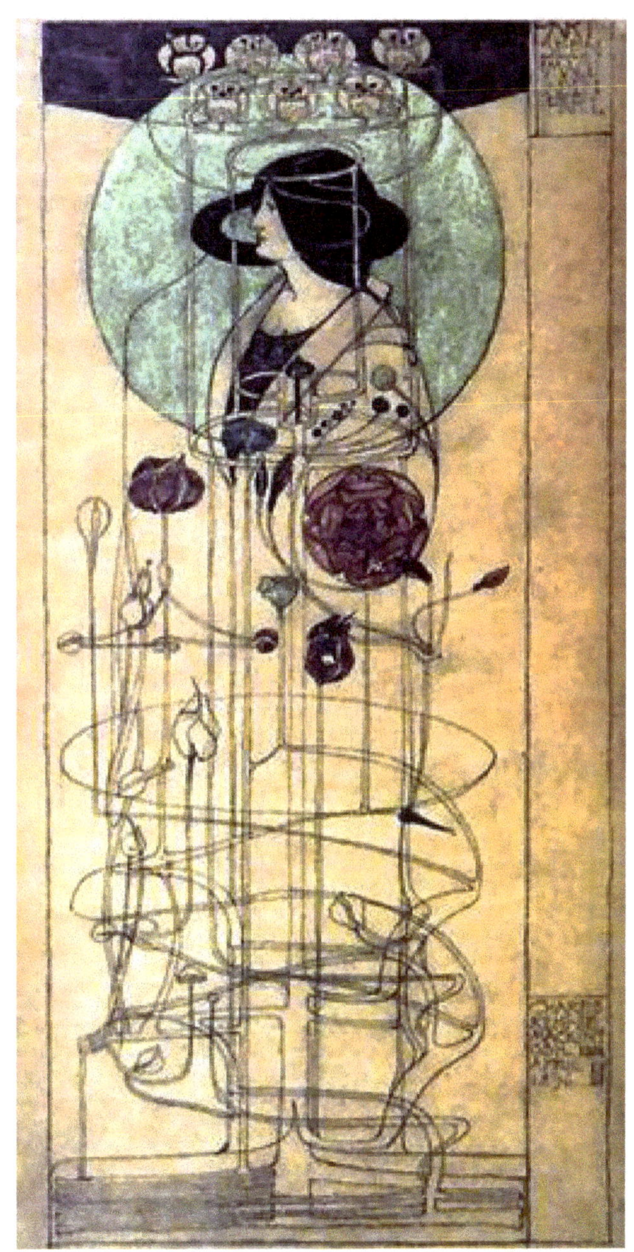

Charles Rennie Mackintosh, *design for frieze, Buchanan Street Tearooms*

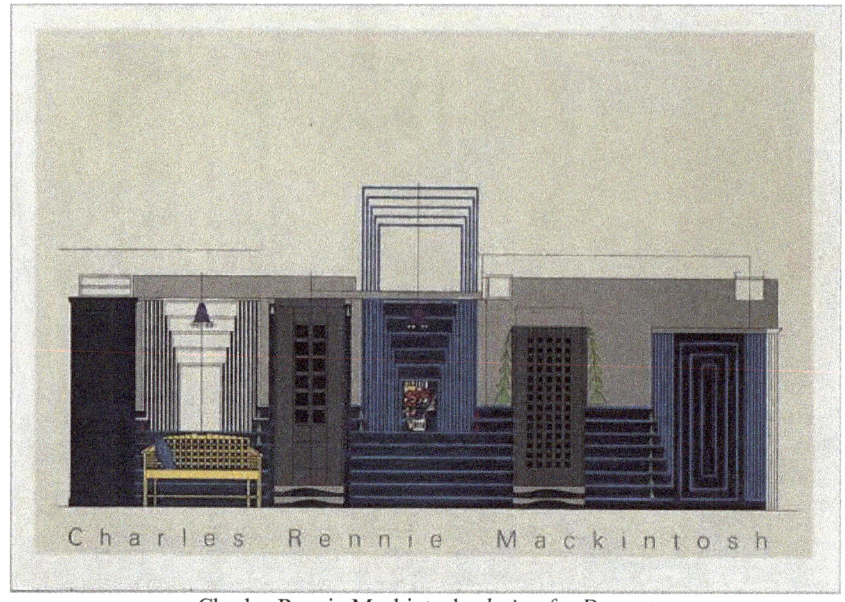

Charles Rennie Mackintosh, *design for Dugout*

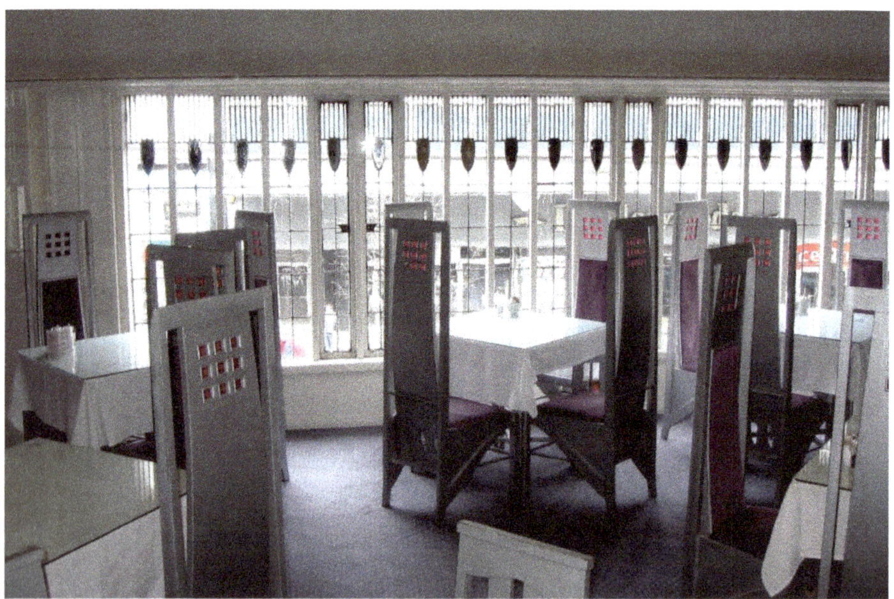

Charles Rennie Mackintosh, *Willow Tearooms, Room Deluxe*

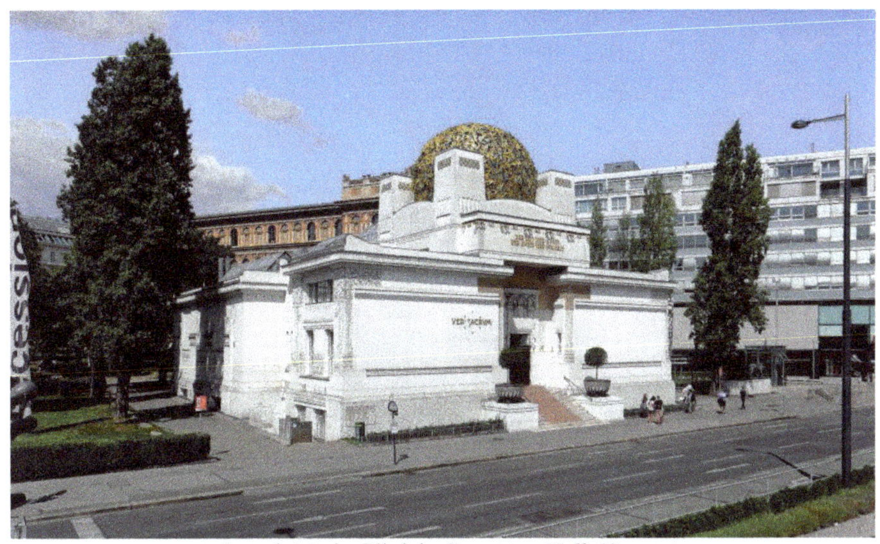

Joseph Maria Olbrich, *Secession Hall, Vienna*

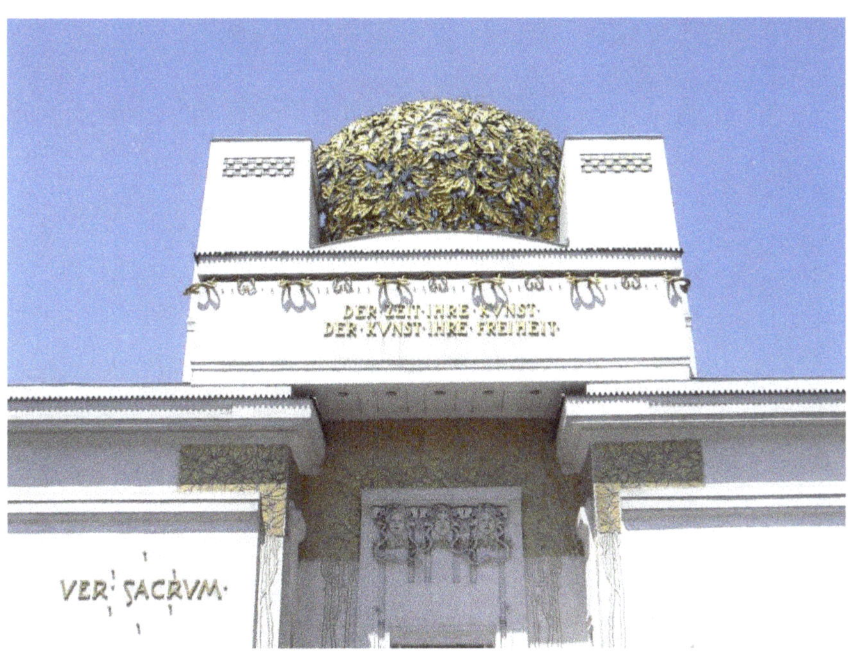

Joseph Maria Olbrich, *Secession Hall, "Golden Cabbage" dome*

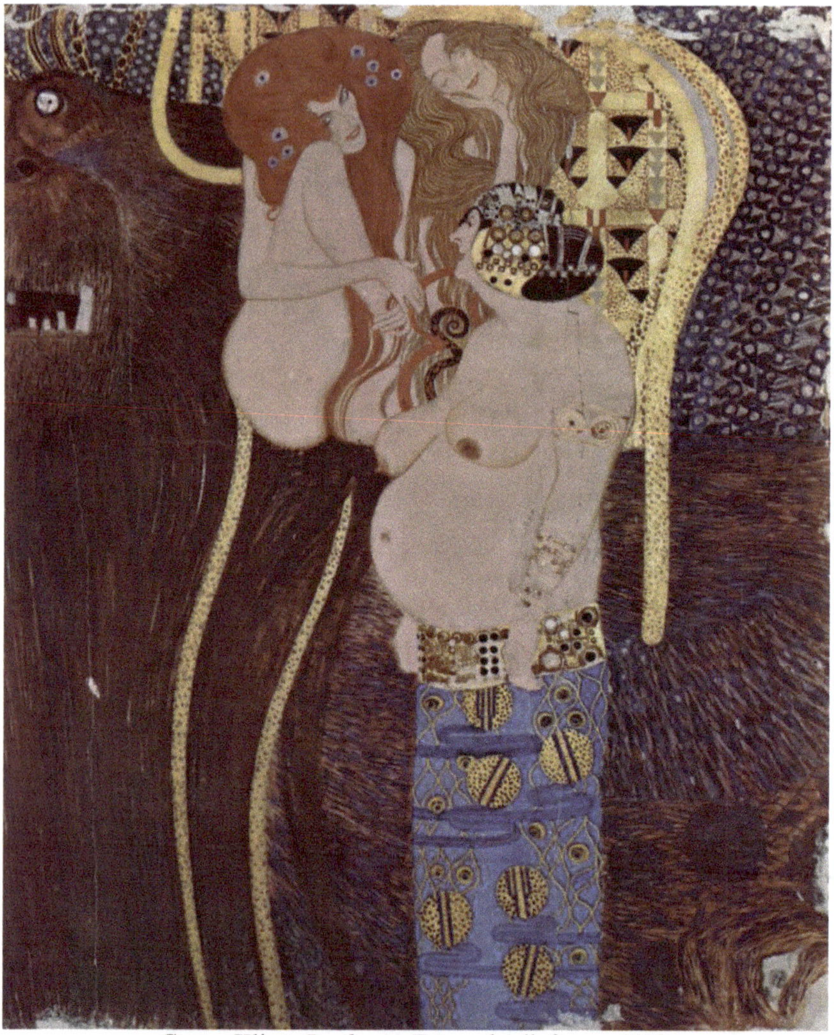

Gustav Klimt, *Beethoven Frieze*, detail, fresco, 1902

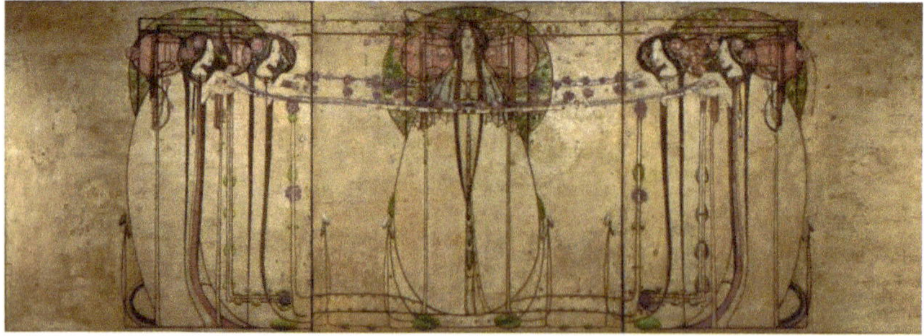

Margaret Macdonald, *"The May Queen,"* gesso panel, 1900

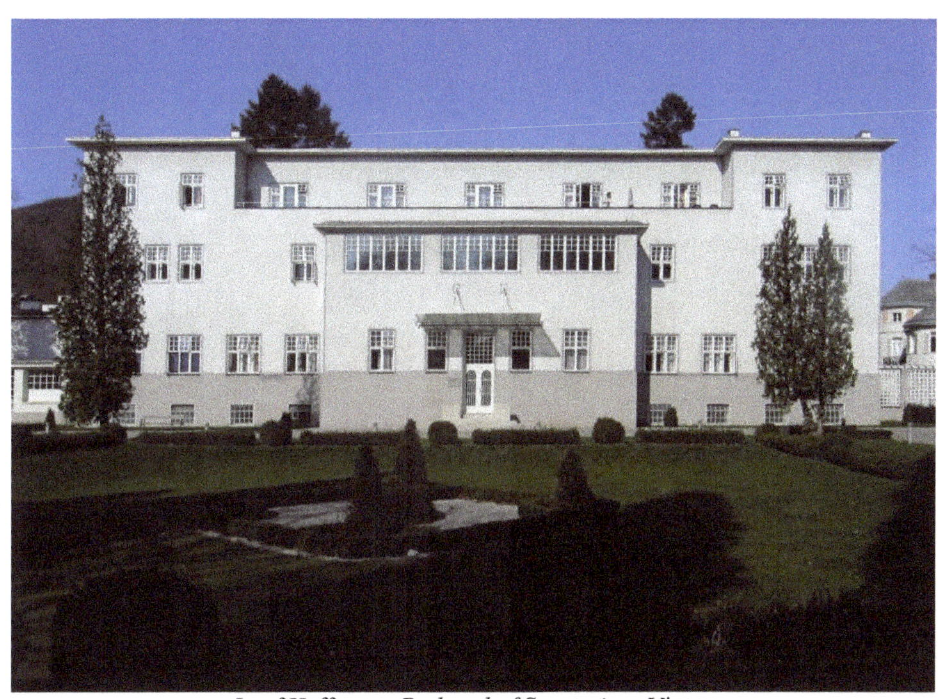

Josef Hoffmann, *Purkersdorf Sanatorium*, Vienna

CHAPTER 10

Internationalism and Nationalism I: Mackintosh and the Four in Vienna

In 1900, the Glasgow Four, known to their Glaswegian detractors as the Spook School, were invited to exhibit their innovative design work in Vienna's Eighth Secession Exhibition, to be installed in Joseph Maria Olbrich's newly constructed Secession Hall. Clearly, given the singular importance of the invitation, Viennese exhibit organizers saw in the art and craft of their Scotch colleagues a stylistic direction in sympathy with their own, as well as a significant step into modernism.

In defining the aesthetic similarities between the work of the Glasgow Four and those of their Austrian hosts, it is useful to begin by outlining the characteristics shared by French, Belgian, and German Art Nouveau designers of the period: fascination with nature; an high degree of involvement in symbolism and spiritualism; preoccupation with abstract curvilinear form. Thus, as is obvious to us now, the stylistic biases shared by Scottish artist/designers in Glasgow and their Austrian counterparts in Vienna stand in marked contrast to those of their French, Belgian and German Art Nouveau peers, at least at first glance. "In aesthetic terms," Stephen Escritt notes, "those who were creating modern art in these cities [Glasgow and Vienna] displayed an increasing tendency towards geometry in both form and decoration" (Escritt: 137).

Escritt elaborates: "In Vienna and Glasgow, stylization became increasingly angular and ornament appeared to be in retreat. Until recently these aesthetic developments have been interpreted as the symptoms of the rationalism that was beginning to take hold in the early years of the twentieth century. The geometry of Josef Hoffmann and Charles Rennie Mackintosh has been seen as the beginning of a functional design in which decoration played no part and fitness for purpose was all" (Escritt: 137).

But, he concludes. a *caveat* must be inserted here, one that undercuts the simple, or simplistic assertion that the French, Belgian, and German Art Nouveau masters worked at total stylistic and conceptual odds with their Scottish and Austrian Art Nouveau peers: "this geometry [that of Mackintosh and Hoffmann] was far from merely functional. It often displayed a subtlety and elegance that betrayed its decorative roots. To contemporaries in 1900, there was no polarization between the geometry of Vienna and the curvilinearity of France. Both were considered as contrasting parts of the same movement" (Escritt: 137).

Two related questions regarding influence have repeatedly been raised here by Art Nouveau scholars. The first centers on the tendency to "square the circle" shared by Mackintosh and his Viennese colleagues, in combination with their rejection of frivolous surface ornament. The second addresses the embrace of strict, unembellished utility manifest in the work of Bauhaus architects and designers of the mid-1920s, and the possibility that both Mackintosh and the Viennese, Hoffmann in particular, had direct influence on the development of Bauhaus built structures and functional ware. The delayed impact of geometric Art Nouveau on Bauhaus innovators such as Walter Gropius and Mies van der Rohe certainly merits further investigation. However, the first question is more germane to a study of the stylistic similarities between the Scotch Maverick Mackintosh and the cultured, urbane Viennese, because it poses interesting questions of originality and/or attribution, that is to say: who got there first?

Early research suggests that Mackintosh, his right-angled, white-painted, clean-surfaced furnishings a welcome antidote to traditional fussy clutter for Secession Hall visitors, had, in fact, set the stylistic standard for *Wiener Werkstätte* designers, directed by the protean Hoffmann and his versatile colleague, Kolomon Moser. More recently, however, scholars of the period counter that the influence may have flowed the other way, or, alternatively, "perhaps Mackintosh and his colleagues in Glasgow and Hoffmann and his fellow designers in Vienna "were responding to similar circumstances and models, including the work of the English designer Charles Ashbee" (Escritt: 133).

According to this more flexible view, the two groups of designers, while historically, culturally, and linguistically far distant, responded with similar stylistic approaches to similar civic needs. Glasgow's pragmatic city fathers,successful industrialists bent on bolstering civic pride, did so by funding architectural innovation, while Vienna's Hapsburg Emperor found the means for discouraging discord within his vast fractious empire by supporting artists, designers, and architects whose efforts opened the door to the future, rather than reiterating Vienna's historicist past.

Vienna, while the historic center of the tradition-bound Austro-Hungarian Empire, had, in fact, earned a reputation for intellectual and artistic radicalism by the early Twentieth Century. Adolf Loos had published his incendiary treatise "Ornament and Crime"; Arnold Schoenberg had composed "Five Orchestral Pieces," in which he rejected the traditional Western tonal system; Sigmund Freud, in "The Interpretation of Dreams," had revolutionized the emerging discipline of psychology by defining and emphasizing the nature and potency of subconscious drives. Nevertheless, when one considers Vienna's otherwise ingrained social, political, and cultural conservatism, it is still surprising that "such a vibrant and radical decorative style [Art Nouveau] flourished in the city." (Escritt: 135) Perhaps the astonishing paradox can be explained by the fact that Secession Hall and its cutting-edge exhibitions enjoyed significant public visibility, while the groundbreaking theories of Loos and Freud, and the atonal musical compositions of Schoenberg, were known only to a select few. Secession Hall and its innovative exhibitions created a cultural fire, and the public raced to witness the flames.

Given this cultural discord, a closer look at turn-of-the-century Vienna seems in order. By 1900, the city was indeed the fourth largest on the continent, but clearly lacked the economic and social dynamism of London or New York in the same period. The Habsburg Empire remained huge, covering "a vast swathe of central and eastern Europe, stretching from Innsbruck in the west to Transylvania in the east, from Prague and Cracow in the north to Zagreb in the south," (Escritt: 135) a geographic spread divided into a host of independent, in many cases antagonistic nations that remain so in our own time.

Obviously, geographic spread does not often necessarily coincide with viability. In 1900, Hapsburg Emperor Franz Joseph was in his seventh decade, and *fin-de-siècle* Vienna was no longer the epicenter of an empire that had become an "increasingly fragile union of nationalities" (Escritt: 135). A result, in part, of Austria's military defeat by Prussia in 1866, Budapest had replaced Vienna as the Empire's politically dominant urban center.

Moreover, by the late nineteenth century, the wave of liberalism that had swept across Europe for decades had made inroads on Viennese politics as well. Be it noted, however, that the "liberal" movement of the late 1800s should not be understood in 20th Century European and American terms. since liberals of the period laid great emphasis on the primacy of the individual, rather than on principles of democratic governance in the modern sense. As a result, the movement's adherents, rather than supporting an egalitarian social and political agenda, sought instead to maintain a time-honored *status quo*. Driven by fear of a disruptive federalism, they argued instead for a centrally administered empire, seen as the only way to "keep together an ethnically disparate, geographically huge and fractious empire through a period of technological progress and political tension" (Escritt: 135).

Technological progress. The subject introduces a further paradox in a discussion of Vienna in 1900. Still steadfastly conservative in social and political matters, while at the same time the seedbed for intellectual and cultural vanguard leaders like Loos, Schoenberg and Freud, turn-of-the century Vienna manifested all the trademarks of urban modernity: electric lighting; a commuter rail network, and a burgeoning automobile culture. That "Viennese society remained characterized by a cossetted predictability and stifling bureaucracy," (Escritt: 136) only serves to drive home the irony.

So, sophisticated technology notwithstanding, it is critical to point out that Vienna's avowed "liberal order" in fact embodied until the 1890s the condition of urban stagnation in art and architecture "that had symbolically rebuilt the city's great arterial road, known as the Ring, in historicist style." (Escritt: 136) The legendary *Ringstrasse* boasted a hodgepodge of revivalist styles: a neo-Greek Parliament; a neo-Gothic City Hall; neo-Baroque apartment "palaces,' an architectural mélange viewed by Kirk Varnedoe as not so much antiquated as *arriviste*, a cheapening of traditional styles. Indedd, the "condition" was so severe that a breakaway group of progressive artists, attracted to the Symbolist, Post-Impressionist, and Art Nouveau avant garde movements gaining momentum beyond Austria's borders, sought to oppose the stagnation they witnessed.

The group comprising the original, core membership of the Vienna Secession began its campaign for change by resigning from Vienna's dominant artists' organization, the *Kunstler hausgenossenschaft* ("Artists' House Organization"). The dissenters opposed the commercialism determining the shape of *Kunstlerhaus* exhibitions, the older organization's control of exhibit venues, and its "stultifying hierarchy" (Escritt: 137), a platform that bears an uncanny resemblance to that supported by

Impressionists Pissarro, Monet, Manet, and Degas in reaction to centuries of tyranny in matters of style and content by the Salon.

That said, the *Kunstlerhaus* should not be dismissed as merely a stodgy, outdated men's club, rigidly controlled by a cadre of painters resistant to artistic change. Sanctioned by the Emperor in 1861, it opened its doors to members in 1870. Ironically, like the Secession, the *Kunstlerhaus* was initially regarded as an essentially progressive institution, whose function was to represent the cause of living artists in Vienna, a significant breakthrough for the Viennese art establishment. (Kallir: 17)

In addition, in its early years, the *Kunstlerhaus* had set itself the task of promoting cultural exchanges with other European countries, while also advocating no fixed stylistic program. Moreover, contrary to much present day scholarly assumption, the group had initiated a policy of democratic rule shortly after its formation, a decision that unfortunately "favored a situation in which the conservative majority came to dictate policy." (Kallir: 18) Further, the taint of corruption that came to define the *Kunstlerhaus* by the 1890s arose from the connection between the dominant conservative faction and the organization's commercial dealings. Since a 10% commission was garnered from the sale of members' work, and since, not surprisingly the work of traditional artists sold better than that of their experimental peers, giving conservative style and content greater play in *Kunstlerhaus* exhibitions led to far greater profit for the group as a whole.

By the mid-1890s, then, the *Kunstlerhaus* indeed no longer served its original purpose and its policies were visibly geared to the preservation of the *status quo*. Shows of foreign art, so sought-after in the 1870s and 1880s, were "deliberately held in check to protect the domestic market" (Kallir: 18). So what had begun as an organization advocating a vanguard program for Viennese artists had become instead a refuge for the city's Old Guard.

The Vienna Secession was officially formed in 1897, its young, all-male members determined to exhibit on their own terms. The painter Gustav Klimt, the group's first elected President, wrote the manifesto that outlined in forceful terms the organization's three primary objectives: "bringing artistic life in Vienna into more lively contact with the continuing development of art abroad; "putting exhibitions on a more purely artistic footing, free from any commercial considerations"; and lastly, "inducing a heightened concern for art in official circles." (Escritt: 138)

The Secession's primary goals thus laid out, a further departure from *Kunstlerhaus* tradition by the group's founders bore heavily on the cordial bond between the Glasgow Four and their Viennese hosts. Echoing cultural upheavals generated forty years earlier by Arts and Crafts movement leaders, this departure rejected the time-honored prioritizing of the fine over the applied arts. This democratizing of the arts would be embodied in the integration of painting and the applied arts in each successive Secession exhibition. Moreover, the integration of fine craft with easel art in exhibition planning should not be surprising, given that Josef Hoffmann and Kolomon Moser, both designers, and Joseph Maria Olbrich, architect, figured importantly among Secession leaders.

While the Secession policy of inclusive internationalism resonated with the provenance of many original Secession members - Olbrich had been born in Silesia;

Hoffmann, in Moravia - Escritt points to more telling political ramifications: "By espousing the ideas of modern internationalist art and design, they [Secession members] set themselves against the nationalist and racist elements that were corroding the unity of the empire, and thus, paradoxically, won friends in establishment circles." (Escritt: 138) These nationalist movements, Hungarian, Czech, and Pan-German chief among them, "tended to thrive on xenophobic solidarity: by the 1880s, for example, the pan-Germans had developed a strong streak of anti-Semitism." (Escritt: 138)

Indeed, by the late 1890s, "Vienna was witnessing the political progressive's nightmare scenario: benevolent autocratic rule taking a stand against a wave of popular intolerance." (Escritt: 139) This mind-bending paradox finds intriguing anecdotal form in the enthusiastic support of the enlightened despot Franz Joseph by the Jewish Sigmund Freud, whose theories laid the groundwork for the modern field of psychoanalysis. However, paradox aside, the odd bedfellows alliance between ossified Habsburg Empire officialdom, with its a inert bureaucracy, and progressive Secession membership boded well for the latter, mainly because both entities opposed divisive nationalism, albeit for quite different reasons. The outcome was the establishment of an Arts Council in 1899 by the Austrian Ministry of Culture "to promote officially approved tendencies in the arts [i.e. the Viennese Secession] and their unifying potential." (Escritt: 139)

In 1898, secure in the largesse of its Habsburg patron, the Secession commissioned one of its own, Olbrich, to design "one of the first and most public expressions of Art Nouveau" (Escritt: 141), the now legendary Secession Hall. Conceived as an exhibition space for Secession artists and designers alone, the building "struck a confident and radical pose against the bombastic, mid-nineteenth century historicism of the surrounding Karlsplatz and nearby Ring." (Escritt: 141) A dazzling white geometric presence, the imposing, cube-like building, "was sparingly adorned with stylized symbolic decoration and crowned with a gilt-bronze cupola pierced into a net of swirling foliage." (Escritt: 141)

Indeed, while certainly standing out as a clean, spare, light-reflective anomaly in a ponderous, historicist architectural context, Secession Hall was by no means devoid of ornament, at least not in the sense that Adolf Loos intended. As Escritt notes, however, it "represented a challenge to convention that the Viennese public was reluctant to accept" (Escritt: 142). Derisively nicknamed "Mahdi's Tomb" or, alternately, "The Assyrian Convenience," the building's chief target for acerbic critics was its cupola, with its elaborate, stylized homage to the natural world. To the ongoing horror of critics in our time, the dome's intricate lacework of swirling gilt and bronze tendrils was derisively dubbed "The Golden Cabbage."

In addition, although in many ways an architectural outlander in its time and place, Secession Hall by no means represented a complete break with Europe's architectural past. Rather, it gave unmistakeable evidence of classical influence, its dome and simplified geometric facade evocative of a Neoclassical temple or mausoleum. The structure's high portico with panelled ceiling, its heavy, stepped frieze, and the fluted panels rising from the base of the blocks flanking the cupola, reinforce the classical effect, obvious to us, but one that apparently escaped its harsher critics.

We can be certain, however, that the building's classical references were not lost on Mackintosh, the Macdonald sisters, and Herbert MacNair, who entered the situation from the remote British Isles and were consequently not burdened by Viennese expectations of what a major exhibition venue *should* look like. Mackintosh, in particular, would have been sensitive to the structure's classical heritage, his awareness informed by his 1891 walking tour of Italy, eyes and mind open to the classical otherness of the country's ancient architectural past. Nor, for that matter, would the botanical sources of Olbrich's gilt and bronze dome have escaped Mackintosh's attention, so closely did Austrian's affinity with the natural world echo his own.

Finally, one must note that, given the wealth of scholarly attention focussed on its exterior, Secession Hall's modernist interior has been largely and mistakenly overlooked. That omission is a serious error. As is evident in his drawings and in the building itself, Olbrich contrived the interior exhibition spaces to accommodate more, not to say better, shows than venues created for *Kunstlerhaus* artists. His goal was to foster harmony between the fine and applied art work on display and the rooms in which they were installed. So, in a bold departure from tradition, he arranged for the construction of moveable walls, to allow for flexibility in both gallery size and proportion. And in yet another break with Viennese tradition, Olbrich arranged for skylights for all the rooms, so that all the exhibits were illuminated from above, thus enhancing the sense of fantasy so dear to Olbrich's well-documented romantic sensibilities. (Varnedoe: 29)

In autumn, 1900, the Eighth Secession Exhibition, destined to be a landmark in Viennese design, was installed in Secession Hall, the blazing white, rectilinear structure in marked contrast to the heavily ornamented architectural leviathans that encircled it on the Karlsplatz. Two central figures in Vienna's *Kunstgeverbeschule* (School of Applied Arts), Felician von Myrbach, Director, and Hoffmann, Professor of Design, were together responsible for organizing the exhibition, which was devoted exclusively to contemporary tendencies in the applied arts. The School of Applied Arts had been a stronghold of Secession principles since 1899, its library stocked with English periodicals introducing the innovative craft of designers from the British Isles to a mainly well-educated Viennese public hungry for change.

The invitation issued to the Glasgow Four, and to the English designer and social reformer Charles Ashbee, followed considerable correspondence between the British innovators and Josef Hoffmann, as well as Fritz Waerndorfer, an anglophile Viennese businessman who would eventually become the sole, and very generous financial backer of the *Wiener Werkstätte.*

Given the stripped-down, right-angled aesthetic informing the Mackintosh's and Macdonald's crafted furnishings, in combination with their equally unconventional wall-hung work, it was virtually inevitable that they, in particular, be invited to participate in the exhibition. And again, the couple's radical elimination of superfluous decoration was clearly consonant with Hoffmann's rejection of decorative flourishes, "stuck on" and serving no functional purpose. The Four readily accepted the invitation, as did Ashbee.

Charles' and Margaret's celebrated Scottish Room comprised a wall-and-furniture ensemble "that mostly, but not exclusively, suggested the interior of a living room" (Kaplan 236). The three enclosing walls were painted a clean white. Of the furnishings, most notable were a tall writing desk and cabinet sideboard, each with beaten metal panels, high-backed chairs and armchairs, and a slim, adjustable, multi-purpose cheval mirror, easily the most elegant and now most frequently reproduced of Charles' creations. The furnishings were also painted a startling white, so that, at a distance, their forms seemed at one with the walls.

To cap their achievement, and acting on the imperative to integrate the fine with the applied arts, the couple seized the opportunity to display Margaret's most recent painting, a large gesso panel entitled. "The May Queen" a technically and stylistically adventurous symbolic image intended for the walls of the Ingram Street Tea Rooms. This imposing, frieze-like mural dominated one wall, whose only other decoration was "a series of tapered posts attached to a narrow wooden frieze, inset with squares of coloured glass" (Kaplan 236).

The couple's uncluttered rooms, where open space seemed as aesthetically critical as solid object, so entranced the exhibition audience that, "according to one report, they were carried through the streets in triumph by students of the *Kunstgewerbeschule* [School of the Applied Arts]." (Billcliffe Burlington Magazine) While many scholars view this anecdote as apocryphal, nevertheless, it does indicate the level of excitement Charles' and Margaret's "exotic" sensibilities stimulated in a sector of Viennese society eager for a new creative vision. More solid proof of their positive impact on Vienna's critical establishment is the following comment appearing in the *Neues Wiener Tagblatt*: "The tea room by Doctor Mackintosh and his wife [*sic*] mus be counted among the most striking achievements that modern art has created" (Escritt: 172).

As an intriguing footnote, it is curious that, given the impact the Scottish Rooms in general, those of Frances and Herbert as well, had on Austrian exhibition guests, it has been until recently hard to pin down precisely the author(s) of each piece. The source of the difficulty lies in the catalogue that accompanied the exhibition, which omitted creative attribution. Instead, photographs and contemporary written accounts, supplemented by Gleeson White's article on the Glasgow School of Design (The Studio, 1897) and a discussion of the Glasgow group in the German periodical *Dekorative Kunst* (1897), are all we have for the important task of identification.

Compounding the sticky issue of attribution is the well-documented indifference among the Four, especially between Margaret and Frances, to the allocation of credit for individual creative and technical contribution to each piece. In the four-way collaborative efforts of The Four, personal vanity was often enough subsumed to success in a combined effort.

However, attribution aside, it is certain that the more significant Scottish contribution to the Eighth Secession Exhibition, in both potential influence and sheer beauty, was that of Charles and Margaret. The Viennese public applauded the impressive large oak cupboard with silver panel, designed by Margaret, and the high back oak chair, conceived and crafted by Charles. The celebrated cheval mirror, now centrally positioned in the Hunterian Museum's recreation of the couple's Mains Street flat, was both the room's focal point, and, by common agreement, the brainchild of Charles' and Margaret's interlocked stylistic instincts.

Further, in fairness, rectilinearity and rejection of ornament was not the hallmark of the Mackintosh/Macdonald collaboration alone. In fact, they were bested in that area by Charles Ashbee, whose room was virtually defined by bare, if not barren, straight-edged, right-angled geometry. As the critic Hevesi stated it: "Next to the Viennese, on this occasion a mixture of Wagner's complex splendour, Hoffmann's elegant logic, and Moser's poetic refinement, it is extraordinary how Ashbee's furniture designs stand out, as if they came from a rectangular planet. Everything vertical, at right angles, ninety degrees" (Escritt: 172).

Oddly, then, while the Scottish Rooms, particularly the environment designed by Charles and Margaret, were in fact more sensual and Symbolist than Ashbee's rigorously rectangular interior, the 1900 issue of the Secession periodical, *Ver Sacrum*, devoted the bulk of its descriptive text and illustration to the Scottish couple's work, backward-looking in some respects though it was.

Indeed, the sumptuous *Ver Sacrum*, itself represented another aspect of the Secession's classical leanings, since its Latin title referred to the Roman tradition of a "Sacred Spring," while the cover of the journal's first issue featured the Greek goddess Athena. (According to the ancient tradition, children born during the Sacred Spring period "were sent away, on maturity, to find new lands and to propagate the tribe's culture and language.") (Escritt: 153) Indeed, Viennese artists of the *fin de siècle* saw themselves as the modern equivalent of that chosen generation in pre-Christian Rome. As self-proclaimed saviors of a faltering society, they viewed their mission as nothing less than rescuing Vienna's culture from the "suffocating grip of their elders." (Escritt: 153) Welcoming fresh approaches to art and design from abroad was certainly the most effective way to accomplish this mission.

Viewed overall, the Eighth Secession Exhibition, while mounted in the cultural heart of Austria, was dominated by cutting edge British designers. The Glasgow Four were the leaders, the Josef Hoffmann and Kolomon Moser, now more celebrated founders of the *Wiener Werkstätte*, the followers. The contrast between the cluttered interiors and dark wood finishes of earlier Secession shows and the minimal decoration, sparse disposition of furniture, and pervasive whiteness of the Scottish Rooms had sizeable impact on future shows, beginning with Albert Roller's spacious Ninth Secession Exhibition, for which small, fussy objects irrelevant to the show's "look" had been omitted

Best known and most visibly indicative of the Scottish influence was the positioning of Gustav Klimt's *Beethoven Frieze* in the Fourteenth Secession Exhibition (1902). Following Margaret Macdonald's lead in her display of "The May Queen," Klimt hung the panels of his cycle of images, far more ambitious in scope and grandiose in content than Margaret's set of gesso panels right up against the gallery ceiling. Logically, then, "it is difficult not to believe that the effect produced by the Mackintosh panels must have lingered in his [Klimt's] mind, influencing the choice of '*mise en scene*' for the Beethoven exhibition." (Billcliffe Burlington

Magazine) In the mnds of both the Scotch and the Viennese artist/designers, the intention was to enhance the viewer's sense of a total environment, a *Gesamtkunstwerk*, rather than a group of vaguely related furnishings and pictures planted randomly in a room.

Indeed the Fourteenth Secession Exhibition was, according to Varnedoe, "the crowning achievement of the Secession's program for unified design (*Gesamtkunstwerk)*, a collaboration of scenography with painting, sculpture, and music." (Varnedoe: 41) At its center rested Max Klinger's sculpture of Beethoven, "enthroned in godlike classical nudity, on rocky heights above the eagle's reach, as a triumphant new Prometheus." (Varnedoe: 41) The exhibit as a whole, as Varnedoe states it, "honors the Germanic ideal of the uncompromising genius divorced from mundane humanity." (Varnedoe: 41) While the mastermind orchestrating this heroic attempt at assimilation of all the arts in a single space was Josef Hoffmann, it is a measure of the impact both Mackintosh and Ashbee had on Hoffmann's stylistic direction that the Viennese designer "imposed a strict, quadratic planarity of snow-white and gold, to express the rarefied atmosphere of the celebration of Olympian genius" (Varnedoe: 41).

The mark made on Viennese design practice by the British participants in the Eighth Secession Exhibition moved far beyond the confines of Secession Hall. In fact, the formation of the *Weiner Werkstätte* by Hoffmann, Moser, and the industrialist Fritz Waerndorfer in 1903 followed closely the model of Charles Ashbee's Guild of Handicrafts, with its concern for equal distribution of duties and income, and a voice in creative and practical affairs for all its designers and craftsmen. As Escritt defines it, "the *Werkstätte* was an attempt to improve the quality and availability of design by giving designers the opportunity to go into business for themselves, rather than have their work exploited and debased by existing manufacturers." (Escritt: 158)Moreover, as the founders plotted the development of an organization that would supply high end design to a large clientèle, they turned to Mackintosh for advice and encouragement.

In practical terms, the element in Mackintosh's *oeuvre* that most influenced *Werkstätte* designers was the Scotchman's white painted furniture, with its subtle curves and exaggeratedly tall proportions, as well as his characteristic groups of little squares as ornamental motif. The critic Ludwig Hevesi singled out the latter feature for special mention in one of his admiring reviews of the Eighth Secession Exhibition's Scottish Rooms. As for Mackintosh's direct impact on Hoffmann's creative decisions, the square latticework, as well as the square panelled doors or windows favored by the Scotch designer, gradually acquired the status of *leitmotif* in the Viennese designer's concepts for *Werkstätte* products.

Most visibly for the Viennese public, the "square" motif informed both the exterior and interior planning for Hoffmann's Purkersdorf Sanatorium, begun in 1904 and completed in 1906. (Interesting, and telling for this study, the construction, furnishing, and detailing of the Sanatorium dovetailed in time frame the completion of Mackintosh's Hill House in Helensburgh, in 1904, and the second stage of the Glasgow School of Design, in 1909). In larger architectural terms, the commission for Purkersdorf provided "the first true opportunity for the artists and craftsmen of the

Weiner Werkstätte to work together to produce a *Gesamtkunstwerk*." (Escritt: 161) Hoffmann was the presiding architect for the project, but the structure as a whole was a collaborative effort, with Kolomon Moser chiefly responsible for the interior furnishings. Purkersdorf Sanatorium was decidedly not built as an asylum for the mentally ill of Vienna's working class. Instead, as Escritt points out, it was planned and constructed as a "retreat for members of Vienna's wealthy bourgeoisie suffering from the stresses of modern life." (Escritt: 161) Yet more cynically, Varnedoe describes Purkersdorf as more a deluxe health spa, where dinner called for formal attire, than a "garrison for the insane." Varnedoe adds that the building, inside and out, reflected Hoffmann's "ambition for total aesthetic control." (Varnedoe: 46) However, whatever one's position regarding both *Werkstätte* intentions for the Sanatorium and Hoffmann's degree of personal ambition, the project satisfied two *Art Nouveau* objectives in *fin-de-siècle* Vienna: (1) in every detail, its planning was an exercise in *Gesamtkunstwerk,* (2) Purkersdorf was a purpose-built response to contemporary psychological concerns, those first identified and analyzed by Sigmund Freud.

As to the latter, the solution arrived at by Hoffmann and Moser "opted for greater simplicity than they had previously attempted." (Escritt: 161) The Sanatorium was an austere, symmetrical, geometric mass constructed in concrete, the "hygienic whiteness of its [interior] walls" and "the simple clarity of Moser's furniture designs" (Varnedoe: 46) conformed to current Viennese notions of the proper environment for psychological cure. The only concession to traditional decoration is two faience figures on the east facade.

Echoes of the classical purism guiding Olbrich in his concept for Secession Hall are also evident in Hoffmann's scheme for Purkersdorf. In photographs of the entrance hall, we see Moser's cube-shaped chairs, with checked cane seats, arranged in geometric positions. (Obviously, the chairs reflect Mackintosh's influence.)The chairs and their arrangement, in turn, complement the concentric square design of the tiled floor.

Hoffmann's taste for rectilinearity is reflected again in the spacious, airy dining room, where rows of pierced-back chairs are positioned along the walls, tables "created further geometric patterns as they contrasted with the walls and tablecloths." (Escritt: 162) As to lighting, the stylistic impact of Mackintosh is immediately visible, since Hoffmann opted for box-shaped lamps hanging from the ceiling to illuminate, unobtrusively, the well dressed, well heeled, but psychologically unstable patients' dining experience.

Finally, even Moser's plant stands became vehicles for Hoffmann's intricate geometry. Their rectilinear supports and black and white checked plant containers playied off the natural, curvilinear forms they were designed to hold. Indeed, the plant stands in particular earned Hoffmann his nickname, "Little Square Hoffmann." In this and other instances, the similarity to the pervasive checked patterning in Mackintosh's work, cannot be attributed solely to coincidence.

At the close of the Eighth Secession Exhibition, Mackintosh, the Macdonald sisters and Herbert MacNair returned to Glasgow. By all accounts, the retreat to the remote, provincial setting, no matter how familiar, was particularly frustrating for Charles.

While still a partner in the Honeyman and Keppie firm, and actually quite busy carrying out commissions for Glaswegian patrons, Mackintosh nevertheless felt isolated in his home city, deprived as he was of the stimulating interchange with students and colleagues enjoyed by Hoffmann and Moser in Vienna (Note that he did periodically travel back to Vienna, in 1902, for the installation of a music room commissioned by Waerndorfer for his family's home, and again in 1906, for the installation of gesso panels created by Margaret, also for the music room.) (Billcliffe and Vergo).

The creative deprivation caused by the distance between Vienna and Glasgow affected the Austrians as well since Hoffmann, Moser, and their Viennese colleagues remained unaware of Mackintosh's significant stylistic evolution in processing commissions for his Glaswegian clients. The changes are most evident in the design solutions he, in concert with Macdonald, formulated for the publisher Walter Blackie's imposing Hill House. Constructed in the period 1902-1904, the elegant interior of the stately home boasted, for one thing, no white furnishings, apart from those in the master bedroom. For another, organic surface decoration had finally disappeared entirely from the tables, chairs, cabinets, desks, and armoires Mackintosh designed for Blackie, producing an overall impression of a handsome, patrician interior that was, nonetheless, surprisingly welcoming.

Indeed, from 1904 on, starting with his elaborate concept for Hill House, Mackintosh used simple geometric shapes as points of departure for the basic forms of all his furniture: cubes, cylinders, rectangles, even segmented circles. His fascination with pure geometry appears most strikingly in the Chinese Room created for Catherine Cranston's Ingram Street Tea Room (1910-1911), as does his abandonment of the brilliant, white-painted surfaces that had so excited visitors to the Scottish Rooms a decade earlier. Again, after 1904, Mackintosh opted chiefly for black stain to both protect his furniture and allow the wood grain to show through. Constructed mainly in sycamore or plane, their rich, dark surfaces were, on occasion, enlivened with inlays of mother-of-pearl or the application of bits of colored glass. (Billcliffe and Vergo)

In the substantial body of scholarship devoted to the participation of The Four in the Eighth Secession Exhibition, followed by Mackintosh's sizeable influence on the *Wiener Werkstätte*, there is only brief mention of the music room Mackintosh designed for Felix Waerndorfer's suburban home on 45 Carl-Ludwig Strasse in 1902. In this writer's view, this critical imbalance, like the paucity of scholarship devoted to Secession Hall's interior, should be redressed.

The facts justify the redress, since Mackintosh's music room, together with the dining room conceived by Hoffmann and the gallery Moser devised for Waerndorfer's art collection, both also commissioned in 1902, served as a promotional tool for the *Werkstätte* at its inception in 1903. (Note that Waerndorfer was an unusually farsighted collector of avant garde art. In addition to paintings by Secession leader Gustav Klimt, ink drawings by Aubrey Beardsley, and figurative sculpture by the Belgian artist George Minne, he was an early supporter of the controversial work of Egon Schiele and Oskar Kokoschka.)

Mackintosh initially met Waerndorfer, the wealthy owner of a cotton spinning mill, in 1900, when the Viennese industrialist travelled to London and Glasgow on behalf of Hoffmann, who was by then Vice-President of the Secession. It was, in fact, Waerndorfer's encounter with the designer/architect, and his first-hand exposure to Mackintosh's built structures and interiors, that generated the invitation issued to The Four, to participate in the Eighth Secession Exhibition.

Hoffmann and Waerndorfer were in accord in believing that what would ultimately be known as the "Scottish Rooms" would both enhance the show and open stylistic doors to the conservative Viennese cultural community. The very foreignness, the "exotic" identity of the Four, they felt, would in itself arouse curiosity and draw greater crowds. Note also that Hoffmann's interest in the Scottish designers had already been piqued by Gleeson White's enthusiastic description of Charles' and Margaret's groundbreaking work in the illustrated journal "The Studio."

The four months, October to December, 1900, that Charles and Margaret spent in Vienna to oversee their rooms in Secession Hall gave Waerndorfer further opportunity to speak with Mackintosh and deepen his appreciation of Charles' singular bead on designing interiors. So positive was his impression that, in 1902, he commissioned Mackintosh to execute a music room, for his family's home in Vienna's Cottage Viertel, or Cottage District. (Many scholars prefer the term "music salon," in referring to a space intended as a meeting-place for Vienna's cultured literati.).

Vienna's Cottage Viertel, a residential district in Vienna's outer suberbs, was established in 1872. Tellingly, given the eventual strong links between the British and the German-speaking cultural communities, the English Garden City movement had been the model for the district, whose purpose was to provide an alternative to the increasing number of grand or grandiose apartment buildings, as well as humbler, often jerry-built tenements, springing up in Vienna's city center and inner suburbs. The proliferation of what we now call "housing developments," of widely varying aesthetic and functional quality, represented an efficient solution to the problem of Vienna's explosive population growth in this decade, but also one in which concern for speedy construction took precedence over aesthetic and stylistic considerations.

An elaborate set of regulations guided both the design of the homes *and* their owners' behavior and activities in the newly established neighborhood. As to the buildings themselves, the regulations specified their dimensions, stylistic detailing, and even the yard space between them. Built for the professional and aristocratic upper classes, the so-called "cottages" were far larger than their name suggests, and, in line with their British ancestry, many boasted red and yellow brick facades, common in England, but not in Vienna, with pyramidal and steeply pitched roofs.

The rigidity of municipal regulations guiding the homes' construction extended to residents' *modus vivendi* as well, presumably in the interest of maintaining a peaceful quality of life for the entire district. The guidelines addressed such delicate, subjectively inflected, touchy issues as excessive noise and unpleasant smells. Especially noteworthy was the prohibition against commerce of any kind, a restriction predicated on the assumption that the hurly-burly of mercantile exchange, accompanied by the invasion of lower class clientele, would inevitably disrupt the neighborhood's well-mannered, and decidedly upper crust, atmosphere.

Only one page of drawings indicating Mackintosh's overall concept for the music room survives, the single sheet exhibiting a set of preliminary sketches thought not to be in the designer's skilled hand. Laying out floor plan, elevation, and sections, the drawing was submitted to the Viennese municipal authorities on June 21, 1902, and, obviously, approved. However, given Mackintosh's prodigious work habits and his sheer love of drawing *per se*, we can speculate that other sheets, including formal perspectives and freehand pencil and watercolor impressions, also emerged from his studio, but were either lost or destroyed during his many journeys back and forth between Glasgow and Vienna.

However, a few photographs of the music room's most important features give us some sense, if a murky one, of Mackintosh's scheme for a domestic venue where enjoyment of music was the central experience. As the photos reveal, the music room's organizational pattern and furnishings closely resembled three examples of Mackintosh's most successful work up to that point: the Eighth Secession Exhibition's Scottish Rooms; the Mains Street apartment where Charles and Margaret merged their aesthetic tastes and individual functional needs after their marriage in 1900; the Rose Boudoir they created for the Decorative Arts Exhibition in Turin, also in 1902.

The pervasive use of white paint, the now-familiar high backed chairs, and geometrization of form spur instant recall of those more celebrated interiors. Moreover, since Waerndorfer had actually purchased many of Mackintosh's Scottish Room pieces, he did indeed install them in the salon he had commissioned. That is not to say, however, that Mackintosh was repeating himself, as though drained of creative energy, in his planning for the Waerndorfer music room. Rather, in conceiving the music room, he solidified a vision for interiors he'd been refining for years.

Apart from the requisite grand piano, the salon's most prominent elements were its built-in seating, in some cases upholstered, in some not, its fitted woodwork, for which Mackintosh prepared full-size drawings (still extant), and the room's intriguing "inglenook." To develop the inglenook, a fireplace set into a corner Mackintosh expanded an already existing shallow bay, in the room's north wall. It is important to emphasize that the exterior chimney corresponding to the fireplace was built of roughcast, in the Scottish manner, its surface sharply contrasting with the smooth stucco typically used for such purposes by Viennese architects. It is a tribute not only to Mackintosh's brash individualism, but to his Austrian patron's exceptional open-mindedness that Waerndorfer both endorsed and financed this departure in structural materials.

Two further elements in the design of the music room merit special attention. The first was a cloth curtain, rather than a solid wall, separating Mackintosh's performance space from Hoffmann's dining room. As a result, at mealtimes, with only a soft, pliable fabric separating musicians from Waerndorfer hosts and guests, all present could listen perhaps to a pianist accompanied by a violinist as they dined and con- versed In focussing on this idiosyncratic feature, we need remember that we are examining an elite private setting in a culture that had produced Wolfgang

Amadeus Mozart, Johann Strauss, and Gustav Mahler. Of all the arts, music reigned supreme in Vienna. Surely, Mackintosh had kept that cultural truth in mind, in favoring a flexible curtain over a rigid wall.

The second element soliciting our attention is more fully "artistic," but not merely in the decorative sense. For the music room walls and furnishings, Margaret Macdonald conceived and carried out two sets of pictorial panels, her substantial, two-fold contribution to the room's overall impact allowing her to capitalize on her skill in gesso painting.

On a smaller scale, Mackintosh had planned for the incorporation of two gesso panels, painted by Margaret, in his concept for a large, protective case for the piano. Entitled "The Opera of the Winds" and "The Opera of the Sea," Margaret's images, alluded to a correlation between the sometimes potent and fearful, sometimes soothing sounds made by natural phenomena and the harmonies, melodies and chords created by man.

On a larger scale, and essential to the salon's cohesion and impact, was Margaret's six-panel gesso frieze illustrating scenes from Belgian Symbolist Maurice Maeterlinck's play, "The Seven Princesses." The panels, with their succession of six interrelated narrative images, demonstrated not only Margaret's gift for depicting stylized figures in a mural-size format, but her familiarity with contemporary literature and drama. Completed in 1906 and installed in 1907, the frieze, in fact, was the music room's riveting center piece.

The sad tale of the Seven Princesses seems an odd, if not inappropriate choice for a multi-panel frieze gracing the walls of a music salon in the home of a prosperous, soptimistic Jewish businessman, albeit a Jewish businessman assimilated into the Austrian Catholic mainstream. But Waerndorfer, respectful of Macdonald's judgement and skill, acquiesced, to her choice of subject.

In developing his play, Maeterlinck, a lapsed Catholic himself, had nonetheless been moved by the legend of the Seven Sleepers, the story of seven Christians who, in 250 A.D., escaped persecution by taking refuge in a cave near the French city of Tours. Their refuge soon discovered by their persecutors, they found themselves not saved, but walled in by the enemy. Good fortune then interposed, however, and the Christians fell into a 200-year preternanatural sleep.

Two centuries later, at the end of the reign of Emperor Theodosius, the cave was opened and the Christians were roused from their slumber, one they believed had only lasted for one night. At this point, sadly, the mythical tale took another bad turn. Finding that their religion was now accepted everywhere, and that they had no longer to fear persecution, the seven Christians were so shocked that they all expired at the same moment, in yet another of the tale's sudden twists of fate.

With this gloomy narrative as stimulus, Maeterlinck transformed the seven, presumably male Christians into seven princesses, introducing his Symbolist drama with precise instructions for costumes and set. According to the playwright, the action, in this relatively static play, takes place in a (simulated) marble hall lined with white porcelain vases. A seven-step staircase divides the hall in half, and on each step, a princess robed in white sleeps on a cushion of pale silk, illuminated by a silver light of mysterious source. At the back of the hall, the audience sees a heavy, bolted door, flanked by large windows through which the setting sun is visible, as well as a dark, forested landscape dotted with pools in the distance. Shooting straight upward through the landscape is a gloomy canal edged by willow trees.

At the start of the play, a man-of-war is seen approaching on the canal. The battleship will be welcomed by an old King and Queen, minor figures in the play's *dramatis personae*. As Patrick Mahony states, "In putting us into the mood for this weird [italics mine] play, it is soon evident that the King and Queen are expecting Marcelius, a handsome prince who wants to marry Ursula, one of the seven young women who are in fact asleep" (Mahony: 72). We then learn, through further exposition, that Marcelius has been delayed and that, in the interim, the seven Princesses have fallen, like the seven Christians into a preternatural sleep.

When Marcelius does arrive, his entry into the marble hall is blocked by the bolted door, and his frantic taps on the windows prove fruitless. Luckily, however, he is helped by the King and Queen, who lead him inside through a secret passage. Upon his arrival, six of the princesses awaken and greet him with joy, but the seventh, his beloved Ursula, remains motionless. We then learn that Ursula is, in fact, not asleep, but dead Ultimately, in the play's final scene, the six princesses, actually Ursula's sisters, carry her lifeless body in slow procession to the top of the seven steps,.

As is no doubt obvious, Maeterlinck's "Seven Princesses" is as morbid in mood and as informed by the fickle nature of fate as its inspirational antecedent, The Seven Christians. "Indeed, Death the intruder has come unheralded, interfering with the best laid plans of all. In the closing dialogue, Maeterlinck symbolizes the external circumstances which close the door of hope forever" (Mahony: 72).

On its face, Margaret's selection of "The Seven Princesses" as thematic source for her multi-panel frieze seems counterintuitive, given the artist's natural ebullience and optimistic outlook. However, a close look at the frieze itself gives us insight into her unlikely attraction to so somber a narrative.

Since Margaret's favored medium was gesso, Maeterlinck's meticulous directions for set and costumes definitely played a part in her decision. In line with the playwright's insistence on an interior setting characterized by whiteness—white silk robes for the young women, white marble for the hall and steps "silver light" illuminating the entire scene—Margaret could allow the white gesso to dominate the surface of her panels, the colorless surface interrupted only by the strategic placement of bits of colored glass.

Moreover, her depiction of the seven princesses suggests dramatically "flat" characters, figures who are not really thinking, feeling individuals, but identical symbolic presences whose bodies are delineated only by thick coils of gesso. These depersonalized young women were obviously the descendants of the female archetypes who inhabited the gesso paintings Margaret had created for Miss Cranston's tearooms in the past. Indeed, as she had for the tearoom murals, Margaret expressed her overall composition not with brush-painted outlines or panes of color, but with loops and swirls of rope-like gesso. Only her handling of the women's faces betrayed any interest in naturalistic specifics.

Moreover, from Charles' point of view, the pervasive pallor of Maeterlinck's sets and costumes, paired with the immobility of the playwright's dramatis personae—for some play-goers compelling, for others dull and bloodless—and the geometricized set of steps at center stage, synchonized perfectly with the white-painted, rectililinear furnishings he planned for the music salon's interior.

Finally, and crucial to understanding Margaret's attraction to "The Seven Princesses," is the artist's sympathy with the play's undercurrent of pessimism. Like Charles, Margaret had been swept up in Scotland's Celtic Revival of the 1890s, spearheaded by the couple's close friend, the urban planner and social theorist Patrick Geddes. While the Revival's pragmatic efforts were directed at generating appreciation for the crafted wood and metal artifacts of Scotland's pre-Roman past, its philosophy rested on a renewed interest in ancient Celtic literature, whose pervasive tone was, in fact, one of melancholy. We can then assume that, in reading "The Seven Princesses" for the first time, Margaret felt instantly at home.

While there is no indication that Waerndorfer's married life was anything but harmonious, there is also no question but that the environment he commissioned for the hearing music was, as today's feminists would phrase it, "male-dominated." The composers whose sonatas, cantatas, and fugues entertained guests in the salon, as well as the musicians who performed their work, were male, across the board. For that matter, Waerndorfer's collection of Symbolist and Expressionist paintings, drawings, prints and sculptures were all accomplished by male artists, mavericks though they were.

So the pale, haunting visual surround created by Margaret's frieze, its panels permanently mounted, rather than temporarily hung on salon walls, provided a valuable counterbalance to what would otherwise have been a uniformly masculine space. Contributing as well to the frieze's success were Margaret's inventive, technique and style, the aloof, imposing female presences that were her subject, and her own gracious, confident bearing. Doubtless all the participants in the fabrication of the music salon were alert to the gender divide, and to Charles' and Margaret's efforts to bridge it. Further, another divide was bridged in the process: that between the fine and the applied arts.

Apart from the installation of Margaret's frieze, the rooms custom-designed by Mackintosh, Hoffmann, and Moser for Waerndorfer's domestic retreat were indeed completed more or less simultaneously in 1902, one year in advance of the founding of the *Wiener Werkstätte*. Both Hoffmann's dining room and Moser's art gallery appear in the *Wiener Werkstätte* photographic archive, "the only example of work by Hoffmann and Moser dating from before its foundation." Consequently, we can surmise that the two leading *Werkstätte* organizers viewed the Waerndorfer commissions as prototypes for their new company, "a means for advertising their work to potential clients." In addition, these in-house catalogues were supplemented by illustrated promotional articles focussed on all three Waerndorfer commissions, including the music room, published in established design journals throughout Germany and Austria. On sale in such cultural meccas as Berlin, Munich, and Cologne, these illustrated periodicals were available to a German-speaking public far beyond the limits of Vienna.

As to the actual construction and detailing of the furnishings and woodwork for the Waerndorfer project, Mackintosh was, for the first time in his career, totally dependent on foreign craftsmen. In this singular instance, he was not collaborating with fellow Glaswegians, many of them skilled artisans in shipbuilding, who "spoke his language," literally and figuratively. Few, if any Viennese carpenters and joiners hired for the task spoke English, much less Mackintosh's impenetrable Highland Scottish. Moreover, some were bemused, if not put off, by his choice of materials, as well as the apparent barrenness of Mackintosh's plans for wood surfaces, particularly those of the walls and door. For his part, Mackintosh shook off the complaints, even the occasional derisive jab, applauding instead the Viennese craftsmen's determination to finish the job in line with his intentions, despite their undisguised discomfort with his stylistic taste.

In terms of response to his idiosyncratic domestic space for the enjoyment of music, Mackintosh fared far better with cultural critics. Vienna's Ludwig Hevesi, an ardent supporter of avant garde fine and applied arts and a friend of Waerndorfer, visited the *Cottage Viertel* home in 1905. In his appraisal of the music room, he concluded that it was "curious," but, at the same time, a site of "spiritual pleasure," just as Mackintosh had hoped it would be. Amelia S. Levitus, writing in an edition of the Glasgow Herald in 1909, went further in her praise, declaring Mackintosh's interior furnishings and Macdonald's gesso panels "perhaps their greatest work, for they were allowed perfectly free scope."

Levitus, an English expatriate living in Vienna, but reporting for the Herald, continued to champion Mackintosh, and Macdonald, through the years when Charles' reputation was on the wane. In 1912, she reminded readers of "The Studio" that some of the couple's best work was to be found in Vienna. Referring specifically to the music room, she urged readers to reflect "on the natural, holistic precision of the design, the free rein Mackintosh had been given, and the regard in which the room was held." With a clever allusion to musical composition, she emphasized the harmonious integration of the room's elements, so in tune with each other as to form "an organic whole, with the same concord as do the passages of a great symphony."

The Waerndorfer music room was indeed a *Gesamtkunstwerk* in its orchestration of visual, aural, tactile, and literary components. It was also one successful component of a successful collaboration between contributors of different nationalities, not to mention gender and, of equal importance, religion. Ironically, the cordial and productive reciprocity between Mackintosh, Macdonald, their *Wiener Werkstätte* colleagues, and Waerndorfer would prove Mackintosh's professional and emotional undoing during the World War I years.

CHAPTER 11

Internationalism and Nationalism II: Van de Velde in Berlin and Weimar, Muthesius, and the Deutscher Werkbund

In 1899, at the urging of German friends, Henry van de Velde, left Uccle with his family for the more vigorous cultural climate of Berlin. In that energetic German capital, his friends insisted, the Belgian Art Nouveau master would find a public and, by extension, potential clients more receptive to both his philosophic bent and his Art Nouveau design practice. As to his departure from Bloemenwerf, the domestic retreat he had so painstakingly planned, built, and furnished as the concrete embodiment of his design ideals, van de Velde's overriding desire for wider acclaim and scope of effectiveness "carried more weight than the sacrifice of concentration and peace inevitably associated with it." (Sembach: 17) In Uccle, van de Velde had relied entirely on occasional visits by friends from Brussels and abroad for the vital exchange of ideas he thrived on and for customers for his furniture design. In Berlin, both were readily available to him every day, without fail, through the wealth of productive encounters the city's culturally-greedy *haute bourgeoisie* allowed him.

In the first years of van de Velde's 17-year sojourn in Germany, his Belgian origins were hardly a professional or personal hindrance in what Sembach terms his "frontier-crossing operation," since neither the recently consolidated German-speaking duchies, nor his own bilingual, bicultural homeland could boast a recognizable, definable national style to either promote or defend. Indeed, Belgium's artistic physiognomy was just as ill-defined as that of Wilhelmine Germany. In truth, the former, an uneasy alliance between Dutch-speaking Flanders and French-speaking Wallonia, had not really become a culturally homogenous state since its own unification 40 years before Germany emerged as a political entity in 1871. On the contrary, and more germane to van de Velde's welcome in Berlin, the Belgian's enthusiastic reception was driven instead by pervasive "curiosity about a man who had such firm theoretical support for his work." (Sembach 18)

Upon his arrival, van de Velde's manifest intellectual and cultural sophistication smoothed his *entrée* into Berlin's élite social circles, where a mood of open-minded liberalism prevailed in the otherwise austere German capital. In Berlin, continental intellectual currents met, collided, and/or coalesced, rendering the German capital the appropriate setting for the introspective, but nonetheless ambitious artist/designer/architect who had earlier been treated with xenophobic disdain by Parisian critics and visitors to Siegfried Bing's *Galérie Art Nouveau*.

Instant social acceptance was soon followed by multiple commissions for clients who, in many cases, were highly respected members of Berlin society. Among them were François Haby, the court hairdresser (Wilhelm was, after all, a traditional, hereditary monarch) Paul Cassirer and Ludwig Loeffler, publishers, Eberhard von Bodenhausen, art lover and industrialist, Harry Graf Kessler, who would become van de Velde's most loyal and consistent patron, and Karl Ernst Osthaus, the banker's son who established the Folkwang Museum in Hagen in 1900.

The commissions that brought van de Velde the most attention and earned him the (dubious) reputation of "fashionable architect" were Haby's hairdressing salon and the headquarters for the Havana Tobacco Company. Sembach examines the motives driving the coveted commissions, emphasizing, on the one hand, the clients' instinct for a showy public image, on the other, genuine appreciation for van de Velde's singular approach to interior design, one determined, in part, by his early years as an easel artist.

> "Undoubtedly, the circles who encouraged van de Velde in Berlin were particularly susceptible to his ideas for differing reasons. There was a mixture of commercial and social, and some artistic interest. The court hairdresser François Haby and the Havana Company probably commissioned him to design their premises to be in vogue, rather than for any other reason. They were concerned to attract attention. When van de Velde came up with particularly imaginative designs for these commissions, his clients' speculative expectations were certainly fulfilled. He was to some extent driving for effect, however, and thus confirmed some of the louder *nouveau riche* traits of which Berlin was rather fond at the time. In fact, there was a community of interest as the still youthful metropolis was generous enough to celebrate van de Velde's experiments as well as support them. In contrast with Paris, Berlin made the artist feel recognized." (Sembach: 91)

Sembach singles out Haby's interior, completed in 1901, as a brilliant demonstration "of the principles van de Velde claimed [sic] to have invented." (Sembach: 20) And indeed, photographs of the salon make it clear that, in Haby's rather stagey precincts, coherence of detail was absolute, so that the process of cutting the hair of well-to-do male clients was carried out in a miniature *Gesamtkunstwerk*. Sembach continues: "The practice of filtering aesthetic effects out of technical necessity reached a peak in van de Velde's use of exposed pipework in his design for Haby's." (Sembach: 20) As is evident in the photos, the pipework, stripped of plaster and other coverings, was mounted on the shop walls in linear patterns as indicative of a taste for elegant ornamentation as for efficient functionality. As a result, "Instead of being concealed, as was customary, they were practically celebrated." (Sembach: 20) Incidentally, not all Berliners were taken with the exposed pipes, as Nikolaus Pevsner points out. "You don't wear your guts like a watch chain across your waistcoat, was the comment of Berliners upon this odd mixture of functionalism and Art Nouveau." [Pevsner: 86]

According to Sembach, the lamps illuminating each customer's station were the salon's "most expressive feature." Jutting from the upper horizontal axis of each mirror, the lamps hung from the termini of two mutually reinforcing metal arms, one rectilinear, the other formed in a wave-like curve, the latter an outgrowth of van de Velde's personal brand of Art Nouveau, which demanded the deployment of the whiplash curve in all his projects. The mirrors themselves, framed in elaborately carved wood, were lined up against the wall with virtually no space between them, so as to create a continuous reflective surface that, in effect, doubled the size of the room. Each mirror was, in turn, functionally and visibly connected to each station's water taps and basin. One might then say that, in net impact, Haby;s interior fell as much into the realm of sculpture or, in our day, installation as into the mundane arena of utility.

Also received with excitement by the Berlin public was van de Velde's more intriguing, unmistakably non-Western scheme for the Havana Company's multi-room tobacco shop. In this particular commission, Sembach's assertion that insufficient attention has been paid to van de Velde's attraction to Islamic architecture is borne out in photographs of the shop's interior spaces. In these images, one sees characteristically Islamic horseshoe-shaped arches framing the passageways leading from one room to another. Fully integrated with the arches are shelf units, which seem to be either "swelling powerfully against the wooden arches," or "forced to bend beneath them" (Sembach: 56), the two elements together creating an overall impression of the near-claustrophobic opulence typical, in the Western mind, of Moorish interiors.

In van de Velde's 1899 design for the Havana Company. the Islamic influence extended to the frieze painted on the walls of the main room, just below the ceiling. The frieze, in keeping with non-figurative Islamic surface imagery, is an abstraction of the smoking process. Smoking is suggested, rather than depicted literally, so that the vertical painted lines, topped by zigzagging and cloud-like shapes, allude to, rather than accurately portray rising smoke. The reference, of course, is to the Havana Company's product, the lowly, but in this case very expensive cigar. The frieze served an integrative purpose as well, providing an even, linear counterpoise to the varying heights of the arches and the shelf units. Needless to say, the very inclusion of a painted wall image, an abstract one at that, in van de Velde's scheme leads one to believe that he hadn't at that point fully shed his painterly urges. While he may not have actually carried out the application of the paint to the walls, the abstract motif was his brainchild.

Van de Velde's stay in Berlin, an experience at once professionally profitable and psychologically reassuring for the hyper-sensitive designer, lasted only a mere three years. In 1902, he answered a call to the Thuringian town of Weimar, a quiet, tradition-conscious city best known as the home of 19th Century literary luminaries Goethe and Schiller. The invitation, while formally issued by the Grand Duke William Ernest, was actually instigated by Harry Graf Kessler, the influential aristocratic polymath who remained van de Velde's staunch advocate throughout his career.

In issuing the invitation, both the Grand Duke and Kessler hoped for the establishment of a *Kunstgewerbeschule*, an academy that would combine fine and applied art study in a single curriculum, similar to that instituted at the Glasgow School of Art by "Fra" Newberry in the early 1890's. In 1902, van de Velde seemed the logical choice for generating what would be an educational upheaval in Weimar's sleepy, conservative setting. For his part, van de Velde readily accepted the invitation, since it clearly validated the principles regarding the necessary link between the fine and applied arts he had begun promulgating in public lectures in Brussels as early as

1894. (He looked forward as well to Weimar's idyllic setting, similar in many ways to the one he and his family had left behind in Uccle.)

In Weimar, van de Velde practiced what he had preached in the mid-1890's, in his Brussels lectures and in his voluminous writings. For nearly a decade, he had maintained that classes in the applied and decorative arts should be incorporated in the curricula of art academies, "which hitherto had mostly confined themselves to turning out large numbers of easel painters and sculptors." (Campbell: 23) At the Weimar Art Academy, best represented by famed graduates Max liebermann and Arnold Böcklin, he did in fact introduce courses in craft techniques, exacting from his students aesthetically pleasing models to be emulated by future artisans. But of perhaps greater importance, he fostered on-site cooperation between the students and local craftsmen, carried out beyond school workshop confines.

In what seemed a charmed professional situation, van de Velde's objective was twofold: to end the social isolation of the artist and to raise the aesthetic quality of craft production as it appeared in its current state. Ideally, with this instructional strategy in place, hand-craftsmen would refine the students' technical skills in their fields of expertise, while, at the same time, profiting from stylistic and aesthetic input offered by *Kunstgewerbeschule* students, who were simultaneously taking classes in painting, drawing and sculpture. (Since there were no large scale industrial firms located near Weimar in 1902, van de Velde's conviction that assembly line production should contribute to the manufacture of well-designed functional goods had no place in his otherwise innovative curriculum. The case for the assembly line would take form twenty years later, midway through the lifespan of the *Kunstgwerbeschule*'s descendant, the Bauhaus.)

Van de Velde's role in Weimar was primarily that of educator. However, in addition to planning the *Kunstgewerbeschule* curriculum, he was also commissioned to design the buildings that would house both fine and applied art lectures and workshops. These two built structures were in fact his first public architectural commissions. Indeed, the very fact that two contiguous, purpose-built structures were commissioned, one devoted only to classes in painting, drawing, and sculpture classes, the other only to courses in carpentry, metalwork, and ceramics, is a telling paradox. While in theory, van de Velde's curriculum encouraged integration of the fine and applied arts, the layout of the school's physical plant suggested otherwise.

Van de Velde's diagram or 'floor plan" of the two structures reveals the topographic relationship between the two strucures, while photographs reveal their distinct qualities. The *Kunstgewerbeschule* is two stories high and L-shaped. Housing small studios for applied arts instruction, it sits on the corner of an rectangular plot, like that of a contemporary university's "quad." Completed in the 1906, the structure seems surprisingly severe and unembellished, its only concession to van de Velde's signature curvilinear tendencies a circular gable overlooking the street. The Director located his own studio, in fact, under that gable and above the building's entrance, providing for himself (but not for other faculty or students) exceptionally large windows. A second van de Velde trademark, the emphasis on visible structural elements, reveals itself in the undisguised iron lintels "skillfully and convincingly linked to the stone design of the gable." (Sembach: 110)

The *Kunstschule*, dedicated exclusively to the fine arts, was begun in 1904, but wasn't completed until 1911. The end result was a building much larger than the *Kunstgewerbeschule*, three stories high, and set on the long axis of the now-meticulously landscaped rectangular plot. As Sembach poetically states it, the two buildings were arranged "in a relationship of mutual tension, based on free movement rather than confrontation." (Sembach: 110) Simply put, the two buildings addressed each other on a diagonal, rather than directly, face to face.

The *Kunstschule*, "unmistakably architectural in concept," takes the severity of its sibling close by many steps further. As Sembach notes, "any reminiscence of furniture design has been successfully eradicated. "(Sembach: 110) With its plain facade and enormous windows, those of the third story embedded in the partially sloped roof, the *Kunstschule* reminds us chiefly of a factory, specifically the AEG Turbine Factory in Berlin, built by Peter Behrens in the same period.

A comparison between van de Velde's *Kunstgwerbeschule* and Charles Rennie Mackintosh's two-stage design for the Glasgow School of Art (1897-1909) is especially valuable here, since the two commissions were developed and carried out with identical objectives. Exercising architectural discipline and self-restraint, van de Velde "approached his commission "in quieter fashion and created a working building. Mackintosh, on the other hand, used the occasion for an artistic demonstration: art [he believed] can only be created inside emphatically artistic architecture." (Sembach: 107)

That Mackintosh's then-cutting edge structure for GSA's innovative curriculum rested on the assumption that easel and applied art courses would be carried on in the same building was doubtless critical to his architectural planning. So also, was the influence of the vernacular Scottish baronial manor on his vision for the school. But certainly, most influential on the planning of GSA's exterior structure and interior spaces, notably its forest-like library, was his own dedication to painting and drawing, which Mackintosh had never, at any point, determined to set aside.

Van de Velde's architectural work in Weimar extended to the design of his family's home, *Hohe Pappeln*, a domestic retreat similar to *Bloemenwerf*, but whose polygonal structure was tighter and more controlled. (*Hohe Pappeln* will be more fully analyzed in the final chapter of this study.) Moreover, in addition to teaching courses in furniture design and masterminding on-site buildings, he took on other projects, including the ultimately aborted planning for the *Théâtre des Champs d'Élysées*. But dominating his professional activities from 1908 until 1914 was his all-consuming involvement in the *Deutscher Werkbund*.

The *Deutscher Werkbund* was formed in 1907, "in response to a widespread feeling that the rapid industrialization and modernization of Germany," a steamroller of industrial expansion that was rapidly surpassing that of other nations on the continent, "posed a threat to the national culture." (Campbell 3) However, as Joan Campbell points out, the *Werkbund* founders emphatically "rejected the backward-looking romanticism of most English and Continental cultural critics, and refused to indulge in the cultural pessimism increasingly fashionable in intellectual circles." Instead, disdainful of such stylish fatalism, they "set out to prove that an organization dedicated to raising the standard of German work in the applied arts through cooperation with progressive elements in industry could restore dignity to labor." At the same time, the founders asserted, the *Werkbund* would "produce a harmonious national style in tune with the modern age." (Campbell: 3)

Uncomfortable with the glorification of Medieval craft traditions espoused by John Ruskin and William Morris, the *Werkbund* pioneers set themselves the task of bridging what they perceived as a destructive gulf between "art," in the large sense, and contemporary industrial practice. As idealistic as the Arts and Crafts leaders, albeit in more future-oriented terms, they sought to "realize their vision of a Germany in which the machine, directed by the nation's best artists, would revitalize the applied arts 'from the sofa cushion to urban planning' (Campbell: 3)." Clearly, the fundament of *Werkbund* philosophy was absolute faith in the machine as the primary agent for the improvement of both the intimate domestic environment and the large scale urban community.

A group of 24 men comprised the Werkbund's original membership: twelve German industrial leaders and twelve well-respected artists, architects, and designers. The hope was to bring about a mutually beneficial encounter between the two groups of men, all of equal achievement in their respective fields, but radically different in education, professional achievement, and concerns regarding to the production of functional objects. Among the major firms represented were Krupp, Daimler, and AEG (*Allgemaine Electricitäts-Gesellshcaft*), Germany's huge, monopolistic electricity company. (Important to note is that, by 1907, AEG had given the protean Peter Behrens, one of the invited artist/ designers, full responsibility for product and factory design, as well as company logo and promotional posters.) Also, affiliated with the *Werkbund* were the more modest, craft-oriented *Werkstätten* of Dresden, Munich, and Vienna. In the latter case, the formidable designer and architect Josef Hoffmann played a dual role: director of *Wiener Werkstätte* business affairs on the one hand; product designer on the other.

According to Stephen Escritt, the *Deutscher Werkbund* story is as relevant to the growth and decline of Art Nouveau as it is to the larger history of modern design, "not least because it attracted so many of the style's leading exponents." (Escritt: 368) *Werkbund* members Peter Behrens, Richard Riemerschmid, Hermann Obrist, and August Endell had all been crucial figures in the development of Munich Jugendstil. Joseph Maria Olbrich had incorporated trademark Art Nouveau features, such as curvilinear form and references to nature, in his plans for Vienna's Secession Hall. Henry van de Velde had been refining his signature whiplash curve in furniture, light fixtures, and serving ware, as well as tapestry, book and poster design, since the mid-1890s.

In Campbell's view, however, the *Werkbund* never realized the goals of its founders. For all its efforts, the organization never "banished the specter of alienation [of the worker] from the world of work,' (Campbell: 3) that is traditional handiwork. Moreover, and more importantly, the *Werkbund* never fully "converted a significant segment of industry to the ideal of quality and good design." (Campbell: 3-4) Nevertheless, the association had established itself on a national scale by 1914 and the start of World War I Moreover, the *Werkbund* did survive the defeat of Germany in 1918 and the demise of the Second Reich, reaching "new heights of activity and influence under the Weimar Republic" (Campbell: 4) in the post-war period. In particular, the mounting of international exhibitions, such as those in Cologne (1914) and later in Stuttgart-Weissenhof (1927), allowed the organization substantial influence beyond Germany's borders.

On the downside, however, from the early 1920's on, links developed with Europe's artistic avant garde, along with the liberal-democratic leanings of Friedrich Naumann and Theodor Hauss, both prominent *Werkbund* members, brought the association under increasing attack by the National Socialists who denounced it as an "agent of cultural bolshevism." (Campbell: 4) Undermined by these attacks, the *Werkbund* was effectively moribund when the National Socialist, or Nazi Party achieved complete control of the German government in 1933.

In discussing the *Werkbund*, we tend to focus exclusively on the 24 men and they were all men who comprised the group's original membership. But, in actuality, the organization's eventual makeup was far more varied and extensive than is commonly assumed Years after its founding, the *Werkbund* brought university professors in direct contact with hand-craftsmen, easel artists with industrialist leaders, and designers with politicians, all of whom had carried on their professional activities in separate professional cocoons until joining the group.

The *Deutscher Werkbund*, then, if for no other reason than sheer inclusiveness, continues to merit our attention for its unprecedented work as a forum, one that raised important questions regarding the relationship between the world of fine and applied art and the world of industry, in a 20th Century context characterized by historically unparalleled economic and social change. The following are three of the major questions the *Werkbund* founders sought to answer, hopefully in concrete, productive terms.

- How to "restore joy in work in the context of industrial society"?
- How to "forge a link between high and popular culture"?
- How to "redefine the role of the handicrafts in a machine age"? (Campbell: 6)

On October 5th and 6th, 1907, approximately 100 prominent artists, industrialists, and art lovers convened in Munich, in response to an appeal by the twelve fine and applied artists and their twelve counterparts in industry noted above. Determined to cast self-directed personal and professional interests aside, the 100 or so *Werkbund* Congress attendees resolved to address the central problem engaging the attention of educated Germans at the time: "how to reforge the links between designer and producer that had been broken in the course of the nation's spectacular economic development." (Campbell: 9) Fired up by an impressively clear-sighted awareness of the drawbacks of rapid-fire industrial expansion, their expressed intention was to inject not only an artistic, but an ethical element into German economic life.

The meeting's keynote speech was delivered by Fritz Schumacher, Professor of Architecture at the Techische Hochshule in Dresden. Schumacher passionately "deplored the destruction of the artistic culture associated with a preindustrial past," but, at the same time, "stressed that the progress of industrialization and mechanization was irresistible." (Campbell: 9) In making these two opposed, but equally valid points, in which he attempted to ascribe equal value to the "artistic culture" of the past and the inexorable expansion of industry in the present, Schumacher distinguished the *Werkbund* agenda from that of the Arts and Crafts movement, with its heavy, some might say undue emphasis on the practical and moral superiority of Medieval craft culture. To reinforce his message, Schumacher went on to insist that the *Werkbund* should "strive to counter the excessive materialism and rationalism that are the by-products of industrial growth, without sacrificing the advantages of modernity" (Campbell: 9). Heady, resounding language that sets the heart to pounding to be sure. But, in concrete terms, a very tall order.

Sensitive to the likelihood of extremes in attitude in the diverse audience before him aesthetically-focused artists here, profit-oriented capitalists there Schumacher emphatically stated not only what *Werkbund* objectives were, but what they weren't. On the one hand, he made it clear that the *Werkbund* had not been "created merely to appease the sensibilities of aesthetes offended by the sheer ugliness of current products." (Campbell: 10) On the other hand, shifting his attention to the captains of industry in the crowd, he declared that the organization had not been formed merely to increase the profits of participating firms.

Instead, he took the middle ground, assuring his audience that elegant, well-functioning goods, their high-volume fabrication enabled by modern machinery and innovative manufacturing techniques, "would both strengthen the nation's competitive position in the markets of the world and foster social peace at home." (Campbell: 10) (It is admittedly easier for us to see the validity of the first, pragmatically-oriented portion of Schumacher's optimistic proclamation than the accuracy or inherent logic of the second. The connection between aesthetically satisfying utilitarian goods and "social peace" seems tenuous at best, at least on its face.)

Among the dominant members of the *Werkbund*, Hermann Muthesius and Henry van de Velde have most commonly attracted scholarly attention, in large part a result of their contrasting views regarding the place and value of individual creative input in the design and manufacturing processes. Their ongoing conflict, fueled by long term personal animosity, came to a head in their well-recorded, violent clash at the opening of the 1914 Cologne Fair, where they debated the critical issue of "typing." It is therefore an historical oddity that neither Muthesius, the *Werkbund*'s central guiding spirit, nor his Belgian colleague and antagonist, attended the initial meeting in Munich. Van de Velde, in fact, didn't formally join the *Werkbund* until 1908, although he is pervasively named a "founder" in *Werkbund* histories.

Nevertheless, their shared influence on *Werkbund* activities, rivalry aside, was enormous and critical to its growth and character. The son of a mason, Hermann Muthesius was born in Thuringia in 1861. Indeed, it is wise to highlight at the outset that Muthesius was reared in the home of an artisan, rather than a household of well-educated professionals, and that he was himself skilled in his father's craft. However, pursuing his father's trade never figured in Muthesius's ambitions. Relocating to Berlin in his late teens, he completed his architectural training in the city's *Technische Hochschule*. That while still a student, he was sent by an architectural firm to Japan, in the capacity of draughts-man, testifies to his precocity, as well as his curiosity about the world beyond Germany's borders. While little has been written of his sojourn in Japan, the impact of Japanese design norms on Muthesius's stylistic inclinations must have been pivotal in his development, especially in light of his highly influential reformist tract on English domestic architecture and design education: *Das Englische Haus* (1903). What seems to have attracted him in both Japan and the British Isles was the felicitous integration of smooth-running utility with unpretentious aesthetic clarity.

Muthesius returned to Germany in 1893 and began his architectural career in the design office of the Prussian Ministry of Public Service. Rising swiftly in government ranks, he was appointed cultural attaché to the German Embassy in London in 1896, "a position apparently created in response to the Kaiser's personal wishes." (Campbell: 12) In that capacity, Muthesius made England his home for seven years.

Disciplined and industrious, thorough in his record-keeping, ceaselessly peripatetic, Muthesius sent frequent reports outlining his observations to the Prussian home office. In them, he described advances in English architecture, craft, and industrial design, "with a view toward adapting the best features of the English experiences to German circumstances." (Campbell: 12)

As noted earlier, his exploratory travels took him as far north as Scotland. In Glasgow, he had illuminating exposure to Charles Rennie Mackintosh's maverick break with historicism, in the Scotch architect's Hill House and Glasgow School of Art, the latter, at that point, still under construction. In London, Muthesius built friendships with the members of the Arts and Crafts Movement, including its guiding spirit, William Morris, while at the same time familiarizing himself with innovative approaches to design education in London's vocational schools.

By the end of his stay on foreign soil, 1896-1903, Muthesius had folded his extensive observations and conclusions into the three bulky, landmark volumes noted above: *Das Englische Haus*. It is telling of his observations' value to Germany that, while in Japan and in England, Muthesius lived and travelled as inquiring acolyte, on his return to his homeland, he quickly assumed the role of vanguard leader in the reform of German design and manufacture.

Back in Berlin, Muthesius moved laterally to a position in the Prussian Ministry of Trade. In his new role, he applied himself to the reform of arts and crafts education, basing his principles on observations made in trade schools in England and securing the appointment of like-minded, progressive practitioners to key positions: Peter Behrens to the Art Academy in Dusseldorf, Hans Poelzig to the Breslau Art Academy, and Bruno Paul to the Berlin School of Applied Art.

In 1907, Muthesius himself entered the educational arena, through his appointment as First Chair of the Applied Arts at the Berlin Commercial University (*Handelshochschule*). While the appointment gave him greater authority to further the cause of reform, his inaugural lecture, in which he laid out his program of basic principles for applied art instruction, set off a storm of protest from conservative elements in the German craft industries. The hostile reaction of entrenched interests in Muthesius's *Handelshochschule* audience was a catalyst for a permanent rift in the heretofore unified German Trade Association to Further the Economic Interests of the Art Industries, thankfully abbreviated to *Fachverband.* In June, 1907, a confrontation between the progressive and traditionalist factions within the *Fachverband* at its annual meeting in Dusseldorf resulted in the secession of the pro-Muthesius firms from the organization. Their defection, in fact, constituted the first step in the formation of the *Werkbund.*

The educational principles laid out by Muthesius in his *Handelshochschule* speech, revolutionary for their time, now seem givens for the informed afficonado of quality design. The three axiomatic guidelines he introduced in 1907 were subsequently incorporated into the *Werkbund* program. And twelve years later in Weimar, for that matter, they served as precepts for the design and fabrication of aesthetically satisfying utilitarian objects at the Bauhaus, under the direction of *Werkbund* alumnus Walter Gropius. They were as follows:

- Increased respect for the innate character of materials.
- Greater emphasis on functional and constructional design criteria for consumer goods.
- Rejection of nostalgic sentimentality, artificiality, excessive ornamentation.

Muthesius was alert to the obstacles he and his colleagues faced in the reform of applied arts education. He was aware that the German "consuming public, corrupted by social snobbery, sudden wealth, and the ready availability of 'luxury' goods cheaply made by machine, would have to be won back to the old ideals" 'old' as Muthesius construed them "of simplicity, purity, and quality." (Campbell: 14) Moreover, deeply invested in the belief that "men are molded by the objects that surround them" (Campbell: 14), Muthesius urged manufacturers to recognize that producing cheap imitations and fashionable novelties, while profitable, was damaging to the national [German] character, "through pollution of the visual environment." (Campbell: 14) Discounting the doubts of both manufacturers and retailers that the new "pure" designs were marketable, he cited the commercial success of the *Dresdner Werkstätten für Handwerkskunst*, which were indicative, he claimed, of the competitive advantage of carefully crafted over shoddy goods.

Muthesius's calculated appeal to German patriotism proved in the long run an effective strategy. Preaching freedom from the "stylistic tyranny of the French, then still dominant in the realm of fashion and design," he stated firmly that German designers should no longer "desperately and ineffectually adapt their designs to foreign tastes and predilections." (Campbell: 15) And he expressed the hope that one day German designers would “dictate good taste to the world, while enriching themselves.” (Campbell: 15) So, in the end, Muthesius hoped to mobilize, all at once, patriotic, economic, and ethical sentiments “in support of fundamentally aesthetic reforms.” His three-pronged rhetorical assault on fusty tradition transfixed the majority of his Berlin audience on three distinct, but interrelated levels.

While the setting out of guidelines for modernizing, German functional design constituted the core of his *Handelshochschule* lecture, it would be an error to overlook the deep distrust of artistic individualism Muthesius expressed in his diatribe (and diatribe it was). As Campbell states it, Muthesius felt that “the style of the future would not be the product of isolated geniuses striving to create new forms, but would develop out of the efforts of many individuals working in a new spirit to utilize available artistic, technical, and economic ideas in the design and production of consumer goods.” (Campbell: 15) Here, Campbell articulates Muthesius’s profound skepticism regarding individual creative activity in the applied arts, a viewpoint anathema to Henry van de Velde, Muthesius’s colleague and ultimately passionate opponent.

Muthesius did in fact avoid the inaugural *Werkbund* meeting in Munich. Having delivered the provocative speech that eventually led to the founding of the organization, he feared that the resulting controversy surrounding his person would jeopardize the survival of the *Werkbund*, still in its infancy. Nonetheless, once the group was established, Muthesius was elected Vice-President. And, since he was still a member of the Prussian Ministry of Trade, he was able to provide the *Werkbund* with useful government contacts. Undeniably, however, the ever more autocratic *Werkbund* founder succeeded in imposing on the organization the views outlined above, until 1914 and the outbreak of World War I.

By 1912, Berlin, headquarters of the German parliament and governmental bureaucracy, had become the meeting place for *Werkbund* designers, artists, and industrialists. Their frequent social gatherings served to reinforce the sense of community “among individuals who often had little in common beyond their desire to further its goals.” (Campbell: 16) In hindsight, it does seem ironic that an organization dedicated to applied arts reform should have chosen as its base raw and raucous Berlin, a government center notable primarily for vigorous commerce and lively, if not frenzied nightlife, rather than Dresden, Munich, or Vienna, more sedate, culturally sophisticated urban centers, whose contributions to innovative design had in the past been so much greater.

Henry van de Velde was, indeed, the only non-German member of the *Werkbund*’s influential central corps. Although he spoke some German, van de Velde’s native languages was Flemish, and, like most well-educated, upper crust Belgians, he was also fluent in French. He had only set up shop in Berlin, as master designer supervising a team of craft specialists, a mere eight years before the founding of the *Werkbund*. However, in that short period, van de Velde had become a popular, respected figure in Berlin society, where his commissioned *Gesamtkunstwerken* for German clients, in addition to his breadth of knowledge in cultural matters and his “theoretical pronouncements on art, the machine, and society” (Campbell: 22) served him well.

In the mid-1890's, van de Velde had established as his creative platform the proposition that "art and architecture must be put in the service of society in order to create a nobler environment for contemporary man," (Campbell: 22) a high-flown sentiment that resonated with that of his *Werkbund* colleagues. Like the initial *Werkbund* membership, van de Velde had little sympathy with the late 19th Century "l' art pour l' art" philosophy. Further, in the tradition of William Morris, the Belgian master regarded himself as a variety of socialist, more specifically a creator of elegant functional objects who posited a direct causal link between the upgrading of the built and furnished environment and a more peaceful, equitable society. In this attitude, he could claim philosophic kinship with Muthesius, Schumacher, and some other *Werkbund* leaders.

While van de Velde had begun his applied arts career at his home in Uccle and, later on, in his workshop in Brussels as master designer of a stunning range of handcrafted furnishings, he'd eventually acknowledged the obvious advantages of mechanized production: high volume, turned out at a faster rate, with greater consistency, leading to greater profit. So, again in true *Werkbund* spirit, he "set out to create a new ornament and style appropriate to the machine age." (Campbell: 22)

In the minds of the founders, then, van de Velde's value to the *Werkbund* rested as much on his role as a progressive educator as on his creative and theoretical achievements, In 1902, after all, as a result of his reputed emphasis on applied arts education, the Belgian designer/ architect had been appointed head of the Weimar Art Academy in 1902, a rare honor for a foreigner in a medieval German town celebrated for its 19th Century literary luminaries, Goethe and Schiller. In Weimar, van de Velde's effort to develop an educational meeting ground between artists and handcraftsmen, had been to some degree successful. Therefore, his welcome into the *Werkbund* seemed all but inevitable.

Initially, from the standpoint of all involved, Henry van de Velde's participation in the *Werkbund* may have seemed a logical step in productive professional symbiosis. But the egocentric Belgian, for all his past accolades and genuine accomplishments, was from the outset disgruntled with the founders' assumptions regarding responsibility for the *Werkbund* agenda. As he asserted in his autobiography, written in exile in Switzerland when he was 96, the *Werkbund* founders had "merely acted as spokemen for a program that he had initiated." (Campbell: 23) Omitting mention of Muthesius altogether, he claimed that Peter Bruckmann, Theodor Fischer, and Richard Riemerschmid had really started the Werkbund, and that all three owed their creative and ethical ideals to him.

According to Campbell, van de Velde's primary mistake was in failing to realize that others might have evolved their ideas, particularly those in line with his own, independently. Labelling his claims exaggerated, she notes that, by 1907, van de Velde's views on the integration of the artist in society through the design of aesthetically satisfying functional goods, as well as his theories regarding the role of the machine in the applied arts and the relationship between the pure and the applied arts, were all common property.

Taking issue with van de Velde's claim of newness for his "new style," she rather dismisses it as "far from reflecting fundamental modern values." (Campbell: 23)

Instead, she argues, he "revealed an unrestrained individualism that seldom went beyond the level of ornament and soon appeared dated." (Campbell: 24) She further asserts that Van de Velde spoke and wrote of the need to serve the public, through the machine production of quality goods, but, "in practice, his designs tended to involve costly handwork and therefore met the needs of only the wealthy few." (Campbell: 24)

So, what was Henry van de Velde's significance for the *Werkbund*, his real contribution to the organization's development? As Campbell sees it the formation of the *Werkbund* had only been possible "because a number of leading artists shared the desire to reform German aesthetic culture and recognized that this entailed cooperation with progressive elements in the crafts and industry." (Campbell: 24) Pure and simple. In 1907, of course, Henry van de Velde's well known, prodigious efforts to merge traditional craft with industrial manufacture easily qualified him as a "progressive element."

The *Werkbund* had its critics and dissenters, whose doubts regarding the feasibility of the group's goals and methods compelled its members to give weight to their voiced intentions through concrete action: entertaining, often even flamboyant *Werkbund* exhibitions; promotional pamphlets and catalogues of products; an intensive educational program.

Among the harshest critics was the Austrian architect and theorist Adolf Loos, best known for the polemical tract in which he condemned all ornament as crime, and for Vienna's Steiner House, unique for its time. Elaborate decoration, according to Loos, wasted the craftsman's time and cost the patron money better spent on only the functional elements of built structures. The austere, unembellished rectilinearity of Steiner House embodied indeed, Loos' purism *vis-à-vis* surface ornamentation.

Loos believed that the *Werkbund*'s very existence was superfluous, given the organization's avowed objective of improving the aesthetic quality of industrially-produced goods. Since, as he saw it, "styles emerge spontaneously as production adapts to new patterns of living, no organization could influence or hasten the process." (Campbell: 29) Stylistic evolution, then, was an organic process, a natural response to gradual changes that took place mainly in the urban environment.

Loos, a true zealot, also opposed the intervention of the artist in the design process, a contrarian point of view that, if followed up in practice, would have eliminated a large segment of *Werkbund* membership. And, taking the argument further, the acerbic Austrian ridiculed the very notion of the "applied artist." Very likely, in fact, had English been his native language, Loos would have favored the term "craftsman," thereby establishing a distinction in professional emphasis, between the artist on the "look" of an object, the craftsman on its utility.

Preternatural in his insight, Loos reacted with hostility to the feverish quest for novelty and modernity he witnessed in turn-of-the-century European culture, a quest all too familiar to 21st Century Americans. Asserting that only the simple—the desk, chair, kitchen cabinet stripped of features inessential for use—could be classed as modern, he insisted that the search for novelty for its own sake was the root cause of much ugliness in the world. (Campbell: 29-30)

However, Loos was not caregorically dismissive of aesthetic concerns in themselves. He conceded that objects of daily use could be beautiful, but went on to refine his position in saying that "if they are aesthetically pleasing it is not because they are artist-designed, but because they perfectly fulfill their function and embody the highest potential of modern technology." (Campbell: 30) Clearly then, "form follows function," the mantra that informs most thinking in architecture and design in our day, seemed axiomatic for the Austrian ideologue long before Walter Gropius and others better known in the field adopted the standard their own.

A caveat: what might be troubling for many is Loos' apparently unexamined assumption that "fine" or easel artists are first and foremost decorators. If that were true across the board, then the greater number of *Werkbund* artist/designers would have had little appreciation for the fundamental *raison d'être* of functional goods: their ability to serve their purpose, and well.

A second *Werkbund* critic, Werner Sombart, had the advantage of an insider's view of the group's operations, albeit for a brief period. Sombart, an economist and political theorist, was a member from 1908 to 1910. His argument with Muthesius focussed on the latter's proposition that the machine age would hasten the development of a superior cultural landscape in Germany. On the contrary, he felt, modern technology, in the hands of the capitalist system, "played the villain in his [Sombart's] account of the [applied] art industries." (Campbell: 30) Consequently, the designers of material goods and the engineers responsible for their efficient function were at the mercy of profit-seeking producers and the mass market. In addition, since Sombart extended his cynicism, not to mention his hard-core elitism, to the greater number of consumers, he professed little faith in the buying public where matters of style were concerned that is, the buying public with shallow pockets: 99% "lacked either the taste or the money to purchase quality goods." (Campbell: 30)

No doubt targetting Muthesius and his *Werkbund* sympathizers, Sombart looked askance at "doctrinaire modernists who tried to develop an aesthetic based on functionalism and the machine." (Campbell: 31) Moreover, clearly ill at ease with the very concept of a necessary link between beauty and practicality, he made a point of distinguishing between useful articles that deserved the artist/designer's attention and those that did not. As he saw it, such mundane conveniences as hot water bottles and umbrellas definitely did not. "Some things are left in undistinguished obscurity and need be formed with practicality rather than beauty in mind." (Campbell: 31)

Sombart's elitism was in a direct outgrowth of his ancestry: he was a born and bred aristocrat. However, his negative, unignorably arrogant appraisal of the tastes of the "masses," even the German masses, seems less off-putting when one takes into consideration his voiced, if grudging approval of the *Werkbund*'s multi-pronged campaign to raise the level of popular taste through education. The organization's ongoing attempt to "combat the preference of producers for cheapness, rather than quality," (Campbell: 31) impressed him as fully and appropriately as it would have a less patrician critic.

Werner Sombart's skepticism regarding the ability of the so-called "common man" to distinguish qualitatively first-rate from second-rate goods found resonance in the writings of the cultural critic Joseph August Lux. In decidedly undemocratic spirit,

Lux dismissed the possibility that advanced technology, itself the engine of industrial growth, could improve "the native bad taste of the masses." (Heskett: 122) Sharing Sombart's elitism, Lux stated that "To make the masses artistic is a hopeless business. The masses can only be made bearable if their [industry's] bad products are withheld and good exclusively provided. They need not be consulted for they have no judgment." (Heskett: 122) As Lux saw it, if the great body of humanity were to inhabit a uniformly tasteful environment on a daily basis, it would be an environment imposed from on high, by a small, select cadre of cultural superiors.

Unlike van de Velde, Mackintosh, and other designer/architects, who stepped gingerly into the realm of factory production, when it suited their needs, Lux posited a sharp line of demarcation between the traditional crafts and modern industry. He saw no hope for a joining of forces, for a sharing of creative obligation between the hand-craftsman, in charge of his product from initial conception to final touches, and the industrial worker adept at one task only.

To a great extent, Lux was an inheritor of the Arts and Crafts mentality regarding the time-honored applied arts: carpentry, metalwork, ceramics, glassmaking weaving, et al. As dismayed, if not horrified, as Ruskin and Morris by the decline in popularity of the craft tradition, he emphatically asserted their "positive value in contemporary culture." (Heskett: 122) Lux's outlook proceeded from the premise that a skilled craftsman contributed more than concrete, utilitarian objects to a nation's political, social, cultural, or aesthetic fabric. Given the artisan's steady, reliable habits of careful, precise workmanship, his intimate familiarity with tools, craft processes, and the qualities of and limitations of materials, he served as a kind of exemplar, a lodestar for the building of a stable, harmonious, productive community.

John Heskett points to a surprising absence of overt social optimism in Lux's thinking. "Whilst echoing Muthesius in recognizing the truly innovative aspects of modern technology in its capacity to produce standard products in large quantities at a consistently high level of quality, the dimension of social idealism was absent from his writing, for he simply didn't believe in its possibilities." On the contrary, it seems to this observer that Lux, passionate advocate of traditional artisanry that he was, instead reserved whatever modicum of "social idealism" he could muster for the shrinking realm of handcraftsmanship, for which he evinced enormous respect, combined with nostalgia and regret at its seemingly inexorable disappearance.

In April, 1912, the organization's head office was in fact moved from Dresden to Berlin, the seat of German government and a far more vigorous commercial center than Dresden. The "city of spires," rich in culture and architectural wonders, was nonetheless ill-suited to the aggressive educational and marketing practices of the Werkbund, not to mention the group's startling growth. By March, 1912, five years after its founding, membership had risen to 971; by March, 1913, it had reached 1,319 and by March, 1914, 1,870. (Campbell: 33)

The increase in membership was, not surprisingly, accompanied by a change of character in the annual meetings. What had begun as "intimate gatherings of a self-selected elite" had mutated by 1912 into "large conventions enjoying public patronage and attracting attention from the national press." (Campbell: 35) One might automatically assume, then, that the *Werkbund*'s growth in sheer size, accompanied by greater visibility in the media, would have worked to its advantage, as would the excitement generated by its lively annual conferences.

A mere recitation of events at the well-publicized 1913 Leipzig Conference, for example, rivals those of earlier expositions in Paris, Glasgow, and Chicago, if only in the variety of entertainments military displays; performances by dance ensembles and dramatic presentations; an evening boat ride, accompanied by a string quartet. (Campbell: 35-36) If nothing else, the energy generated by the wide spectrum of crowd-pleasing events at the conferences should have in turn nourished support for the *Werkbund*'s more serious, central agenda: the manufacture of high quality, aesthetically pleasing functional goods. And to some extent, it did.

However, as Campbell points out, the growth in numbers, in particular, was not necessarily a good thing. As informed intuition suggests, such an expanded, unfiltered group of participants "could not possibly consist only of outstanding personalities," (Campbell: 36) that is, individuals exceptionally gifted in technological innovation or the fledgling field of industrial design. More-over, further damaging the once-convivial atmosphere of *Werkbund* meetings and diluting the idealism of its original policies, an amendment made to the group's constitution in 1912 opened the membership door to commercial corporations. These corporate newcomers were, in the most literal sense, "strictly business." They were neither involved directly in industrial manufacture, nor guided in any way by artistic concerns. Each of these newly admitted corporations was entitled to a voting representative, an egalitarian decision whose unfortunate consequence was greater dissonance in the *Werkbund.*

The generally welcome, but somewhat unwieldy expansion in individual and corporate membership led, moreover, to increased centralization of the *Werkbund*'s decision-making powers. The core leadership, now settled in Berlin, was dominated by Muthesius, his ever-more authoritarian dicta moderated by the liberal, more flexible Frederick Naumann. Given this narrow concentration of power, the opinions of the great mass of Werkbund members, those not representing industrial or commercial giants, inevitably counted for less. "Increasingly, the association was controlled by a small inner circle at headquarters [in Berlin], a circumstance that aroused resentment and reinforced the feeling that the *Werkbund* was falling into the hands of bureaucrats out of touch with important sections of the membership." (Campbell: 36)

However, what did meet with universal approval was the *Werkbund*'s strengthened financial position. The group's financial sources were multiple: receipts from dues, exacted on a sliding scale; the sale of *Werkbund* publications, such as yearbooks, informative pamphlets and product catalogues; infusions of cash from public bodies, such as the Prussian Ministry of Trade, a bureaucratic agency whose largesse inevitably came with hooks.

In pre-World War I years, *Werkbund* activities were divided into three main areas: reform of product design; propaganda, in the positive, promotional sense; consumer education, this last critical not only to the *Werkbund*'s success, but to its very survival.

The organization's strategy for instructing a diverse public on the importance of quality in mass-produced goods rested on its recognition that "it would be self-defeating to ask manufacturers and craftsmen to adopt the ideal of quality without first ensuring that a market for their work existed." (Campbell: 39) Indeed, diversity in the target audience posed the greatest challenge for the educational staff, because the hopefully persuasive pitch for high quality and stylistic refinement was, in fact, directed at three distinct populations in German society: the financially solvent, but not affluent middle class; the university-educated, but often financially strapped intellectual elite; the deep-pocketed wealthy, whether the wealth be inherited or recently amassed, (i.e., the *nouveaux riches*).

The instructional pitch directed at the middle class was contrived with a distinct moral edge, one that acknowledged the primacy of cleanliness in the German ethical hierarchy. As a result, the German bourgeoisie had to be convinced that "good taste [was] as important as cleanliness as part of the morality." (Campbell: 39-40) As to the intelligentsia, for whom ideas, not earthly goods, were essential commodities in their daily lives, *Werkbund* educators had to overcome the "fanatical frugality prevalent among intellectuals, who often disdained material possessions, contenting themselves with tasteless furnishings as long as they were cheap." (Campbell: 40)

And finally, in addressing the wealthy, in general a conservative sector in German society, the educators directed their efforts at undercutting the assumption that only the purchase of antiques qualified as profitable, long term investment. This cautious class of buyers had to be convinced that "carefully selected modern designs would keep their value in the long run." (Campbell: 40)

Admittedly, and sadly, there was no overcoming the refusal of many well-heeled customers to purchase industrially-produced furnishings for their upscale homes at all. They persisted in demanding custom-designed, hand-crafted goods, with an elitist resistance that ran counter to the *Werkbund*'s program. The cultural superiority they boasted in their persons should, they believed, extend to and be reinforced by the possessions that surrounded them. It is indeed ironic that this portion of a larger contingent of wealthy consumers should have so frequently figured in van de Velde's clientèle, and he a prominent *Werkbund* leader, no less.

By 1914, the *Werkbund* had come to be regarded as the authoritative body on issues of functional design in Germany. Its membership had risen from 472 in 1908 to 1870 in 1914, and included most of the outstanding design and architectural talent of the time. Its annual conferences, held in such meccas as Munich, Frankfurt, Dresden, and Vienna, had been well-attended events, promoted throughout Germany in major newspapers and in journals devoted to cultural affairs.

Of the *Werkbund* conferences lively experiences more accurately termed "fairs" the 1914 Cologne Fair was by far the most significant in terms of the future direction of the association. Its program was completed by Cologne architect Carl Rehorst, whose initial plan was to group exhibitions of only *Werkbund* products under thematic heads. However, since the site chosen for the Fair was very extensive, additional exhibits by non-member manufacturing firms and regional organizations were included, so as to ensure the *Werkbund* some profit for its organizational efforts. (The non-*Werkbund* participants paid a fee to show their wares on the Cologne Fair grounds.) The result was a set of disparate exhibitions, whose stylistic diversity would have well suited international expositions, such as those mounted in Paris,

Glasgow, and Chicago in past decades, but ill fit the more focussed *Werkbund* agenda for uniformly high quality design.

This visual cacophony was exemplified by the stylistic contrasts between the most important buildings. Peter Behrens' Festival Hall, Josef Hoffmann's Austrian Pavilion, and Muthesius' pavilion for the Hamburg-Amerika Line were all constructed in "stripped Neo-classical style" (Heskett: 131). Van de Velde's theater was a Jugendstil derivative, "its curving organic lines attempting to integrate both exterior and interior elements into a whole, but never succeeding entirely in overcoming the basic, rectangular constructional features," (Heskett: 131) according to Heskett's uniquely negative, rather mean-spirited appraisal. Walter Gropius, who would direct the Bauhaus from its inception in 1919, contributed a model factory, using state-of-the-art glazed elements for its exterior wall surfaces, but falling back on an architectural framework based on neo-classical principles absorbed from his mentor, Peter Behrens.

By common agreement, Bruno Taut's Glass Pavilion was the most riveting attraction of the Cologne Fair, owing primarily to its intricate play with light and color. An inventive departure from any familiar architectural norm, the pavilion took the form of a multi-faceted, polygonal dome, resembling nothing so much as a pineapple on its exterior. The dome rested on a concrete plinth, the walls of its 14-sided, lozenge-like form fabricated of thick glass brick. Two entrances, each reached by a flight of stairs, allowed access to the dome's interior. For many Cologne, Fair visitors, the initial impression of Taut's visionary structure was that of a sacred space. As they ambled or strode toward the Glass Pavilion, some reflexively slowed their pace, as though approaching a religious shrine.

Intended to demonstrate the potential for glass in architectural planning, the pavilion was in fact the first building to be constructed entirely of glass bricks. It had, of course, distinguished ancestors, beginning with the magisterial iron and glass Crystal Palace, designed by Joseph Paxton for London's International Exhibition of 1850-51. Given Taut's strong links with German Expressionism, and the movement's stress on on the symbolic value of rich, saturated color, it should come as no surprise that Taut himself publicly celebrated the effect of the light-reflecting, inlaid glass plates on the dome's facade. Dark blue at the base, they rose up through moss green and golden yellow, culminating in luminous pale yellow at the top. In Taut's romantic view, transparent or translucent glass was the material most appropriate for the orchestration of human emotions and therefore most suitable for the design of a building conducive to spiritual enlightenment.

The pavilion interior was, if anything, more magical, the source of the magic Taut's strategic use of technology considered advanced for the period. Glass-treaded staircases led to a small upper room, where a "modern machine" projected a kaleidoscope of color. Reinforcing the mood of celestial immateriality was a glistening waterfall, lit from beneath. The falls cascaded between the staircases, so that, as guests descended, they felt they were moving through sparkling water. (Obviously, but still "magically," they emerged dry.)

Lastly, and further enhancing the other-worldly ambience, were floor-to-ceiling interior glass walls, composed of rhombus-shaped colored panes arranged in a mosaic pattern. Acting as prisms, the panes processed sunlight through to the interior, so that one's experience inside the pavilion suggested that one might have inside a large, polychrome crystal.

Unlike most of the buildings on the fairgrounds, the Glass Pavilion served no practical purpose, other than the promotion of an unconventional material for built structures. Like van de Velde's *Werkbund* theater, Taut's dome was eventually razed. Only a small number of black and white, rather murky photographs remain to inform us, albeit inadequately, of the architect's transformative manipulation of light, through the deployment of clear and colored glass, falling water, and a primitive device for projecting shafts of light through colored lenses.

It is then a most satisfying paradox that, of the buildings specifically designed for the Cologne Fair, some quite imposing, only van de Velde's theater and Taut's Glass Pavilion are now commonly featured in expensively printed, illustrated architecture and design books. (That those extraordinary structures are represented only through a limited group of black and white photographs is, however, not so satisfying.)

As to the Fair's overall impact, Heskett sums it up as follows: "The great variety of forms demonstrated the extent to which *Werkbund* members had succeeded in gaining commissions, often in new fields of activity. At the same time, however it was abundantly clear that the formal unity so often declared as an aim of the cultural reform movement was as far away as ever." (Heskett: 135)

The official opening of the Cologne Fair took place on July 5, 1914, in Behrens' Festival Hall. At that inaugural event, the accumulated tensions underlying the diversity of the Fair's exhibits reached critical mass, followed by an explosion. The detonator was Muthesius' keynote address, entitled "The *Werkbund*'s Task of the Future." As central theme, Muthesius introduced the concept of *Typisierung* or "standards of good form and good taste." (Heskett: 135) The *Werkbund* leader and architectural theorist claimed he had seen these standards qualities typical of *Werkbund* products gradually emerge, across the board, in functional goods manufactured by *Werkbund*-related firms since the organization's founding in 1907.

In his advocacy of *Typisierung*, Muthesius further predicted that the standards, once defined, codified, and uniformly applied to every product manufactured in Germany, would serve as a kind of platform for foreign export and the dissemination of German culture abroad. The intensely nationalistic tenor of Muthesius' address, with its ominous subtext for present day readers, is both evident in his wording and prophetic of Germany's aggressive future actions on the European continent.

Prior to the conference, Muthesius had printed and circulated ten theses that would together comprise the basis of his address. While the tone of the theses in written form was stridently polemical, Muthesius' presentation was far less so, according to the accounts of those actually in attendance at the Fair opening. Nevertheless, van de Velde, who had read the theses in advance, took the floor immediately after Muthesius concluded his speech, and delivered a set of ten counter-theses, in which he vehemently asserted the freedom of the individual artist. He then went on to brand the *Typisierung* a flagrant restriction of that freedom and an intolerable infringement on the artist's creative self-determination:

> "As long as there are artists in the *Werkbund,* they will protest against any proposed canon and any standardization. The artist is essentially and intimately a passionate individualist a spontaneous creator. Never will he, of his own free will, submit to a discipline forcing upon him a norm, a canon." (Pevsner: 26)

Van de Velde's retort didn't end with the impassioned defense of creative independence quoted above. According to the outraged Belgian designer, whose clients been a cultured, well-educated, well-heeled elite throughout his career, the best in style could only be achieved in products designed and fabricated for a limited group, or better stated, class of patrons. Only close collaboration between a designer and a wealthy, tasteful client could result in both well-functioning, aesthetically pleasing objects for daily use and similarly well-functioning built structures. This intimate, one-on-one process he believed, was "a precondition of any concept of *Typisierung*, which bore the mark of the individual artist/designer and would inevitably vary from situation to situation, according to the specifics of the designer/client relationship." (Heskett: 135)

In light of the *Werkbund*'s stated goal, high volume industrial production of quality goods which would thereby make them available to large numbers of consumers, van de Velde's argument seems radically at odds with the *Werkbund* agenda. However, easily perceived in his thinking is what present-day economists term "trickledown effect." That is, once the well-crafted, aesthetically satisfying light fixture, dining room set, mirror frame, armchair has been created by the individual designer for the individual patron, it could then serve as template for reproduction through efficient mass production.

At first glance, the confrontation between Muthesius and van de Velde seems a heated argument carried on in the realm of high flown theoretical generalities. However, a closer look reveals that underlying the rhetorical clash between the two Werkbund leaders were "longstanding conflicts of personality and policy." (Heskett: 135) By no means the least of the conflicts "was accumulated resentment shared by van de Velde with other *Werkbund* artists against "decisions leading to the commercialization of the 1914 exhibition, and pique at the allocation of space and building commissions associated with it." (Heskett: 135-136) Feeding the mutual hostility as well was Muthesius' oft-voiced dismissal of the Jugendstil movement and its decidedly non-functional curvilinearity, the very stylistic elements so fully realized in van de Velde's Cologne Theater.

A simple listing of well-respected *Werkbund* artist/designers in sympathy with van de Velde's objections to *Typisierung* gives one a sense of how influential a group they were, and how threatening to Muthesius' dominance in the organization. Among them were Walter Gropius, Bruno Taut, Hans Poelzig, and August Rendell. And while not himself an artist, Karl Ernst Osthaus, a wealthy, enterprising expert on German and foreign craft and a van de Velde client, also gave the artists his full support. At the root of the artists' attempt to undermine Muthesius' ever-tightening grip on *Werkbund modus operandi* was "deep-seated dissatisfaction with the entire direction of *Werkbund* policy," so that "seizing control would assert the claims of the artists even if it split the organization." (Heskett: 136)

Muthesius, in his very person, epitomized the source of the artists' growing discontent. Throughout his involvement with the *Werkbund*, he had retained his position with the Prussian Ministry of Culture, which rendered him a de facto "heir to the tradition of bureaucratic manipulation of society for dynastic ends." (Heskett: 136) Certainly, if one takes into account his earlier independence in observing and appraising British architecture, Muthesius was too strong-minded an individual to operate as a mere puppet of officialdom. However, his day-to-day contact with the Ministry was naturally conducive to a point of view that saw cultural uniformity as a path to social unity. "Germany's role in the world and the importance of trade in furthering it, were precisely in accordance with the overall trend of government policy." (Heskett: 136)

There were, in fact, genuine differences between Muthesius and van de Velde in the realm of design aesthetics. But an immeasurably more important factor in their feud was van de Velde's rejection of the notion that artists should play a subservient role in the conduct of pragmatic architectural or design affairs. He had, after all, until his epiphanic months on the shores of the North Sea, spent a significant portion of his youth as an easel artist, driven solely by the need to create images that were beautiful and evocative.

Ultimately, it seemed that van de Velde and his fellow artists had won the war for *Werkbund* control, when Muthesius, to everyone's amazement, withdrew his ten theses. But further attempts by Walter Gropius to force Muthesius' resignation as *Werkbund* Director failed. (Obviously, Gropius was by then no longer a passive observer of Werkbund conflicts.) In the end, *Werkbund* membership as a whole concluded that, personal alliances and animosities notwithstanding, the more critical issue was the preservation of the group's unity, "fragile though it was, since it appeared that affairs of greater moment lay ahead." (Heskett: 136) The "affairs of greater moment," of course, were the events that led to the outbreak of war in August, 1914 and the premature shutdown of an historically critical exhibition that was, despite the fractious climate it engendered, a crucible for competing notions of quality design and its manufacture that would play themselves out in years to come. The Cologne Theater virtually embodied those competing notions.

Van de Velde had been commissioned for the design of the theater in 1913, so that he actually worked on the project in tandem with his *Werkbund* colleagues in architecture, Muthesius, Taut, Behrens, and Gropius, for at least a year. According to his biographer, Klaus-Jürgen Sembach, the structure van de Velde ultimately contrived for the sprawling Cologne Fair was both "an unexpected pinnacle of achievement for its time." and "a remarkably isolated phenomenon within its creator's development." (Sembach: 183) The Latin term *sui generis* comes swiftly to mind, as we consider Sembach's double barreled accolade, because the theater was indeed unique in two ways: it did represent a stylistic advance over other public structures of the period, and it was, in more personal terms, a departure from van de Velde's earlier schemes for buildings intended for public use.

Moreover, as Sembach points out, the impressive visual sweep of the theater's design, combined with its functional efficiency, served to rehabilitate van de Velde's reputation as an architect of consequence. This was particularly the case for *Werkbund* members allied with the Belgian Art Nouveau master in his passionate defense of creative individualism. (Van de Velde's influence had, in fact, gradually waned as the centrality of craft-based Jugendstil in German design had been supplanted by the national focus on the economic advantages for Germany of mechanized mass production.)

Following the convoluted trail of the Cologne Theater's development, manifest in van de Velde's many sketches and plaster models, is a fascinating journey in itself. Initially, the architect was asked to contrive a building on a much smaller scale than the theater he ultimately completed. With a mere 450 seats, the structure was at first conceived only as a cinema and, in the earliest planning stages, looked paltry alongside "festival halls, parades of shops, and terrace restaurants which other architects had been asked to design." (Sembach: 183) Nevertheless, this particular commission had its charms, both for van de Velde and for those curious *Werkbund* members who looked on, as the sole non-German speaker among them attempted to integrate the theater's specific functional and decorative features into its overall form. Buildings constructed for the sole purpose of showing films were, after all, rare for the time.

Van de Velde's first ground plan was, in fact, unprecedented in Western theater design. Sembach sets out the rationale for the novel elements as follows: "As a cinema does not require a deep stage or backstage apparatus, he [van de Velde] designed a foyer which encircled the entire auditorium and this became the enclosed passage, making it possible for patrons to circulate uninterruptedly." (Sembach: 183) His next step, "a logical consequence of the first," was to swivel the inner part of the building 180 degrees, thereby placing the film screen on the entrance side. As a result, most of the audience would enter the theater with a view of the raised rear stalls the norm for movie theaters in our day while only those seated in the last few rows had access to the auditorium through a back entrance that faced the screen.

In a further break with tradition, the interior of van de Velde's proposed structure had almost no right angles. Similar to those of the Barcelona's Antonì Gaudi, interior walls were pervasively curved, their intersections soft and perceptible only as lines, rather than the sharp edges created by walls set at angles to each other. Sembach makes an astute distinction here. He observes that van de Velde's plan "seems free in form, as though derived from laws of linear harmony, rather than functional requirements." (Sembach: 184) He adds that "the curved outlines [in van de Velde's plans] of necessity enclose useless empty spaces. Pure utility would have demanded a different line." (Sembach: 185)

For those familiar with van de Velde's biography, it is logical to think back 25 years or so, to his brief, but impassioned career as an easel painter, a vocation that absorbed him until 1893, when his creative focus shifted to utilitarian design. His initial drawings for the theater seem, in fact, to straddle the fence, at some points reflecting his early philosophic musings on line itself, "a line is a force," at others satisfying the concrete demands of what we now term "purpose-built" architecture.

Not long after van de Velde completed the first stage of his plans, the stated purpose for the theater was revised, a consequence either of a change of heart on the part of Cologne Fair organizers, or a request from van de Velde himself. (The source is still uncertain.) According to the updated concept, the theater would now facilitate both cinema and traditional theatrical productions. The site, however, remained the same, still cramped and still allowing for only 450 seats, so that the dual-purpose venue, once completed, would very likely resemble an intimate studio theater. Moreover, in planning for the altered concept, van de Velde was now compelled to rotate the interior elements 180 degrees once more, a return to convention that permitted a stage for live theater.

Thankfully for architectural posterity, however, the tradition-flouting quality of van de Velde's thinking continued to inform his sketches and models, this time in his plan for a tripartite stage. In this proposal, two clusters of columns would divide the stage into irregular thirds, to be 'used in sequence without tiresome pauses for scene changes, or simultaneously, or all as one." (Sembach: 185) Referring to van de Velde's years in Weimar, Sembach notes that the "notion of increasing flexibility by allowing action to take place at several places at once had been developed during the preparation of designs for the summer theater in Weimar," (Sembach: 185) a project that, like his aborted plans for *Le Théâtre des Champs Elysées*, had never come to fruition.

The columns, while imposing, were not load-bearing and could be moved, or even removed, according to the dramatic requirements of each production. As to the benefit of the three-part stage for actors and directors, the "result would have been very lively theater, and particularly useful for plays with a large number of scenes." (Sembach: 185) On the downside, the sheer width of the planned stage, with dramatic action shifting rapidly from one section to another, demanded a more flexible orientation of the audience and greater corresponding breadth, rather than depth, in seating. Obviously, the expansion of the theater's seating capacity was limited by its confining site. So, once again, van de Velde's cutting edge vision was stalemated, at least temporarily.

Fortunately, yet another change issued from on high worked in favor of that very vision, when Cologne Fair organizers lifted the projected structure entirely from its initial location between the wings of Muthesius's stately, but stodgy *Farbenschau*, and placed it on a larger site far distant from the Fair's most significant exhibits and events. As Sembach points out, "It was not until this point that the design was able to evolve and develop autonomous legitimacy." (Sembach: 186)

In pragmatic terms, the new site permitted more workable storage areas for props, sets and costumes. Of equal, social importance, the more expansive site would work to the advantage of theatergoers, since now van de Velde could further expand the already generous foyers, a gift for audience members who delighted in leaving their seats at intermission, and eat, drink, stroll and converse. The extended foyers were, in fact, no trivial issue for van de Velde, who was himself an ardent theatergoer, with full, first-hand understanding of audience needs. Be it noted, however, that the new site was not chosen by Muthesius for its suitability to van de Velde's Jugendstil influenced plans, or to address the obvious need for more space. The site, in fact, was uncomfortably remote from the epicenter of Cologne Fair exhibits and related activities. Moreover, the theater would now rest side by side with Gropius's and Meyer's model factory, a spare, no frills, rectilinear building obviously geared only for pragmatic, as opposed to cultural ends. The juxtaposition of the down-to-earth utilitarian with the loftily artistic struck many as ludicrous. So, the move, while ultimately a creative boon to van de Velde, had its real origin in Muthesius's opposition to the Belgian's intransigent individualism, paired with envy of what seemed the foreigner's excessive influence on *Werkbund* objectives.

More specifically, in terms of location, the theater had been transplanted to the shores of the Rhine, so that the building would now rest on a riverside embankment and its entrance placed at a high level. With entrance, vestibule, and the highest point of the stalls now located at the top of the embankment, it was possible for the audience to access the auditorium directly from the back. (Sembach: 187) Van de Velde is here to congratulated for successfully exploiting a situation that may have seemed, at first glance putting it mildly logistically problematic: a broad hillock of land overlooking a legendary waterway resonant with German history. Undaunted, he devised a layout roughly corresponding to that of a Greek open air theater, with the onstage columns reinforcing a classical reference familiar to cultured German theatergoers.

The larger site, of course, offered van de Velde more flexibility in the planning of the interior, starting with the widening of the auditorium and the addition of 175 more seats. (It is, by the way, interesting to note that somewhere in the process of accommodating entrance, vestibule, foyers, seating, storage areas, and the *sine qua non stage* to the larger site, provision for cinema projection and a film screen had been dropped altogether. Possibly, lack of interest in or familiarity with the nascent medium, on the part of both Fair organizers and van de Velde himself, contributed to its disappearance.)

While we no longer have the Cologne Theater structure to appraise and appreciate, we do have numerous photographs, shot from multiple viewpoints, of the building's exterior, as well as interior views of its gracious, elegant foyers and what appears an enormous auditorium. The photos, admittedly, do inform us that the furnishings of the auditorium, unlike those of the foyers, were disappointingly conventional and, at least in Sembach's mind, "ponderous," while the huge lamp suspended from the ceiling, pedestrian in design, bore no stylistic relationship to the architect's innovative tripartite stage.

The exterior photographic views present us with a low-slung structure, distinguished by an intriguing, if disconcerting mix of rectilinear and curvilinear forms coinciding with the variety of functional spaces inside. The walls are uniformly swept clean of extraneous ornament. As Katherine Kuenzli states it, the theater's "smooth, alternately convex and concave surfaces set off a lively interplay of light and shadow across the building's facade." (Kuenzli: 251) She adds that van de Velde's "rational massing of volumes" signals his "embrace of affordable modern materials." (Kuenzli: 251) Indeed, his use of inexpensive metal and brick, faced with equally affordable stucco, resulted in an edifice whose exterior wall texture suggests reinforced concrete to viewers with only the photos as reference points. (Van de Velde had actually experimented with reinforced concrete in the first decade of the 20th Century, but limited time and financial restrictions prevented him from trying out the still-novel and pricier material in the construction of the theater. Clearly, a more flexible construction schedule and a deeper pool of funds would have allowed him the innovative deployment of a new material, reinforced concrete, equal in importance to Bruno Taut's use of glass for his pavilion.)

In discussing the multiplicity of forms that characterize the theater's exterior, Sembach emphasizes van de Velde effort to "develop a composition which differed according to the point from which it was viewed," noting that a "preconceived unified appearance" played no part in the architect's vision. (Sembach: 194) In fact, the prismatic exterior encouraged visitors to absorb its intricacy actively, by circumambulating around it. A walk around the theater, a kinetic, rather than static experience, offered exposure to the building as a whole that was, for some, puzzling and frustrating, but for others, aesthetically stimulating.

A thoughtful examination of van de Velde's Cologne Theater its shifts in purpose and location, its successive stylistic incarnations is bound to be an exercise in paradox. While the theater was van de Velde's most compelling, visually challenging structure to date, it also marked the end of his design and architectural work in a country that had extended an enthusiastic welcome to the Art Nouveau master 15 years earlier. (Van de Velde was expelled as an enemy alien in 1916.) And while the design and construction of the theater had absorbed his creative time for at least a year, as he adjusted his plans to each change in site and purpose, the theater only hosted only a small number of performances before Cologne Fair events were short circuited by the outbreak of war.

Most disturbing of all, the Cologne Theater, from the outset never planned as a permanent fixture on the German landscape, was razed in 1920, along with the greater number of other, in a few cases magisterial Cologne Fair buildings. The destruction of the theater, reflecting a stunning lack of foresight, constituted a serious loss to architectural posterity, since, in planning the structure, van de Velde had broken away from traditional ideas "according to which interior arrangements had to be governed by exterior rules." (Sembach: 198) Instead, in what is best termed his "shell design," he "followed the logic of showing only the volume necessary to contain the space required." (Sembach: 198) The apparent incoherence of the shell, the constantly shifting impression one would have as one circled the theater, was a direct outgrowth of van de Velde's striking architectural audacity. Thus, the greatest paradox we find in discussing the Cologne Theater is the following: what was audacious in 1914 has become the norm in 2015, in public projects of many 20th and 21st Century architects we now applaud.

The Cologne Theater may have vanished as a concrete, physical artifact, but it has nonetheless remained a significant milestone in architectural history, starting with the writings of van de Velde's peers and *Werkbund* colleagues, particularly those involved in the Bauhaus. In 1925, Walter Gropius, who had stood quietly on the sidelines while the titanic theoretical battle between van de Velde and Muthesius raged, included the theater in his book, International Architecture. In one sense, Gropius was accurate in perceiving the theater "as a precursor to an international architecture and eventually to what was labeled the International Style." (Kuenzli: 251) The building did represent a bold foray into the structural precepts that guide modernist architects to this day: elimination of excess surface embellishment; functionality as primary goal. However, as Kuenzli correctly observes, the Bauhaus Director's exclusive focus on the theater's functionality has unduly swayed the critical outlook of historians who followed Gropius's lead. These scholars "have downplayed the building's complex political and elaborate relations between architecture, painting, and stage design in favor of overdetermined notions of simplicity and functionality." (Kuenzli: 251)

It is certainly true that the ensuing decades of scholarly appraisal conditioned by Gropius's near-tunnel vision make it easy to overlook the sculptures, murals, bas reliefs, and ceramics available to the eye in the photographs discussed above. These works of art, the greater number fully integrated with the theater's exterior and interior forms, spaces and wall surfaces, are clearly emblematic of van de Velde's concern for more than bare utility in his plans for the building.

In front of the theater, for example, stands a fountain in the form of a bather by the German sculptor Georg Kolbe. Kolbe's streamlined "Bather" reflects the artist's effort to echo and reinforce the optical qualities of van de Velde's facade. Superfluous anatomical detail is eliminated and abstract form in itself accentuated, so as to create "continuous dynamic contours." (Kuenzli: 251) Kolbe's Matisse-like bather was contained in a large water basin, "where it appeared as an ocular vision and sprayed water jets." (Kunezli: 251) As in Taut's Glass Pavilion, the jets of spray became themselves sculptural elements.

Equally as telling of van de Velde's lifelong attachment to the fine arts, despite his personal abandonment of painting, are quasi-naturalistic sculptures by his *Werkbund* colleague, Hermann Obrist. These included two bas reliefs set into the theater's facade and two more free-standing pieces positioned in side gardens located on the north and south of the theater complex. Of the many artists who contributed murals, bas reliefs, sculpture, and ceramics to the Cologne Theater, only Obrist was, like van de Velde, a *Werkbund* founding member. The two artist/designers, along with ten other artist members, had been dubbed the Twelve Apostles, the Christian reference certainly no accident of careless speech. Indeed, the hint of patronizing sarcasm is hard to ignore.

As Kuenzli, a delightfully lyrical writer, puts it, Obrist's sculpture presented "elaborate, tactile surfaces grounded in the natural world." The undulating plant tendrils carved in the free-standing piece "Movement" expressed "the never-ending vitality of plant life," while the clusters of sculpted grapes Obrist nestled in windows above the garden "appeared more abstract, alternately wave- or leaflike ornaments." (Kuenzli: 251) Moreover, in a daring rejection of convention that would be carried on by the mid-20th Century American sculptor David Smith, Obrist did away with pedestals, in order to make his pieces "more physically present and an integral part of nature." (Kuenzli: 251) So, while in its elaborate detail and realistic borrowings from the natural world, Obrist's sculpture worked at aesthetic odds with van de Velde's ornament-free surfaces and abstract forms, he did share with his *Werkbund* colleague the willingness to circumvent convention, thereby risking adverse criticism by conservative's parties within and without the *Werkbund.*

Are we approaching *Gesamtkunstwerk* here, as we examine piecemeal a brick, metal, and stucco edifice whose purpose or function was the effective presentation of theatrical performances? The building itself, for Muthesius and his followers a somewhat frivolous, self-indulgent Jugendstil caprice, was to those *Werkbund* members with foresight a courageous *démarche* into the future of public architecture and an evocative presence as well. Moreover, the stealthy integration of bas reliefs, murals, ceramics, and sculptures by German artists in sympathy with van de Velde's aesthetic go far in suggesting a Wagnerian "total work of art." But most central in determining the Cologne Theater's contribution to the *Gesamtkunstwerk* ideal is the nature of the performances fostered by van de Velde and his colleagues as they planned the theater's schedule.

Billed as an "Artists' Theater," the Cologne Theater, played host mainly to avant garde Symbolist and Expressionist drama, that is, dramatic events that dispensed with traditional story lines, deploying instead sets, props, costumes, elaborate lighting effects, mime-like gesture and ambient sound contrived to target the audience's emotions directly. Traditional plot trajectory, character development and dialogue played little to no part in these experiences. The theater also welcomed innovative dance ensembles to its exceptionally broad, flexible stage. The predomiminance of avant garde productions reflects an element in van de Velde's wide-ranging interests not commonly appreciated: his abiding fascination with the lively arts, especially when their creators ventured into unfamiliar, experimental terrain.

From 1890 to 1914, for instance, he collaborated with the Symbolist group *Les Nabis* (the Prophets) in numerous interior design projects, most notably those prepared for Siegfried Bing's *Galérie Art Nouveau.* Aware that *Les Nabis* extended their efforts to stage design, he was thus naturally drawn to sets for Symbolist theater contrived by Maurice Denis, the leading member of the group. Those very sets found a home in the Cologne Theater. Onstage, the *Nabis*' attraction to dazzling color materialized in sets consisting mainly of monochromatic panels painted in saturated hues. Moreover, the group's obsession with mystery and ambiguity took concrete form in the shooting of colored light through gauze curtains hung from a scaffolding above the stage. The result, one that transformed actors and stage scenery "into abstract rhythms of line and color" (Kuenzli: 258) spoke to van de Velde's own penchant for abstraction.

By 1914, over two decades separated Henry van de Velde from his relatively brief, but impassioned career as an easel painter. The drawing or painting he did in the intervening period, all of it impeccable in execution, had served mainly to body forth his concepts for built structures and their furnishings. However, perhaps it is not too much of a stretch to name his final project in Germany a work of art in itself, a collaborative piece, his canvas the theater's site on the banks of the Rhine. In addition to designing the intricate structure, he had mobilized sculptors, muralists, and ceramicists to raise the building from the strictly useful to the genuinely beautiful Then, he had brought the static structure and its thoughtfully chosen and integrated artistic elements to life, in favoring dramatic performances whose directors, set and costume designers, lighting experts, and performers dancers, singers, and actors had been deeply influenced by contemporary movements in the visual arts, specifically Symbolism and Expressionism. That is, van de Velde took his final bow in Germany, if not as an easel painter, definitely as an architect whose bedrock gifts and instincts were essentially artistic.

CHAPTER 12

Strange Bedfellows; Bedfellows Nonetheless

Charles Rennie Mackintosh and Henry van de Velde represented divergent channels of *Art Nouveau*: the geometric and the curvilinear. They differed as well in their decision to continue working as easel artists, or not, in tandem with a long term professional focus on design and architecture. Mackintosh, while passing through many phases in the watercolor medium, never fully abandoned his career as a studio artist. In contrast, van de Velde simply stopped painting altogether in the early 1890s, apart from draughting formal perspective drawings for clients. Both men, however, extended their stylistic inclinations, always informed by technical expertise, into the orchestration and furnishing of their domestic environments.

Van de Velde's first foray into the planning and construction of a home for his family, resulting in the masterful, innovative *Bloemenwerf*, discussed in an earlier chapter. But up until now in this study, attention has *not* been paid to the equally groundbreaking domestic environment Mackintosh, in concert with Margaret Macdonald, fashioned as their first living space. Their Mains Street apartment, unlike van de Velde's succession of three spacious, separate houses set on large plots of land, comprised two stories of an already existing building on one of Glasgow's city streets.

Charles and Margaret occupied their Glasgow apartment at 120 Mains Street from 1900, the year of their marriage, until 1906, when they moved to 78 South Park Avenue. In both the planning and the crafting of their first shared home, they pooled their notions of the most aesthetically satisfying *and* the most workable fit-out for their two-floor living space. The end result was a Mackintosh/Macdonald *Gesamtkunstwerk*, in which everything, "from the general interiors to the cutlery and fire tongs" (Cooper 57), reflected their personal tastes alone, with no conceptual input accepted or interior furnishings purchased from outsiders, apart from the Japanese prints that graced their walls. (Of necessity, however, Charles did hire local artisans to help construct the furniture he and Margaret designed.)

Indeed, the couple was so pleased with the interiors they had together created at the Mains Street address that they went so far as to dismantle the fireplace fittings and move them, along with chairs, tables, wardrobe, bed, light fixtures, screens, and mirrors, to their second address on South Park Avenue. The Mains Street rooms, so progressive for their time, have now been installed a third time in the University of Glasgow's New Hunterian Gallery, with substantial scholarly attention to accurate reproduction of the originals. Visitors to the Hunterian have full access to the surprisingly modernist, two-storey space, but only in the company of a guide, an essential requirement given the age, vulnerability, and irreplaceable nature of the rooms' contents.

Critical to note, at this point, is the University's cavalier demolition of the home's original exterior in 1963. For its reconstruction in 1981, completed a full eighteen years later, the architects chose to erect a "puzzling reinforced concrete shell hung on the side of New Hunterian Gallery." (Crawford 333) While distinctly uninviting, the shell, with its coarse, industrial surface, does re-create the height and orientation of the South Park Avenue home, which stood about a hundred yards away. The parallel here, albeit limited, with the destruction of van de Velde's sweeping, modernist theater, at the close of the 1914 *Deutsche Werkbund* Cologne Fair, is unignorable. In both cases, those responsible for the demolition were either unaware of or indifferent to the historical and architectural significance of the structures they heedlessly sacrificed to the wrecking ball.

In each of the Mains Street rooms, the overall effect, as Cooper notes, is "one of bare and spacious elegance," achieved through the pervasive "white walls, plain grey carpet, and natural pine or black-stained furniture." (Cooper 57) The term "elegance" applies as well to the "dark intimacy" of the dining room on the first level. That so spare and distilled an interior, one that we in our own time would find neither shocking nor off-putting, should have been created in an era when public taste ran to the cluttered and overstuffed, is a tribute to Charles' and Margaret's shared individualism, not mention their exceptional insight into the future of design.

It is probable, for that matter, that the couple, especially the more pragmatic Margaret, construed their private space not only as a domestic haven, but as an experimental prototype that would serve to promote their careers. As, in fact, it did. In 1901, the pacesetting British periodical *The Studio* published an illustrated article by Gleeson White celebrating the apartment in a special summer issue entitled "Modern British Domestic Architecture." And not long afterward, Herman Muthesius, as impressed with the Scottish couple's collaboration as White, singled out the Mains Street rooms for inclusion in his magisterial *Das Englische Haus*. Finally, and further nourishing their reputations, Germany's design periodical *Dekorative Kunst* published a photograph of Mackintosh's ornament-free double wardrobe in its annual 1902 issue. That is to say, Mackintosh and Macdonald had, perhaps inadvertently, perhaps not contrived a living space that became a model for avant garde design in both Great Britain and on the continent.

Two elements in the Mains Street interiors merit particular attention, since they are emblematic of Mackintosh's maverick take on traditional features in British and European homes. The first is the drawing room fireplace, always a necessary, pre-central heating presence in a northern country where winters are long, precipitation frequent, and the atmosphere chilly and damp even in summer. The fireplace Mackintosh installed in the Mains Street drawing room is stunningly sleek. A harmonious integration of straight and curved edges, its unembellished frame is unusually shallow, nearly flush with the wall. Moreover, Mackintosh, in his effort to avoid the intrusive bulk of the conventional fireplace, made little concession to comfort. Guests desirous of basking in the flames' warmth were offered only two flat floor cushions at either side of the fireplace frame. Alternatively, they could resort to a straight-backed chair nearby. In this decision, Mackintosh had obviously favored stylistic refinement over the the easy, inviting welcome of a traditional fireplace setting.

The second feature claiming our attention is the bedroom's four-poster bed, an imposing structure that provides evidence of what Steele terms Mackintosh's "rare ability to transform various divergent references into a cohesive statement." (Steele 99) The bed, virtually a room within a room, is a stripped-down, compact, rectilinear adaptation of a centuries-old structure contrived to ensure uninterrupted sleep in a warm, insulated cocoon. Fashioned of oak, Mackintosh's four-poster is painted white, with glass panels rising at both ends of the bed's frame. As is typical of the four-poster, curtains on either side protected Charles and Margaret from winter's bite when closed or allowed them to savor rare moments of Glasgow's fitful sunlight when open. Importantly for both Mains Street visitors and the Mackintosh scholar, the four-poster's general appearance, streamlined and stripped of surface ornamentation, goes far in disguising the designer's reference to sleeping arrangements that originated in the Medieval period.

For the visitor to the Hunterian, other aspects of the Mains Street rooms will likely be as striking, starting immediately as one enters the two-storey space. Moving through a dark hallway, one eventually confronts a large mirror, mounted so as to catch light from a window in the first room. The mirror is clearly positioned both as an antidote to the hallway's gloom and a strategy for visually expanding a cramped urban space. Charles' and Margaret's (for the most part) successful attempt at enlarging what could have been a claustrophobic urban space visually, if not physically, is again evident in the elimination of all ornament above eye level on the walls of all the Mains Street rooms, downstairs dining room, upstairs drawing and bedroom inclusive.

As to artificial lighting, Charles' affinity with Japanese norms guided his design of simple, geometric hanging lamps, rather than the heavy, elaborate chandeliers favored by his Victorian peers. The lamps, suspended from the ceiling by thin cords, were indeed the apartment's only light source, in a period when electric light was rapidly replacing gaslight throughout Glasgow. So unobtrusive as to escape notice altogether, the rectangular fixtures reinforce the airy quality that defines the Mains Street home as a whole, in particular the second level, where easy access from study-drawing room to master bedroom presages the "open plan" strategy common later in the Twentieth Century.

While Mackintosh, like van de Velde, selectively capitalized on the advantages of industrial production when issues of cost and speed were dominant, he was always mainly preoccupied by what he would have termed the "spiritual experiences" generated by the built and furnished projects he planned, and whose completion he oversaw. In the Mains Street apartment, the primacy of this concern is manifest in the progression from dark to light one experiences as one climbs the stairs from the somber first floor dining room, with its black-stained table and chairs, to the second-floor studio-drawing room and bedroom, open not only to each other, but to the light streaming in from tall windows on all sides. Here, again, both walls are painted white, as is the adjustable, full-length, standing mirror that so captivated Viennese visitors to Scottish Rooms at the Eighth Secession Exhibition.

In sum, the impact of one's ascension from the first to the second Mains Street level can be described as one of emotional, spiritual, and straightforward optical illumination, with an undercurrent of relief and joy at entering so bright and open a space. Of course, this dramatic transition was precisely the experience Charles and Margaret had hoped for in their preparations for their first shared dwelling.

While the development of the Mains Street interior drew on the couple's applied art skills and stubbornly idiosyncratic tastes, the home asked nothing of Charles' architectural, engineering, or infrastructural expertise. The stylistic and functional decisions were made in response to the spatial and material realities of an existing built structure. In fact, throughout their marriage, a deeply loving, but childless one, Charles and Margaret applied their respective craft skills and stylistic predilections only to the Mains Street apartment, later transported "as is" to South Park Avenue. In Walberswick and in Provence, they either rented rooms or cottages or stayed in hotels, while carrying out their creative work elsewhere, in rented studios.

Van de Velde, by contrast, was responsible for both the overall architectural form *and* the interior layout and furnishing of three successive homes, all of them intended as welcoming havens for his large family, as well as sites for his professional work. Starting with *Bloemenwerf,* he purposely arranged for a smooth elision between living and office/studio space, so that he could easily shift his attention from family to professional matters without leaving the house. (Note that, from the mid-1890s until his move to Berlin in 1901, h maintained and expanded his commercial design firm, with its show rooms, expert craftsmen, and specialized tools and machinery, in Brussels, while living in *Bloemenwerf.* Nevertheless, clients often paid visits to his model home in Uccle, and much of his theoretical work was carried on there.) In addition, van de Velde and Maria Sethe invariably chose tracts of land in natural settings for their villa-like houses, in areas where urban growth had not yet begun its encroachment.

Bloemenwerf, built in 1896, was van de Velde's initial foray into domestic planning. *Hohe Pappeln*, constructed twelve years later in Weimar, was the second. Co-opting the name his five-year-old son Thyl gave to the new residence, van de Velde called the impressive structure, built in the period 1907-1908, "The House Under the Tall Poplars" (*Hohe Pappeln*). Its completion in 1908 coincided with the year of van de Velde's initial involvement with the *Deutscher Werkbund*, an intense engagement that seems not to have interfered with his administrative and teaching duties at the *Kunstgewerbeschule.*

Given the stunning range of his intellectual, political, educational, and creative activities in the years 1907-1908, van de Velde's state of mind should have been a stable and optimistic one. Instead, the period marked a crisis in his career, and for good reason. Van de Velde's appointment to the directorship of Weimar's Applied Arts Academy, as well as his welcome into the predominantly German *Werkbund*, are indeed well documented. But a series of proposals for major architectural projects that were ultimately rejected, such as an elaborate plan for a museum on the *Champs Élysées*, have not received nearly as much scholarly attention. These rejections, for proposals whose guiding concepts, as well as carefully wrought renderings, he had labored over for months, were deeply disheartening for the sensitive Belgian.

Therefore, *Hohe Pappeln,* with its quiet, peaceful setting and spacious, multi-room interior geared primarily for comfort, was a refuge not only from the demands placed on van de Velde at the *Kunstgewerbeschule* and at *Werkbund* meetings, but from psychological distress.

In general appearance, *Hohe Pappeln* closely resembled its Uccle predecessor, although there were marked differences in general layout and structural detail between van de Velde's first residence in Belgium and his second in Germany. Like *Bloemenwerf*, the Weimar home was sited in a leafy, secluded neighborhood, but, in this case, the guiding objective was the creation of a retreat for van de Velde's family. Consequently, while van de Velde did use his private study in *Hohe Pappeln* for theoretical and polemical writing, as well as renderings for prospective clients, he did not, as he had *Bloemenwerf*, envison *Hohe Pappeln* as a showcase for his stylistic innovations.

The sheer size of his family surely accounted, at least in part, for the change in focus. By the time van de Velde and Maria Sethe moved to Weimar from their lodgings in Berlin. They had four daughters and one son, a fact that explains the greater emphasis not only on comfort, but on privacy and security than in earlier years. (That is not to say, however, that van de Velde was indifferent to the aesthetic and stylistic impression his Weimar home made on his Weimar colleagues and students, and guests from Berlin.)

The exterior structural similarities between *Hohe Pappeln* and *Bloemenwerf* noted above are clear. As in his ground plan for *Bloemenwerf*, in his scheme for *Hohe Pappeln,* van de Velde avoided conventional boxy, right-angled, straight-edged forms "in favour of bevels, curves, and protrusions." (Sembach: 130) As Sembach points out, the end product, a polygonal structure whose "entire design [is] broken at a number of points," looks "more formally complex than its actual volume would lead one to expect." Moreover, "As you walk around it, the house presents far more aspects than the usual four viewpoints could possibly offer" (Sembach: 130), an observation Sembach also applies to his description of the process of circumambulating van de Velde's Cologne Theater. Thus, a pattern in the architect's priorities and biases emerges: avoidance of sharp right angles, along with a taste for intriguing, usually sudden, sometimes befuddling changes in the viewer's perception of the three-dimensional whole as he or she circles the structure.

Photographs of *Hohe Pappeln* reveal not only the rather confusing variety of functional elements on its exterior—window groupings of different widths and heights set into the walls, multiple balustrades, also of different sizes—but a cape-like shingled roof that seems to envelop the building more fully than its counterpart for *Bloemenwerf.* Indeed, the roof "almost completely encloses the end of the upper storey," (Sembach: 130) suggesting again that van de Velde's chief preoccupation in *Hohe Pappeln*'s design, conscious or not, was the safety and protection of his family. The roof does in fact suggest a sheltering, impermeable carapace.

That the Weimar home was conceived above all as a family retreat, rather than an experimental prototype open to the public, is yet more evident in its interior. The general configuration is that of a ship, with the main and side hallways, or axes, running parallel to each other, as opposed to intersecting at right angles as they would in a traditional private home. As a result of this organizing principle, the ground floor rooms—dining room, living room, drawing room, and study—run in linear succession through the length of the house.

That said, however, van de Velde's concept was not driven by the need for the symmetrical spatial arrangement essential to the design a ship. The original ground floor rendering bears this observation out, since, in the distribution of interior spaces, one side of the house is decidedly more complex, or simply more extensive and busier than the other. So, we can conclude that, as was true of *Hohe Pappeln*'s exterior structure and detailing, van de Velde's mapping of his home's interior reflected his characteristic independence in its departure from predictable, time-honored norms.

As for the rooms, themselves, their shapes, dimensions, and furnishings, the van de Velde predilections outlined above are again apparent in period photographs. The architect's study is a case in point. Initially envisioning a perfect octagon, van de Velde eventually chose to break into the study's matched eight sides and thereby extend the total area of his work space by 50%. (Symmetry, again, was not a concern.) The locus of the architect's theoretical and creative efforts, the study, is fitted out with two desks, their slim, unobtrusive forms installed, again idiosyncratically, so as to face two separate walls set at 45 degree angles to each other. One desk is aligned with a wall surface literally coated with bookshelves, while the other looks directly out a window. The desks are strictly utilitarian presences, "almost melting into the other fitted furniture," (Sembach: 134) as was frequently true of the seating in Mackintosh's projects in the same, early Twentieth Century period.

Not at all surprising, in the work space of a designer/architect who had devoted years of his youth to easel art, is the presence in the study of two sculpted portraits of van de Velde by contemporary masters: a bronze portrait head by the Constantin Meunier, and a second, also in bronze, by the Georg Kolbe, the latter sculpted in 1913 in celebration of van de Velde's 50th birthday. The presence of fine sculpture by accomplished practitioners in van de Velde's study is telling in terms of his evolution toward design and away from easel art.

As discussed earlier, van de Velde, while an accomplished, versatile, and disciplined painter, had decided to dedicate himself to the applied arts exclusively in 1893, a decision made neither hastily, nor, psychologically speaking, easy.While throughout his long career, van de Velde continued to apply his gift for drawing to meticulous perspectives for clients, his abandonment of easel art for its own sake, *l'art pour l'art*, after 1892, was indeed total. Instead his passionate attachment to the fine arts was re-directed into an active appreciation of the painting, sculpture, and graphic work of his European peers. While he no longer painted himself, he collected the work of others.

We see further proof of this fervent appreciation in the *Hohe Pappeln* drawing room. Prominently displayed in this rather cluttered, but comfortable *and* comforting environment was a portrait of Maria Sethe with three of her children, painted by Théo van Rysselberghe. In close proximity was a sculpture by Georges Minne. Like Meunier, Kolbe, and von Rysselberghe, Minne was, in his own time, a well-respected studio practitioner with decidedly modernist leanings. The presence of his experimental work in van de Velde's domestic environment indicates that, while the Belgian master had for years been uncertain of his own artistic bent, he recognized and appreciated singular stylistic clarity in his fine art contemporaries.

Informally furnished, with relaxation in mind, the *Hohe Pappeln* drawing room, was hardly a showroom, as was its Mackintosh/Macdonald counterpart on Mains Street. Fitted, or more accurately put, jammed into a limited space was a grand piano, Maria Sethe's desk, three small sofas, and a group of chairs designed, of course, by van de Velde himself. The curvilinear, upholstered chairs, unlike much of the furniture installed elsewhere in *Hohe Pappeln*, were not designed expressly for the Weimar residence, but did epitomize an earlier period in van de Velde's development as an *Art Nouveau* designer.

Given this mix of elements, the furnishings representative of successive stages of van de Velde's stylistic evolution in the applied arts, combined with the painting and sculpture signifying his steady devotion to the fine arts, the drawing room gives us a solid grasp of a singularly protean designer. But, like *Hohe Pappeln*'s exterior, whose visual impact was altered with each change in the observer's viewpoint, the drawing room and the interior as a whole also generated a fair amount of visual confusion. It is all the more noteworthy, then, that the museum he designed for a Dutch couple's massive, selectively chosen art collection in 1925, two decades later, should stand out for its minimalist exterior, well lit, uncluttered galleries, and quality of serenity throughout. The museum is not only van de Velde's paean to the visual arts themselves, but representative of a major sea change in his stylistic outlook, one that, stylistically speaking, severs his connection to the *Art Nouveau* movement.

His Van de Velde's climactic argument with Muthesius regarding standardization now three years past, and acutely aware of his perceived status as "enemy alien," van de Velde left Germany with his family for Switzerland in 1917. Politically neutral, the trilingual, tricultural nation, with its mountainous terrain, provided what the Belgian artist/designer/ architect clearly needed at the time: an escape from the growing suspicion and hostility he and his family faced every day in Weimar.

Fortunately for both van de Velde and architectural posterity, the wealthy Dutch couple Anton and Helene Kröller-Muller contacted him in 1919 with a request for the design of a museum that would house their sizeable collection of modern art. For van de Velde, both the scope of the project and the potential financial reward were most welcome. Of even greater importance, given his ongoing dedication to the visual arts as an appreciator and collector, if no longer a practitioner, the project gave him the opportunity to create an exhibition space on his own, idiosyncratic terms.

Van de Velde's original plans for the museum, while radically altered later, were nothing short of grandiose. The scheme reflected a short-term, wrongheaded bent for monumental structures poorly suited to his native architectural gifts *and* to the buildings' practical purposes. Nevertheless, like many architects in high middle age, van de Velde tended at that point to focus his attention on large scale public projects he felt would ensure his place in the architectural canon. With the sweeping, innovative Cologne Fair Theater reduced to rubble, the opportunity to design and supervise the construction of another expansive architectural landmark, again in service to the arts, seemed the perfect antidote to the horror of the *Werkbund* theater's demolition.

The first stage of van de Velde's plans offered his patrons a fortress-like edifice of "quasi-Egyptian massiveness" (Sembach: 23). Sembach points to what is obvious to us now: the lack of correspondence between the prospective structure's internal function and its external extravagance. "Cyclopean walls were designed to enclose gigantic halls, intended to contain only a few pictures." (Sembach: 29) In fact, like so many major contemporary museums designed by 21st Century "starchitects," the building itself, if completed, would have surely pre-empted the curiosity of visitors, distracting them from the art work on display inside. Fortunately, however, the museum in its initial form, an expensive proposition in both materials and labor costs, was never completed. Rampant inflation throughout Europe, especially in Germany in the years following its defeat in 1918, rendered the museum in its earliest incarnation unaffordable for the Kröller-Mullers.

While the notion of a museum for the couple's collection floated in limbo for years after van de Velde's first abortive effort, he did become the Kröller-Mullers' private architect, a position that was at once secure and professionally isolating. Freed temporarily from financial worries, he was nonetheless cut off from mainstream architectural developments, certainly those that had their seeds in Bauhaus theories and design workshops, as well as collegial connections in Belgium and Germany.

By 1925, however, it had become clear to all three parties invested in the museum's creation that, while bringing the structure as originally envisioned into being was impossible, a smaller, pared-down version lay within financial reach. The resulting "transitional museum," the term applied to van de Velde's distillation of his initial concept, had a liberating effect on the long-frustrated architect. In Sembach's eloquent words, "from the heart of the colossus sprung the modest core. The massive chrysalis fell away, releasing clear, simple architecture." (Sembach: 29)

Fortunately, we can glean from aerial photographs both the vision behind the original plans and the museum's eventual, concrete realization. In the photos, we see two architectural wings with bulbous ends built on to a roughly square central section, forming what must have initially been a symmetrical pattern. But, as is characteristic of many van de Velde projects, there is a break in the symmetry, caused by an extension of one wing, an addition visible on the photo's left side. According to Sembach, the extension played no part in the original scheme. Doubtless, then, van de Velde's aversion to settled regularity, an aversion manifest in so many of his earlier projects, generated this upset of the building's original, and quite pat symmetry.

Van de Velde's radical alteration of his original plan is further evident in the museum's strikingly plain exterior surfaces, surfaces devoid not only of ornament or protrusions, decorative or functional, but also of windows, save small ribbon windows set very high on the walls. Indeed, the modified structure, with its remarkable modernity, "seems like a simplified model for an old design," since, "the exterior is not overloaded, but determined by precise organization of mass" (Sembach: 208). "Mass," in fact, is the noun best applied to the Kröller-Muller Museum exterior, which is a series of clean, seemingly impenetrable walls defining a low-slung structure whose contents, those meticulously chosen paintings, drawings, and sculptures, will reward those who enter its precincts with their innovative qualities.

The museum's central core, a "wreath-like sequence of rooms around an inner courtyard," (Sembach: 208) presents another break with architectural tradition. In a then-highly unusual procedure, van de Velde fit alternate galleries with open corners. "Every second corner is missing, a bonus, as corners are not useful in museums." (Sembach: 208) Indeed, the minimizing of sharp distinctions between one exhibition space and another permits smoother movement from one room to the next, thus enhancing the visitor's grasp of the Kröller-Muller collection as a cohesive corpus of modernist art. Moreover, ill at ease as well with conventional right angled corners, van de Velde chamfered those that remained, so that their faceted edges contributed further to the fluidity noted above.

The broken symmetry, the plain, unembellished exterior surfaces, the softening or elimination of sharp corners inside, all indicate a momentous change in van de Velde's handling of purpose-built architectural structures, and a radical, rather than a gradual rejection of Nineteenth Century European norms and expectations.

The departure makes itself known again in the enclosed courtyard, the tower-like presences in each corner of the sculpture garden, and the transfer of the museum entrance from the north to the west side. The insertion of a courtyard within an opaque, somewhat forbidding exterior was a successful strategy for opening up the surrounding gallery spaces to more natural light which pours in through the large windows cut into the interior gallery walls. The light, of course, flooded the courtyard on sunny days, slanting as well into the adjoining sculpture gallery.

The mark made by Moorish design conventions on van de Velde's stylistic decisions, especially visible in his Berlin interiors. is obvious here as well. The courtyard has its antecedents in Middle Eastern and North African domestic architecture, as it does in Spanish and Italian homes. A secluded space, the courtyard is insulated from the hurly-burly of the outside world. by thick, seemingly impregnable walls. In like manner, a visit to the Kröller-Muller Museum is a quiet, intimate meditative experience, one protected from mundane intrusions.

As for the corner towers in the sculpture garden, they serve no utilitarian purpose. "In spatial terms, they are not compulsory, but they are extremely solid, in order to counterbalance the pellucid architecture. Their function is essentially *artistic* [italics mine]." (Sembach: 201) The shift of the museum entrance from the north to the west side was, in Sembach's view, the most significant change made to van de Velde's original plan. "The most important alteration, only adapted at the last minute, was the transfer of the entrance to the narrow, western end, entirely changing the orientation of the building, which is now based on a single axis, rather than two intersecting ones as originally planned." (Sembach: 210)

Sembach goes further in noting the similarity between the Kröller-Muller Museum entrance facade and a front view of the demolished *Werkbund* theater, now only available to us in photographs. "Although more austere in detail, it is surprisingly close to the theater in approach and organization. In the interior, movement occurs first from the light and entirely unsolemn entrance hall to the inner courtyard, which is also very light in its effect. All the doorways are open; visitors are never disturbed by doors" (Sembach: 210).

Conceivably, as he supervised the construction of a light-permeated *inner sanctum* for the display of fine art, its modest entryway leading into its spacious, radiant galleries, van de Velde was remembering the luminous stretch of beach on Belgium's North Sea coast, where he had experienced the epiphany that profoundly altered his creative direction. In that solitary setting, the prime mover in the change in his professional intentions had indeed been light itself, the luminosity generated by the reflection of the sun's rays on the shifting waters.

Henry van de Velde neither started, nor bequeathed to posterity, a clearly defined, easily recognized "school" of architecture, as did, for example, Bauhaus leader Mies van der Rohe. However, the Kröller-Muller Museum, finally open to visitors in 1953, did represent a remark-able departure from the *Art Nouveau* stylistic features that characterized van de Velde's craft work and built structures from the mid-1890s on. Its organizational pattern departed as well from the often-maddening irregularity, the seemingly *ad hoc*, intuitive structuring of two of his private homes, *Bloemenwerf* and *Hohe Pappeln*. For that matter, the museum's nearest predecessor, the *Werkbund* theater, its sleek, low-slung exterior prophetic of Finnish architect's Alvar Aato's parabolic forms, also signals the Belgian master's growing impatience with Nineteenth Century stylistic fussiness, including his own.

The Cologne theater was, in fact, a turning point in the development of van de Velde's personal brand of modernism, the development virtually embodied in his succession of plans for the Kröller-Muller commission. Indeed, the result of the evolving plans, the Otterlo Museum, was to ultimately stand as one of many stripped-down, strikingly modernist projects conceived and carried out by van de Velde when he has already well into old age. So, we can conclude that, while he left neither a rigidly codified agenda nor direct descendants in the architectural field, what van de Velde did leave was an impressive record of architectural maturation

Here, three points made earlier merit further consideration, if one is to locate the sources of van de Velde's series of stunning architectural turnabouts. First of all, in the mid-1920s (when he was in his early 60s), he did reach the liberating realization that building large was neither an essential, nor even a useful strategy for winning the fame and respect of his peers he longed for. The initial, failed attempt at placing an imposing behemoth of a museum on the Otterlo urbanscape, a setback that was a blessing in disguise, certainly contributed to his newfound willingness to plan at a more modest, less ostentatious scale. A smaller edifice allowed for tighter focus on the distribution of spaces and greater precision in detail, even as it reduced costs for its patrons. More to the point, the reduction in size compelled the architect to find other ways to convey visually the *significance* of a building, such as eliminating superfluous ornament and protrusions from exterior surfaces.

Secondly, van de Velde's tendency to avoid social and professional contact with fellow architects, a predilection formalized by his contractual obligation to the Kröller-Mullers, may have served him well in the end, since the distance he maintained from fellow architects at no point precluded friendships with artists, writers, composers, engineers, and politicians. This broad spectrum of personal connections served to nourish both his wide-ranging, acquisitive intellect and his deep appreciation of *all* the arts, without intruding on the creative processing that informed his design and architectural decisions. For that matter, he had only to observe and analyze the innovative structures emerging in Belgian, Dutch, and German cities in the early Twentieth Century, in order to profit from their inventiveness in form and materials enabled by technological advance. Socializing with the architects who conceived them might well have proven more distracting than rewarding.

Thirdly, and crucial to a full understanding of van de Velde's creative trajectory, was the steadfast devotion to the (non-utilitarian) fine arts emphasized repeatedly in earlier chapters. Admittedly, that none of his carefully crafted, often moving paintings graced the walls of his private homes, not to mention the museums he designed, does give one pause. Was he too dissatisfied with his own efforts to exhibit his own work side by side with that of established artists, one might ask? Would the day-to-day presence, particularly on his own walls, of paintings accomplished in his youth, generate nostalgia too painful to be endured? Or were his the pieces simply ill-suited to the interior design schemes he conjured for clients and for his own family? Very likely, all three factors informed, to some degree, his decision to exhibit only the paintings, sculpture, and graphic work of celebrated contemporaries, while storing, or hiding his own.

Nevertheless, throughout his long career, van de Velde carried into his applied art and architectural projects the thoughtful, idiosyncratic approach to stylistic decision-making, which he'd developed as a young man dedicated to making works of art with no practical function. Trusting his instincts, he'd drawn from more than one ethnic, cultural, and national tradition—Japanese, Moorish, Dutch, and, of course, Belgian—in designing furniture, servingware, carpets, mirror frames, book covers, and buildings that bore little resemblance to those of other designers and architects.

Moreover, in none of his projects was concern for utility prioritized at the expense of expressive or aesthetic considerations. The creative individualism he'd fought for so passionately at the 1914 *Werkbund* Congress, the outrage at the very *notion* of standardization, finds its embodiment in the eclectic corpus of work left by an *Art Nouveau* master who began his extraordinarily productive 70-year career as an easel artist.

While van de Velde endured a particularly disturbing exile from his adopted country, Germany, toward the end of World War I, Mackintosh suffered another sort of exile from his own a year before the war began, albeit one not so existentially threatening as demoralizing. The year 1913 marked the dissolution of Mackintosh's partnership with Honeyman and Keppie, followed by a frustrating and ultimately failed attempt at starting an independent practice. Professionally stalemated and in serious financial straits, Mackintosh and Macdonald closed down their home on South Park Avenue, their last in their native Glasgow, and moved to Walberswick, in Suffolk, England. At this point in his career, Mackintosh was suffering a personal crisis of confidence, one echoed,and probably fed by a general crisis affecting the whole of Glasgow's architectural profession. Geographically remote as was this once-vibrant shipbuilding center, its economic vitality was now sapped by the threat of the war that would break out in 1914. It is both sad and ironic to note that, just fifty years earlier, Glasgow had seen a flowering of architecture that would never be matched in the Scottish city again.

Mackintosh's personal crisis was twofold. In 1913, at the mature age of 45, he confronted on a daily basis clients and colleagues whose faith in his ability to complete architectural projects successfully and on time was rapidly fading. Further, routinely fielding expressions of distrust in those who had eagerly sought his services in the past went far in eroding the self-esteem essential to his productivity. By 1913, the public view of the Scottish master, a view Steele deems "exaggerated and scurrilous," was of an arrogant, drunken man who had been "carried" for years by his Honeyman and Keppie colleagues. (Steele 63)

However, Steele, an ardent Mackintosh champion, does concede, that there was justification for the derision levelled at the maverick Scottish designer, a protean creative figure who had long been deemed Great Britain's leading architect by such influential critics as Hermann Muthesius. Severely criticized for his failure to meet deadlines, Mackintosh was in fact ill-suited to the strictures of office routine. (steele: 63) He was also, in truth, a notoriously heavy drinker. In lean times, such as those in 1913, his erratic work habits and alcoholism could only be destructive to a firm already on shaky ground financially.

The move to Walberswick was not a voyage into unknown territory. Charles and Margaret had already visited the English fishing village in 1897, and in again in 1900, for a stay with their friends, the Newberrys. Although the specific dates remain uncertain, we know that the couple's final, extended sojourn in Walberswick ran from late 1913 to summer, 1915. Moreover, their choice of Walberswick as a haven, an escape from public and professional calumny, *and* the demoralizing ebbing away of architectural commissions, rested on more than its peaceful atmosphere, its proximity to water, and its inexpensive lifestyle. For Mackintosh, an erstwhile painter of Scotland's wildflowers and native plants, Walberswick was a treasure trove of flora, a lush, verdant paradise.

During his months in Suffolk, he produced more than forty superb watercolors, mostly of plants and flowers. "intended to be compiled into a book by a German, rather than a British publisher, until the First World War intervened." (Steele 63) Steele not only applauds the high quality of the paintings, but sees them as irrefutable evidence of Mackintosh's mental clarity at the time, notwithstanding his chronic resort to alcohol for solace. "The assurance of line, judicious use of colour and composition and skill in detail mark them as some of the best watercolours of his career, hardly the product of someone suffering from delirium tremens." (Steele 63)

Walberswick itself was in economic decline when Charles and Margaret arrived in late autumn, 1913. The town had lost its two pillars of economic stability. A once-thriving cloth industry, conducted as a cottage enterprise before the Industrial Revolution, had been displaced by large, mechanised factories to the north, while Walberswick's fishing fleets were severely diminished. Nevertheless, "the village retained sufficient character to become a haven for creative people, especially artists who were described as working against time to finish before the buildings fell down." (Steele 63)

So, resettled in a quiet community composed, in large part, of fellow artists, far from Glasgow's troubled and troubling architectural scene, Charles could reset his emotional gears and return to his first love: painting. Significantly, in Walberswick, his bitter turn against architecture in recent years extended to the subjects he chose to paint. Not one of his Walberswick watercolors records the town's two outstanding historic landmarks: St. Andrews Church and a windmill dating back to England's pre-industrial past.

For Mackintosh, the town's main appeal was indeed its abundance of flora. Suffolk fen was covered with flowering plants sea pinks, sea milkwort, slender trefoil, and sea lavender, while both its private manorial holdings and parish lawns and gardens were alive with laurel, oxlip, anemone, wood spurge, and butcher's broom. In Suffolk, then, Charles was rediscovering a varied natural cosmos he had been forced to marginalize during the years devoted exclusively to architectural commissions. However, nearing middle age and with substantial professional achievement under his belt, Mackintosh could not simply duplicate the experiences of his youth. The Walberswick watercolors reflect his evolution from wide-eyed, spontaneous draughtsman, setting to paper all he encountered in the Scottish countryside, to seasoned designer/architect, always alert to the specific visual qualities that had driven his work from the outset.

While he frequently walked the uncultivated fields around the village, in Walberswick, Mackintosh focused his artistic energy primarily on gardens, even, in a few cases, pressed flowers, rather than untended stretches of wildflowers and plant life in the Suffolk countryside. It is estimated that two thirds of the documented flower drawings and watercolours illustrate cultivated plants the herbaceous perennials, bushes and trees of gardens. (Steele 71) Of course, accessible, freshly cut annuals and perennials, such as jasmine, rosemary, and petunias, planted in groomed gardens, could be arranged in and out of vases to fit a compositional pattern Mackintosh had already begun visualizing in his mind.

The Mackintosh eye for particularity was as keen and observant as any in art history, his hand as deft, but the Scottish master was never as concerned with botanical accuracy as, for example, his Florentine ancestor, Leonardo da Vinci. For example, "Larkspur" (1914) illustrates the "mixture of botanical correctness and individual expression that characterizes Mackintosh's flower designs during this [Walberswick] period." (Steele 69) In these watermedia paintings, paintings, his instinctive tendency to reshape, as well as respond accurately to existing shape, is complemented by what Steele terms "interesting parallels" between the Walberswick paintings and his work in other media, "especially in the balance of curvilinear and rectilinear forms." (Steele 71) In "Fritillaria" (1915), for instance, the balance is obvious, as is the similarity between the plant's lattice-like patterning and the checked patterning so pervasive in the furnishings designed for patrons in Glasgow and Vienna.

Throughout the Suffolk years, Charles and Margaret kept their domestic and studio lives separate. Once settled in a cottage, they proceeded to rent a riverside studio, an affordable shared space where Charles could resolve to his satisfaction watercolors he had roughed out and and partially completed outdoors. Of course, in the weatherproof studio, he could also develop floral images taken from cut flowers arranged in vases or resting, untouched by the elements, on table surfaces.

But, in the end, Mackintosh had always been most comfortable painting outdoors. In the 1880s and 1890s, he had roamed in and around Glasgow and the north of Scotland, then into England, there sketching local homes, churches, and public buildings in Dorset, Norfolk, Devon, and Somerset His tour of Italy in 1892 had also been an outdoor walking experience, where first hand observation of Classical, Renaissance, and Baroque large scale architectural structures and small functional or decorative details mattered equally.

In Suffolk, Mackintosh lit on Westwood Garden as his primary outdoor workplace. A "landscape in miniature," the garden's stillness and the privacy it offered suited his need for "seclusion, contemplation, and undisturbed study." (Steele 71) Doubtless, at the same time, his mind fairly seethed with memories of the furniture, light fixtures, screens, and mirror frames he had fashioned for clients in past decades. The recollection of their forms and surfaces so infiltrated his Walberswick watercolors that visual continuity between Mackintosh's multi-pronged work in the applied arts in Glasgow and his fine art efforts in Walberswick was inevitable.

Regarding Mackintosh's brief, but immensely productive stay in Walberswick, three additional points should be made. Firstly, while the paintings, as a group, always appear self-validating, the watercolor was actually applied very quickly, with portions of the penciled outline occasionally left incomplete or bare of watermedia. As a result, even when a piece is seemingly "in progress," its meticulous compositional framework and spare, but deft application of color seduces the viewer through a potent impression of freedom and spontaneity. Secondly, and sadly, the promised publication of the work by a German publisher never materialized. And thirdly, despite the floral content of the Walberswick watercolors, there is no documented indication that Mackintosh was, at that point, ready give up altogether his career in architectue. That would not happen until 1923, when Mackintosh and Macdonald made their last move together to Provence. Nevertheless, it is obvious that there was a decided shift in Charles' creative interest in this interim period.

With the outbreak of World War I and the possibility of infiltration or outright invasion by German forces, tensions rose along the British coast. (Steele 73) Mackintosh was obviously neither German nor Austrian, but his strong Scots accent, a nearly impenetrable Highland brogue, combined with his eccentric dress and behavior, maded him an object of suspicion for local townspeople. In daytime, he was an elusive figure, disappearing for long periods in Westwood Garden, or for solitary walks in the fields surrounding Walberswick. At night, he commonly sat alone in the village pubs, the Bell or the Anchor Inn, sporting a Sherlock Holmes deerstalker cap and cape, rather than the familiar fishermen's wool and oilcloth. On some nights, he could be seen walking on the beach, again alone So, in speech, dress, and habits, Mackintosh was definitely an odd man out in Walberswick, even in his relations with other resident artists.

Most suspect of all was Mackintosh's connection to the Viennese cultural community, common knowledge even in tiny, impoverished Walberswick. As Steele relates it, "Things came to a head," when Mackintosh was seen shining a lantern from the top floor window of his Westwood cottage in late 1914. Not surprisingly, given his reputation as an outlander, the gesture was taken as an attempt to signal an enemy ship at sea. In fact, opening the door to his hotel room that very evening, a shocked Charles found a soldier standing guard, "since a search of his belongings had uncovered correspondence from the Viennese Secessionists." (Steele 73)

Although letters from a group of foreign artists hardly suggest subversive dealings with an enemy government, Mackintosh was nonetheless summoned to appear before the Suffolk magistrates and charged with spying. He narrowly avoided detention, "largely due to the efforts of Lady Norah Mears, the daughter of the town planner and leader of the Celtic Revival Patrick Geddes, who pleaded his case with the war office in London" (Steele 73).

The arrest itself, although a legal calamity rather than a professional setback or rejection, was deeply disturbing for Mackintosh, as it appeared to encapsulate all the misunderstandings that preceded it, those directed at his spare, geometric interior design and his innovative built structures. Adherents of the English Arts and Crafts Movement ethos judged Mackintosh a defector from the group's central tenet: a purist return to Medieval handcraftsmanship, unpolluted by modern industrial techniques of manufacture. Conservative Glaswegian architects, designers, and tastemakers saw his progressive stylistic biases as outlandish and uncomfortably avant garde.

With hindsight, then, we see the paradox in Mackintosh's situation: "he was arrested for possession of letters from those who did recognize his talent and singular position in history." (Steele 75) And those admirers were indeed German-speaking foreigners. Soon after the traumatizing arrest and subsequent exoneration, now ill at ease in a setting that had been once a refreshing haven, Charles and Margaret left Walberswick for London in August, 2015.

In London's Chelsea, Charles and Margaret rented studio space at 43A Hans Studios and adopted a lifestyle very much in contrast with their quiet routine in Walberswick. They indulged in extravagant dress, attended and hosted parties, and displayed few signs of the financial distress they had confronted in their last years in Glasgow. In London's "painterly hub of the 1880s and 1890s," their circle of friends included not architects, but painters, musicians, writers and sculptors. They joined theatrical groups, the Plough and Margaret Morris's Theater Club, became involved in the Allied Artists Association and the London Salon of the Independents, and dined at the popular Blue Cockatoo on Cheyne Walk. Chelsea's bohemian, artistic setting was a welcome antidote to the social and creative isolation the couple had felt in Walberswick, even among the town's colony of painters.

Almost immediately, Mackintosh set to work on a residential project that would be his final commission He was asked to make alterations to a small home in Northampton, at 78 Derngate Road. His client, Whynne J. Bassett-Louke, was an engineer who had prospered by supplying the Cunard Shipping Lines with model ships to be used for testing each new design under simulated conditions. Collaborating with an nautical engineer certainly worked to Mackintosh's advantage.

In this, his last achievement as a designer/architect, his own experience working with craftsmen in Glasgow's shipbuilding trades served him well.

The 78 Derngate home was a red brick structure whose overall dimensions were 15' x 24'6." That is to say, Bassett-Louke's living quarters were very small indeed. The modest size, however, was well suited to Mackintosh's gifts He'd shown skill in the past "when faced with the challenge of restricted space, as the tea room projects (especially the Willow) indicate." (Steele 85) This was fortunate, since Derngate offered the architect "a most tightly circumscribe programme," (Steele 85) one that would hopefully make a narrow space seem larger than its measurements and proportions indicated. The Derngate remodeling project required the planning and construction of a 9' 6" x 5' extension on the home's garden side, in addition to transformation of an existing window facing the street into a wider projecting bay window. Mackintosh was also asked to enlarge the home's front room, now named the "lounge hall," by repositioning the staircase, as well as cutting into an exterior wall to create a second, 6' wide bay.

In Mackintosh's imaginative strategy, the repositioned staircase became a sculptural entity set directly opposite the home's entryway. Its location in the lounge hall once accomplished, the staircase was then faced with a gridded wooden screen, which in turn incorporated the door to the dining room beyond. In a feat of harmonious compression, Mackintosh shaped the door so that its stepped upper edge followed the stepped ascent of the staircase (Steele 8).

As noted earlier, Mackintosh had by this time left behind the white-painted surfaces that had marked his domestic interiors in Glasgow and Vienna. Instead, at Derngate, walls, ceiling, woodwork, and furniture were uniformly stained black,so as "to make all the colour seem more vivid." (Steele 85) And rich color there was. Steele writes eloquently of the frieze Mackintosh developed for the lounge hall, which carried across the top of the room's fireplace surround, and along the wall behind the stair. The frieze featured a repeated motif of stylized trees, applied in a chevron pattern and painted in vivid vermilion, gold, grey, blue, green, and white. The stenciled repeat ran along the top third of the wall, "an echo of the tripartite spatial division evolved in increasingly three-dimensional expression from 120 Mains Street to the drawing room of the Hill House. A rarity in our own time, Mackintosh's frieze, its stylized pattern shifting direction with the shifts in direction of the walls, expanding and contracting according to the viewer's perspective, served to increase the sensation of depth in the room.

In addition, in his "determination to use every square inch available to best advantage," (Steele 85) Mackintosh equipped the Derngate residence with an expanded kitchen, the primary element in the extension he formulated for the back of the house facing the garden. Like the facing for the staircase in the lounge hall, the extension's roof did double duty, in this case providing a balcony for the second storey master bedroom which overlooked the lush garden below.

For this last, and thankfully successful project, Mackintosh engaged in what we would now term "subcontracting," supplying expert London craftsmen with drawings for furniture, curtain and upholstery fabric, custom-made lighting, and staircase screen. As was always true of his formal renderings, plans, sections, elevations and perspectives inclusive, the drawings were exhibition-worthy themselves. Most importantly, however, throughout the design and production process, Mackintosh envisioned, as he had for decades, a 'unified space in which each component, at various levels of scale, plays an important part." (Steele 85) One is bound to recall here his insistence on putting his personal stamp even on the landscaping for Hill House, for which he produced masterful ink drawings of trees and bushes as guides for the manor's future gardeners.

This writer is in accord with Steele's high praise for this elegant, efficient *Gesamtkunstwerk*, a model of architectural concision *and* the inadvertent finale to Mackintosh's career as designer/architect. Steele goes so far as to assert that 78 Derngate is "a masterpiece of space planning, the paramount case study for all designers and students today who feel that true creative expression can only be achieved in grandiose proportio" (Steele 85).

During the eight years Mackintosh spent in London, 1915-1923, he continued, however, to address the challenge of still life painting for its own sake, in tandem with his, for the most part frustrating pursuit of architectural commissions. (To bulk up their income, he and Margaret carved out a new creative enterprise, textile design, with moderate success.) Indeed, since the Walberswick years, drawing and painting with no pragmatic goal in sight had become critical to Mackintosh's wellbeing. In his Chelsea paintings, he focused exclusively on bouquets of flowers in watercolors that displayed not only his accumulated wealth of botanical knowledge, but a "hitherto unseen richness of colour" (Robertson 309).

In conjunction with the stylistic changes in his painting, the sojourn in Chelsea witnessed another significant turning point for Mackintosh. While sketching and painting had been largely a private activity for Mackintosh after the mid-1890s, in London he mounted solo exhibitions of his still lifes with the International Society of Sculptors, Painters, and Gravers, in 1916, 1917, and 1918, and at the prestigious Goupil Gallery. These ventures into the public eye, in highly respected venues, run in sharp contrast to the nearly two decades, ca. 1895-1915, when none of his botanical or architectural drawings were exhibited or published. In fact, it puzzles us now to learn that Mackintosh declined to display his sketches and watercolors even in his Glasgow homes, at least as far as contemporary photographs indicate.

And in Turin, in 1902, while Margaret, Frances, and Herbert all showed new watercolor panels in their respective installations, Charles showed instead commissioned graphics and plates from the House for an Art Lover competition folio. What the change indicates is an alteration in self-image: in London, Mackintosh increasingly perceived himself as much an easel artist as an architect.

Pamela Robertson presents an illuminating analysis of the technical and stylistic attributes that distinguish Mackintosh's work on paper (and the surface was always paper) from that of his peers, not only in architecture and design, but in easel art. She points, more than once, to the artist's heavy emphasis on line, but later qualifies her statement in noting that, in all the work, line is limited to *outline,* whose purpose is the expression of form. Shading and cross-hatching, traditional Western strategies for expressing volume, found no place in Mackintosh's technical arsenal (Robertson 293). Clearly, owing to this deceptively simple, but very effective approach to expressing form, Mackintosh's watercolor paintings bear a strong resemblance to the Japanese prints he and Margaret had not only appreciated in friends' homes and in galleries, but collected themselves.

Robertson goes on to define the Mackintosh line as economic, but "eloquent and unhesitating," adjectives commonly applied to the graphic work of Toulouse Lautrec, the Nineteenth Century French artist most influenced by the Japanese *ukiyo-é* printmakers. In terms that border on the poetic, Robertson elaborates in noting that, as Mackintosh deploys his drawing tool, he develops a "continuously moving outline, which crosses and touches and intertwines, defining space as eloquently as it does form." (Robertson 310) There is a *caveat* here, however. in the suggestion of uninhibited spontaneity implicit in Robertson's comment, for rarely did Mackintosh begin the draughting of a pencil, pen, and watercolor image without advance planning. His drawing "required rigorous analysis and editing of the subject prior to placing any mark on the sheet." (Robertson 293) Indeed, Mackintosh would carry on this methodical process of organization and distillation, without resort to preparatory sketches, into the 38 watercolor paintings, some edging up to abstraction, he accomplished during his and Macdonald's last years together in southern France.

As to subject matter, one can trace its evolution from sketchbook studies made in Scotland, England, and Italy, through the Symbolist and decorative paintings completed in Glasgow in the 1890s, followed by floral paintings in the Walberswick and Chelsea years, to the culminating watermedia paintings in Provence. In these final pieces, built structures intersect seamlessly with natural setting. Predictably, each of these evolutionary stages initially demanded uneasy experimentation. However, be it noted that, while willing to venture into new image content, Mackintosh never experimented with materials. Pen, pencil, and watercolor remained his media constants, which he manipulated with ever greater proficiency.

By the early 1920s, Mackintosh was finding himself increasingly estranged from current architectural taste in London. (Robertson 310) This mood of alienation seems unjustified to us now, given that his remodeling of 78 Derngate for Bassett-Lowke shows definite signs of a move into Art Deco's sleek geometry, so popular in the later 1920s. But, 78 Derngate notwithstanding, Mackintosh still saw as little prospect for establishing an independent architectural practice in London as he had in Glasgow in 1913. And once again, he and Macdonald found themselves financially hard pressed.

So, in 1923, in a state of severe disillusionment and depression, Mackintosh and Macdonald prepared for their last move in what had become a peripatetic life. The couple left London for Provence, a destination we instantly recognize as that of other canonic modernists, Vincent van Gogh and Henri Matisse among them. The combined attractions of a (mainly) sunnier climate, dramatic landscapes, and a decidedly less expensive way of life promised a salubrious escape from professional disheartenment. By 1924, Charles and Margaret had settled into a routine, also peripatetic, but with a regularity adjusted to seasonal changes in weather. From 1924 to 1927, they were based largely in the Pyrénées-Orientales, renting rooms in Amélie-les-Bains, Île-sur-Têt, Mont-Louis, and Port Vendres, this last their home base for the greater part of each year. Port Vendres had special appeal for Mackintosh, for reasons of familiarity and attendant nostalgia. The town boasted a bustling port, one whose commercial activity and nautical atmosphere, big ships and small dinghies, piers and loading docks, fog horns, bells, and lapping water, were moving reminders of Glasgow's thriving port on the river Clyde. Port Vendres, in fact, became Mackintosh's favored site for painting. Of the 38 surviving paintings accomplished in Provence, nearly half depict the town, its harbor and the low hills beyond.

In the four years Mackintosh spent in southern France, his chosen subject matter was land-scape, but always landscape in conjunction with the area's manmade structures, many tracing their origins back hundreds, in some cases, thousands of years. As Robertson states it, "The relationship of a hill town to its surrounding landscape of a port to a sea and hills beyond, or a fort to its rock and approaching roads, were rigorously explored from different vantage points" (Robertson 312). Moreover, his interest in landscape had actually surfaced late in his painting career. Only two views of the Suffolk countryside, completed in 1914 and 1915, survive, as do two views of Dorset's rolling hills, executed during a holiday with the artist Randolph Schwabe's family in 1920. In Provence, paintings of an unpeopled landscape, bare of built structures, were also rare. Again, only two remain.

Robertson carries her discussion of Mackintosh's working practice further in her perceptive analysis of his culminating achievement in painting, the body of watercolors he completed in Provence. In forming her conclusions, she synthesizes information taken from the "physical evidence," the paintings themselves, with that taken from the stream of letters written to Macdonald over a six-week period in 1927, when she was in London and Mackintosh remained alone in Port Vendres (Robertson 213).

Robertson begins by addressing the related issues of speed and productivity, always a critical issue for artists who are both invested in excellence and needy of income through the sale of their work. While we tend to understand the creation of a watercolor as a rapid, spontaneous, process, one requiring a deft, confident hand with brush and medium and permitting little or no revision, in Mackintosh's case, technical progress for each piece was actually slow and painstaking. "The Rock," for example, with its stunning frontality, was still unfinished after five weeks of steady work. This is especially surprising, in light of the work's size: a mere 12" x 14 1/2". As was true for all the Provence paintings, the focal subject, the rocky outcropping, was "closely observed and analysed in advance. The lack of any preliminary sketches suggests that this was largely a visual process and the picture made in front of the subject, never indoors" (Robertson 213).

Reiterating her earlier comment, that Mackintosh never worked from preparatory sketches, Robertson now adds that he never developed an image from memory. "Even the earlier flower studies and still life's, though worked in the studio, were painted from life." (Robertson 213) Of course, painting from life, or painting *plein air*, demands that one equip oneself with an artist's paraphernalia, tools and materials essential for getting the image started and, depending on the individual artist's' process, concluded. As *plein air* painters go, Mackintosh travelled exceptionally light. His equipment was minimal: prepared, paper-mounted millboard, tubes of watercolor, enameled palette, dish for mixing the colors, eraser, ruler, pocket knife, brushes, water container, brush washing cup. There is no recorded indication that he also brought with him umbrella, stool, or easel during his daily expeditions, although they certainly would have made his task both easier and more comfortable. More importantly, however, unencumbered as he was, Mackintosh could "scramble to the best locations on rocks or hillsides from which to secure his preferred vantage point" (Robertson 213).

A central issue in any painter's set of concerns is that of composition. Arriving at a satisfying composition was inevitably an exacting process for Mackintosh, given the decades he had spent "composing" interiors for homes, schools, and municipal buildings that, in the main, incorporated influences from a variety of architectural traditions. The composition for each of the nearly fifty watercolors he accomplished in Provence was always predetermined before he began working on-site, Thus, a pencil outline set to paper in advance provided Mackintosh with a compositional framework. Then, his outdoor vantage point established, he applied the watercolor, gradually erasing most, but not all of the outline. Indeed, the remaining residue of the pencil outline is a major factor in the paintings' singular energy.

Perhaps most innovative in Mackintosh's interpretation of his Provençal subject matter was his bold manipulation of content elements. In each piece, different views of each element, natural and manmade, organic and geological, are dovetailed to produce a seamless whole. For "The Rock," for example, Mackintosh painted in the background view of Port Vendres first, from a vantage point in Anse Christine, a bay south of Port Vendres. Then, he moved west to a second point, one that gave him his desired view of the rocky outcropping. Intensifying the drama generated by the three-part counterpoint of sweeping landscape and angular architecture in the back-ground, and steep, imposing rock in the foreground, is Mackintosh's strategic use of dark and light areas played off against each other. (Robertson 213) In other paintings, the dramatic impact is further heightened through his adoption of particularly high or low vantage points, as in the Fort Mailly studies.

A discussion of Mackintosh's astonishing Mediterranean watercolors must necessarily pinpoint not only what they are, but what they are not. Moody and emotionally charged as was their maker, the paintings themselves are not at all concerned with mood or atmosphere in the natural world, as were those of the German Romantic Caspar Friedrich, or with potent natural forces, as were those of the English Romantic J.M.W. Turner, or with nature's textures, as were those of the Dutch landscape masters Hobbema and von Ruisdael. Furthermore, despite Mackintosh's obvious delight in the vigorous, clamorous human activity on the Port Vendres docks there is no depiction of human interchange, not even a sign of human presence, in any the paintings. "Rather, his watercolors depict an immobilized world, unruffled and unpeopled. Out of mundane reality a diminutive rock formation, a modest, ruined fort, or a roadside straggle of houses Mackintosh formulated patterns from shadows, rocks, terraces, fields, and reflections that transformed the subject wthout sacrificing its identity." (Robertson 213)

Charles Rennie Mackintosh passed away in 1928 at age 60, an age that seems to us now relatively young. Unable or unwilling to sacrifice to good sense and the prospect of longevity his dependence on alcohol and tobacco, he died of jaw and throat cancer just as his painted response to the Provence environment was bearing unprecedented fruit. While van de Velde, in maturity, channeled his enduring passion for painting into structures intended not only to house, but to present at their best the studio work of others, Mackintosh, in his last years, was evolving into a maker of two-dimensional images increasingly reflective of his experiences as an architect. The operant term here is "abstraction."

"Fort Mailly," completed one year before his death in 1927, best exemplifies the gradual, but relentless merging of graphic and water media skill with residual architectural instincts that drove Mackintosh's efforts in painting during the final years of his life. Its title notwithstanding, the image is dominated not by the fort, "our fort,' as Mackintosh described it to Macdonald, but by sloped layers of deep gray and taupe-colored rock face. Fort Mailly is a looming, intimidating white structure in the background, and is almost entirely obscured by the front-and-center rock face, which seems itself a fortress. A broken strip of intense blue Mediterranean sky is visible at the top, a small concession to the brilliant, saturated color that betokens Provence in most minds. The seemingly accidental resemblance between the Kröller-Muller Museum's barren exterior walls and the textureless, abstracted forms of both the sloping rocks and the fort itself in "Fort Mailly" is perhaps, in the end, no accident. Van de Velde, while never an on-site member of the Bauhaus group in Weimar, or later in Dessau, was certainly aware of the severe rectilinearity of architectural forms, not to mention the extensive use of glass, that characterized the almost other-worldly structures of Mies van der Rohe and his adherents.

By the same token, Mackintosh was sensitive to, and deeply marked by, the virtually irresistible wave of abstraction that swept through British and continental artistic circles in the early decades of the Twentieth Century. While always moved chiefly by the rich and varied complexity of the organic cosmos, by the late 1920s the impressionable Mackintosh had nevertheless fully absorbed into his artistic vocabulary both the riveting omnipresence of inorganic rockface in Provence *and* the machine-like forms generated by the British vorticists, themselves inheritors of European Cubism and Futurism. No doubt still stubbornly resistant to the possibility that his worsening illness was serious, indeed fatal, he remained until his death the extraordinary creative figure who integrated in his *oeuvre* a host of external influences, while producing a startling range of crafted objects, built structures, and paintings that were entirely original and his own.

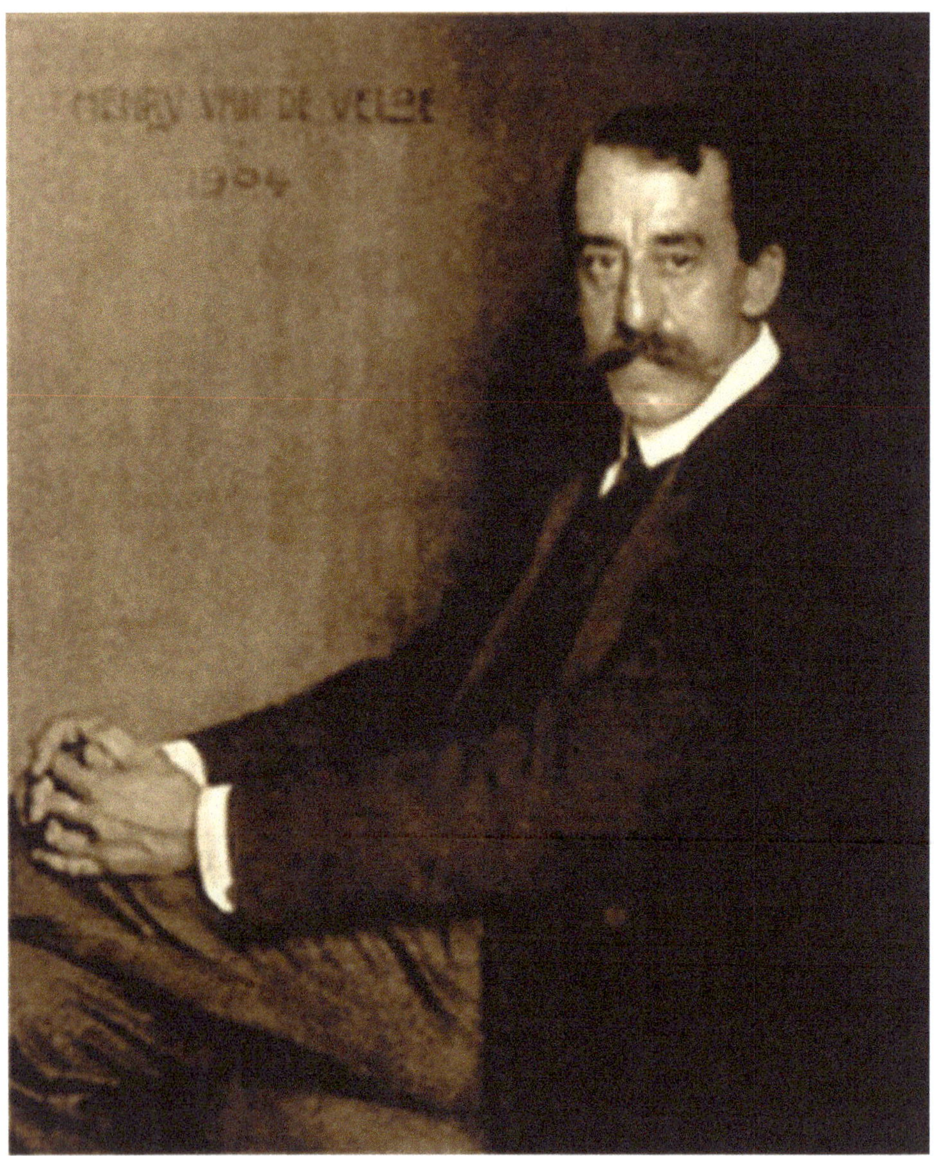

Photograph of Henry van de Velde

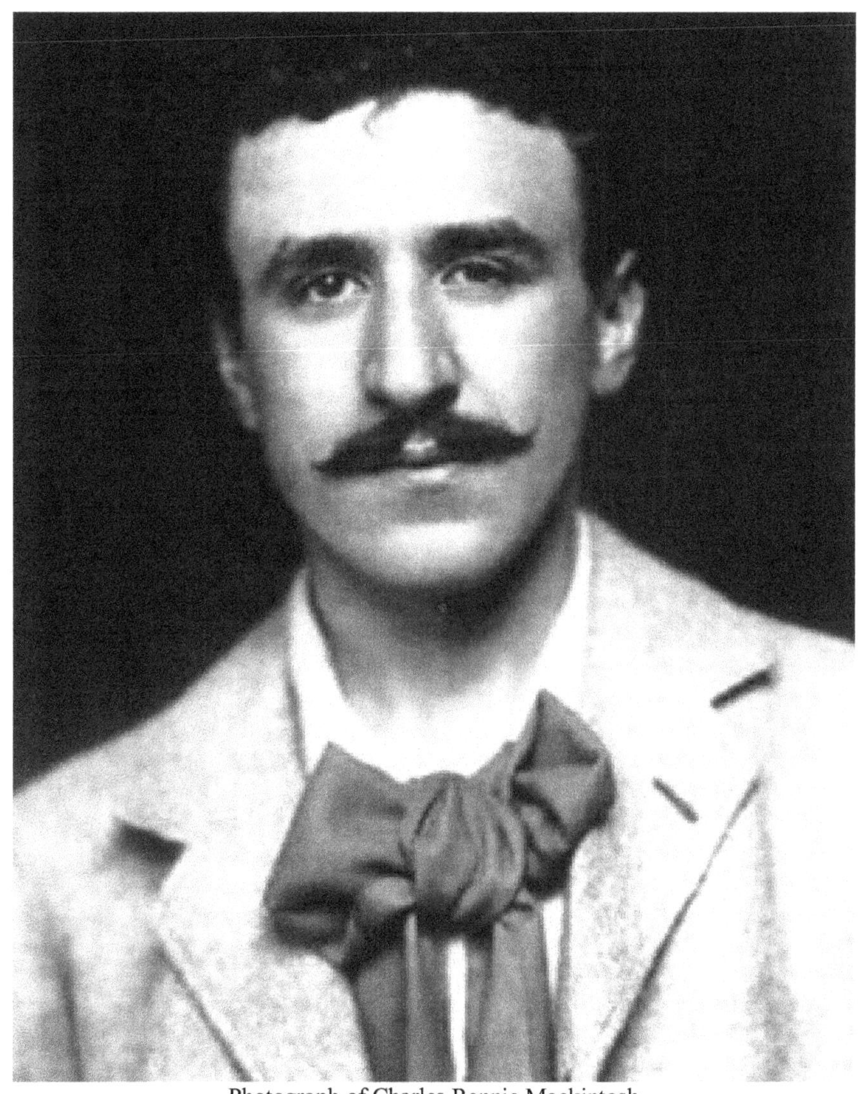
Photograph of Charles Rennie Mackintosh

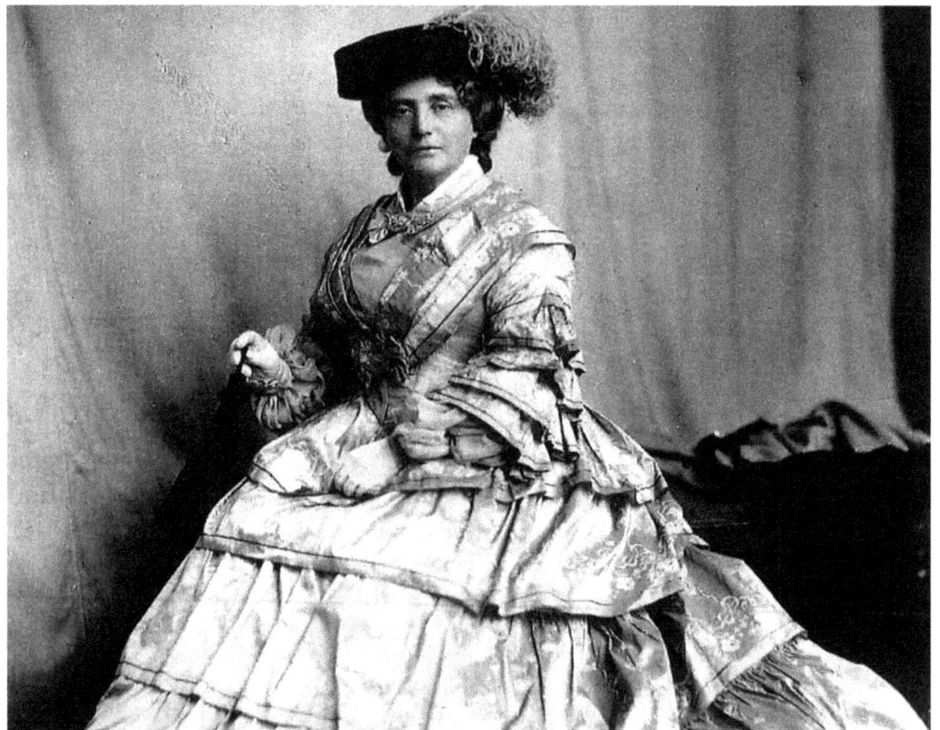

Photograph of Catherine Cranston

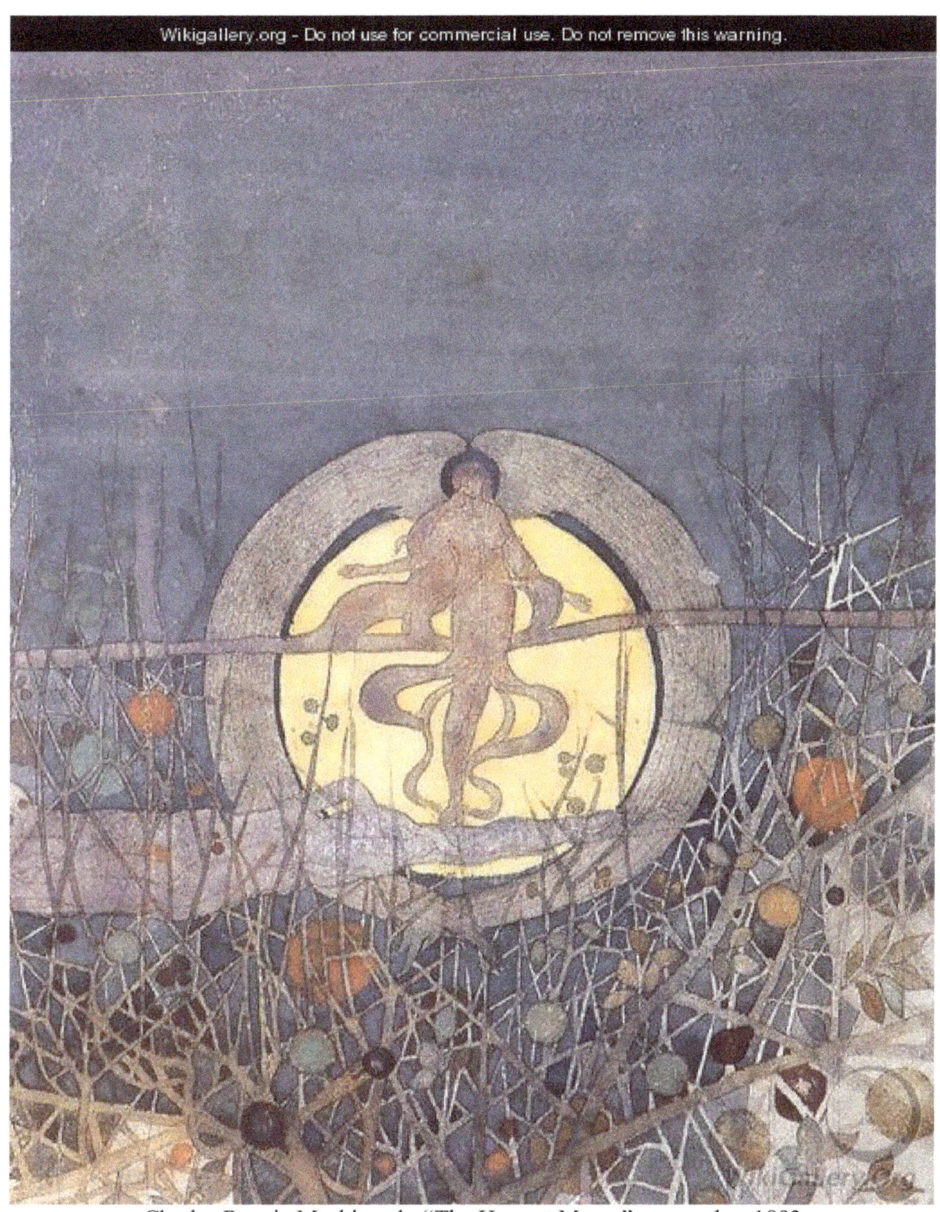

Charles Rennie Mackintosh, “The Harvest Moon,” watercolor, 1892

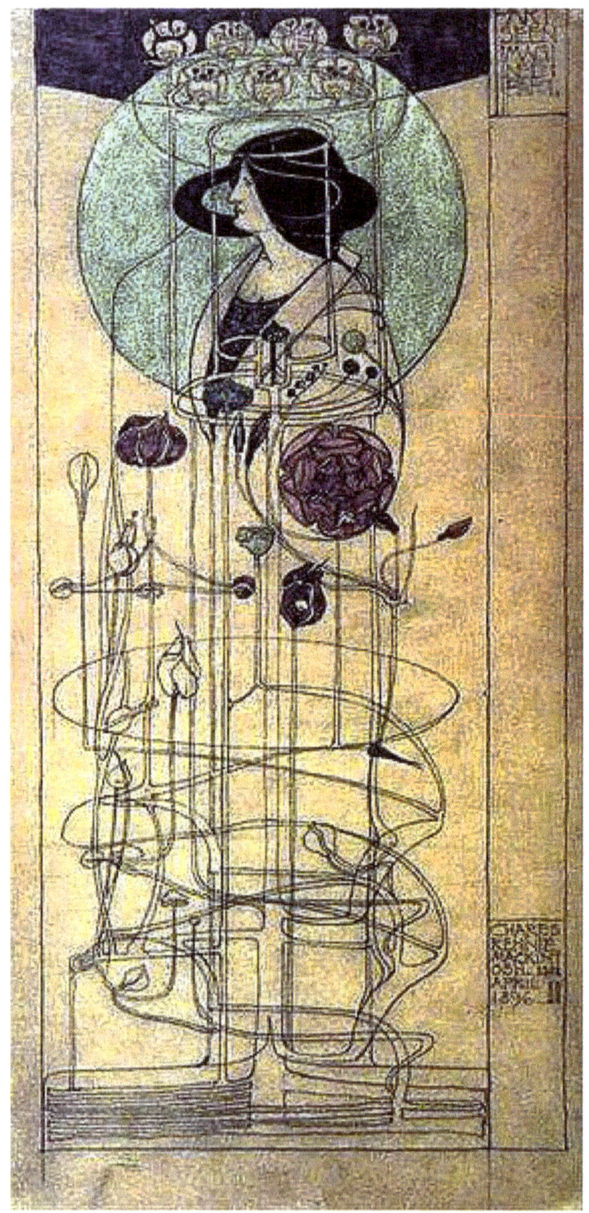

Charles Rennie Mackintosh, “Part Seen, Part Imagined,” watercolor, 1896

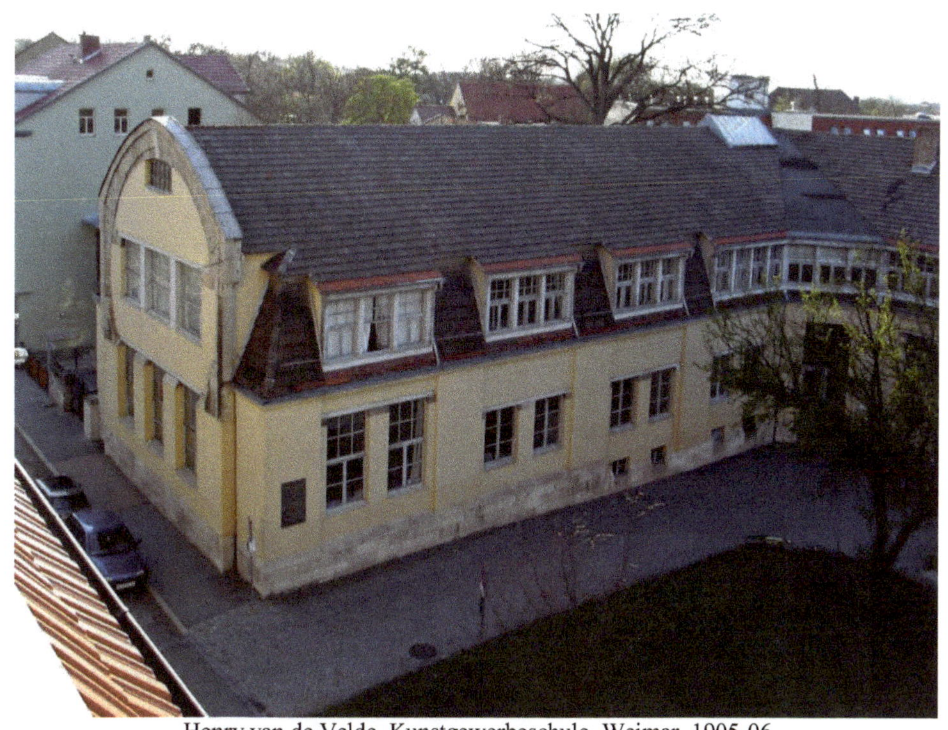

Henry van de Velde, Kunstgewerbeschule, Weimar, 1905-06

Henry van de Velde, Exhibition Theater, Deutscher Werkbund Fair, Cologne, 1914

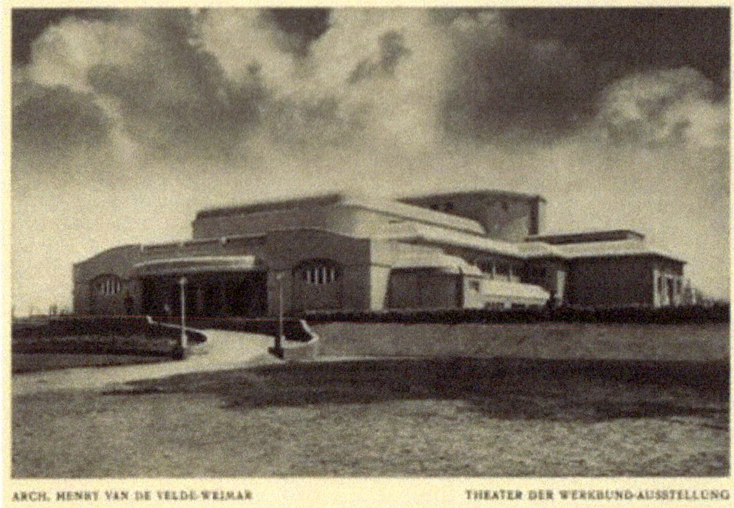

a. Exhibition Theater, exterior view

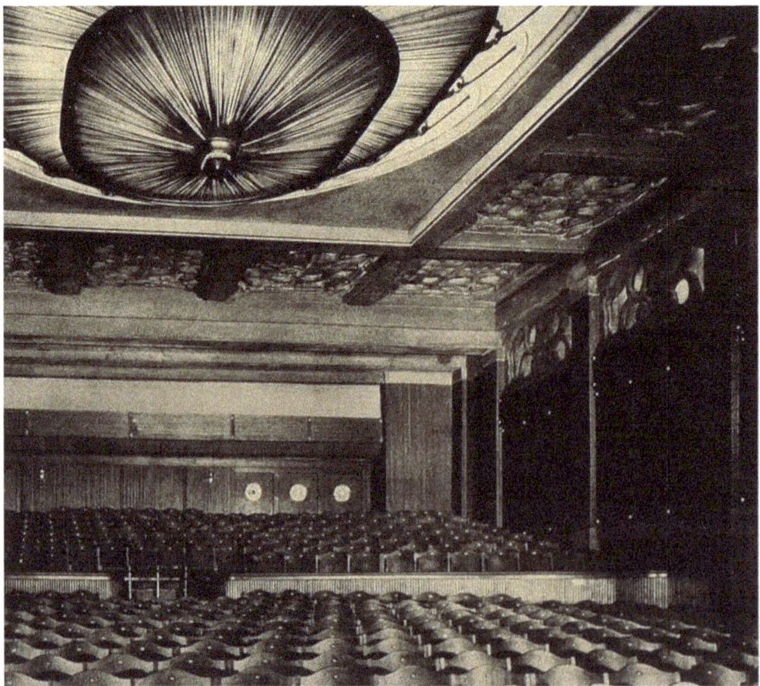

b. Exhibition Theater, auditorium

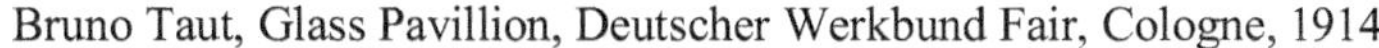
Bruno Taut, Glass Pavillion, Deutscher Werkbund Fair, Cologne, 1914

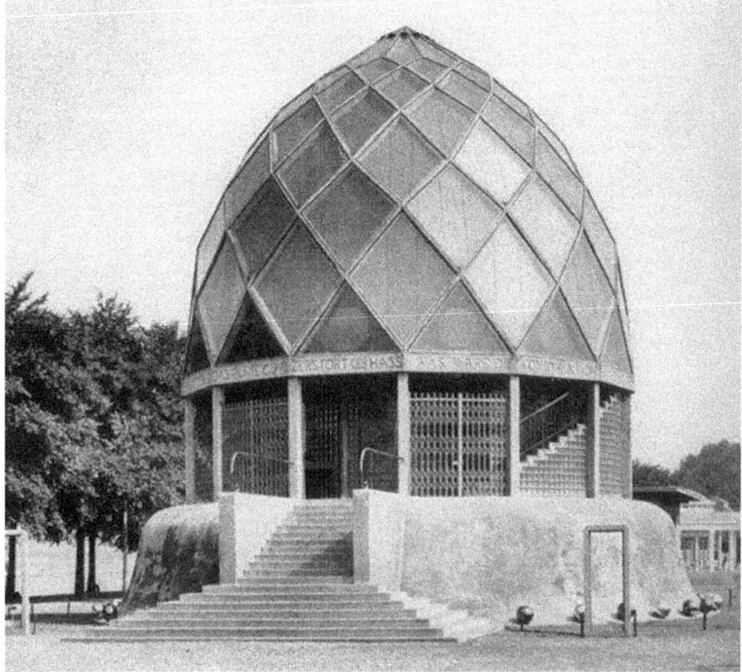
a. Glass Pavillion, exterior view

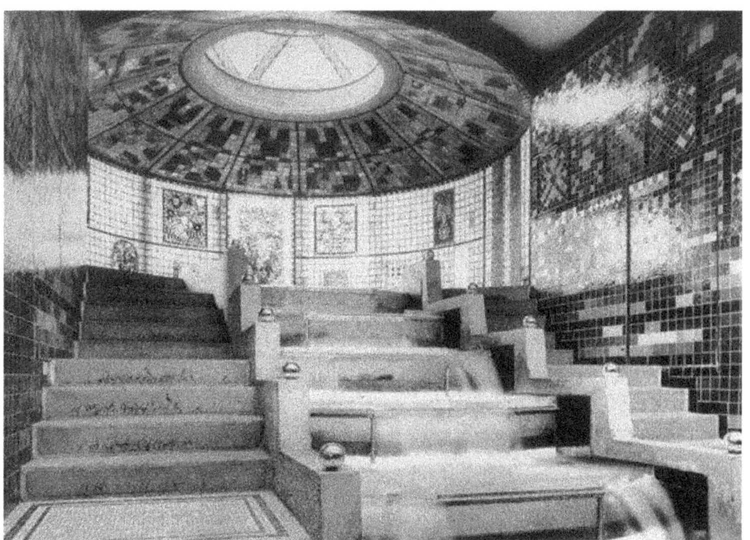
b. Glass pavillion, interior view, staircase

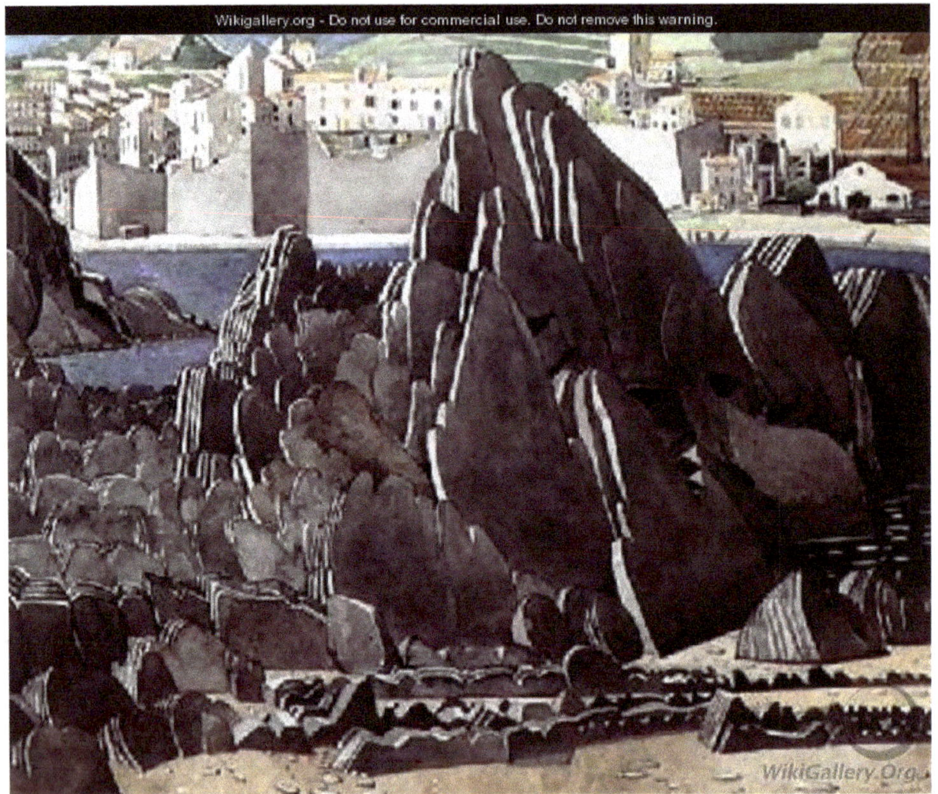

Charles Rennie Mackintosh, “The Rocks,” watercolor, 1926

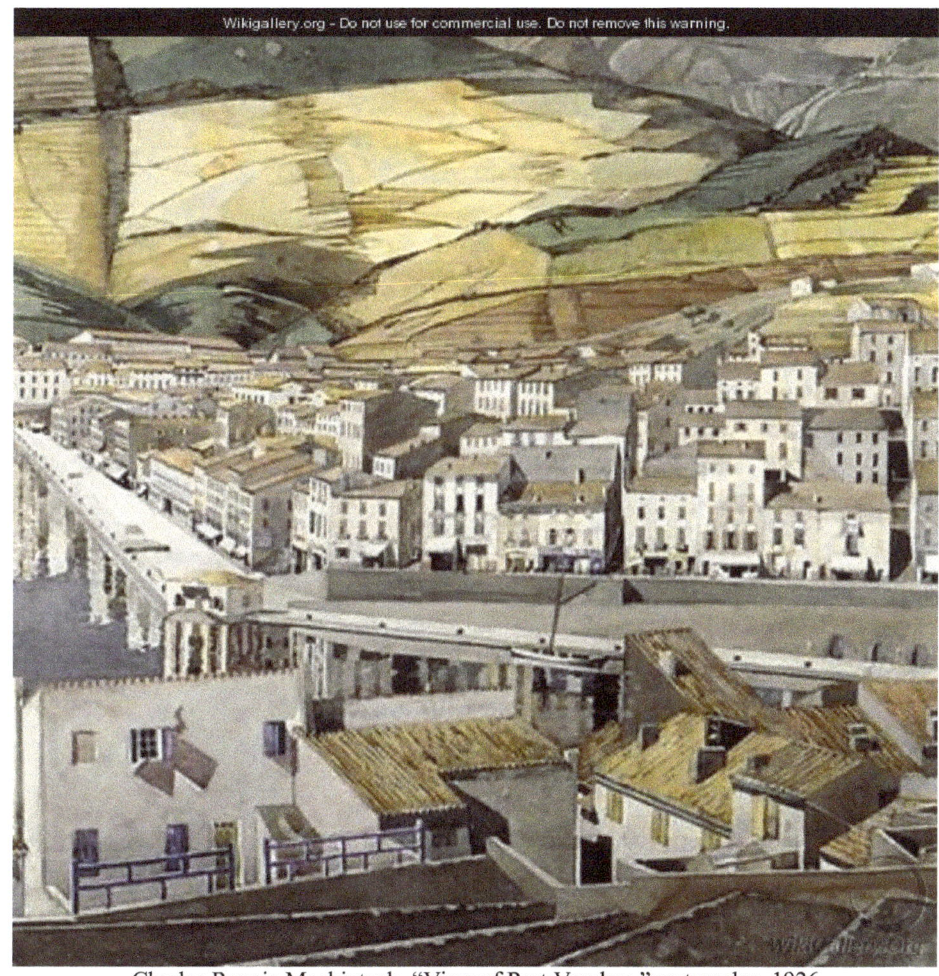

Charles Rennie Mackintosh, “View of Port Vendres,” watercolor, 1926

Bibliography

Berkley, George I, Vienna and Its Jews: *The Tragedy of Success, 1880s-1980s*, Abt Books: Cambridge, MA, 1988.

Billcliffe, Roger and Vergo, Peter, "*Charles Rennie Mackintosh and the Austrian Art Revival*," *The Burlington Magazine*, Number 896, Volume CXIX, November 1997.

Billcliffe, Roger, The Glasgow Boys: *e the Glasgow School of Painting*, 1876-1895, Murray Publications: London, 1985.

Billcliffe, Roger, Charles Rennie Mackintosh: Architectural Sketches and Flower Drawings by Charles Rennie Mackintosh, *Rizzoli International Publications*: New York, 1977.

Blakesley, Rosalind, *The Arts and Crafts Movement*, Phaedon Press: New York and London, 2006

Block, Jane, *Les XX and Belgian Avant-Gardism, 1868-1894*, *UMI Research Press*: Ann Arbor, MI, 1989.

Brett, David, Charles Rennie Mackintosh: *The Poetics of Workmanship, University of Chicago Press*: Chicago, 2004

Burckhardt, Lucius, *The Werkbund, Hyperion Press*: New York, 1987.

Burkhauser, Jude, ed., *The Glasgow Girls*: *Women in Art and Design*, 1880-1920, Canongate Books: Edinburgh, 1993.

Callen, Anthea, *Women Artists of the Arts and Crafts Movement*: 1870-1914, Pantheon Books: Edinburgh, 1979.

Campbell, Joan, *German Werkbund: The Politics of Reform in the Applied Arts*, London, 1978.

Canning, Susan, "*In the Realm of the Social,*" *Art in America*, February, 2000.

Canning, Susan, "*The Symbolic Landscapes of Henry van de Velde,*" *College Art Association Journal*, Vol. 45, No.2, Summer, 1985.

Clement, Russell T., *Four French Symbolists: A Sourcebook on Pierre Puvis de Chavannes*, Gustave Moreau, Odilon Redon, and Maurice Denis, *The Greenwood Group*: *Westport*, CT, 1996.

Cooper, Jackie, ed, (Barbara Bernard, Introduction) Mackintosh Architecture*: The Complete Buildings and Selected Projects, Rizzoli International Publications*: New York, 1980.

Emboden, William, Sarah Bernhardt, *Macmillan Publishing Co., Inc.*: New York, 1979.

Escritt, Stephen, *Art Nouveau, Phaedon Press*: London, 2000.

Exhibition Catalogues

Goddard, Stephan H., ed., Les Vingt and the Belgian Avant Garde, *The Spencer Museum of Art: The University of Kansas*, 1992.

Gold, Arthur and Fizdale, Robert, *The Divine Sarah, Alfred A. Knopf*: New York, 1979.

Gottlieb, Robert, *The Life of Sarah Bernhardt, Yale University Press*: New Haven, CT, 2010.

Günther, Sonia and Posener, Julius, eds., (Dennis Sharp, Introduction), Hermann Muthesius, 1861-1927, *The Architectural Association*: London, 1979.

Hauptmann, Jodi and van Zeylen, Marina, eds., Beyond the Visible: *The Art of Odilon Redon. The Museum of Modern Art*: New York, 2005.

Helsinger, Kathryn Bloom, ed., Art Nouveau in Munich: *Masters of Jugenstil, Philadelphia Museum of Art and Prestel Verlag*: Berlin, 1988.

Heskett, John, German Design: *1870-1918, Taplinger Publishing Co*: New York, 1986.

Holland, Janice, *The Studios of Frances and Margaret Macdonald, Manchester University Press*: Manchester, 1996

Irwin, D. and Irwin, F., *Scottish Painters at Home and Abroad, 1700-1900, Faber and Faber, Inc.*: London, 1975.

Jarzombek, Mark, "Joseph August Lux: Werkbund Promoter; Historian of a Lost Modernity," *Journal of the Society of Architectural Historians*, June, 2004.

Kallir, Jane, *Viennese Design and the Wiener Werkstätte, Galérie St.Étienne, Paris and George Braziller*, New York, 1986.

Kleeblatt, Norman, ed., *The Dreyfus affair: Art Truth and Justice, U. of California Press*, Berkeley, Los Angeles, London, 1987.

Kobayashi, Tadash, Ukiyo-e: *Great Japanese Art, Kodansha International Ltd.*: Tokyo, New York, San Francisco, 1982.

Livingstone, Karen, and Parry, Linda, eds, *International Arts and Crafts, Victoria and Albert Publications*: London, 2009.

Mahony, Patrick, Maurice Maeterlinck: Mystic and Dramatist, *The Institute for the Study of Man: Washington*, D.C., 1979.

Marcus, George H, *Masters of Modern Design: A Critical Assessment, The Monacelli Press*: New York, 2005.

Martin, David, *The Glasgow School of Painting, Paul Harris Publishing*: Edinburgh, 1976.

McKean, John, *Charles Rennie Mackintosh: Architect, Artist, Icon, Lomond Publishing*: Broxburn, Scotland, 2000.

Moffat, Alistair, *Charles Rennie Mackintosh, Baxter Photograph, Ltd.*: Edinbrugh, 1998.

Mucha, Sarah, ed., *Alphonse Mucha, Frances Lincoln, Ltd.*: London, 2005.

Neat, Timothy, Part Seen, Part Imagined: *Meaning and Symbolism in the Work of CharlesRennie Mackintosh and Margaret Macdonald, Canongate Books*: Edinburgh, 1994.

Pattemans, Pierre, *Modern Architecture in Belgium, Mette Willert*, trans., Marc Vokaer: Brussels, 1976.

Pevsner, Nikolaus, Pioneers of Modern Design: *From William Morris to Walter Gropius (Fourth Edition), Yale University Press*: New Haven and London, 2005

Pool, Phoebe, Impressionism, *Thames and Hudson*: London, 1967.

Posener, Julius, *From Schinkel to the Bauhaus, Lund Humphries*: London, 1972.

Robertson, Pamela, ed., Doves and Dreams: *The Art of Frances Macdonald and J. Herbert MacNair, Lund Humphries*: London, 2006

Robertson, Pamela, ed., The Chronicle: *The Letters of Charles Rennie Mackintosh to Margaret Macdonald Mackintosh, Lund Humphries*: London, 2005

Russell, Frank, ed., *Art Nouveau Architecture, Rizzoli International Publications*: New York, 1979.

Salmon, Eric, *Bernhardt and the Theater of Her Time, Greenwood Press*: Westport, CT, 1984

Schwartz, Frederic J., The Werkbund: *Design Theory and Mass Culture before the First World War, Yale University Press*: New Haven, 1997

Sembach, Klaus-Jürgen, *Henry van de Velde, Michael Robinson, trans, Rizzoli International Publications*: New York, 1989

Stanley-Baker, Joan, *Japanese Art, Thames and Hudson*: London, 1984

Steele, James, *Charles Rennie Mackintosh: Synthesis in Form, St. Martins Press:* London, 1994

Stevens, Mary Anne and Hoogee,Robert, eds., *Impressionism to Symbolism: The Belgian Avant Garde, 1880-1900, Royal Academy of Arts*: London, 1995.

Taranov, Gerda, Sarah Bernhardt: *The Art within the Legend, Princeton University Press*, Princeton, N.J., 1972

Varndedoe, Kirk, Vienna 1900: *Art, Architecture and Design, Museum of Modern Art: New York and The Little Brown Company*: Boston, 1986.

Weisberg, Gabriel P., *Art Nouveau Bing: Paris Style, 1900, Harry Abrams*: New York, 1986

Wistrich, Robert S., *Austrians and Jews in the Twentieth Century, The Macmillan Press*, Ltd.: London, 1992

www.ingramcontent.com/pod-product-compliance
Lightning Source LLC
LaVergne TN
LVHW052350100826
845147LV00013B/807
9781863350235